A MESSAGE FROM KANNA, THE ARTIST.

"TEACH ME ♥ BUD-DHA!"
PICK IT UP, PWEEZ ...
Agh! No way!!
BOINK

Ema Toyama

MANGA DOGS

Vol. 1

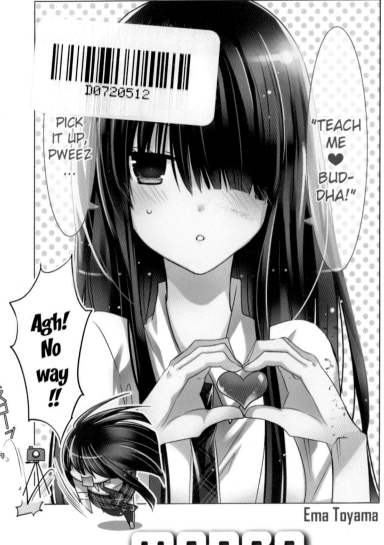

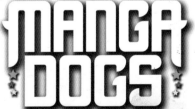

contents

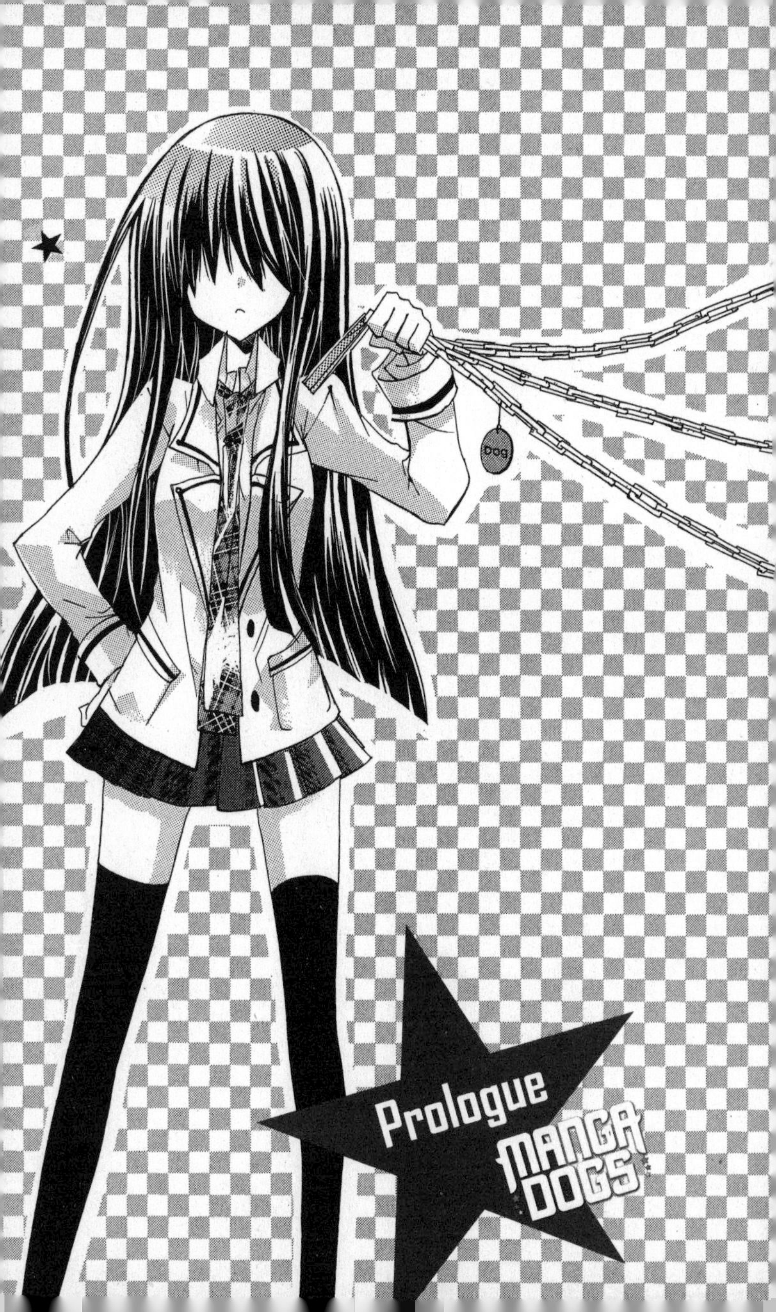

DOG
Prologue
MANGA DOGS

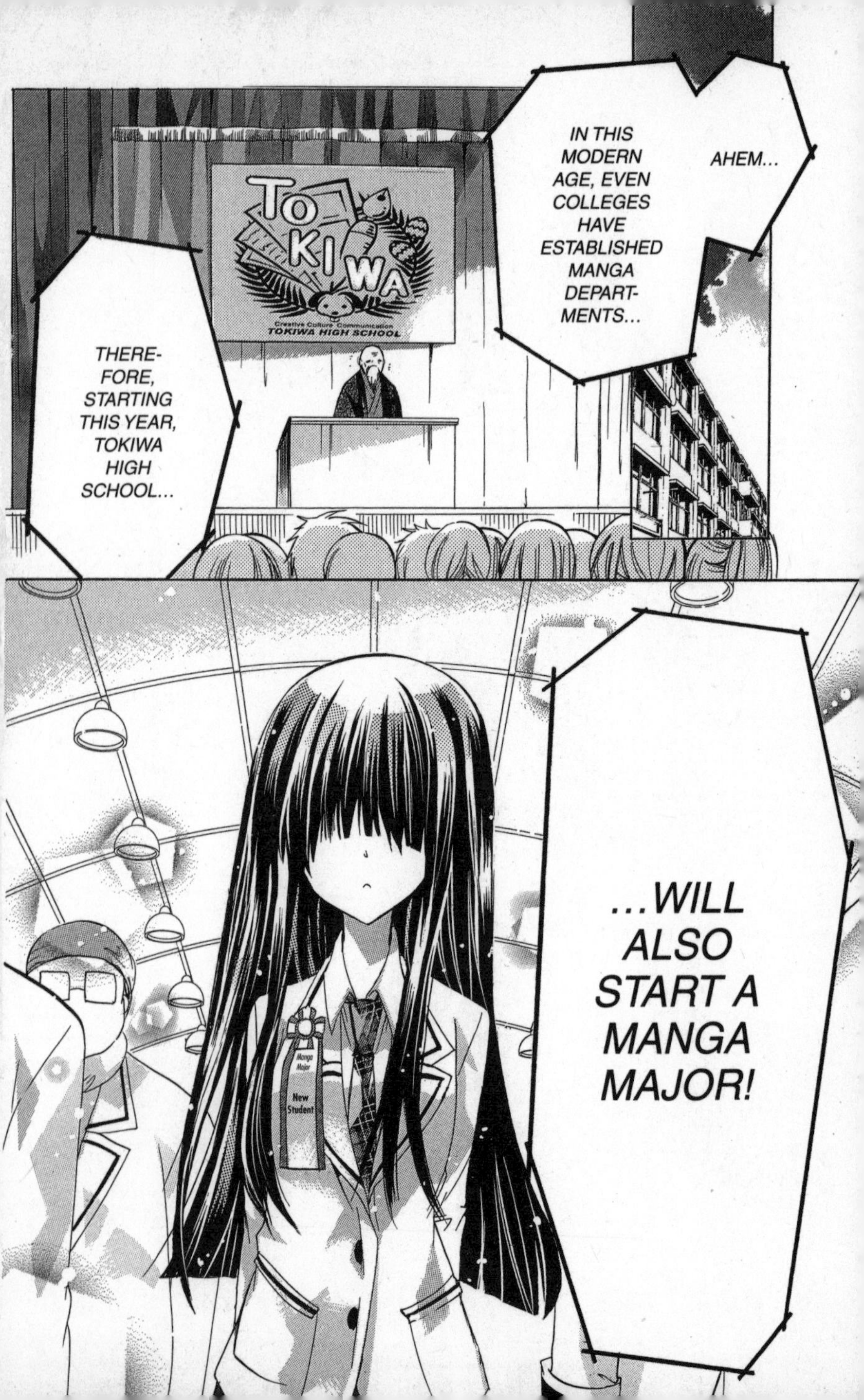
AHEM...
IN THIS MODERN AGE, EVEN COLLEGES HAVE ESTABLISHED MANGA DEPART-MENTS...
TOKIWA
Creative Culture Communication
TOKIWA HIGH SCHOOL
THERE-FORE, STARTING THIS YEAR, TOKIWA HIGH SCHOOL...
...WILL ALSO START A MANGA MAJOR!
Manga Major
New Student

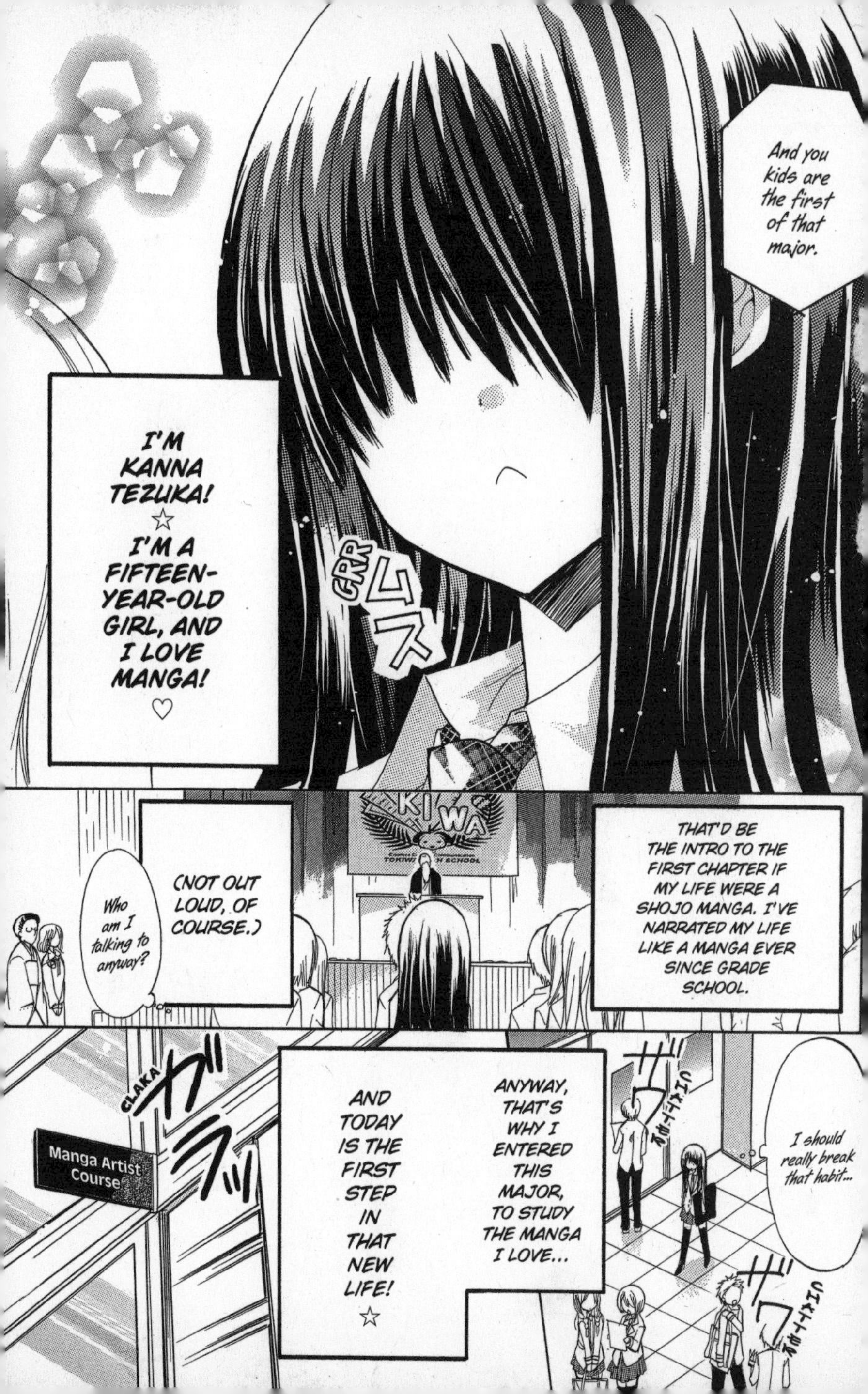
And you kids are the first of that major.
I'M KANNA TEZUKA! ☆ I'M A FIFTEEN-YEAR-OLD GIRL, AND I LOVE MANGA! ♡
GRR
THAT'D BE THE INTRO TO THE FIRST CHAPTER IF MY LIFE WERE A SHOJO MANGA. I'VE NARRATED MY LIFE LIKE A MANGA EVER SINCE GRADE SCHOOL.
(NOT OUT LOUD, OF COURSE.)
Who am I talking to anyway?
I should really break that habit...
CHATTER
CHATTER
ANYWAY, THAT'S WHY I ENTERED THIS MAJOR, TO STUDY THE MANGA I LOVE...
AND TODAY IS THE FIRST STEP IN THAT NEW LIFE! ☆
CLAKA
Manga Artist Course

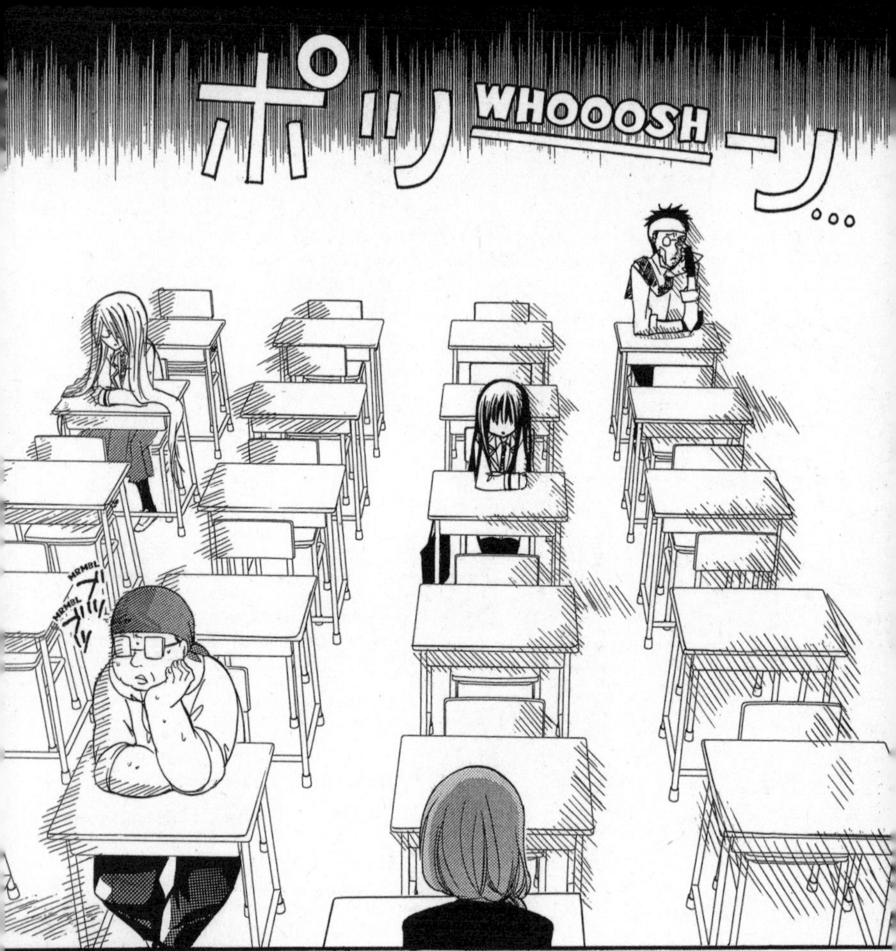
WHOOOSH
MRMBL
MRMBL
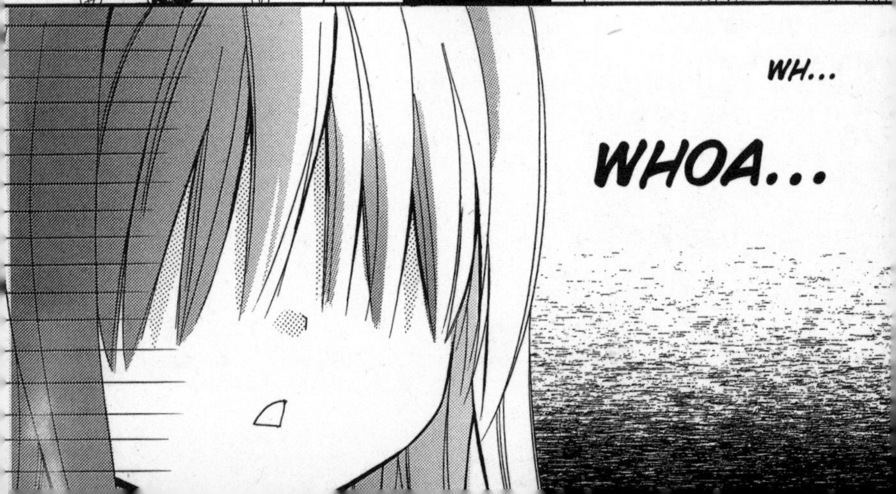
WH...
WHOA...

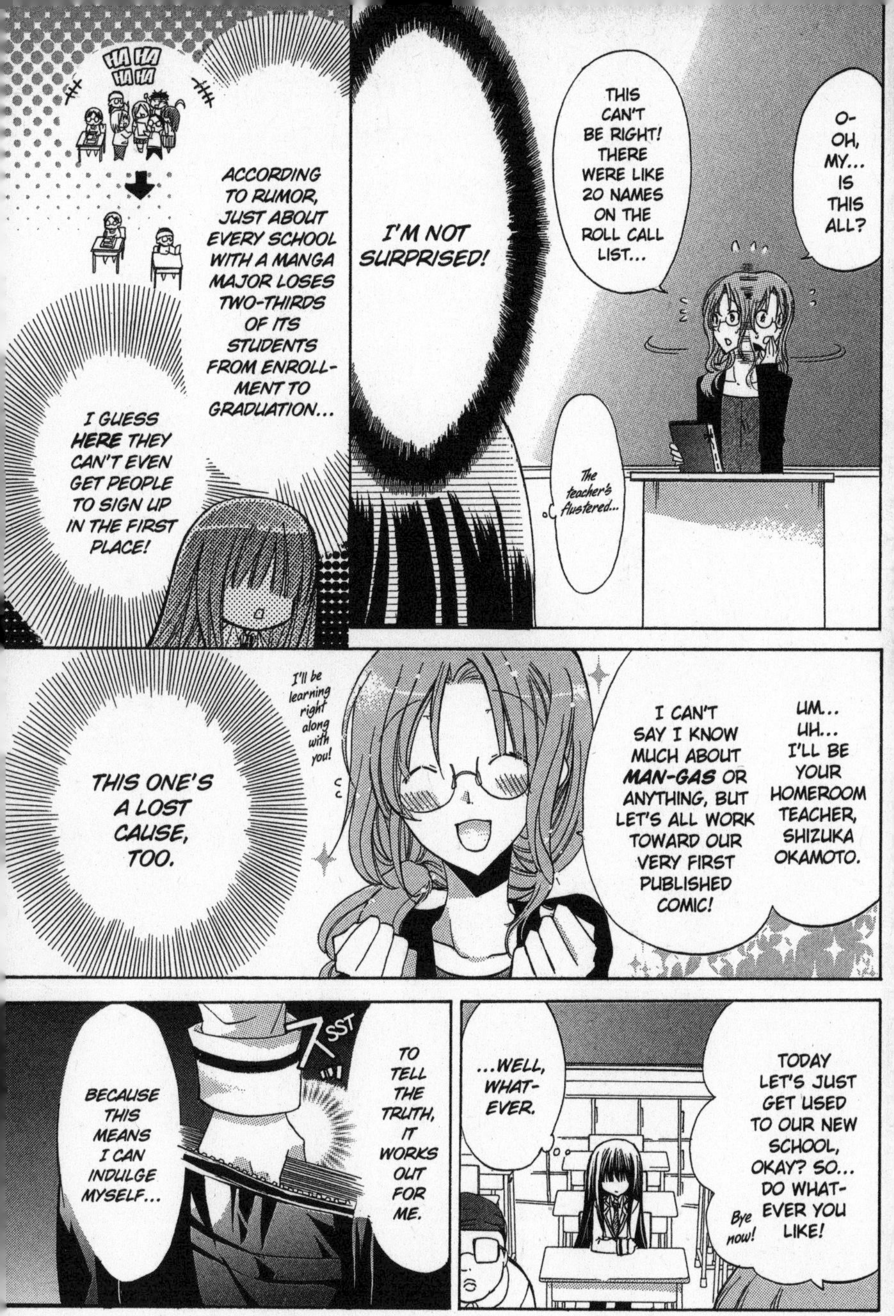
O-OH, MY... IS THIS ALL?
THIS CAN'T BE RIGHT! THERE WERE LIKE 20 NAMES ON THE ROLL CALL LIST...
The teacher's flustered...
I'M NOT SURPRISED!
HA HA HA HA
ACCORDING TO RUMOR, JUST ABOUT EVERY SCHOOL WITH A MANGA MAJOR LOSES TWO-THIRDS OF ITS STUDENTS FROM ENROLL-MENT TO GRADUATION...
I GUESS HERE THEY CAN'T EVEN GET PEOPLE TO SIGN UP IN THE FIRST PLACE!
UM... UH... I'LL BE YOUR HOMEROOM TEACHER, SHIZUKA OKAMOTO.
I CAN'T SAY I KNOW MUCH ABOUT MAN-GAS OR ANYTHING, BUT LET'S ALL WORK TOWARD OUR VERY FIRST PUBLISHED COMIC!
I'll be learning right along with you!
THIS ONE'S A LOST CAUSE, TOO.
TODAY LET'S JUST GET USED TO OUR NEW SCHOOL, OKAY? SO... DO WHAT-EVER YOU LIKE!
Bye now!
...WELL, WHAT-EVER.
TO TELL THE TRUTH, IT WORKS OUT FOR ME.
SST
BECAUSE THIS MEANS I CAN INDULGE MYSELF...

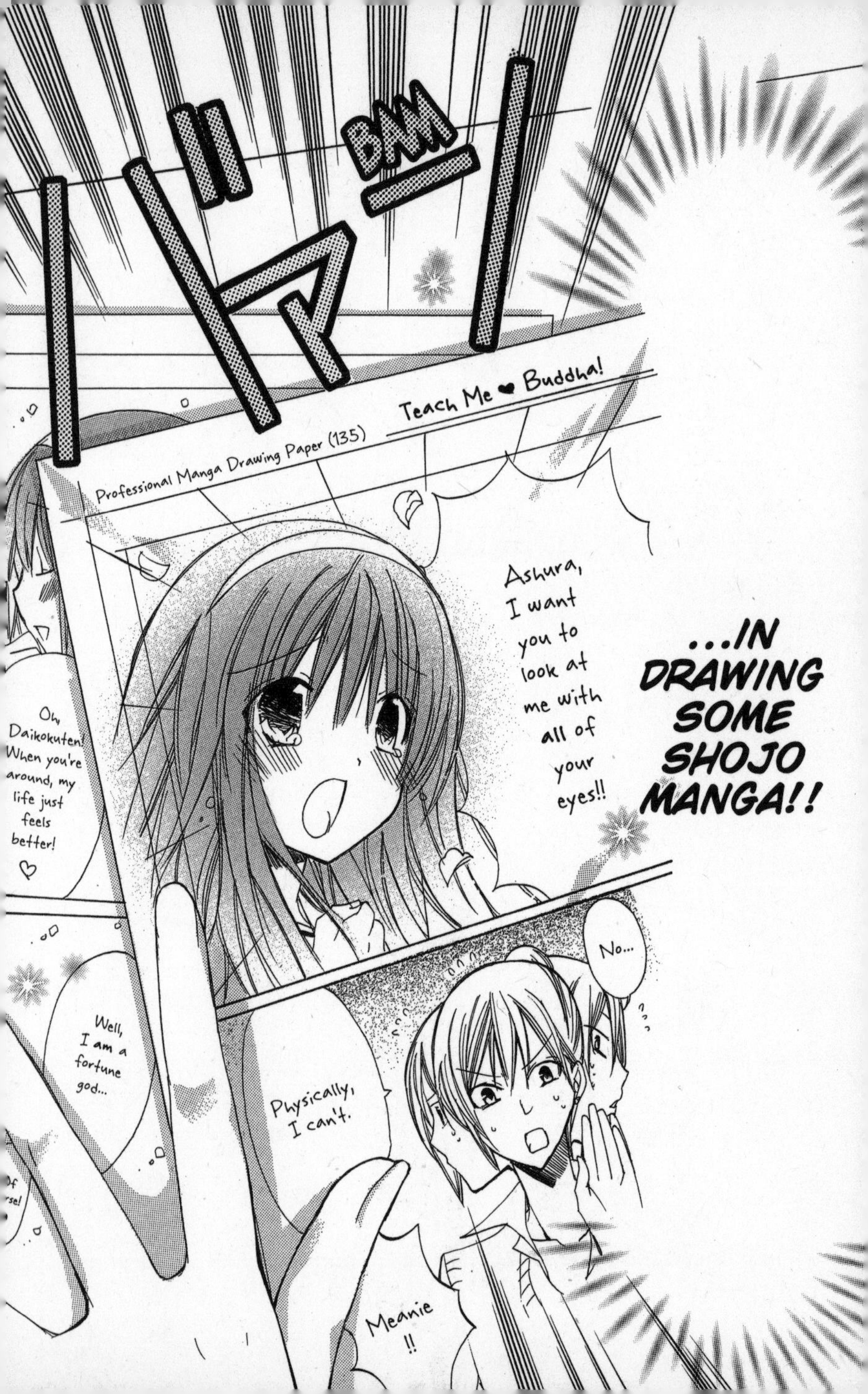

BAM
...IN DRAWING SOME SHOJO MANGA!!
Teach Me ♥ Buddha!
Professional Manga Drawing Paper (135)
Ashura, I want you to look at me with all of your eyes!!
Oh, Daikokuten! When you're around, my life just feels better! ♡
Well, I am a fortune god...
No...
Physically, I can't.
Meanie!!

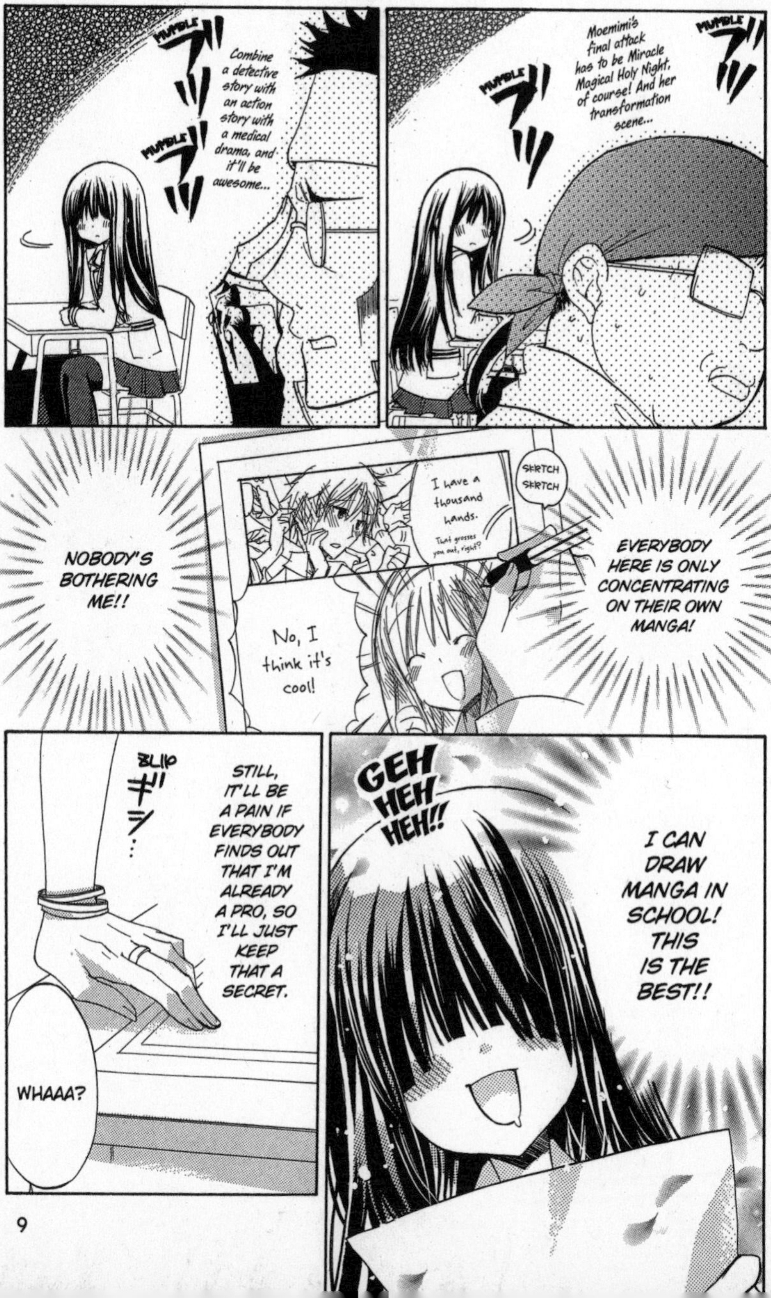
MUMBLE
MUMBLE
Moemimi's final attack has to be Miracle Magical Holy Night, of course! And her transformation scene...
MUMBLE
MUMBLE
Combine a detective story with an action story with a medical drama, and it'll be awesome...
SKRTCH SKRTCH
EVERYBODY HERE IS ONLY CONCENTRATING ON THEIR OWN MANGA!
I have a thousand hands.
That grosses you out, right?
No, I think it's cool!
NOBODY'S BOTHERING ME!!
GEH HEH HEH!!
I CAN DRAW MANGA IN SCHOOL! THIS IS THE BEST!!
BLIP
STILL, IT'LL BE A PAIN IF EVERYBODY FINDS OUT THAT I'M ALREADY A PRO, SO I'LL JUST KEEP THAT A SECRET.
WHAAA?

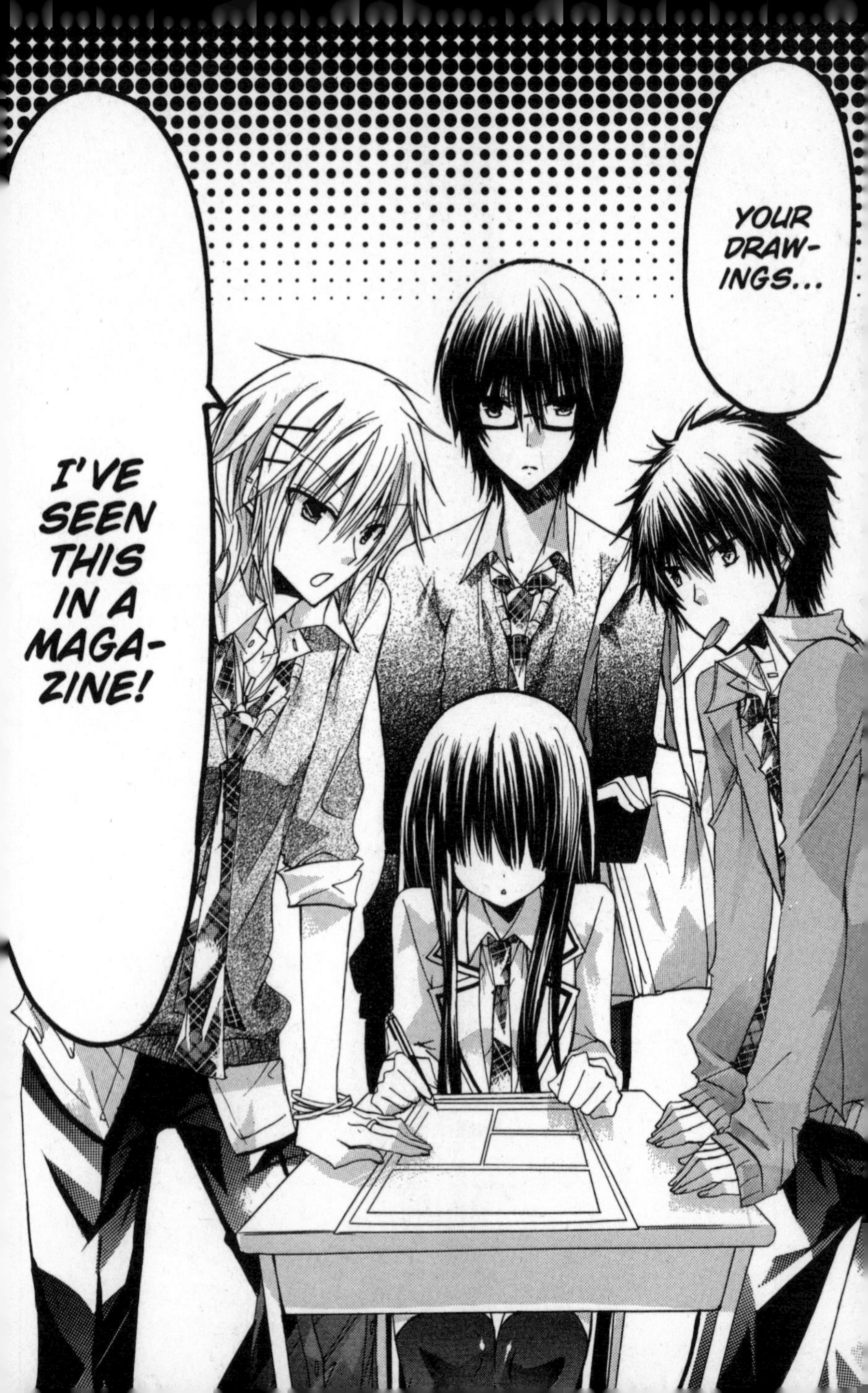
YOUR DRAWINGS...
I'VE SEEN THIS IN A MAGAZINE!

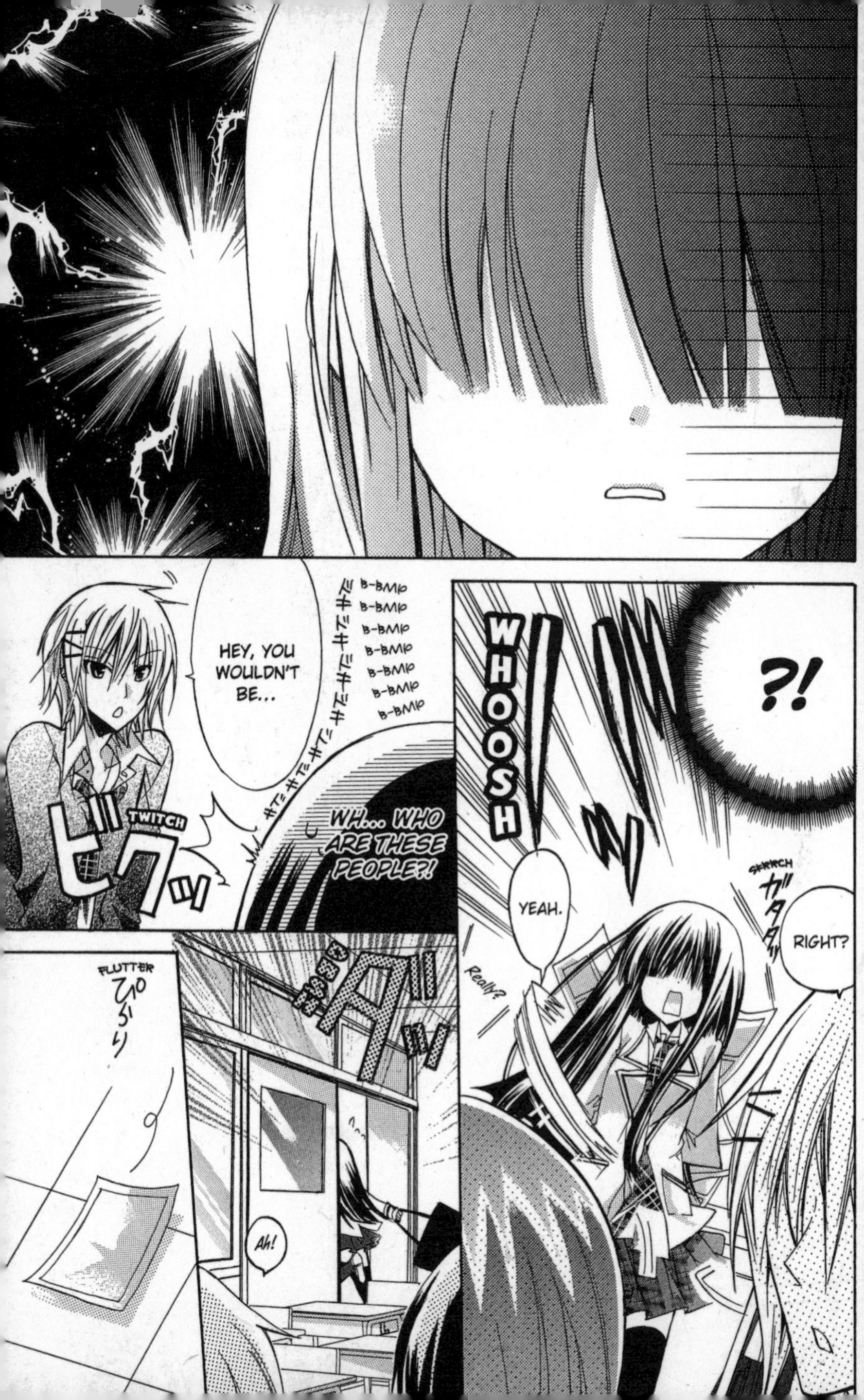

?!
WHOOSH
SKRRCH
RIGHT?
YEAH.
Really?
B-BMP
B-BMP
B-BMP
B-BMP
B-BMP
B-BMP
B-BMP
HEY, YOU WOULDN'T BE...
WH... WHO ARE THESE PEOPLE?!
TWITCH
Ah!
FLUTTER

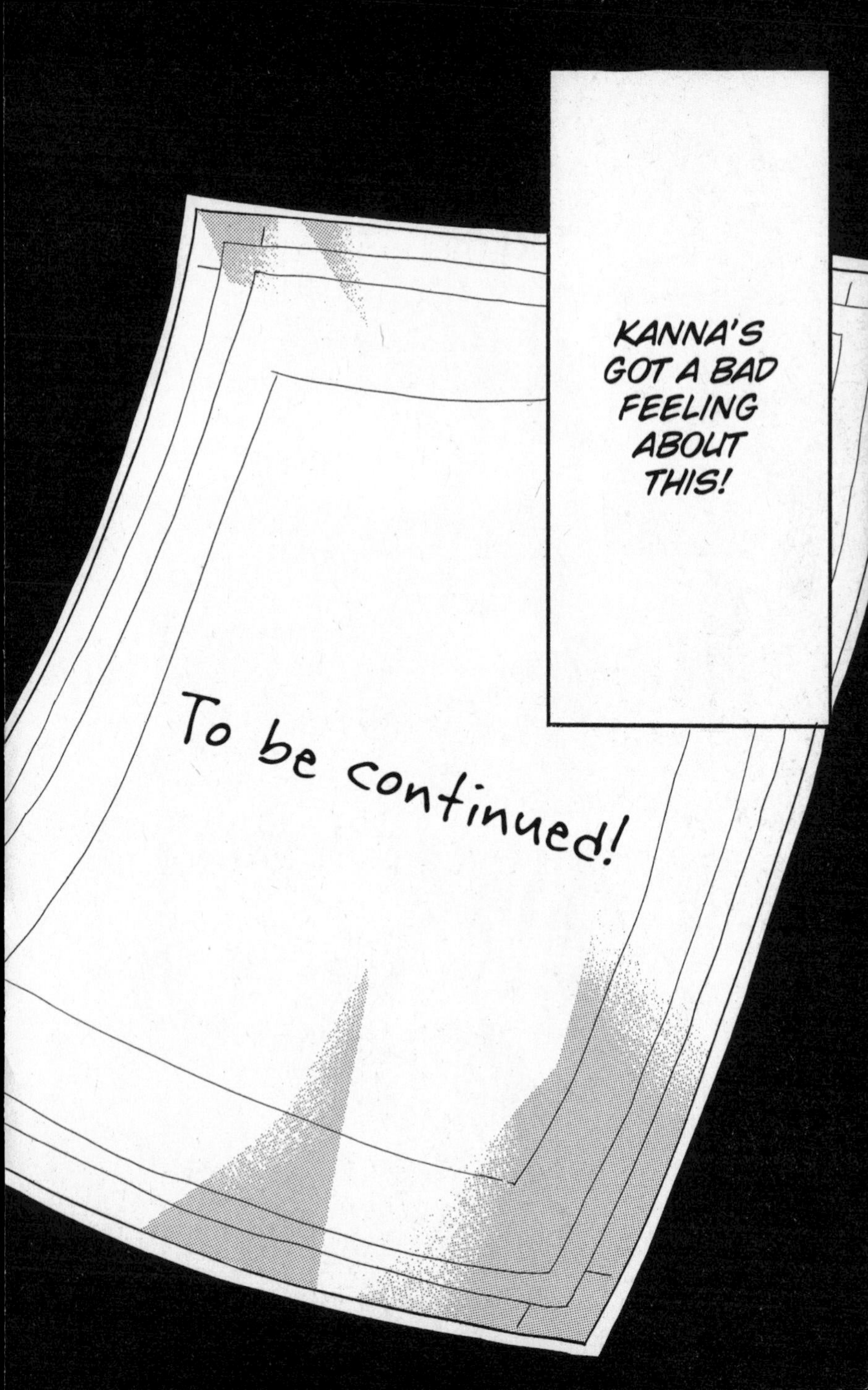
KANNA'S GOT A BAD FEELING ABOUT THIS!
To be continued!

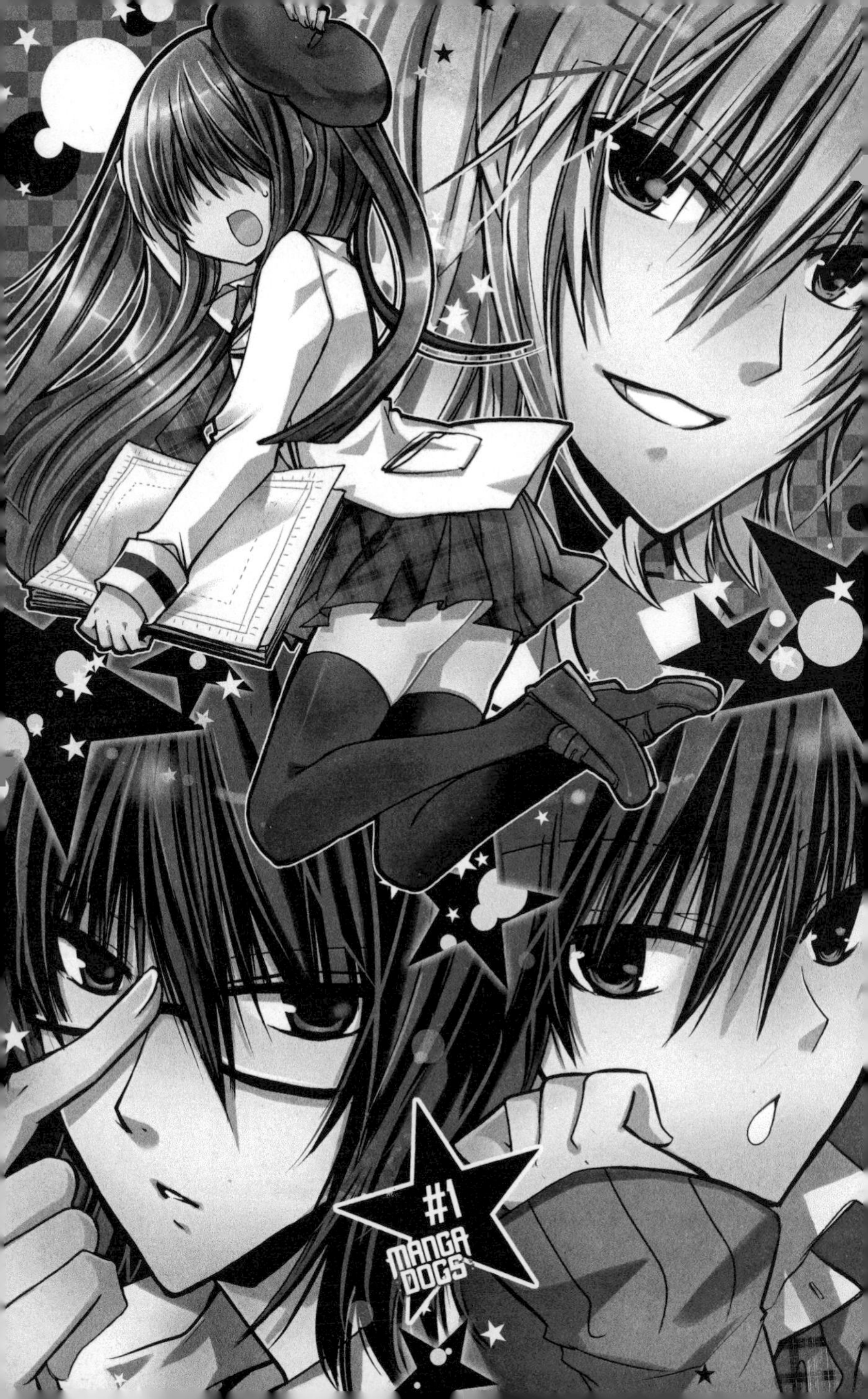
#1
MANGA DOGS

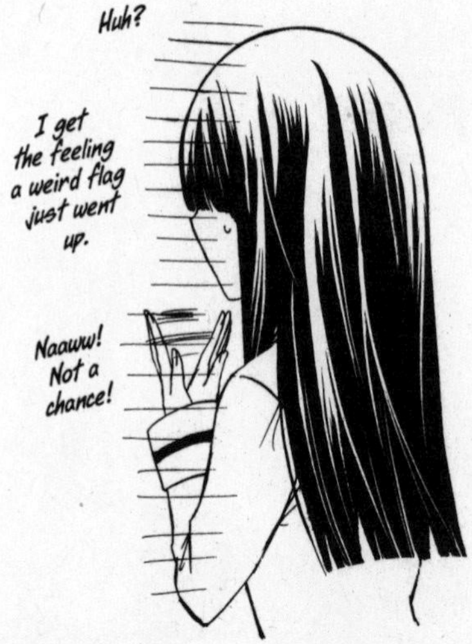
Huh?
I get the feeling a weird flag just went up.
Naaww! Not a chance!

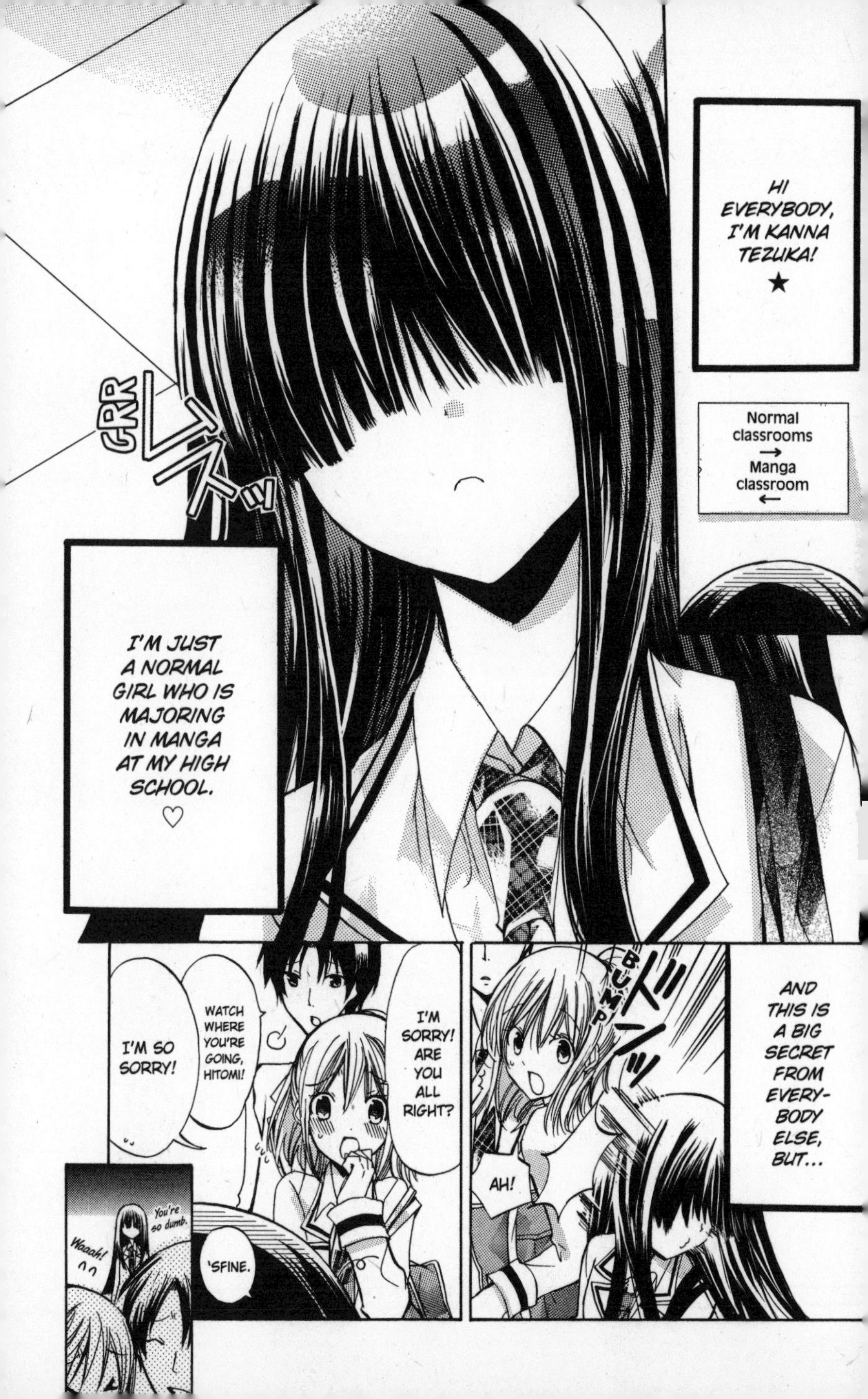
HI EVERYBODY, I'M KANNA TEZUKA! ★
Normal classrooms → Manga classroom ←
GRR
I'M JUST A NORMAL GIRL WHO IS MAJORING IN MANGA AT MY HIGH SCHOOL. ♡
AND THIS IS A BIG SECRET FROM EVERY-BODY ELSE, BUT...
BUMP
AH!
I'M SORRY! ARE YOU ALL RIGHT?
'SFINE.
WATCH WHERE YOU'RE GOING, HITOMI!
I'M SO SORRY!
You're so dumb.
Waaah!

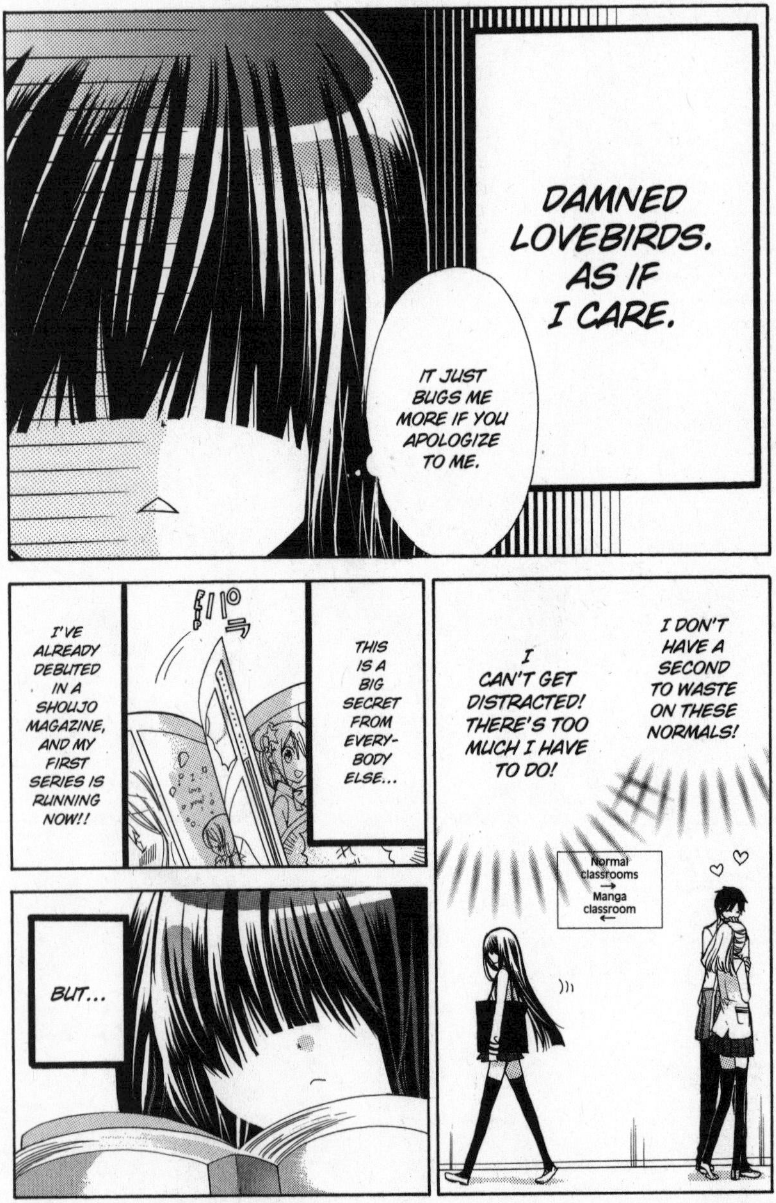
DAMNED LOVEBIRDS. AS IF I CARE.
IT JUST BUGS ME MORE IF YOU APOLOGIZE TO ME.
I DON'T HAVE A SECOND TO WASTE ON THESE NORMALS!
I CAN'T GET DISTRACTED! THERE'S TOO MUCH I HAVE TO DO!
Normal classrooms →
Manga classroom ←
THIS IS A BIG SECRET FROM EVERYBODY ELSE...
FLIP
I'VE ALREADY DEBUTED IN A SHOUJO MAGAZINE, AND MY FIRST SERIES IS RUNNING NOW!!
BUT...

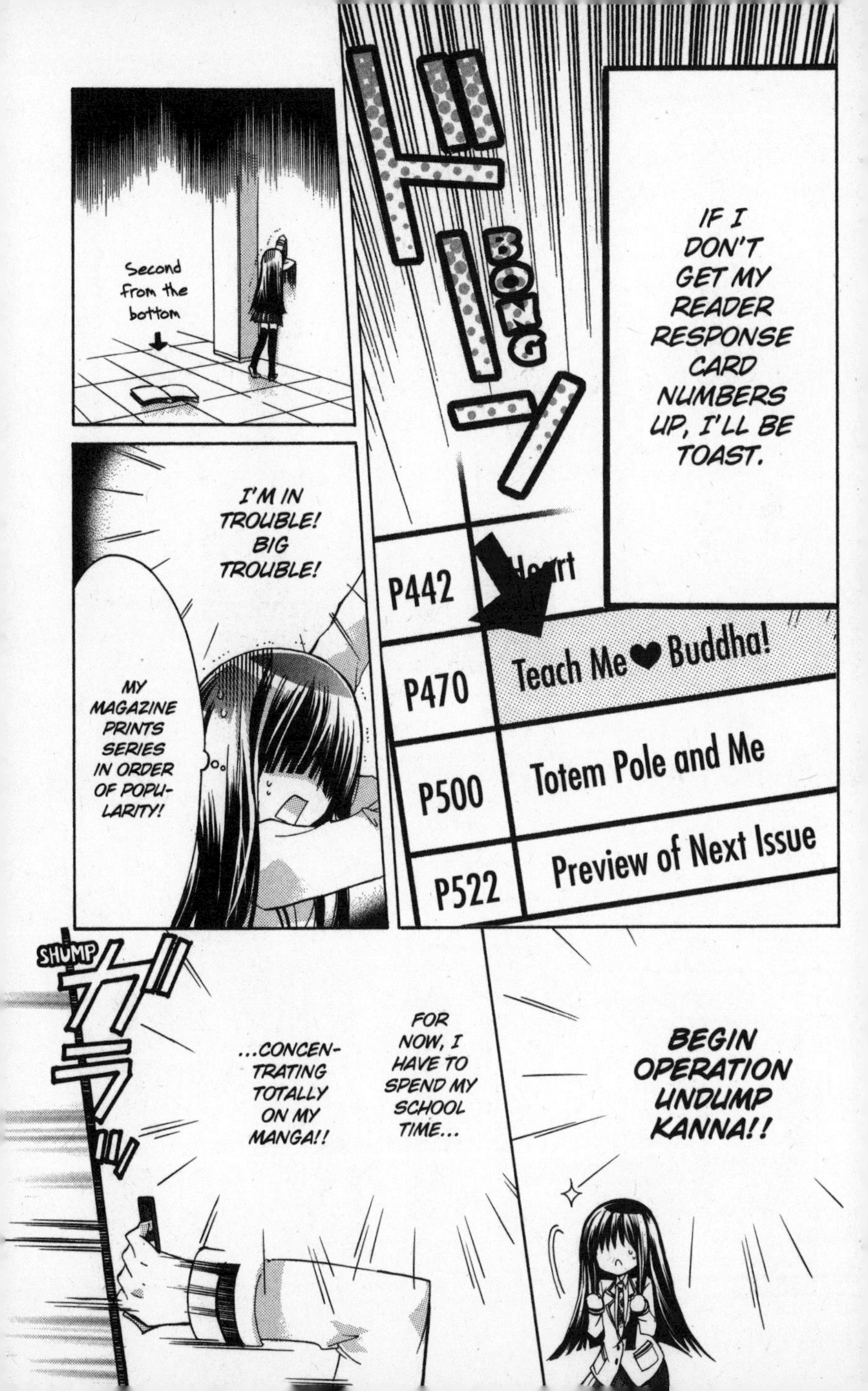
IF I DON'T GET MY READER RESPONSE CARD NUMBERS UP, I'LL BE TOAST.
BONG
P442
P470 Teach Me ❤ Buddha!
P500 Totem Pole and Me
P522 Preview of Next Issue
Second from the bottom
I'M IN TROUBLE! BIG TROUBLE!
MY MAGAZINE PRINTS SERIES IN ORDER OF POPULARITY!
BEGIN OPERATION UNDUMP KANNA!!
FOR NOW, I HAVE TO SPEND MY SCHOOL TIME...
...CONCENTRATING TOTALLY ON MY MANGA!!
SHUMP

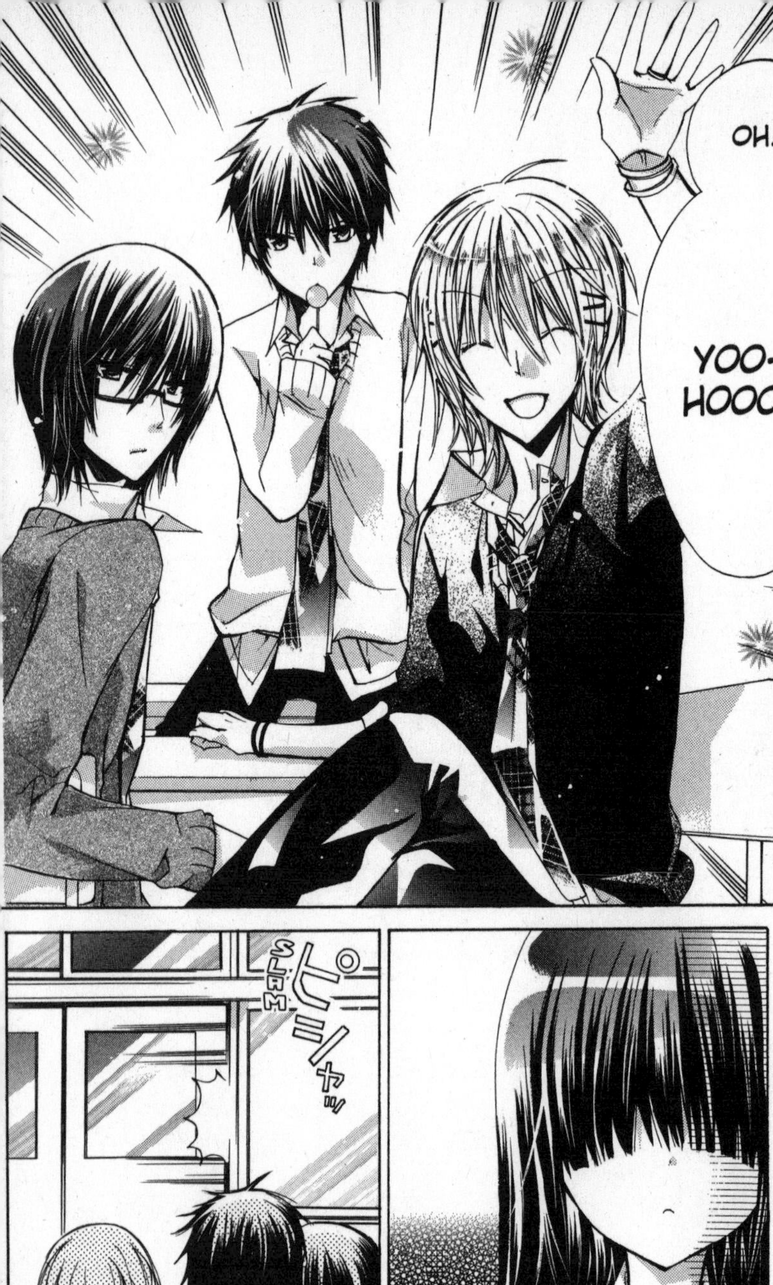
OH!
YOO-HOOO!
ピシャッ
SLAM

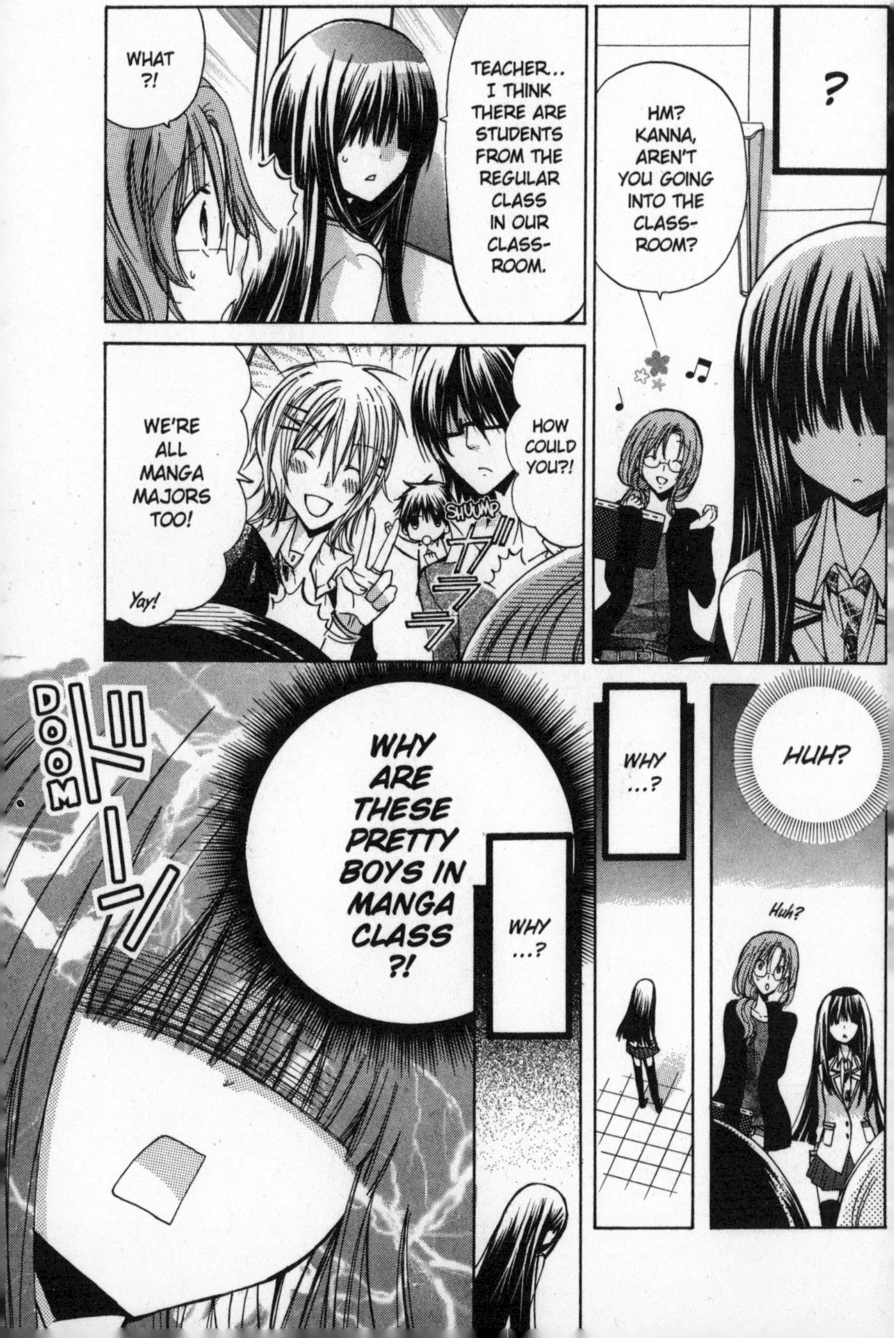
?
HM? KANNA, AREN'T YOU GOING INTO THE CLASSROOM?
TEACHER... I THINK THERE ARE STUDENTS FROM THE REGULAR CLASS IN OUR CLASSROOM.
WHAT?!
HOW COULD YOU?!
SHUUMP
WE'RE ALL MANGA MAJORS TOO!
Yay!
HUH?
Huh?
WHY...?
WHY...?
WHY ARE THESE PRETTY BOYS IN MANGA CLASS?!
DOOM

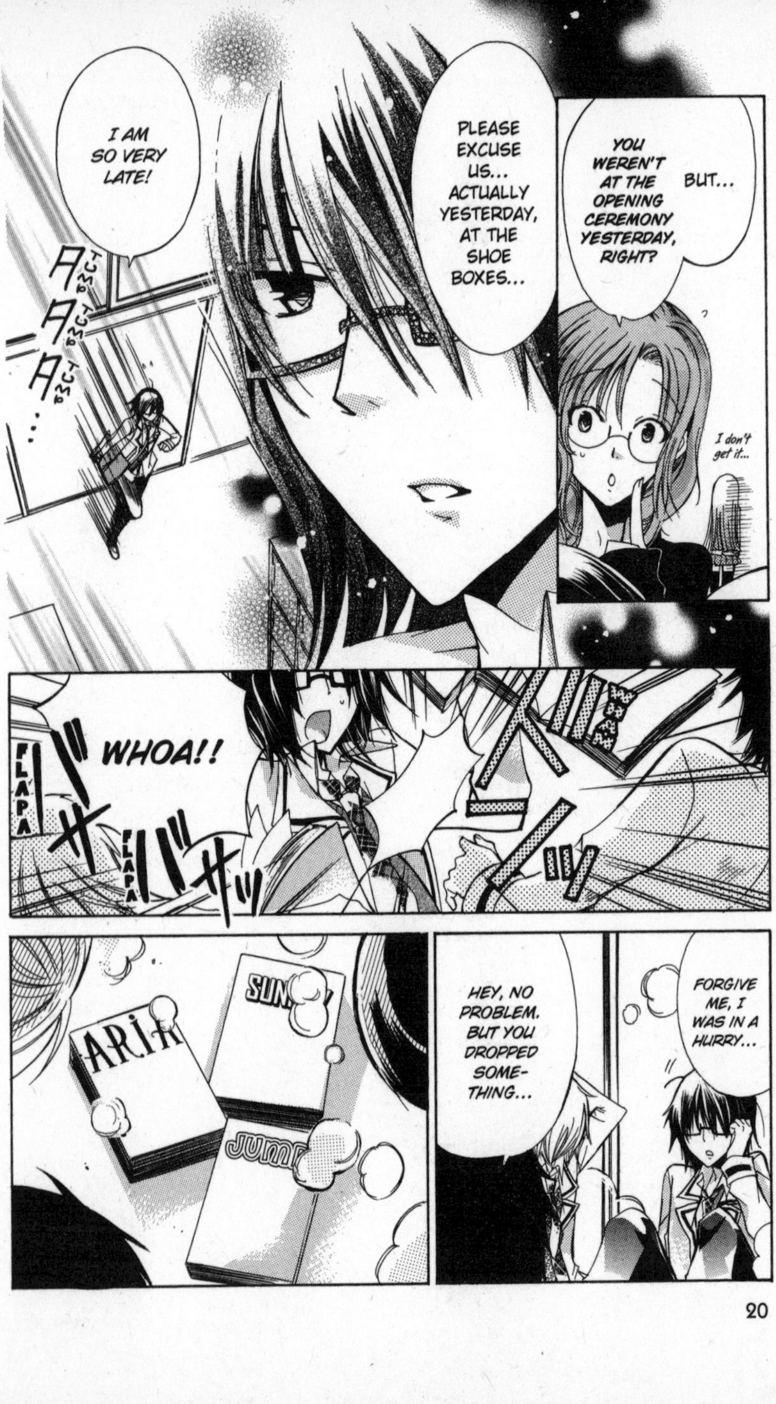
YOU WEREN'T AT THE OPENING CEREMONY YESTERDAY, RIGHT?
BUT...
I don't get it...
PLEASE EXCUSE US... ACTUALLY YESTERDAY, AT THE SHOE BOXES...
I AM SO VERY LATE!
TUMP TUMP TUMP...
WHOA!!
FLAPA FLAPA
FORGIVE ME, I WAS IN A HURRY...
HEY, NO PROBLEM. BUT YOU DROPPED SOME-THING...
ARIA
SUN
JUMP

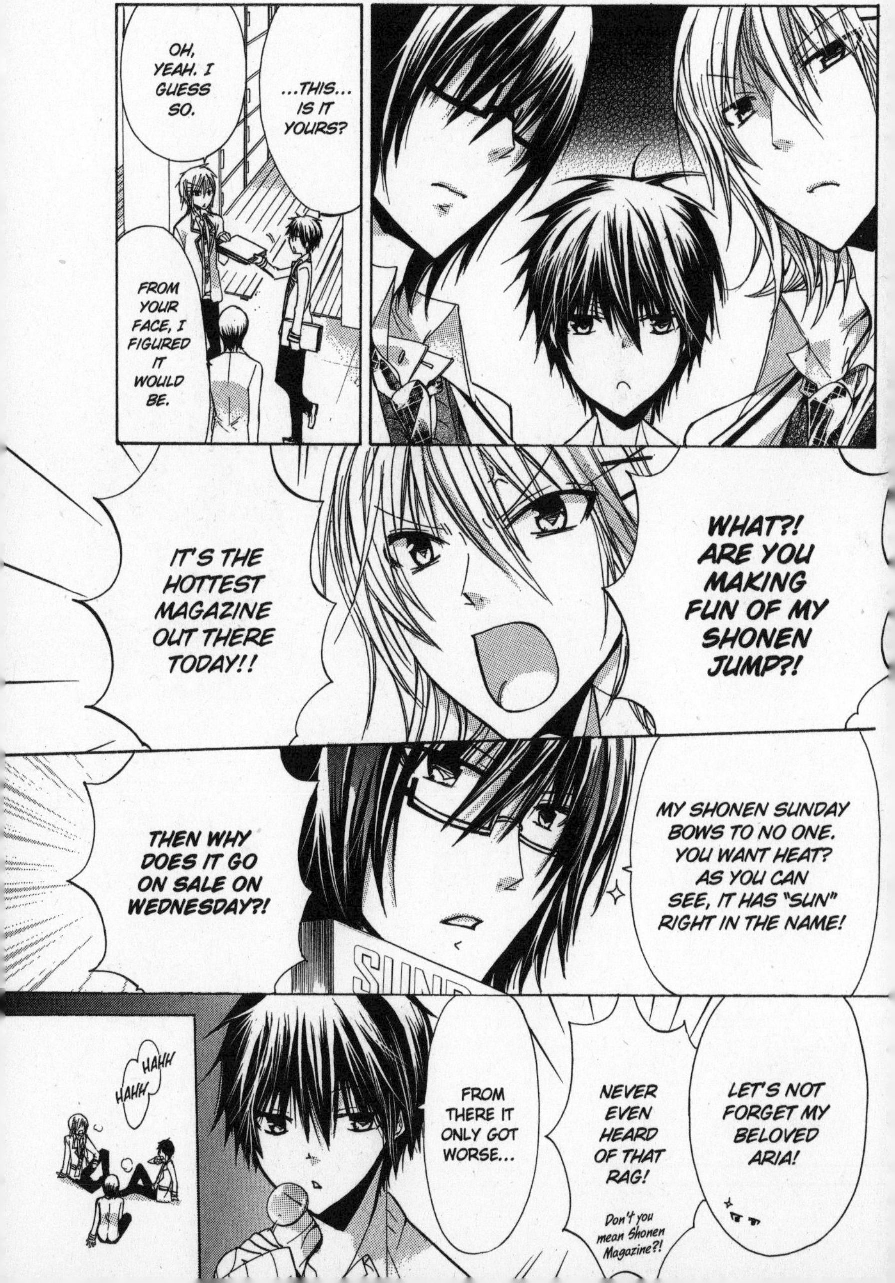
...THIS... IS IT YOURS?
OH, YEAH. I GUESS SO.
FROM YOUR FACE, I FIGURED IT WOULD BE.
WHAT?! ARE YOU MAKING FUN OF MY SHONEN JUMP?!
IT'S THE HOTTEST MAGAZINE OUT THERE TODAY!!
MY SHONEN SUNDAY BOWS TO NO ONE. YOU WANT HEAT? AS YOU CAN SEE, IT HAS "SUN" RIGHT IN THE NAME!
THEN WHY DOES IT GO ON SALE ON WEDNESDAY?!
LET'S NOT FORGET MY BELOVED ARIA!
NEVER EVEN HEARD OF THAT RAG!
Don't you mean Shonen Magazine?!
FROM THERE IT ONLY GOT WORSE...
HAHH HAHH

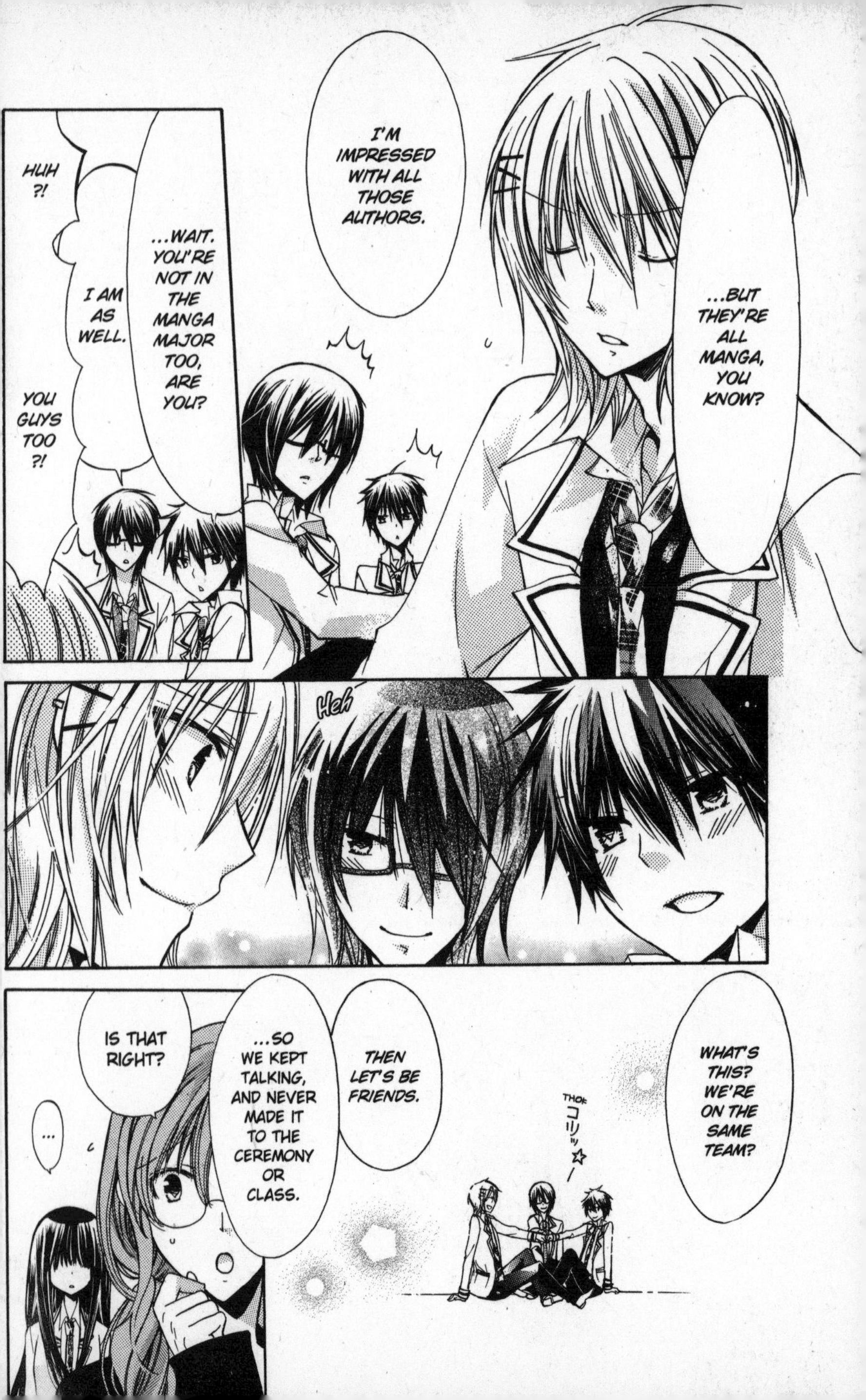
I'M IMPRESSED WITH ALL THOSE AUTHORS.
...BUT THEY'RE ALL MANGA, YOU KNOW?
...WAIT. YOU'RE NOT IN THE MANGA MAJOR TOO, ARE YOU?
I AM AS WELL.
HUH?!
YOU GUYS TOO?!
Heh
WHAT'S THIS? WE'RE ON THE SAME TEAM?
THOK
THEN LET'S BE FRIENDS.
...SO WE KEPT TALKING, AND NEVER MADE IT TO THE CEREMONY OR CLASS.
IS THAT RIGHT?
...

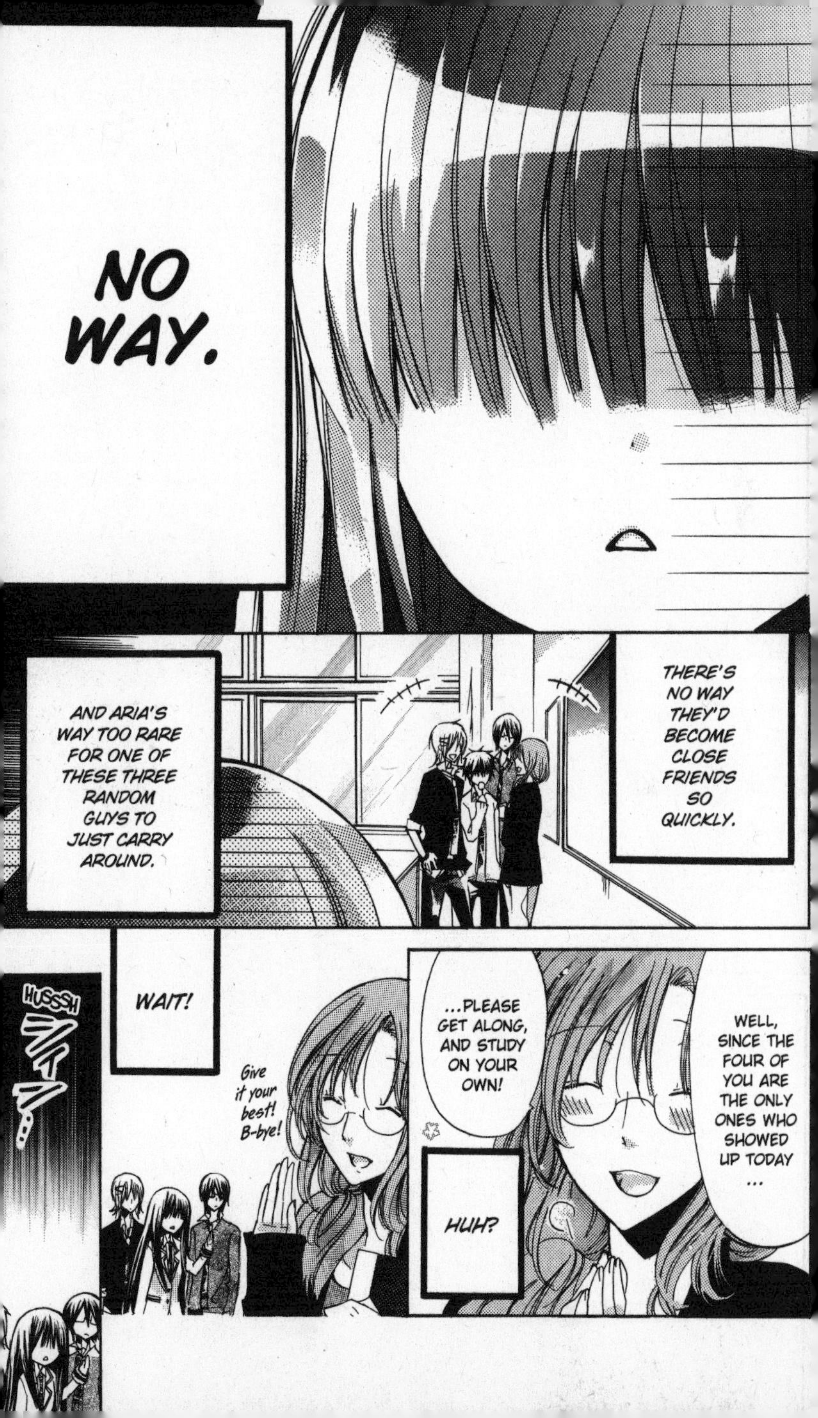
NO WAY.
THERE'S NO WAY THEY'D BECOME CLOSE FRIENDS SO QUICKLY.
AND ARIA'S WAY TOO RARE FOR ONE OF THESE THREE RANDOM GUYS TO JUST CARRY AROUND.
WELL, SINCE THE FOUR OF YOU ARE THE ONLY ONES WHO SHOWED UP TODAY ...
...PLEASE GET ALONG, AND STUDY ON YOUR OWN!
HUH?
Give it your best! B-bye!
WAIT!
HUSSSH

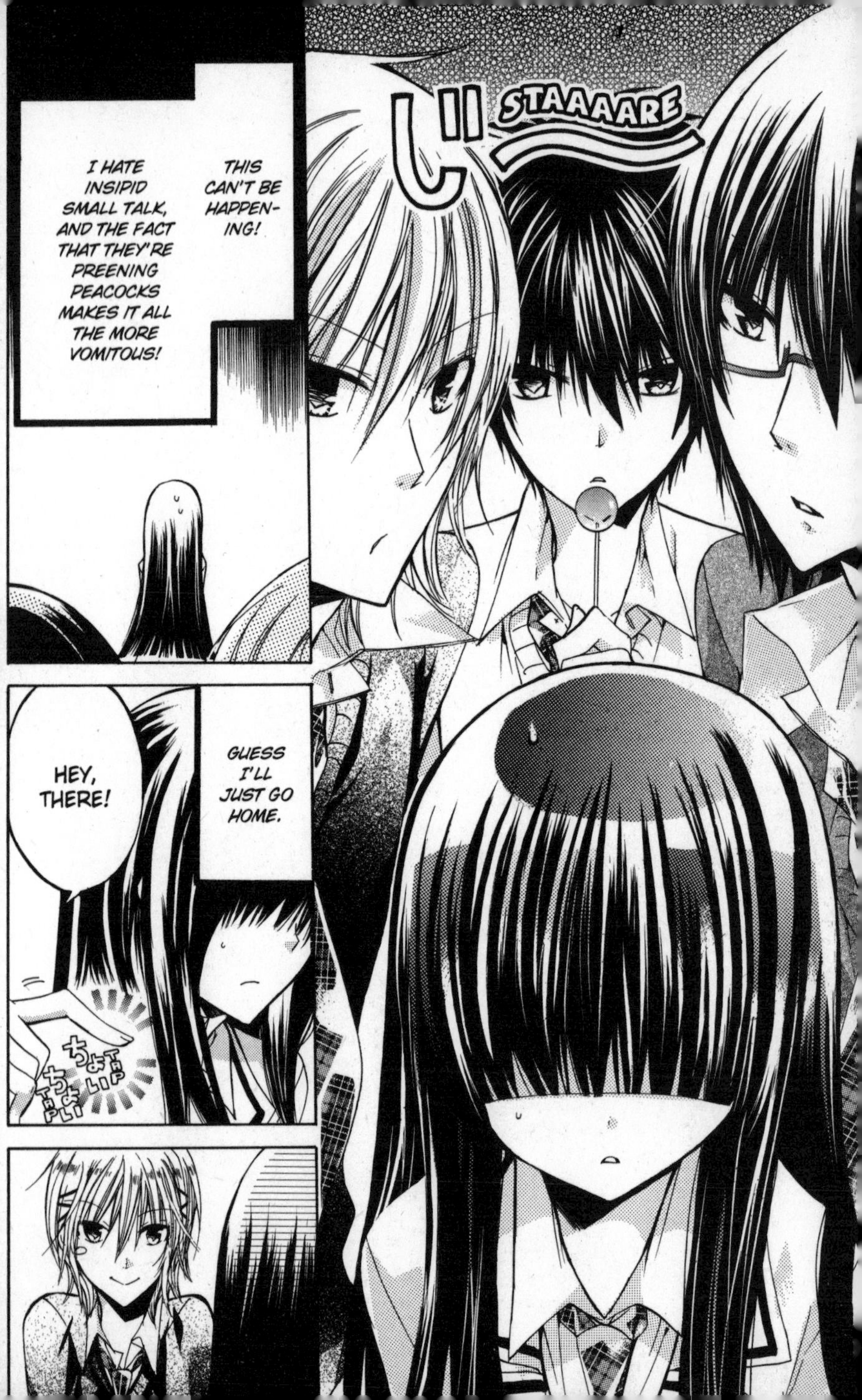
じーー
STAAAARE
THIS CAN'T BE HAPPENING!
I HATE INSIPID SMALL TALK, AND THE FACT THAT THEY'RE PREENING PEACOCKS MAKES IT ALL THE MORE VOMITOUS!
GUESS I'LL JUST GO HOME.
HEY, THERE!
TAP TAP

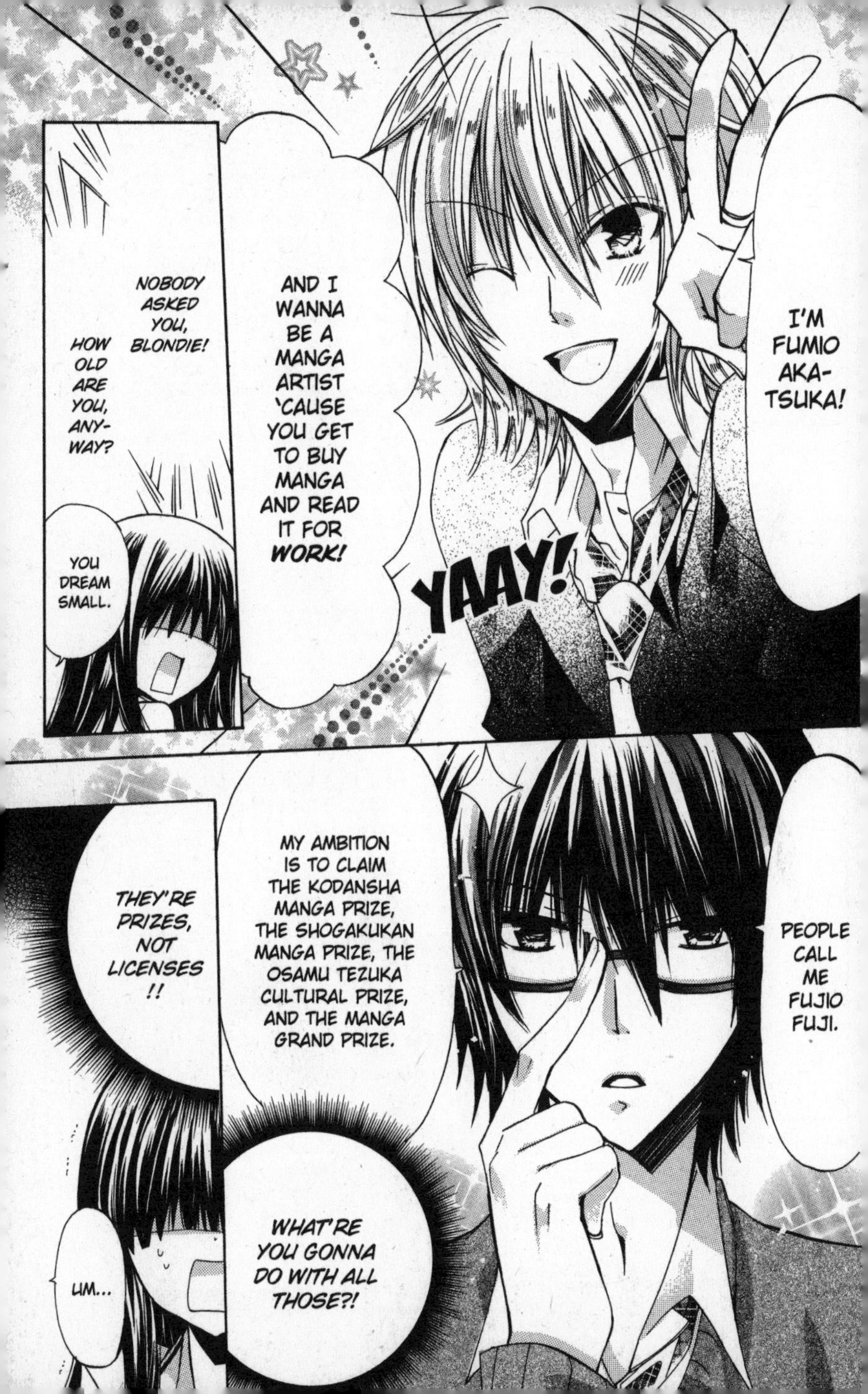
I'M FUMIO AKA-TSUKA!
YAAY!
AND I WANNA BE A MANGA ARTIST 'CAUSE YOU GET TO BUY MANGA AND READ IT FOR **WORK!**
NOBODY ASKED YOU, BLONDIE!
HOW OLD ARE YOU, ANY-WAY?
YOU DREAM SMALL.
PEOPLE CALL ME FUJIO FUJI.
MY AMBITION IS TO CLAIM THE KODANSHA MANGA PRIZE, THE SHOGAKUKAN MANGA PRIZE, THE OSAMU TEZUKA CULTURAL PRIZE, AND THE MANGA GRAND PRIZE.
THEY'RE PRIZES, NOT LICENSES !!
WHAT'RE YOU GONNA DO WITH ALL THOSE?!
UM...

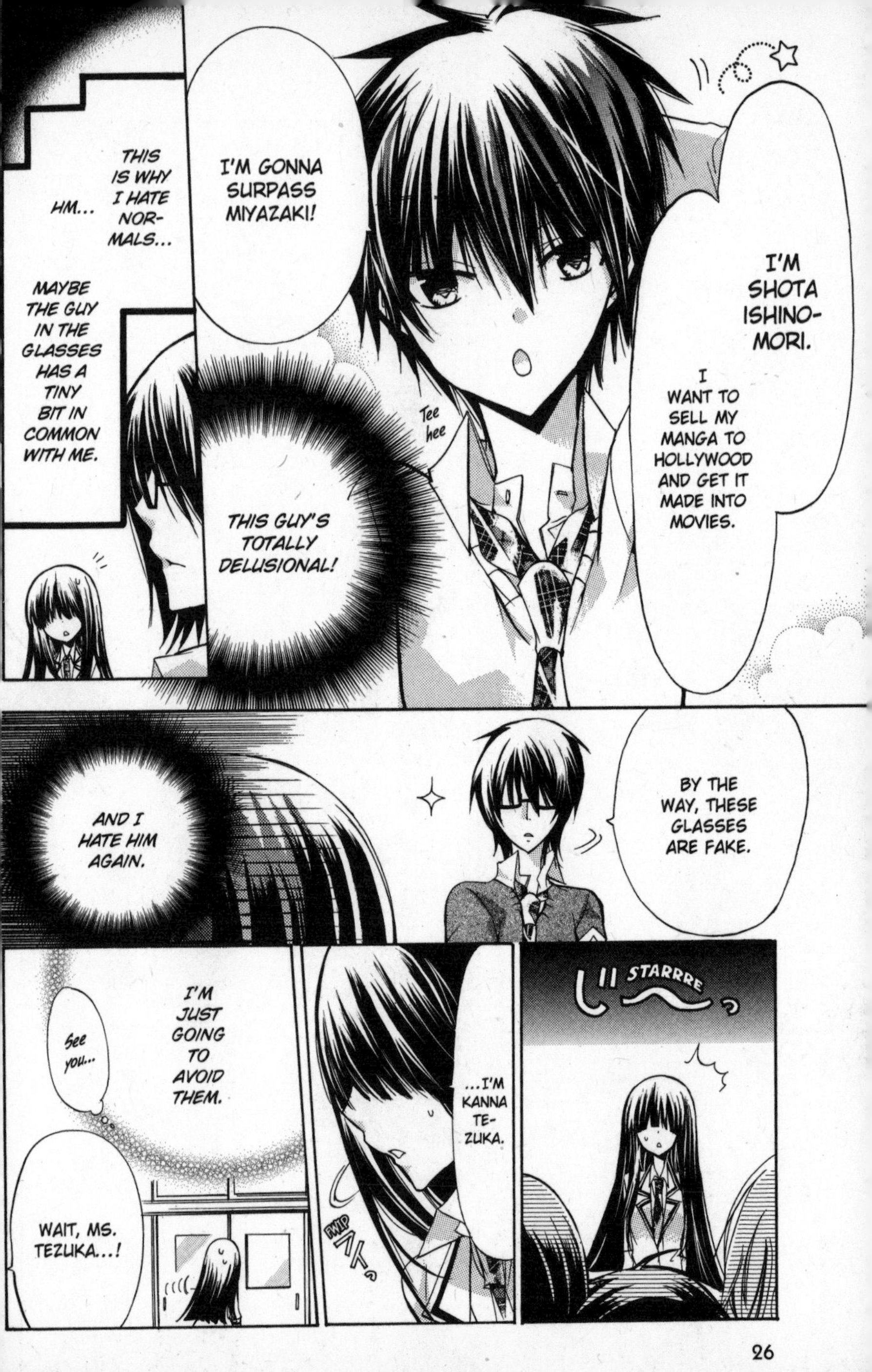
I'M SHOTA ISHINO-MORI.
I WANT TO SELL MY MANGA TO HOLLYWOOD AND GET IT MADE INTO MOVIES.
I'M GONNA SURPASS MIYAZAKI!
Tee hee
THIS GUY'S TOTALLY DELUSIONAL!
THIS IS WHY I HATE NOR-MALS...
HM...
MAYBE THE GUY IN THE GLASSES HAS A TINY BIT IN COMMON WITH ME.
BY THE WAY, THESE GLASSES ARE FAKE.
AND I HATE HIM AGAIN.
じーっ STARRRE
...I'M KANNA TE-ZUKA.
FWIP
I'M JUST GOING TO AVOID THEM.
See you...
WAIT, MS. TEZUKA...!

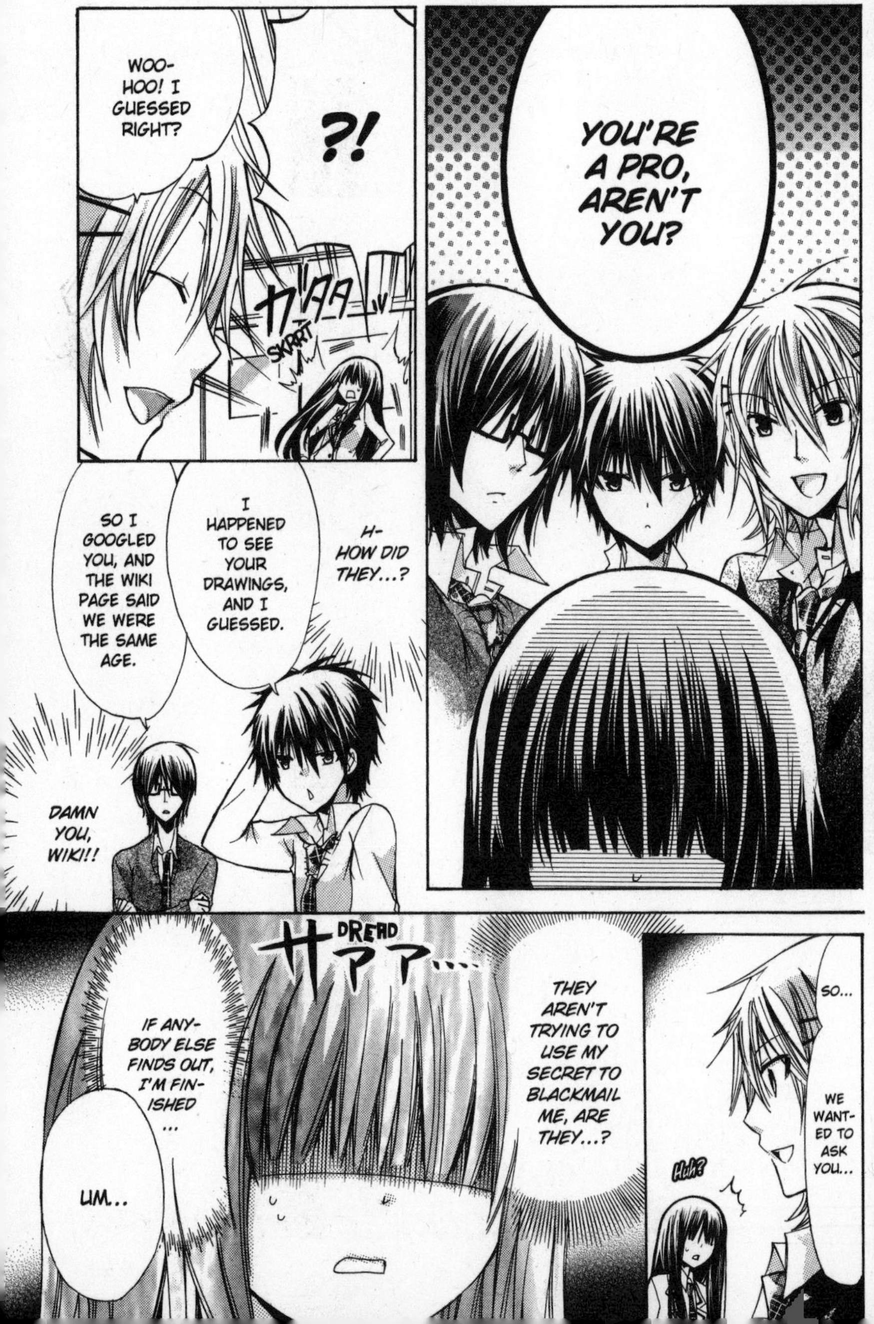
YOU'RE A PRO, AREN'T YOU?
WOO-HOO! I GUESSED RIGHT?
?!
カタタ
SKRRT
H-HOW DID THEY...?
I HAPPENED TO SEE YOUR DRAWINGS, AND I GUESSED.
SO I GOOGLED YOU, AND THE WIKI PAGE SAID WE WERE THE SAME AGE.
DAMN YOU, WIKI!!
SO...
WE WANTED TO ASK YOU...
Huh?
THEY AREN'T TRYING TO USE MY SECRET TO BLACKMAIL ME, ARE THEY...?
サアア...
DREAD
IF ANYBODY ELSE FINDS OUT, I'M FINISHED...
UM...

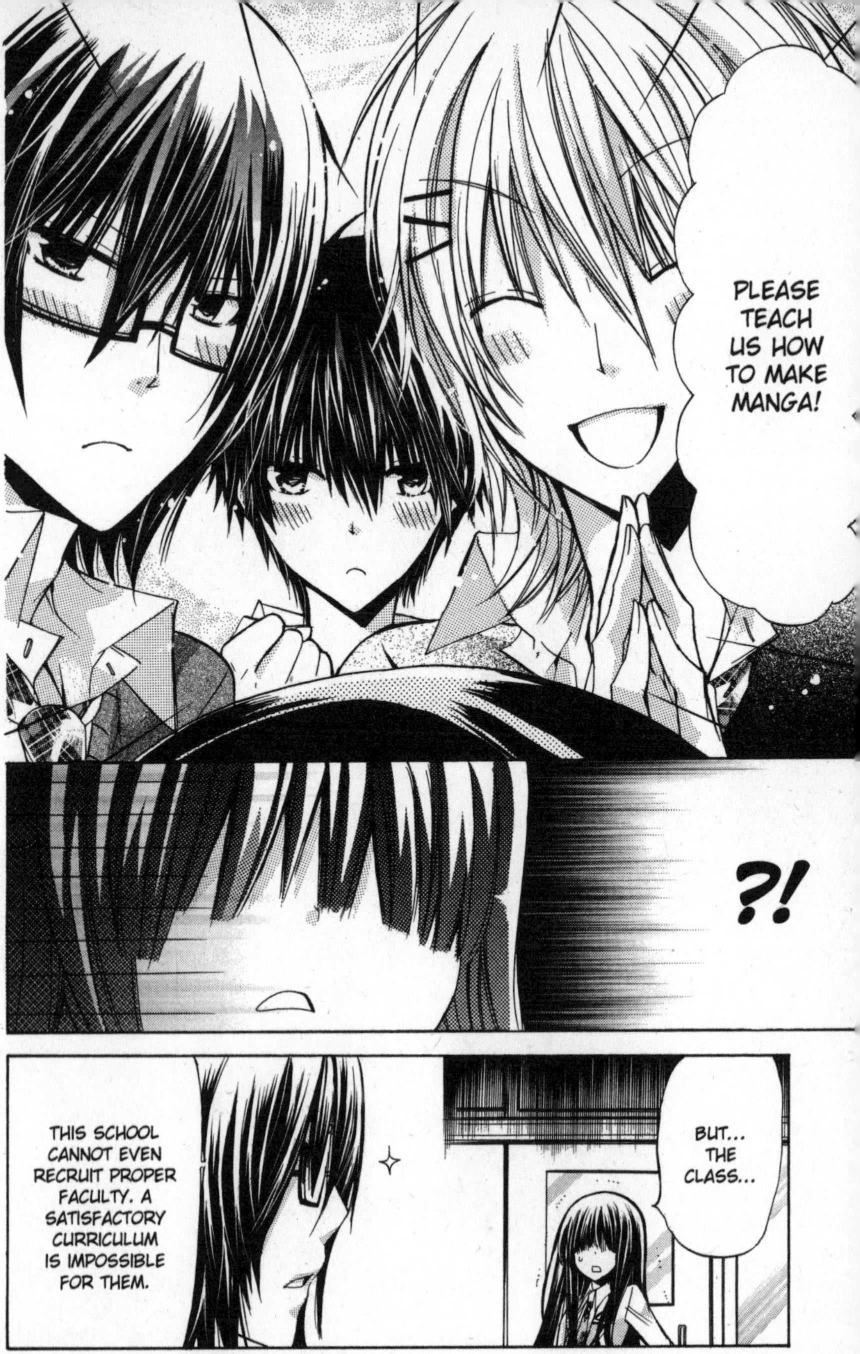
PLEASE TEACH US HOW TO MAKE MANGA!
?!
BUT... THE CLASS...
THIS SCHOOL CANNOT EVEN RECRUIT PROPER FACULTY. A SATISFACTORY CURRICULUM IS IMPOSSIBLE FOR THEM.

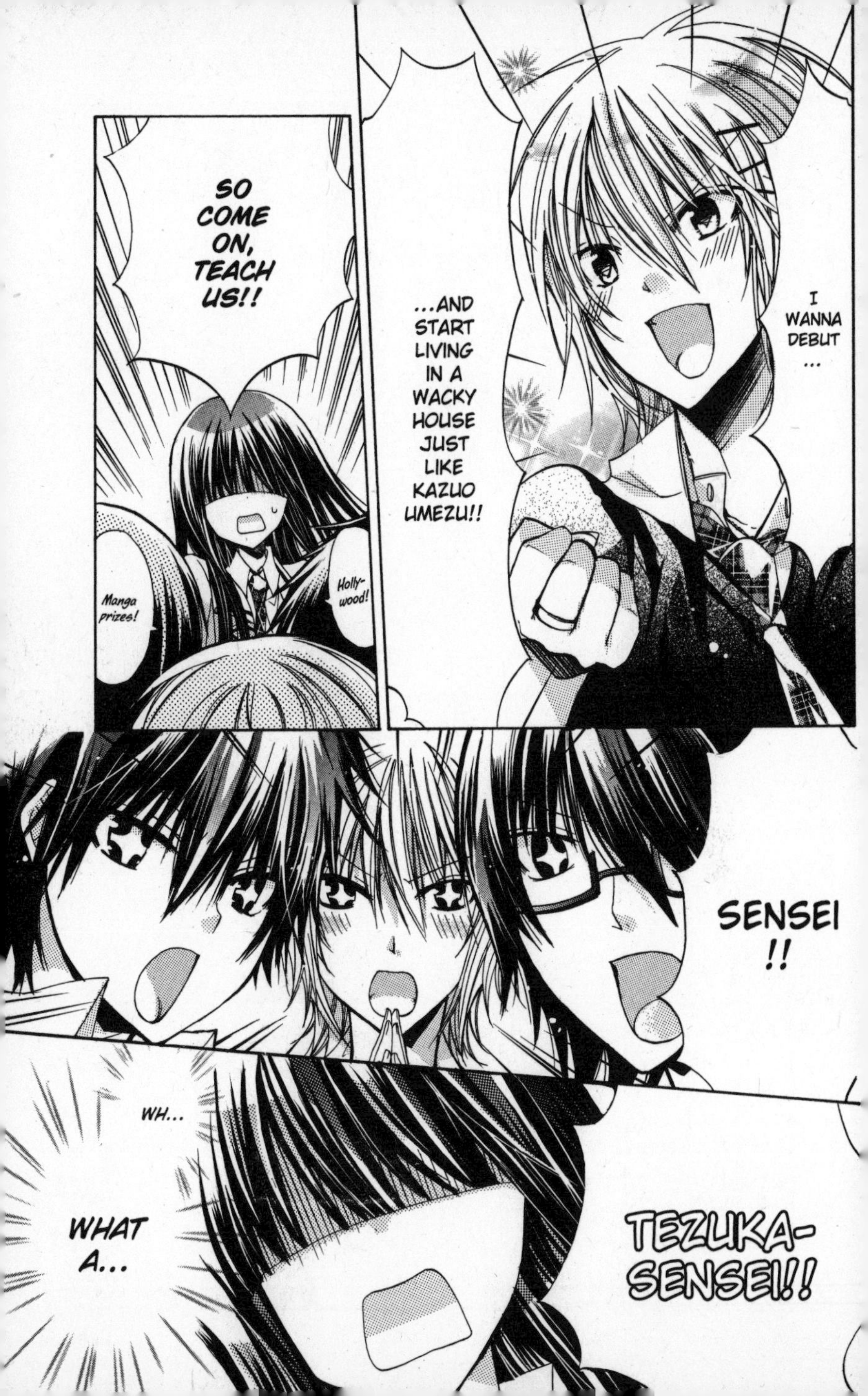
I WANNA DEBUT ...
...AND START LIVING IN A WACKY HOUSE JUST LIKE KAZUO UMEZU!!
SO COME ON, TEACH US!!
Holly-wood!
Manga prizes!
SENSEI !!
TEZUKA-SENSEI!!
WH...
WHAT A...

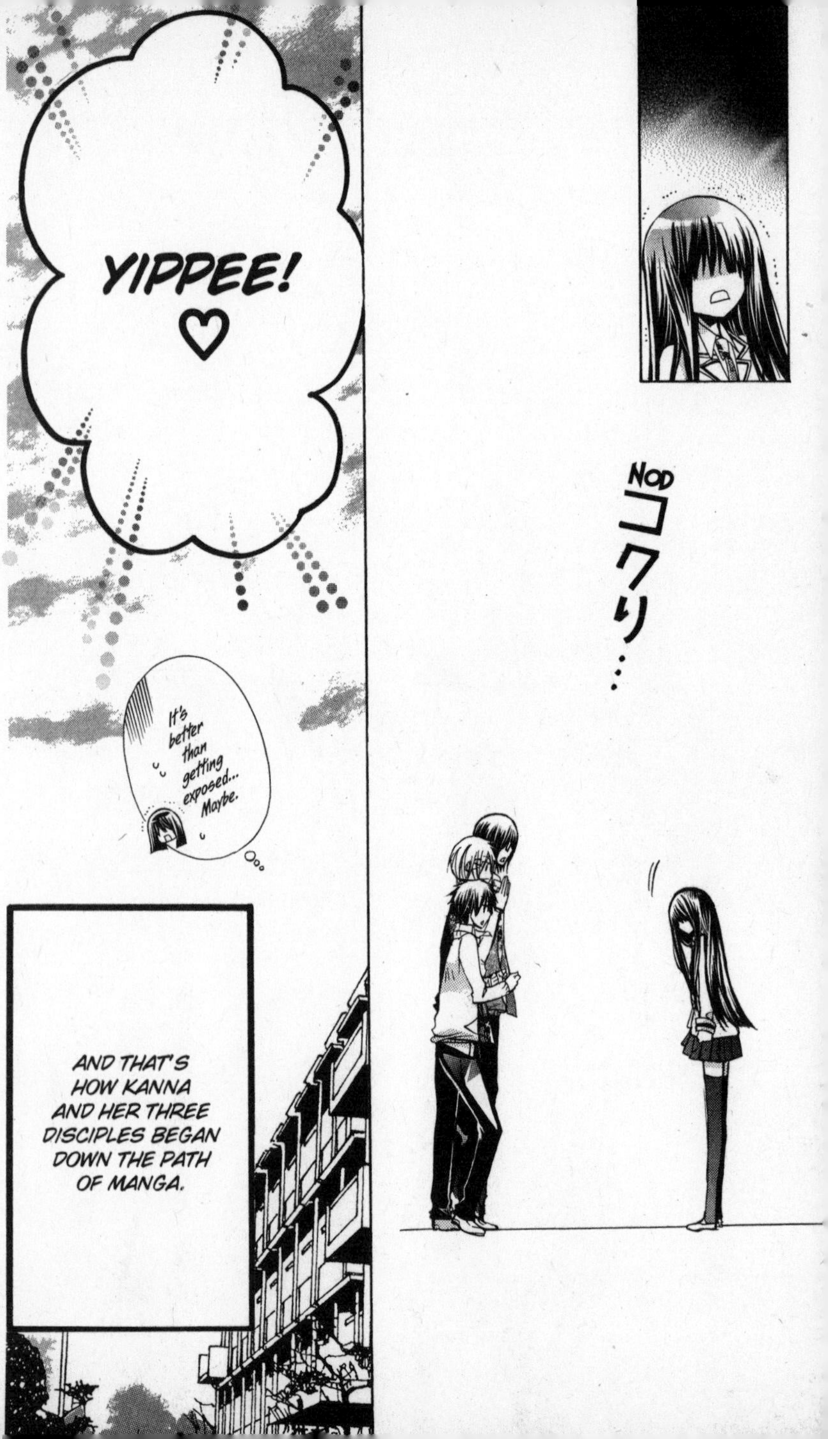

NOD
コクリ…
YIPPEE! ♡
It's better than getting exposed... Maybe.
AND THAT'S HOW KANNA AND HER THREE DISCIPLES BEGAN DOWN THE PATH OF MANGA.

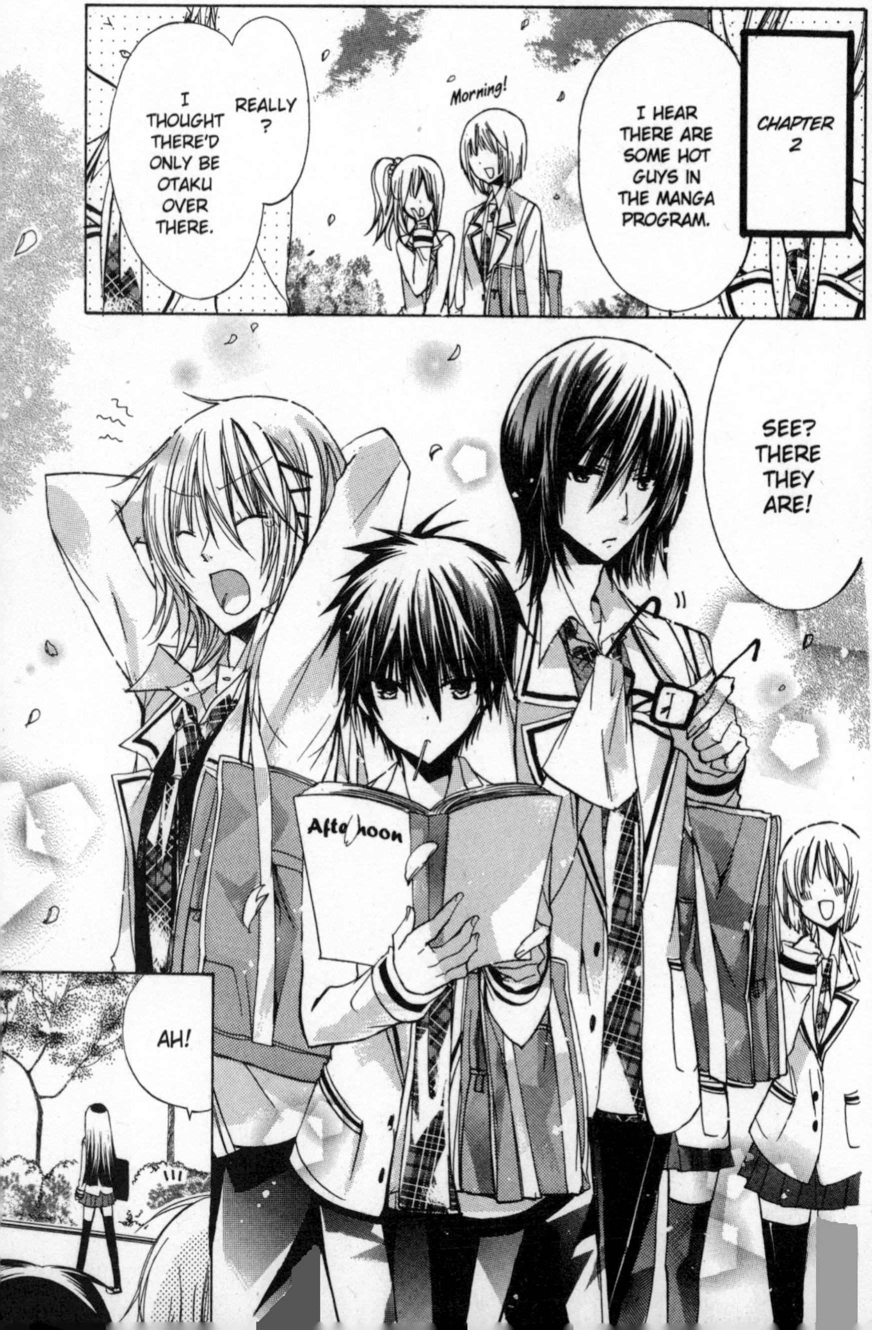
CHAPTER 2
I HEAR THERE ARE SOME HOT GUYS IN THE MANGA PROGRAM.
Morning!
REALLY?
I THOUGHT THERE'D ONLY BE OTAKU OVER THERE.
SEE? THERE THEY ARE!
AH!

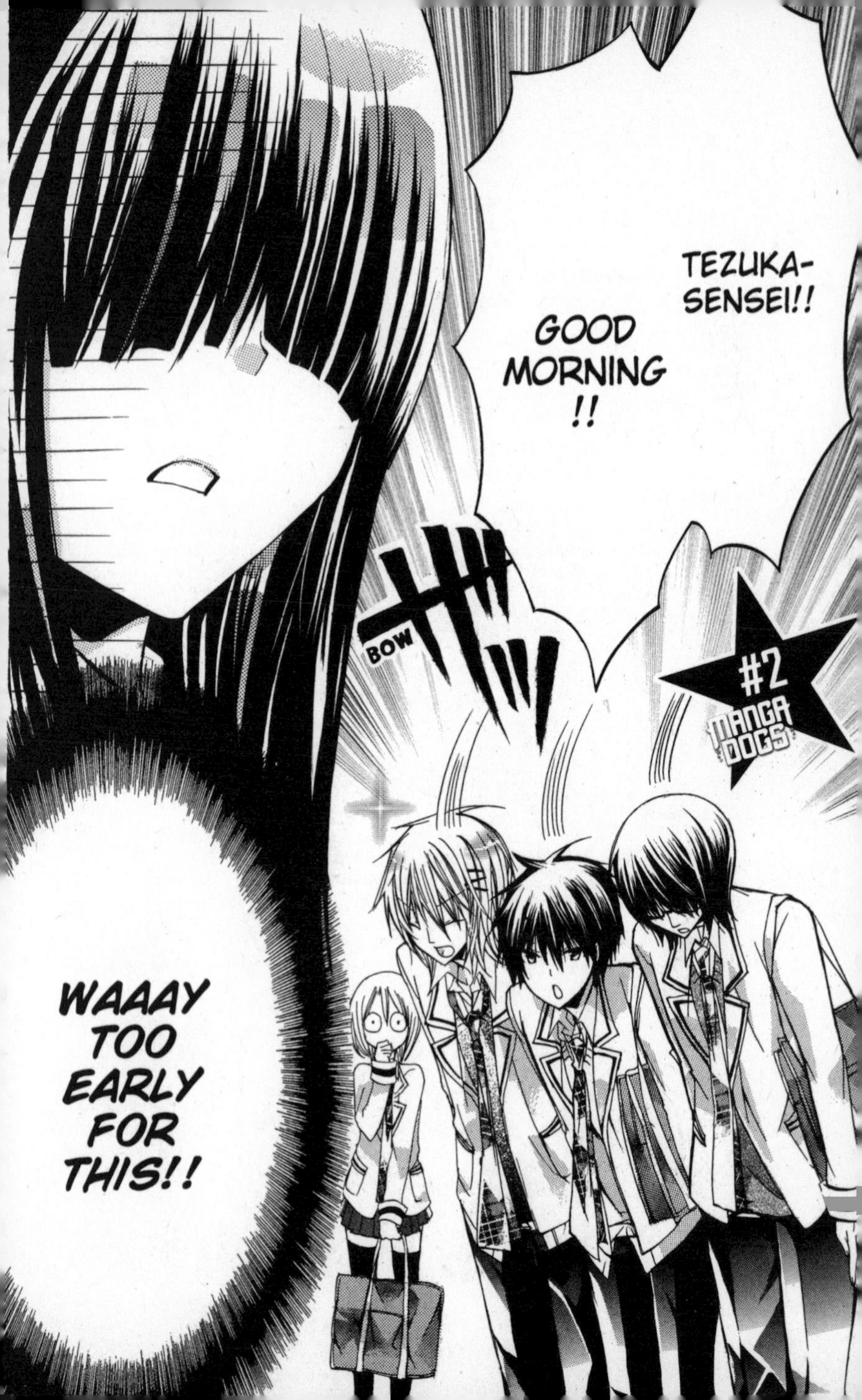
GOOD MORNING!! TEZUKA-SENSEI!!
BOW
#2 MANGA DOGS
WAAAY TOO EARLY FOR THIS!!

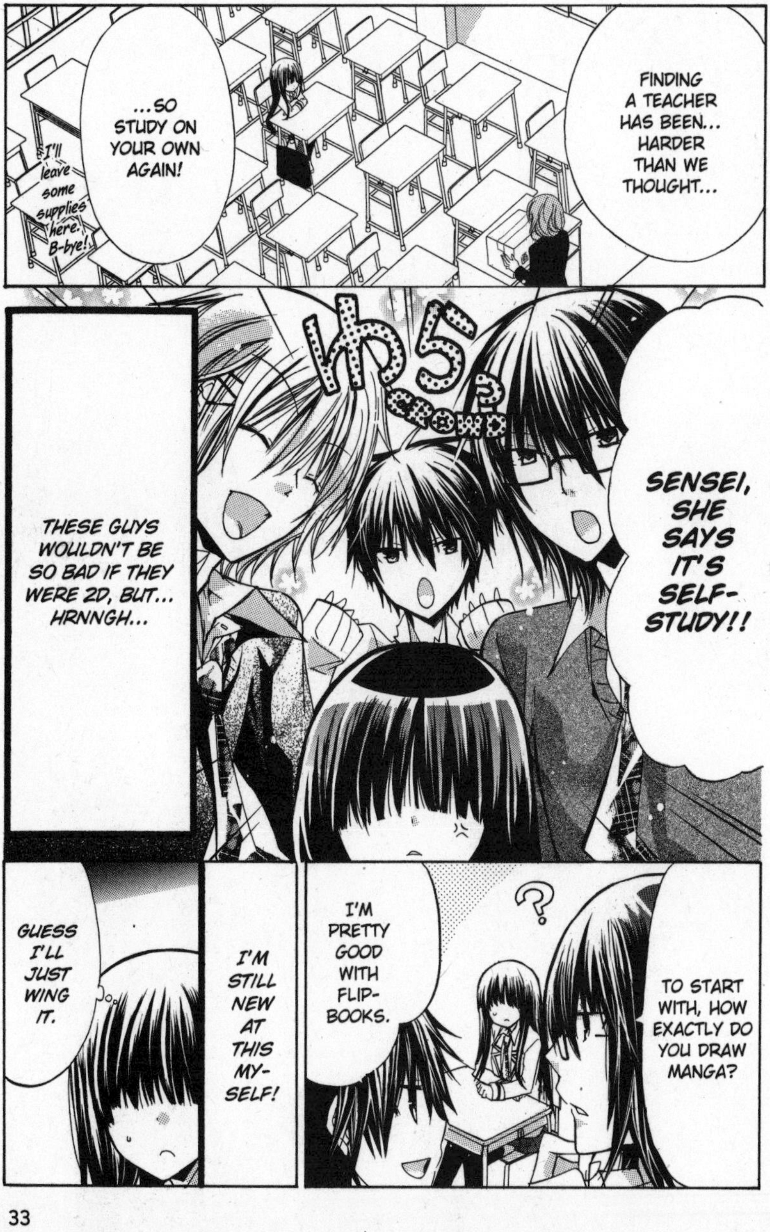

FINDING A TEACHER HAS BEEN... HARDER THAN WE THOUGHT...
...SO STUDY ON YOUR OWN AGAIN!
I'll leave some supplies here. B-bye!
わら
CROWD
SENSEI, SHE SAYS IT'S SELF-STUDY!!
THESE GUYS WOULDN'T BE SO BAD IF THEY WERE 2D, BUT... HRNNGH...
?
TO START WITH, HOW EXACTLY DO YOU DRAW MANGA?
I'M PRETTY GOOD WITH FLIP-BOOKS.
I'M STILL NEW AT THIS MY-SELF!
GUESS I'LL JUST WING IT.

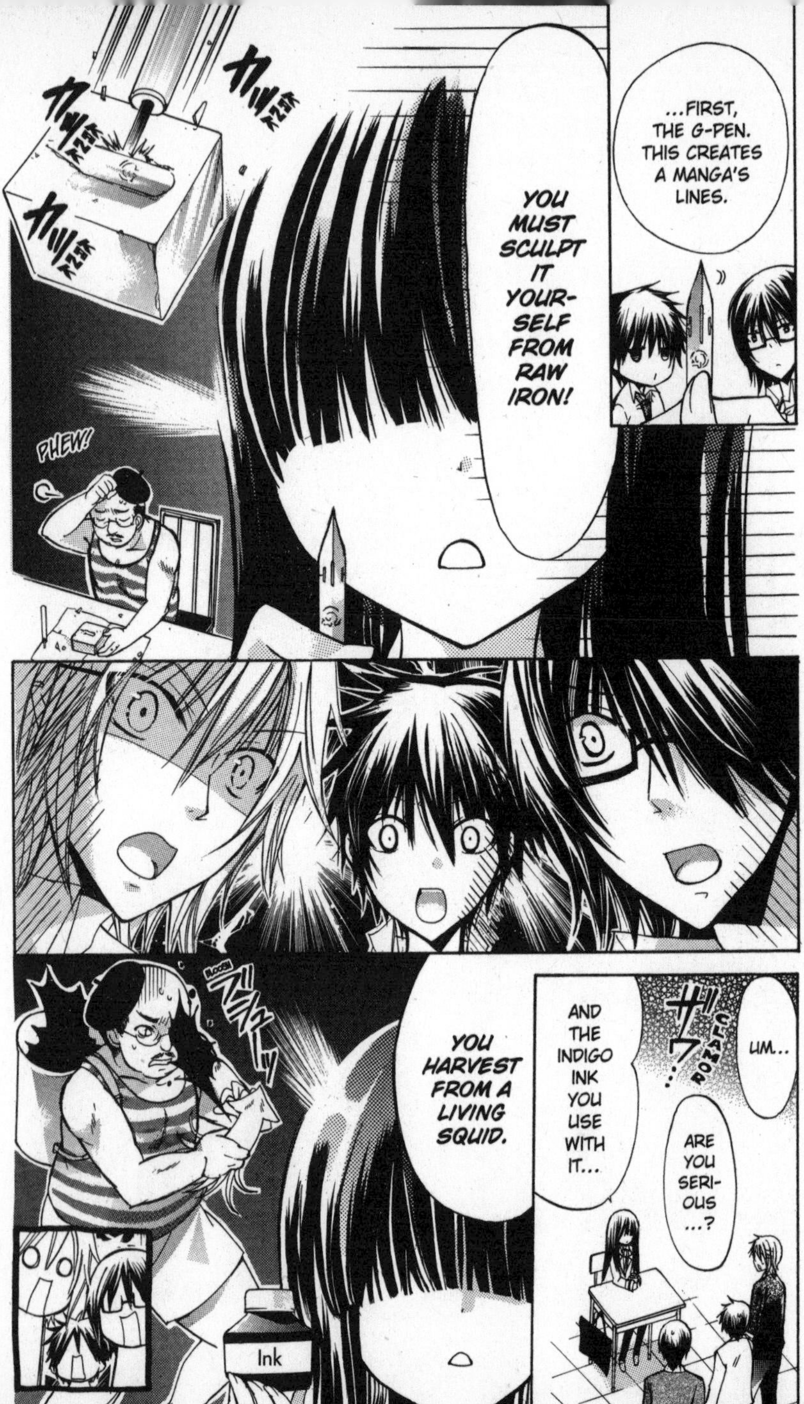
...FIRST, THE G-PEN. THIS CREATES A MANGA'S LINES.
YOU MUST SCULPT IT YOURSELF FROM RAW IRON!
PHEW!
UM...
CLAMOR
ARE YOU SERIOUS...?
AND THE INDIGO INK YOU USE WITH IT...
YOU HARVEST FROM A LIVING SQUID.
Ink

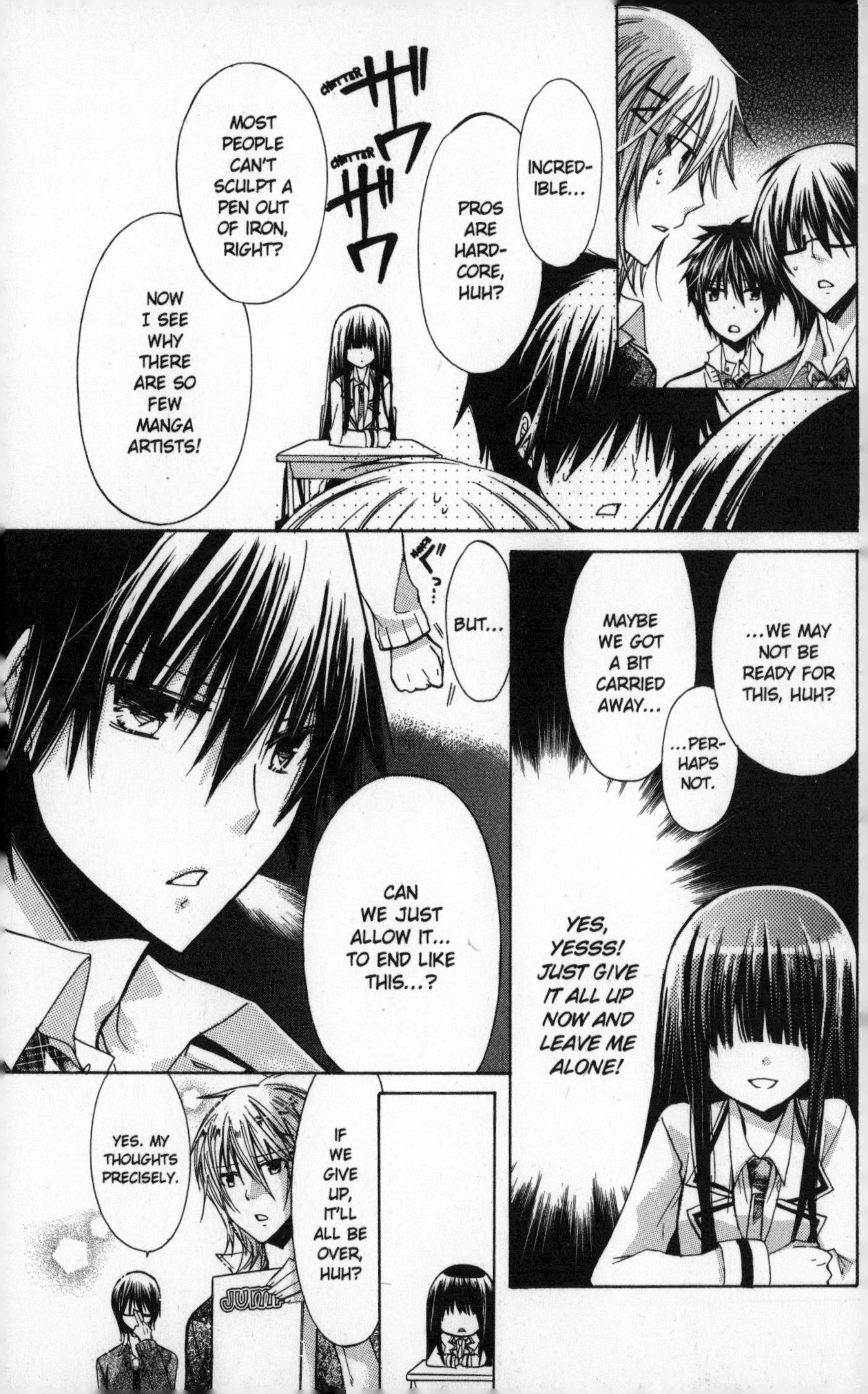
INCRED-IBLE...
PROS ARE HARD-CORE, HUH?
CHATTER
CHATTER
MOST PEOPLE CAN'T SCULPT A PEN OUT OF IRON, RIGHT?
NOW I SEE WHY THERE ARE SO FEW MANGA ARTISTS!
...WE MAY NOT BE READY FOR THIS, HUH?
MAYBE WE GOT A BIT CARRIED AWAY...
...PER-HAPS NOT.
YES, YESSS! JUST GIVE IT ALL UP NOW AND LEAVE ME ALONE!
BUT...
CAN WE JUST ALLOW IT... TO END LIKE THIS...?
IF WE GIVE UP, IT'LL ALL BE OVER, HUH?
YES. MY THOUGHTS PRECISELY.

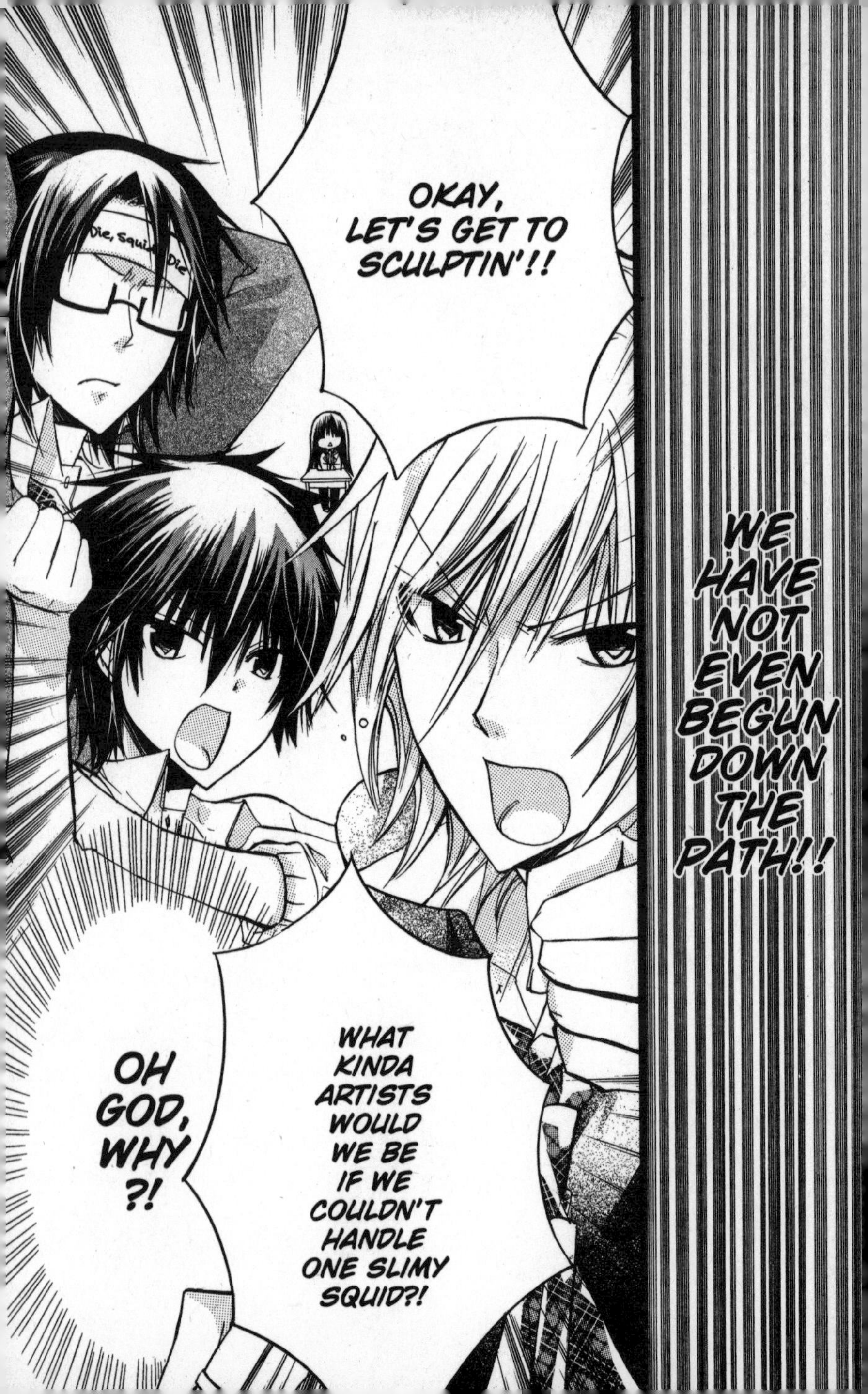
WE HAVE NOT EVEN BEGUN DOWN THE PATH!!
OKAY, LET'S GET TO SCULPTIN'!!
WHAT KINDA ARTISTS WOULD WE BE IF WE COULDN'T HANDLE ONE SLIMY SQUID?!
OH GOD, WHY?!

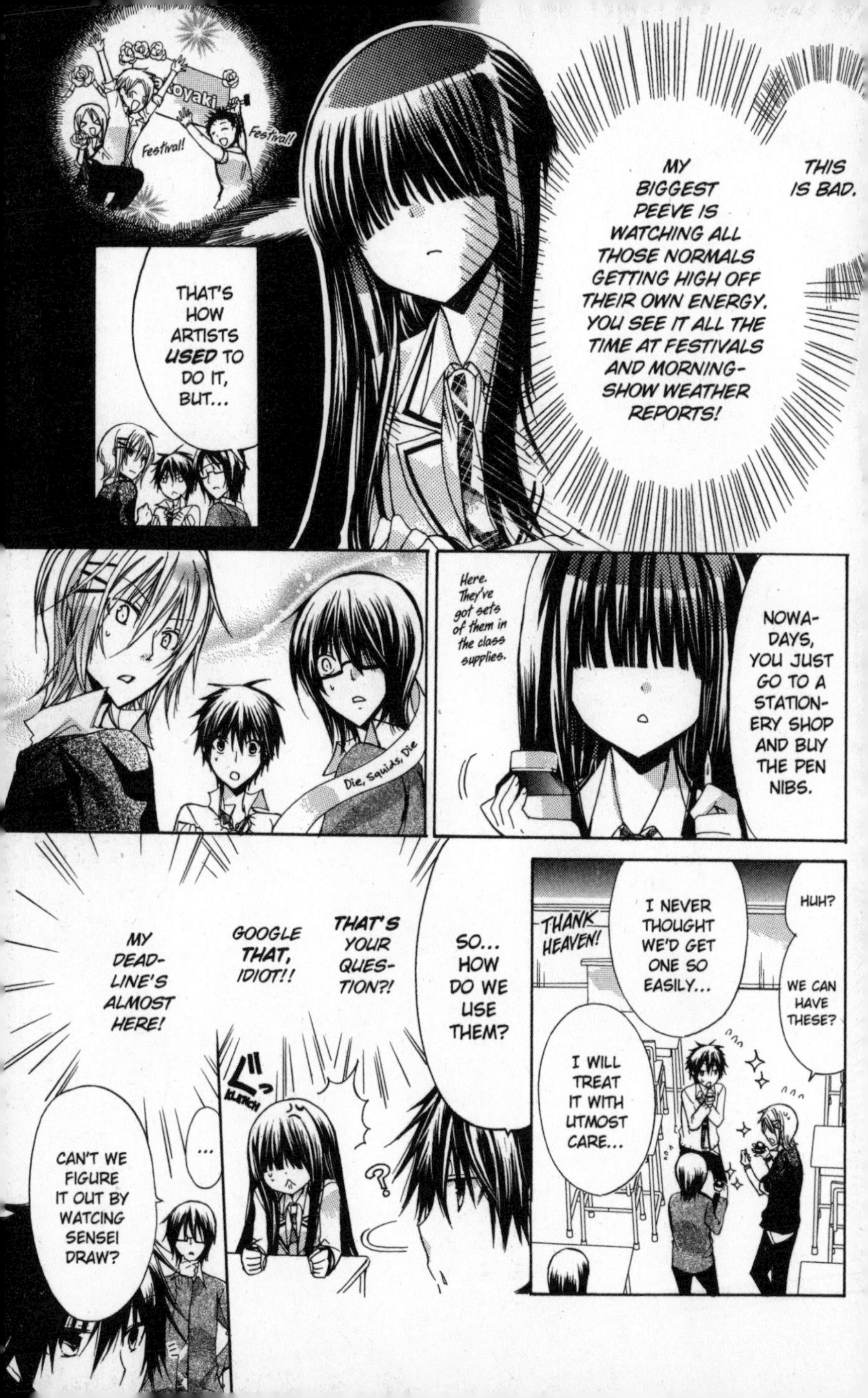
THIS IS BAD.
MY BIGGEST PEEVE IS WATCHING ALL THOSE NORMALS GETTING HIGH OFF THEIR OWN ENERGY. YOU SEE IT ALL THE TIME AT FESTIVALS AND MORNING-SHOW WEATHER REPORTS!
Festival!
Festival!
THAT'S HOW ARTISTS *USED* TO DO IT, BUT...
NOWADAYS, YOU JUST GO TO A STATIONERY SHOP AND BUY THE PEN NIBS.
Here. They've got sets of them in the class supplies.
Die, Squids, Die
HUH?
WE CAN HAVE THESE?
I NEVER THOUGHT WE'D GET ONE SO EASILY...
THANK HEAVEN!
I WILL TREAT IT WITH UTMOST CARE...
SO... HOW DO WE USE THEM?
THAT'S YOUR QUESTION?!
GOOGLE *THAT*, IDIOT!!
MY DEADLINE'S ALMOST HERE!
KLENCH
...
CAN'T WE FIGURE IT OUT BY WATCING SENSEI DRAW?

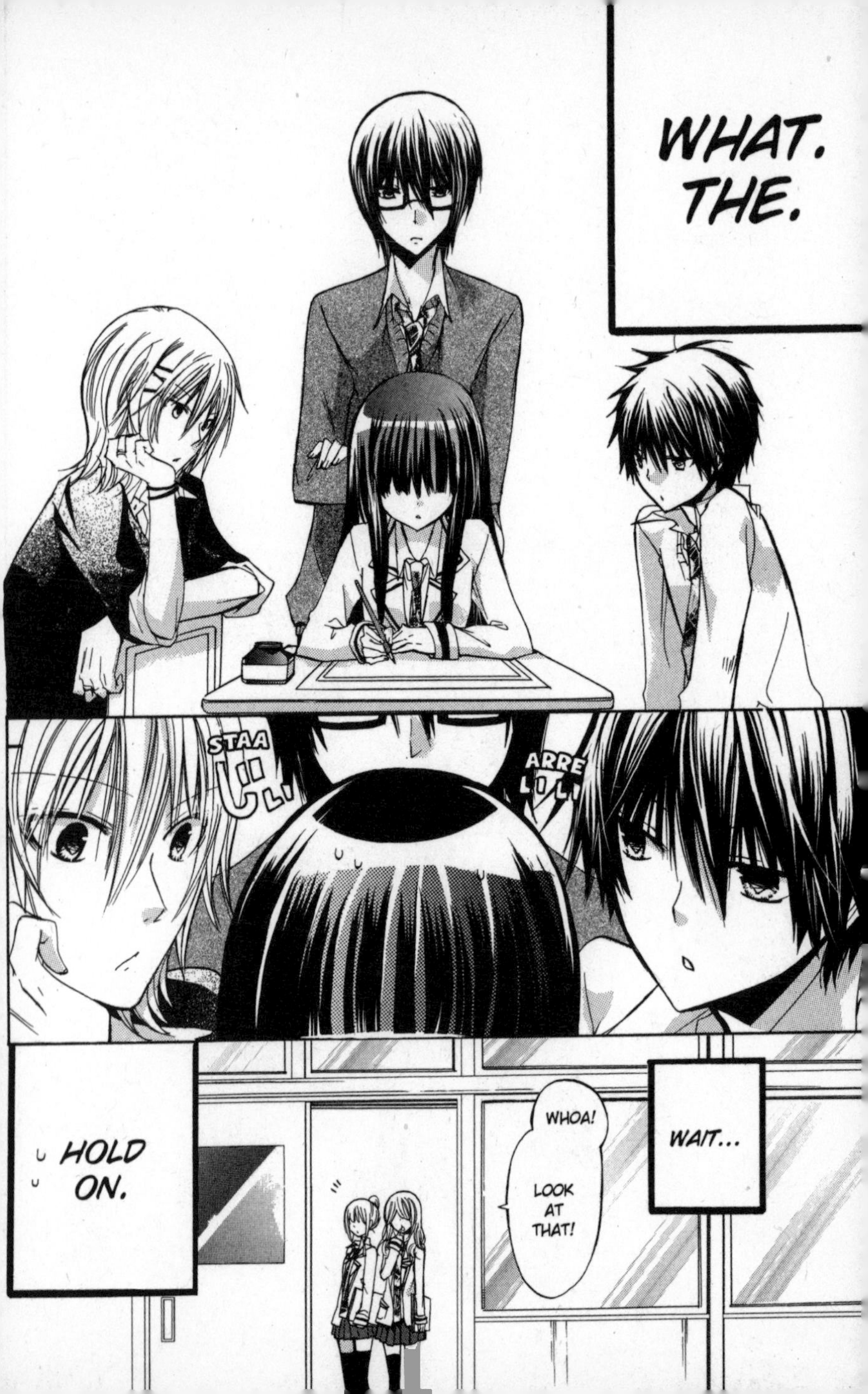
WHAT. THE.
ARRE
STAA
WAIT...
WHOA!
LOOK AT THAT!
HOLD ON.

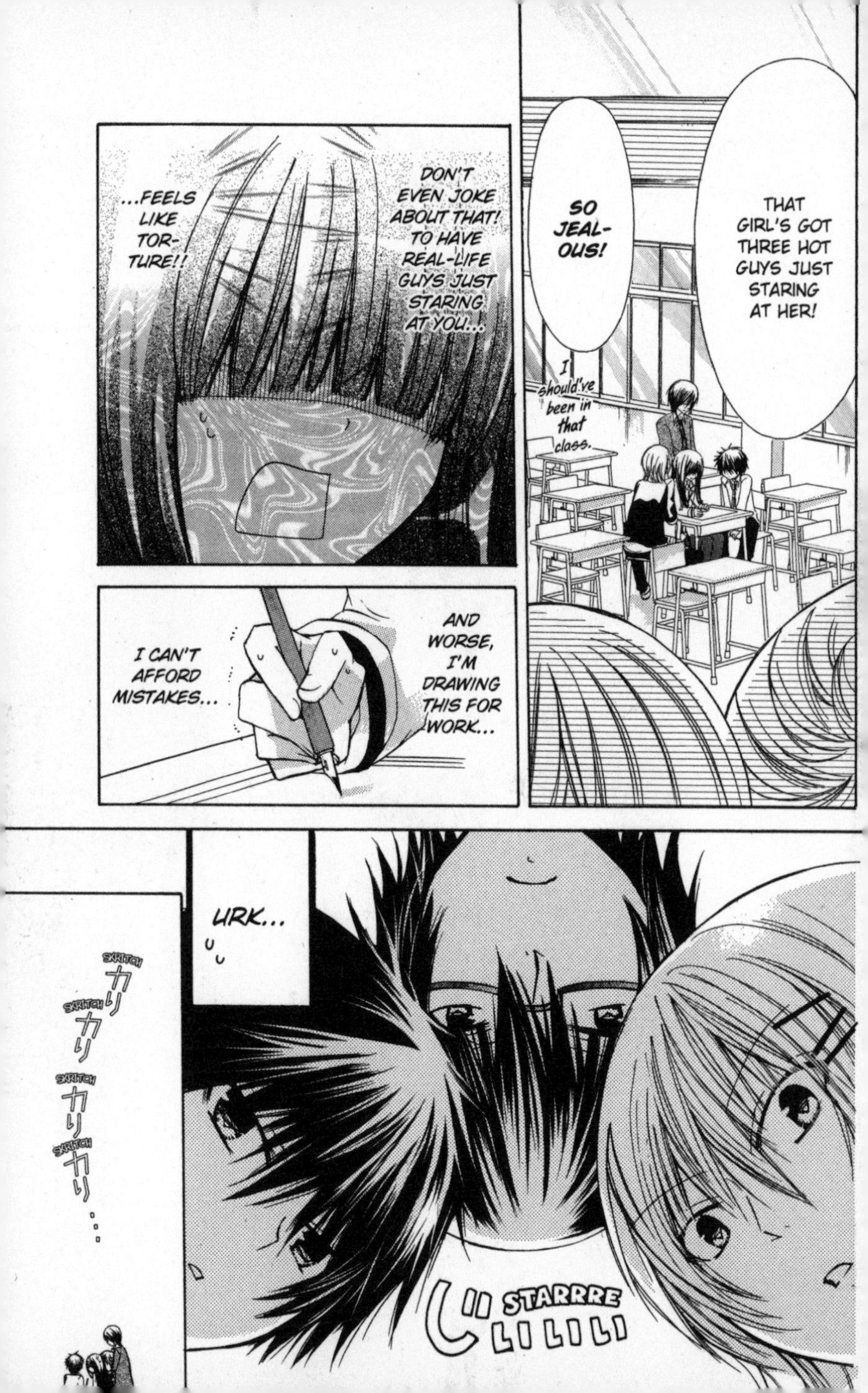
THAT GIRL'S GOT THREE HOT GUYS JUST STARING AT HER!
SO JEAL-OUS!
I should've been in that class.
DON'T EVEN JOKE ABOUT THAT! TO HAVE REAL-LIFE GUYS JUST STARING AT YOU...
...FEELS LIKE TOR-TURE!!
AND WORSE, I'M DRAWING THIS FOR WORK...
I CAN'T AFFORD MISTAKES...
URK...
STARRRE
SKRITCH カリ
SKRITCH カリ
SKRITCH カリ
SKRITCH カリ...

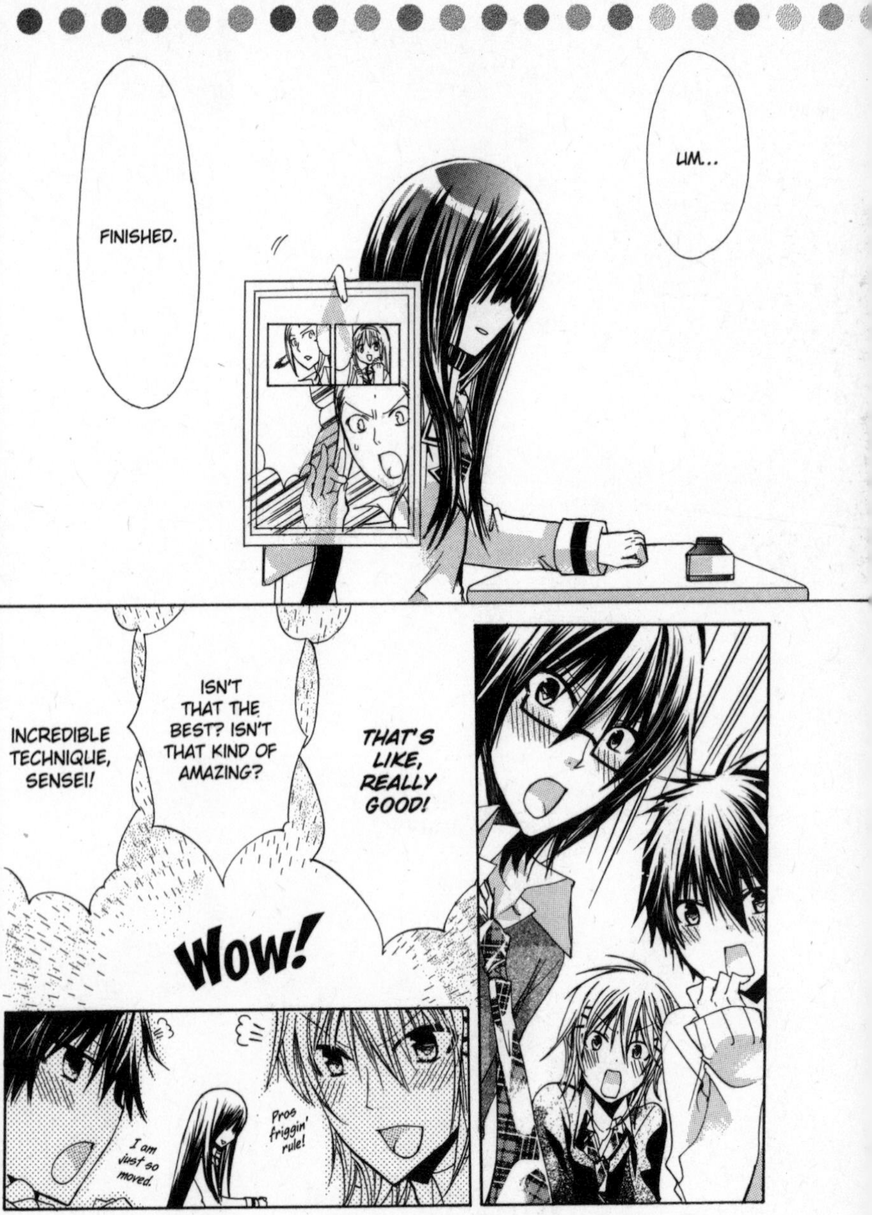

UM...
FINISHED.
THAT'S LIKE, REALLY GOOD!
ISN'T THAT THE BEST? ISN'T THAT KIND OF AMAZING?
INCREDIBLE TECHNIQUE, SENSEI!
WOW!
Pros friggin' rule!
I am just so moved.

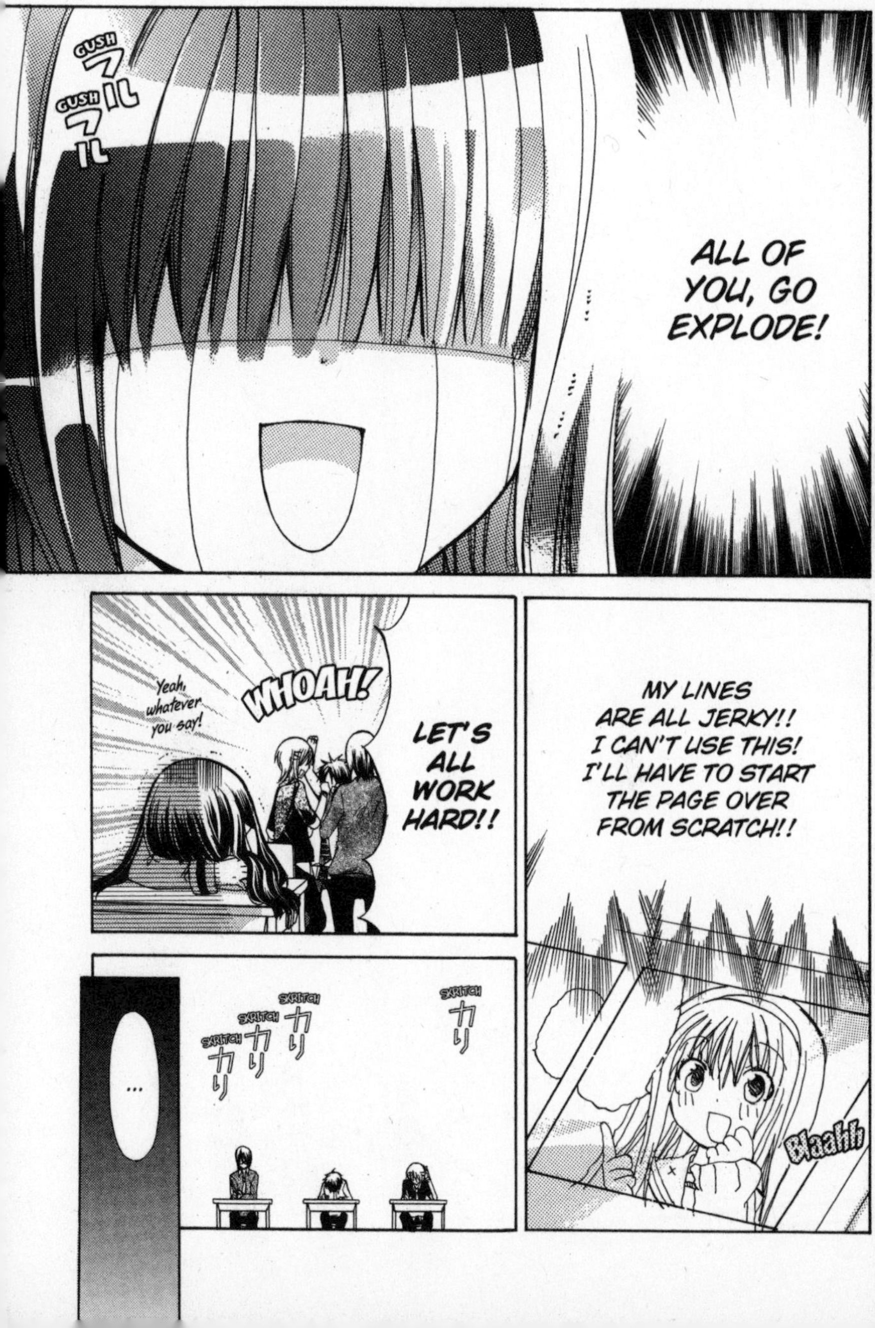
ALL OF YOU, GO EXPLODE!
...
GUSH フル
GUSH フル
MY LINES ARE ALL JERKY!! I CAN'T USE THIS! I'LL HAVE TO START THE PAGE OVER FROM SCRATCH!!
Blaahh
LET'S ALL WORK HARD!!
WHOAH!
Yeah, whatever you say!
SKRITCH カリ
SKRITCH カリ
SKRITCH カリ
SKRITCH カリ
...

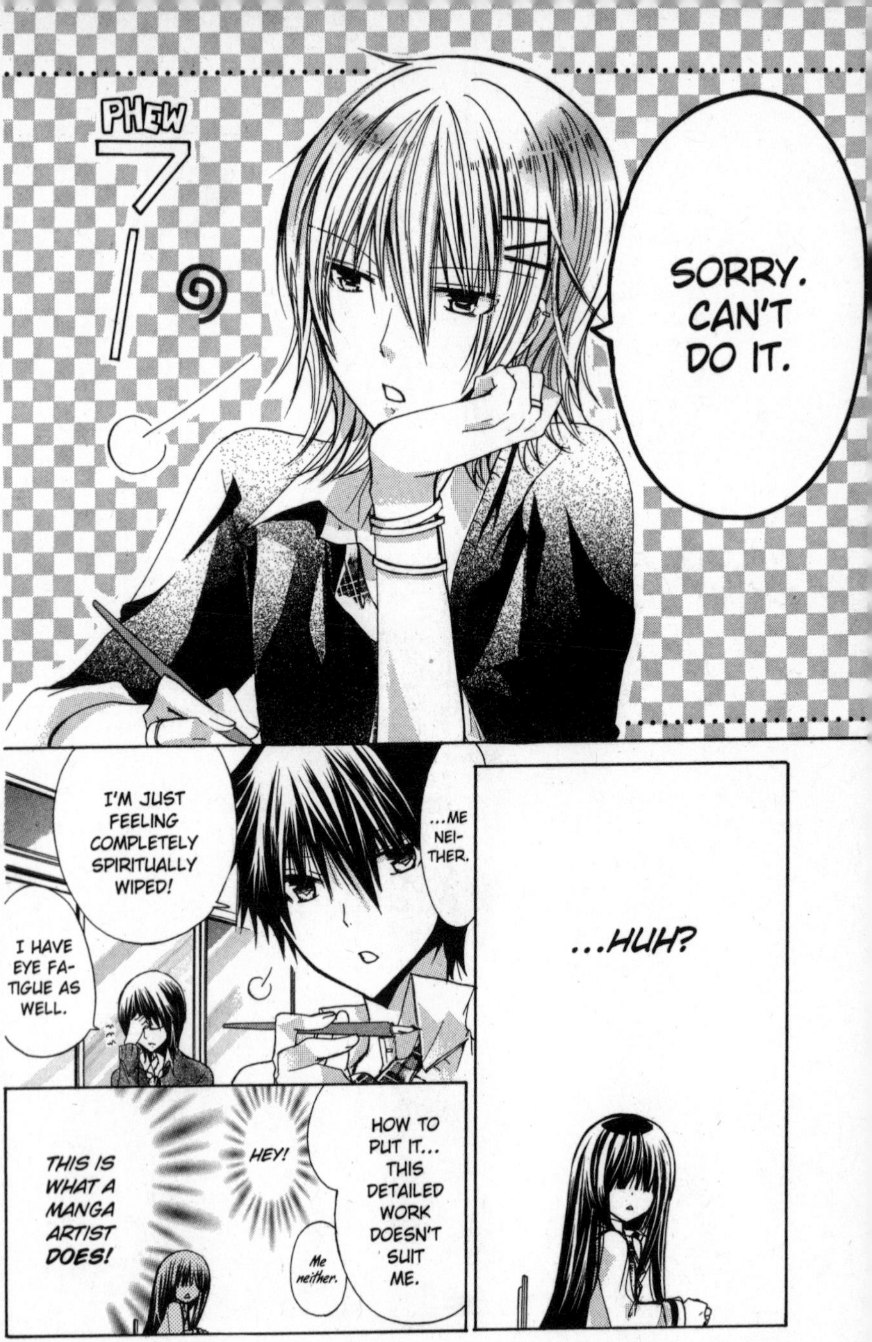
SORRY. CAN'T DO IT.
PHEW
...HUH?
...ME NEI-THER.
I'M JUST FEELING COMPLETELY SPIRITUALLY WIPED!
I HAVE EYE FA-TIGUE AS WELL.
HOW TO PUT IT... THIS DETAILED WORK DOESN'T SUIT ME.
Me neither.
HEY!
THIS IS WHAT A MANGA ARTIST DOES!

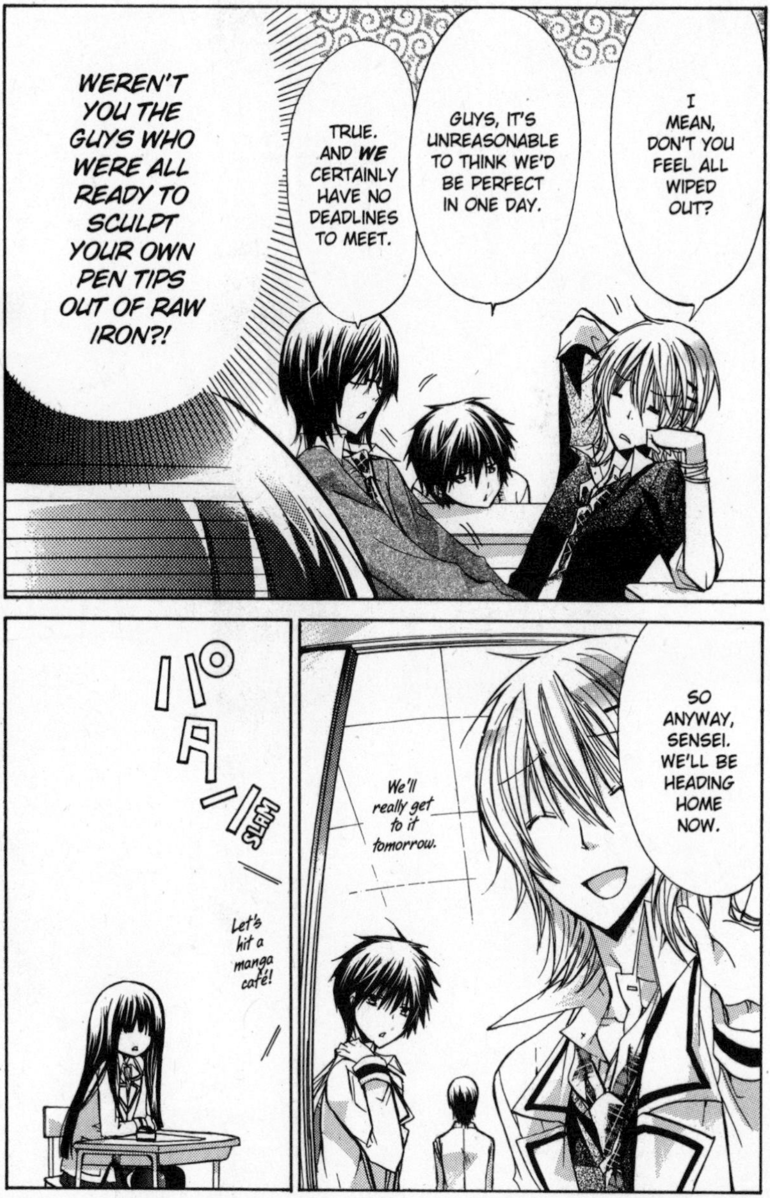
I MEAN, DON'T YOU FEEL ALL WIPED OUT?
GUYS, IT'S UNREASONABLE TO THINK WE'D BE PERFECT IN ONE DAY.
TRUE. AND **WE** CERTAINLY HAVE NO DEADLINES TO MEET.
WEREN'T YOU THE GUYS WHO WERE ALL READY TO SCULPT YOUR OWN PEN TIPS OUT OF RAW IRON?!
SO ANYWAY, SENSEI. WE'LL BE HEADING HOME NOW.
We'll really get to it tomorrow.
SLAM
Let's hit a manga café!

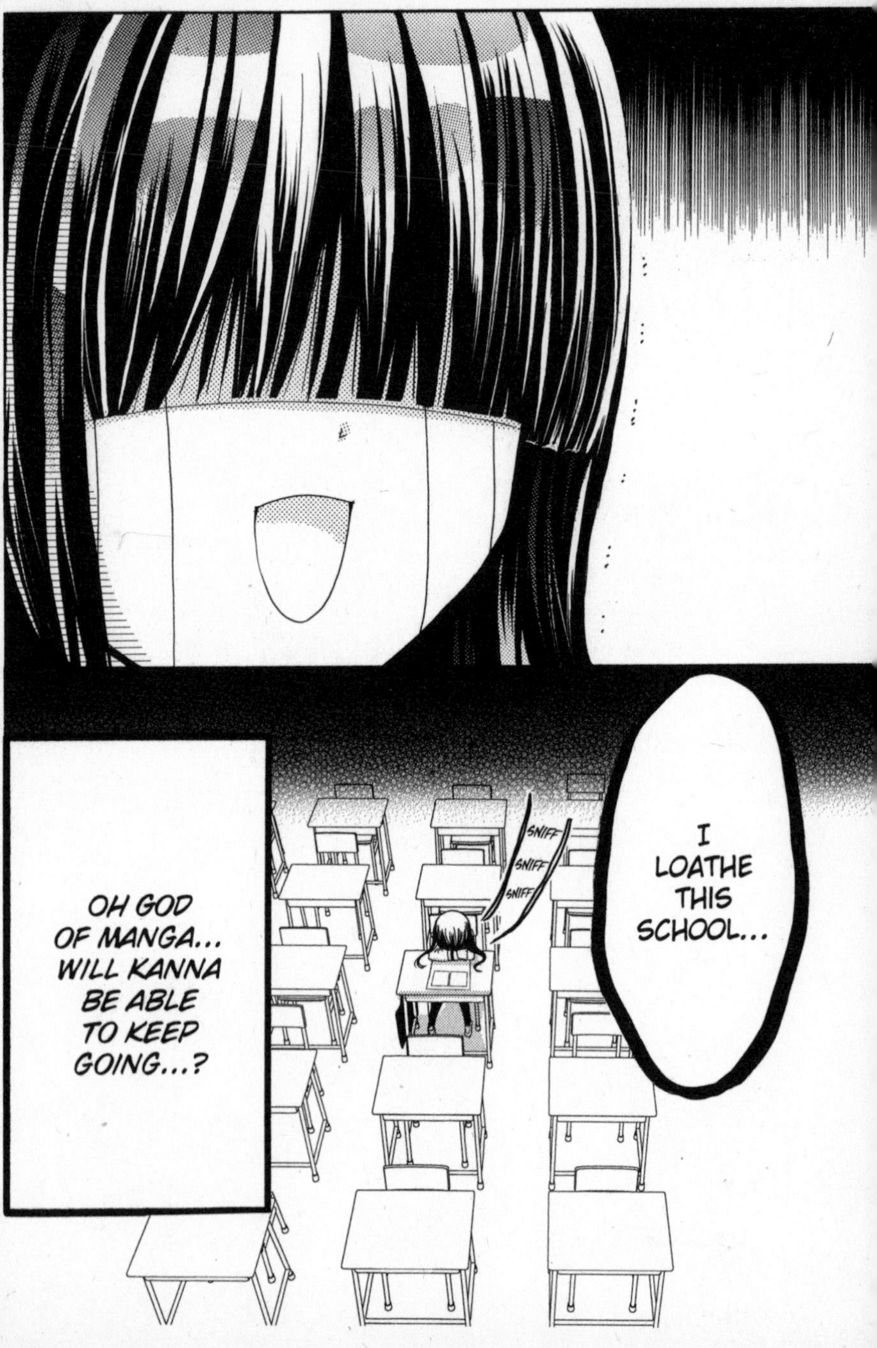
I LOATHE THIS SCHOOL...
SNIFF
SNIFF
SNIFF
OH GOD OF MANGA... WILL KANNA BE ABLE TO KEEP GOING...?

This...
is just the
time for an
"and then
she woke up"
ending.

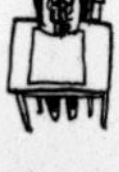

MANGA DOGS

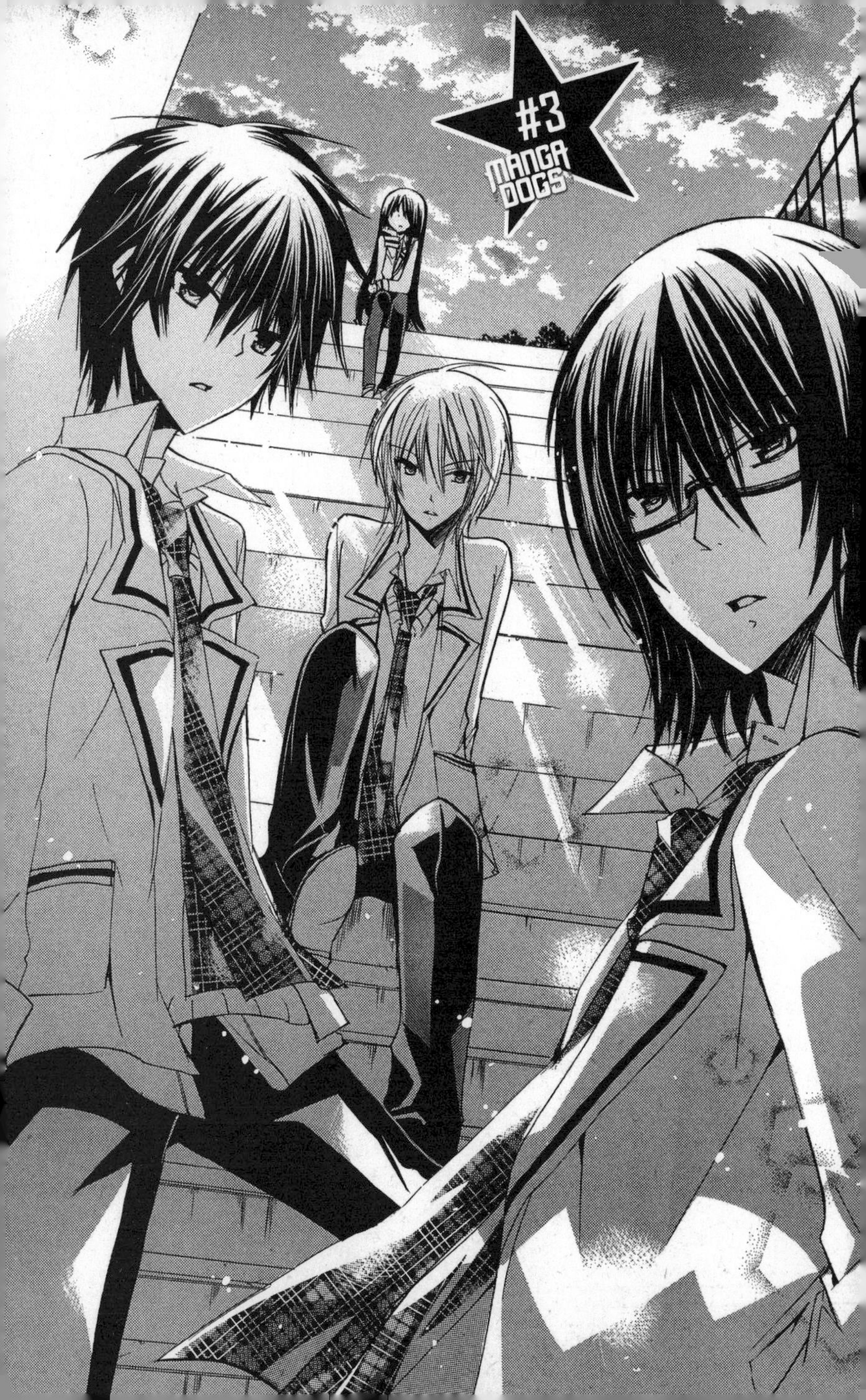
#3
MANGA DOGS

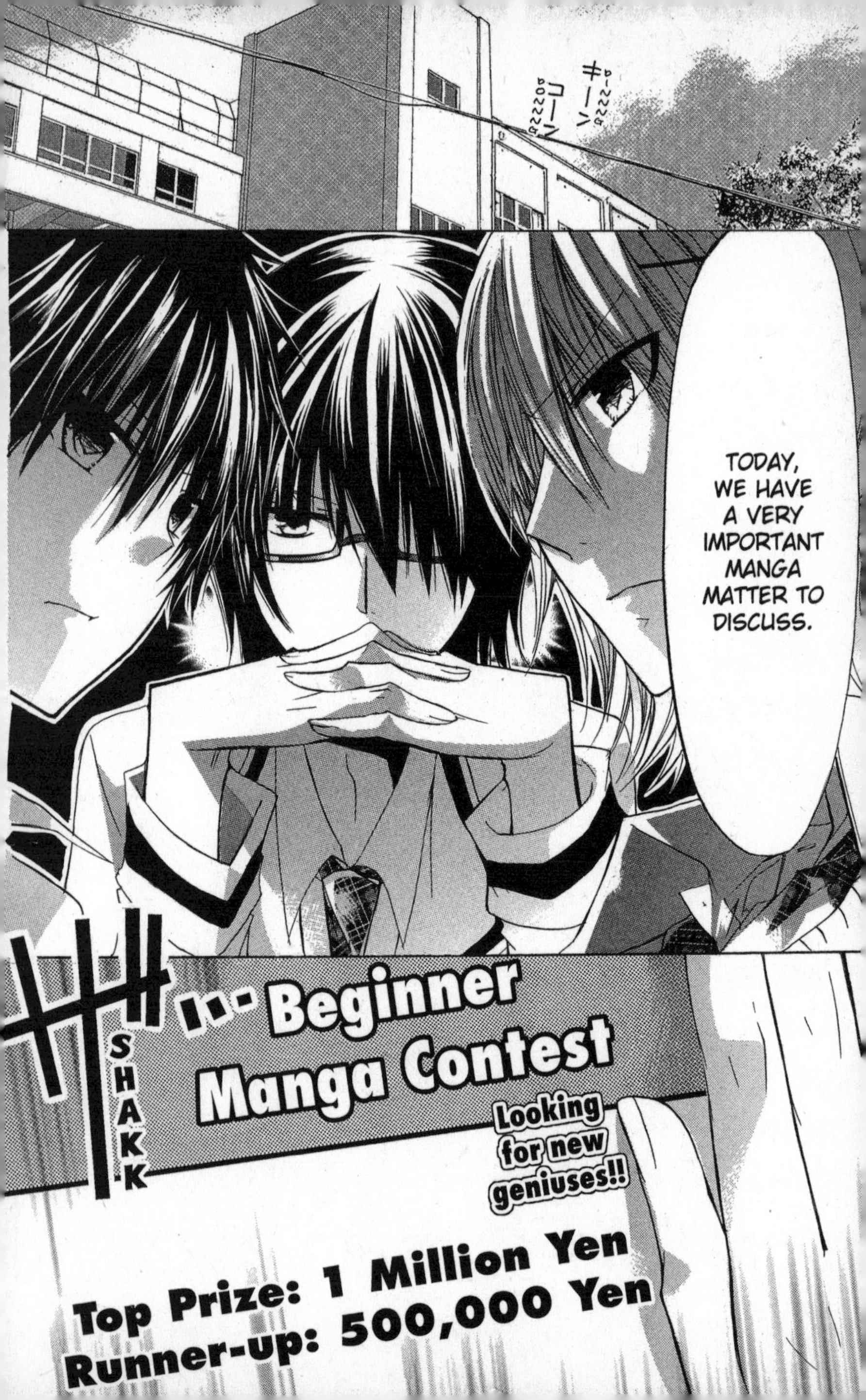
キーン
DINNNG
コーン
DONNNG
TODAY, WE HAVE A VERY IMPORTANT MANGA MATTER TO DISCUSS.
SHAKK
I... Beginner Manga Contest
Looking for new geniuses!!
Top Prize: 1 Million Yen
Runner-up: 500,000 Yen

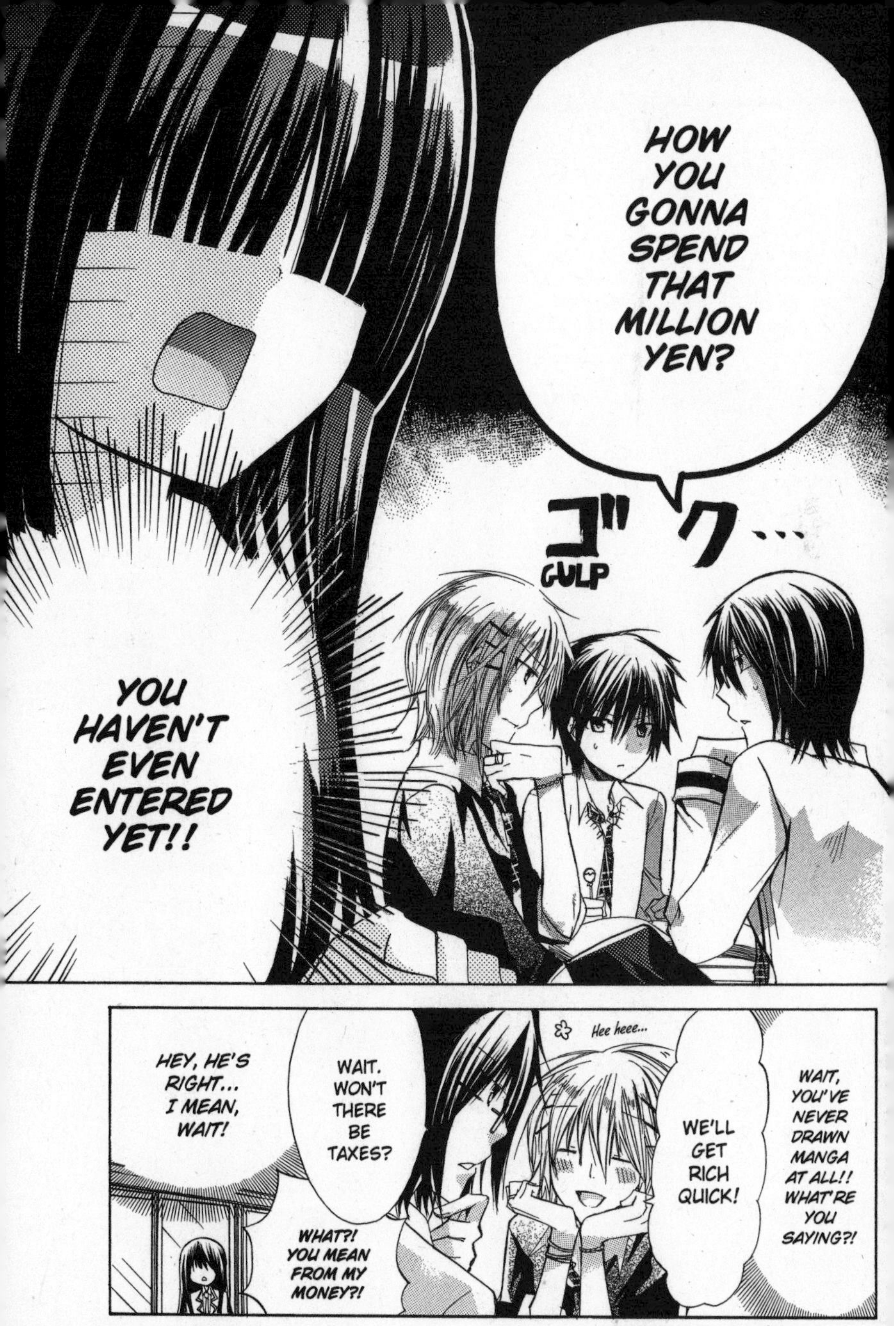
HOW YOU GONNA SPEND THAT MILLION YEN?
ゴク…
GULP
YOU HAVEN'T EVEN ENTERED YET!!
WAIT, YOU'VE NEVER DRAWN MANGA AT ALL!! WHAT'RE YOU SAYING?!
Hee heee...
WE'LL GET RICH QUICK!
WAIT. WON'T THERE BE TAXES?
WHAT?! YOU MEAN FROM MY MONEY?!
HEY, HE'S RIGHT... I MEAN, WAIT!

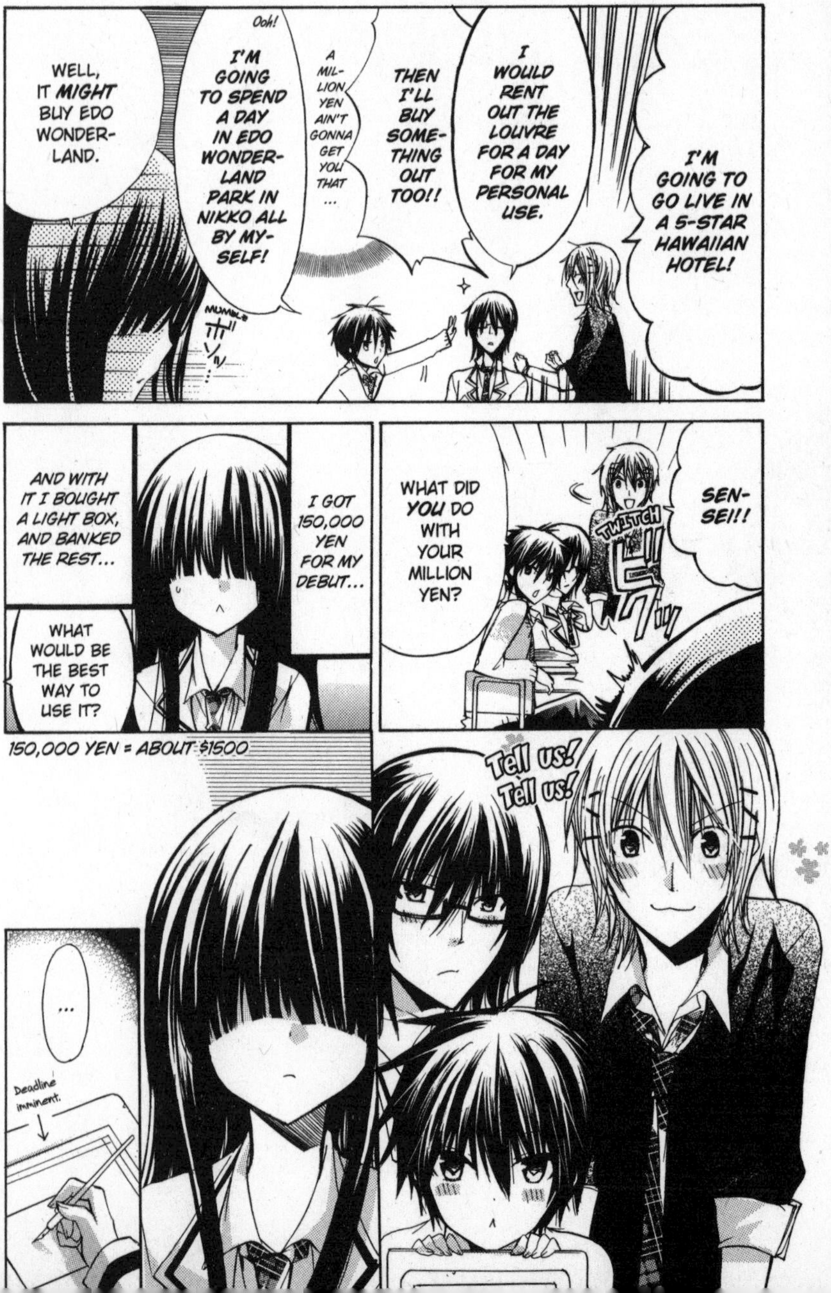
I'M GOING TO GO LIVE IN A 5-STAR HAWAIIAN HOTEL!
I WOULD RENT OUT THE LOUVRE FOR A DAY FOR MY PERSONAL USE.
THEN I'LL BUY SOME-THING OUT TOO!!
A MIL-LION YEN AIN'T GONNA GET YOU THAT ...
Ooh!
I'M GOING TO SPEND A DAY IN EDO WONDER-LAND PARK IN NIKKO ALL BY MY-SELF!
MUMBLE
WELL, IT *MIGHT* BUY EDO WONDER-LAND.
SEN-SEI!!
TWITCH
WHAT DID *YOU* DO WITH YOUR MILLION YEN?
I GOT 150,000 YEN FOR MY DEBUT...
AND WITH IT I BOUGHT A LIGHT BOX, AND BANKED THE REST...
WHAT WOULD BE THE BEST WAY TO USE IT?
Tell us! Tell us!
...
Deadline imminent.

150,000 YEN = ABOUT $1500

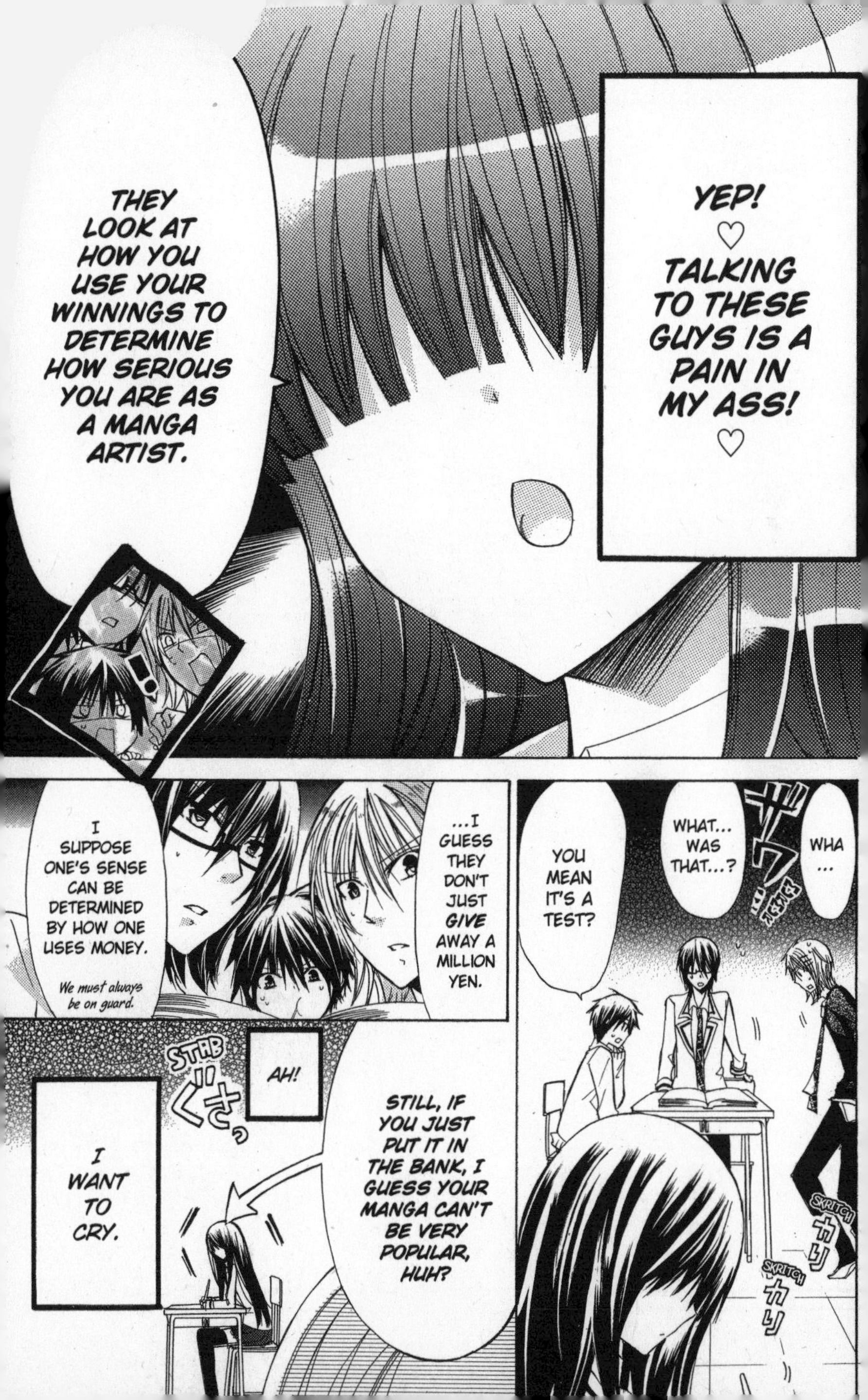

YEP! ♡ TALKING TO THESE GUYS IS A PAIN IN MY ASS! ♡
THEY LOOK AT HOW YOU USE YOUR WINNINGS TO DETERMINE HOW SERIOUS YOU ARE AS A MANGA ARTIST.
WHA...
WHAT... WAS THAT...?
YOU MEAN IT'S A TEST?
SKRITCH カリ
SKRITCH カリ
...I GUESS THEY DON'T JUST GIVE AWAY A MILLION YEN.
I SUPPOSE ONE'S SENSE CAN BE DETERMINED BY HOW ONE USES MONEY.
We must always be on guard.
STILL, IF YOU JUST PUT IT IN THE BANK, I GUESS YOUR MANGA CAN'T BE VERY POPULAR, HUH?
AH!
STAB ぐさっ
I WANT TO CRY.

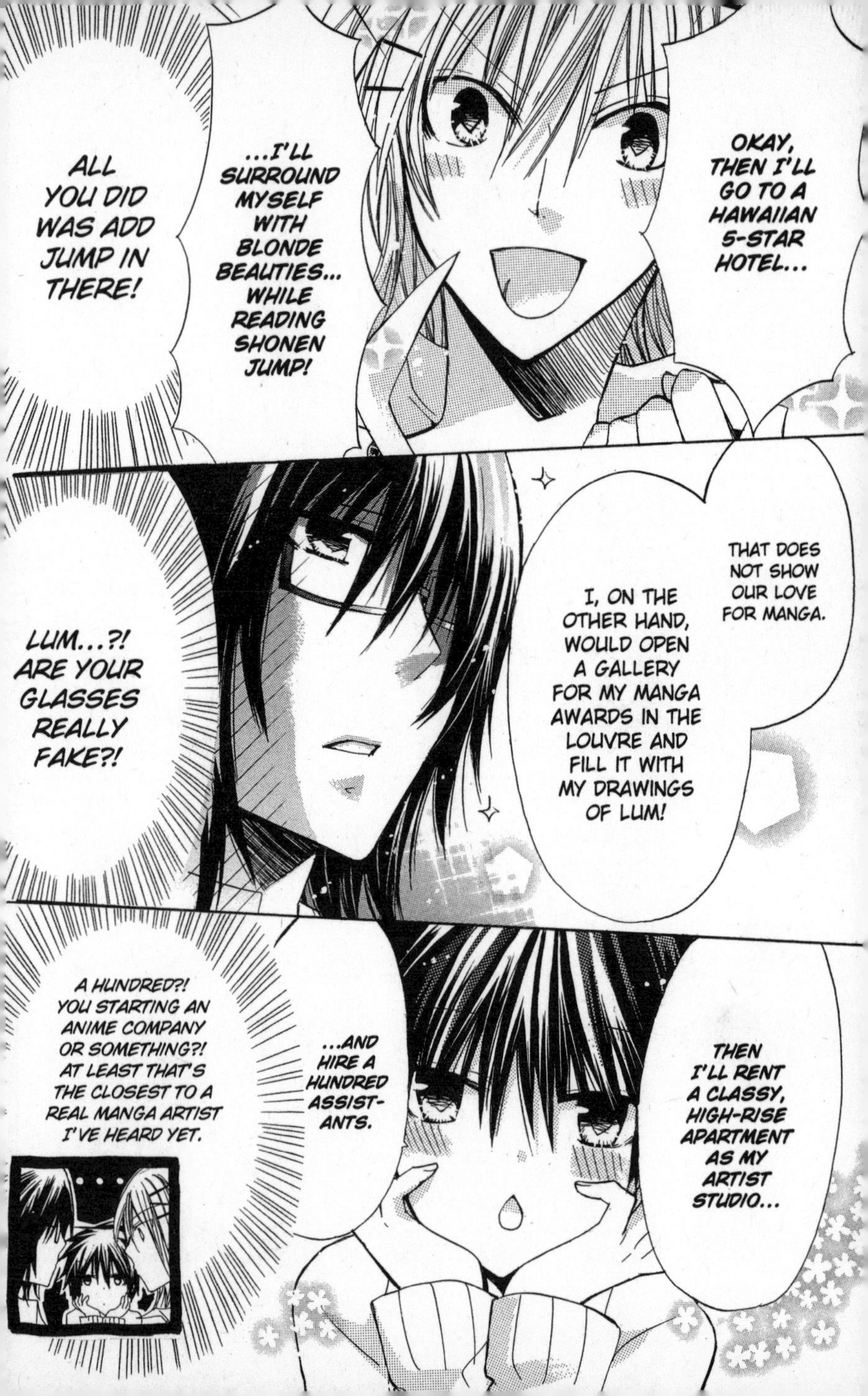
OKAY, THEN I'LL GO TO A HAWAIIAN 5-STAR HOTEL...
...I'LL SURROUND MYSELF WITH BLONDE BEAUTIES... WHILE READING SHONEN JUMP!
ALL YOU DID WAS ADD JUMP IN THERE!
THAT DOES NOT SHOW OUR LOVE FOR MANGA.
I, ON THE OTHER HAND, WOULD OPEN A GALLERY FOR MY MANGA AWARDS IN THE LOUVRE AND FILL IT WITH MY DRAWINGS OF LUM!
LUM...?! ARE YOUR GLASSES REALLY FAKE?!
THEN I'LL RENT A CLASSY, HIGH-RISE APARTMENT AS MY ARTIST STUDIO...
...AND HIRE A HUNDRED ASSIST-ANTS.
A HUNDRED?! YOU STARTING AN ANIME COMPANY OR SOMETHING?! AT LEAST THAT'S THE CLOSEST TO A REAL MANGA ARTIST I'VE HEARD YET.
...

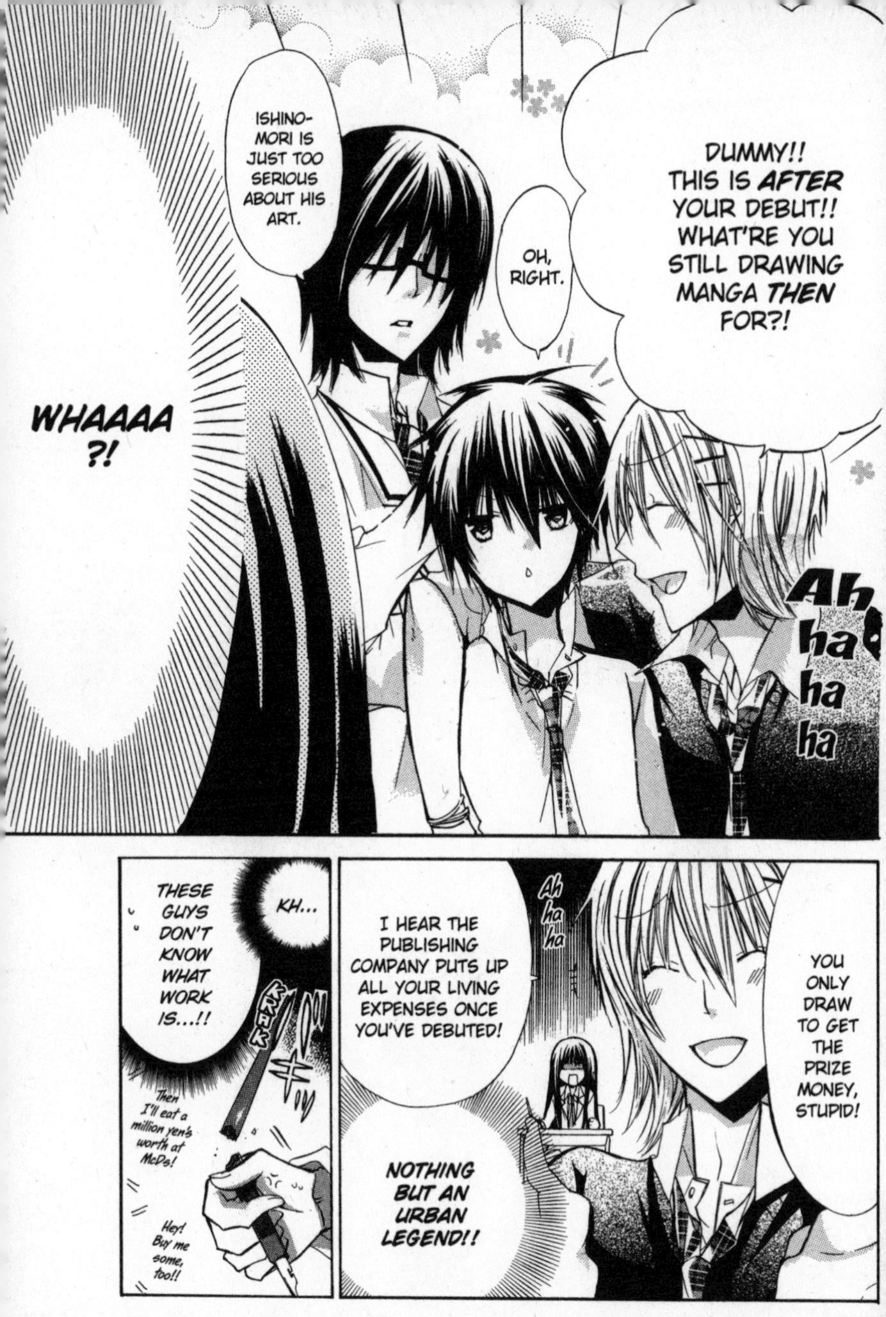
DUMMY!! THIS IS AFTER YOUR DEBUT!! WHAT'RE YOU STILL DRAWING MANGA THEN FOR?!
OH, RIGHT.
ISHINO-MORI IS JUST TOO SERIOUS ABOUT HIS ART.
Ah ha ha ha
WHAAAA ?!
YOU ONLY DRAW TO GET THE PRIZE MONEY, STUPID!
Ah ha ha
I HEAR THE PUBLISHING COMPANY PUTS UP ALL YOUR LIVING EXPENSES ONCE YOU'VE DEBUTED!
NOTHING BUT AN URBAN LEGEND!!
KH...
THESE GUYS DON'T KNOW WHAT WORK IS...!!
KRAK
Then I'll eat a million yen's worth at McDs!
Hey! Buy me some, too!!

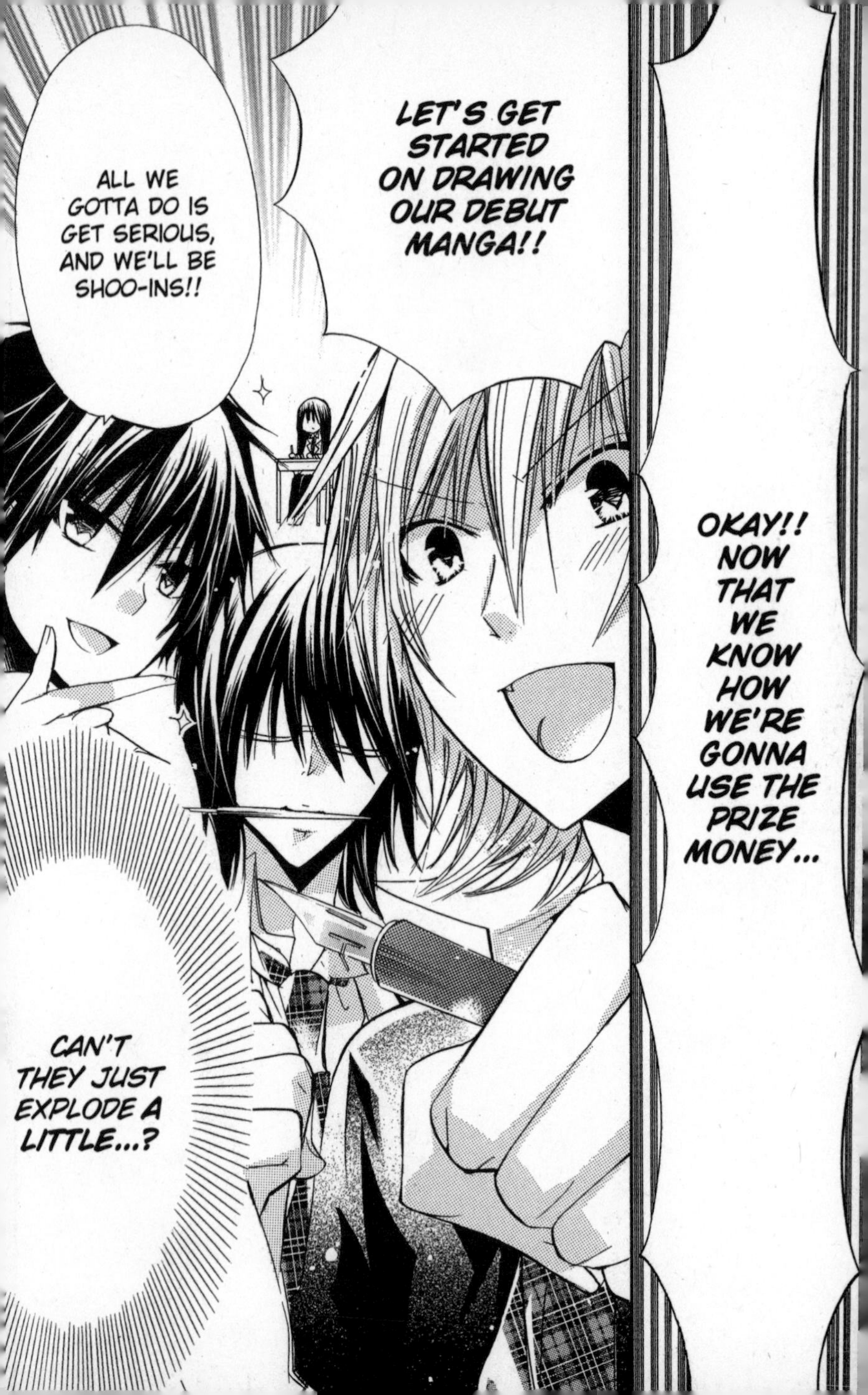
OKAY!! NOW THAT WE KNOW HOW WE'RE GONNA USE THE PRIZE MONEY...
LET'S GET STARTED ON DRAWING OUR DEBUT MANGA!!
ALL WE GOTTA DO IS GET SERIOUS, AND WE'LL BE SHOO-INS!!
CAN'T THEY JUST EXPLODE A LITTLE...?

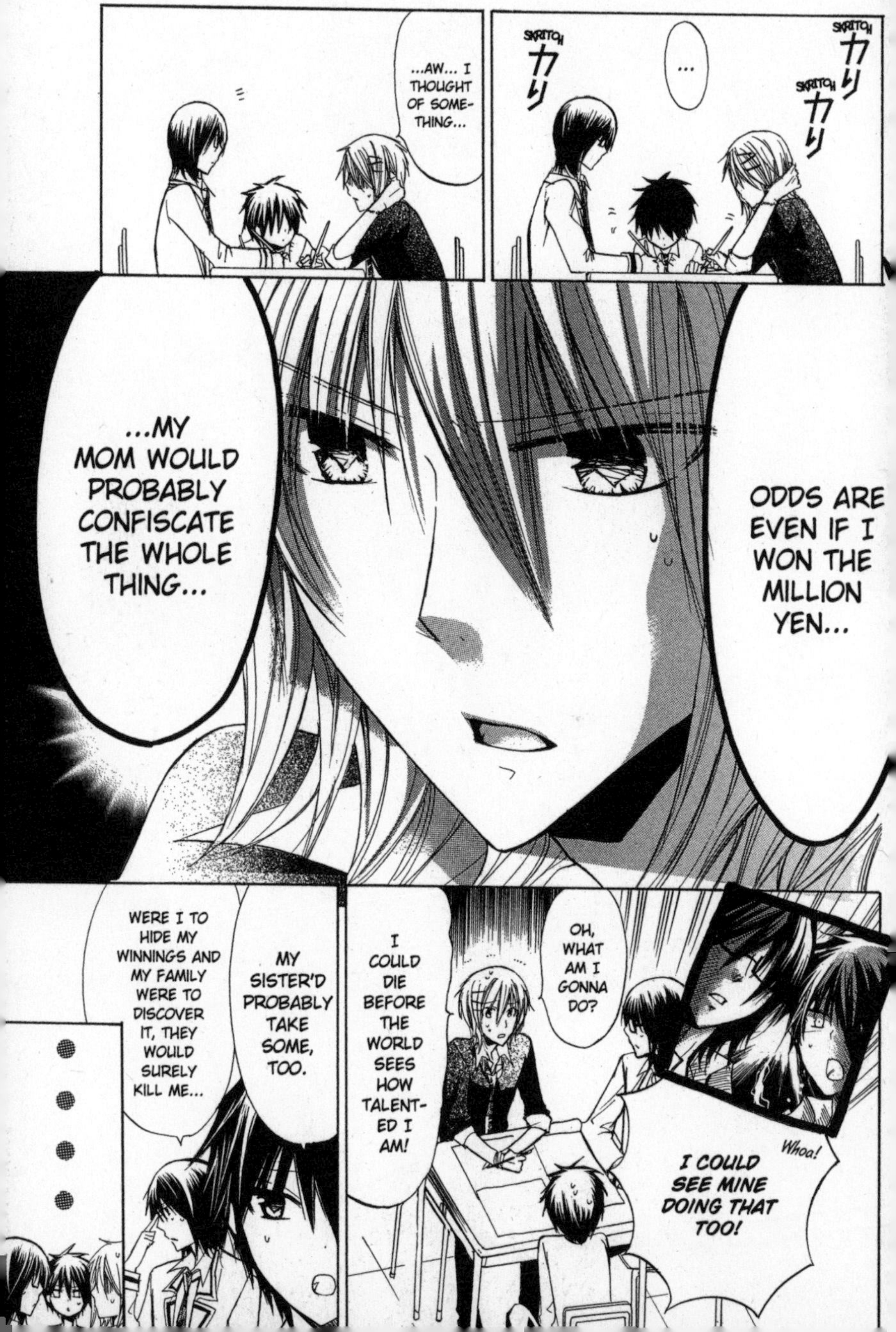
SKRITCH カリ
SKRITCH カリ
...
SKRITCH カリ
...AW... I THOUGHT OF SOME-THING...
ODDS ARE EVEN IF I WON THE MILLION YEN...
...MY MOM WOULD PROBABLY CONFISCATE THE WHOLE THING...
OH, WHAT AM I GONNA DO?
I COULD DIE BEFORE THE WORLD SEES HOW TALENT-ED I AM!
Whoa!
I COULD SEE MINE DOING THAT TOO!
MY SISTER'D PROBABLY TAKE SOME, TOO.
WERE I TO HIDE MY WINNINGS AND MY FAMILY WERE TO DISCOVER IT, THEY WOULD SURELY KILL ME...

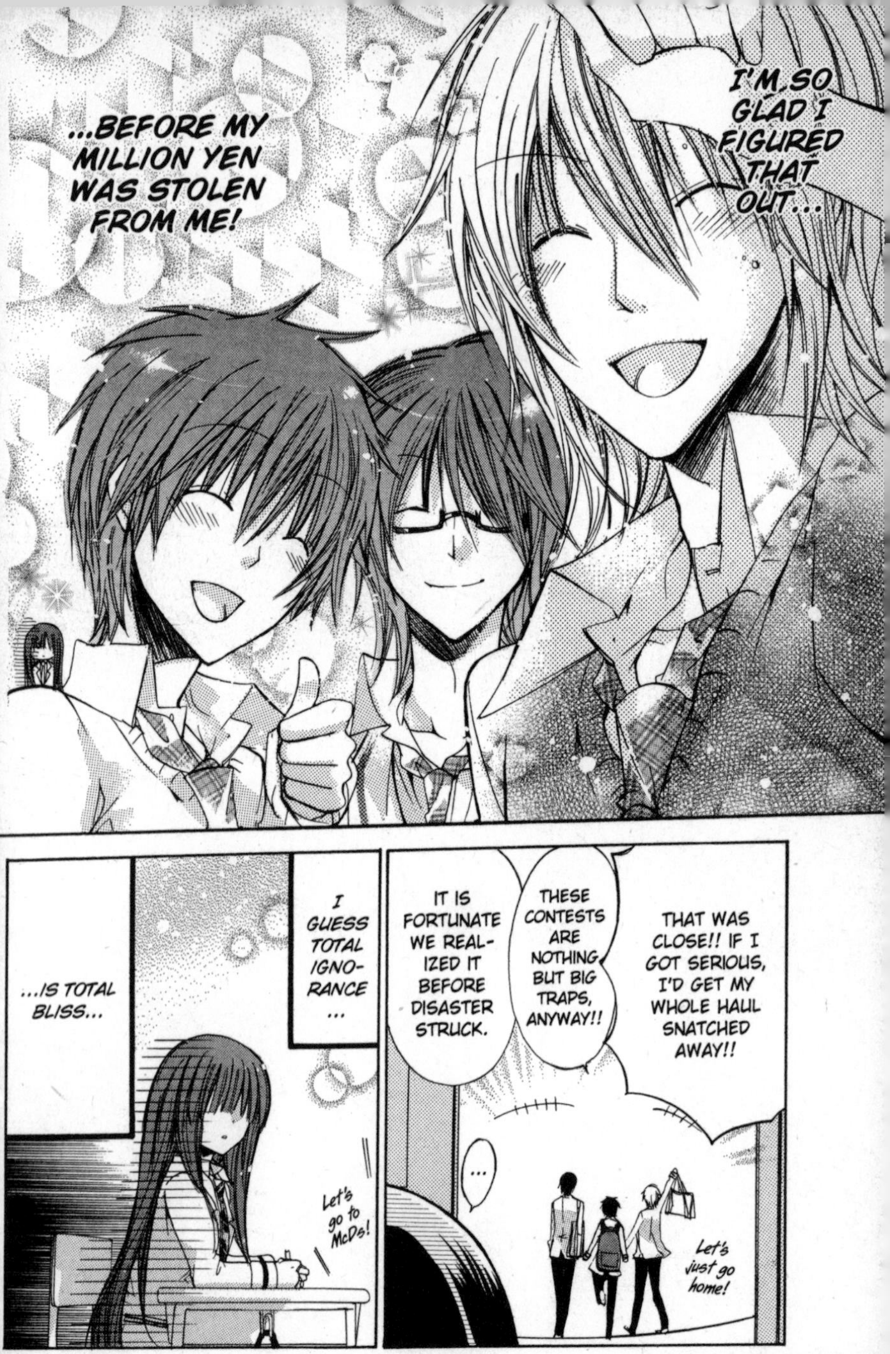
I'M SO GLAD I FIGURED THAT OUT...
...BEFORE MY MILLION YEN WAS STOLEN FROM ME!
THAT WAS CLOSE!! IF I GOT SERIOUS, I'D GET MY WHOLE HAUL SNATCHED AWAY!!
THESE CONTESTS ARE NOTHING BUT BIG TRAPS, ANYWAY!!
IT IS FORTUNATE WE REAL-IZED IT BEFORE DISASTER STRUCK.
...
Let's just go home!
I GUESS TOTAL IGNO-RANCE...
...IS TOTAL BLISS...
Let's go to McDs!

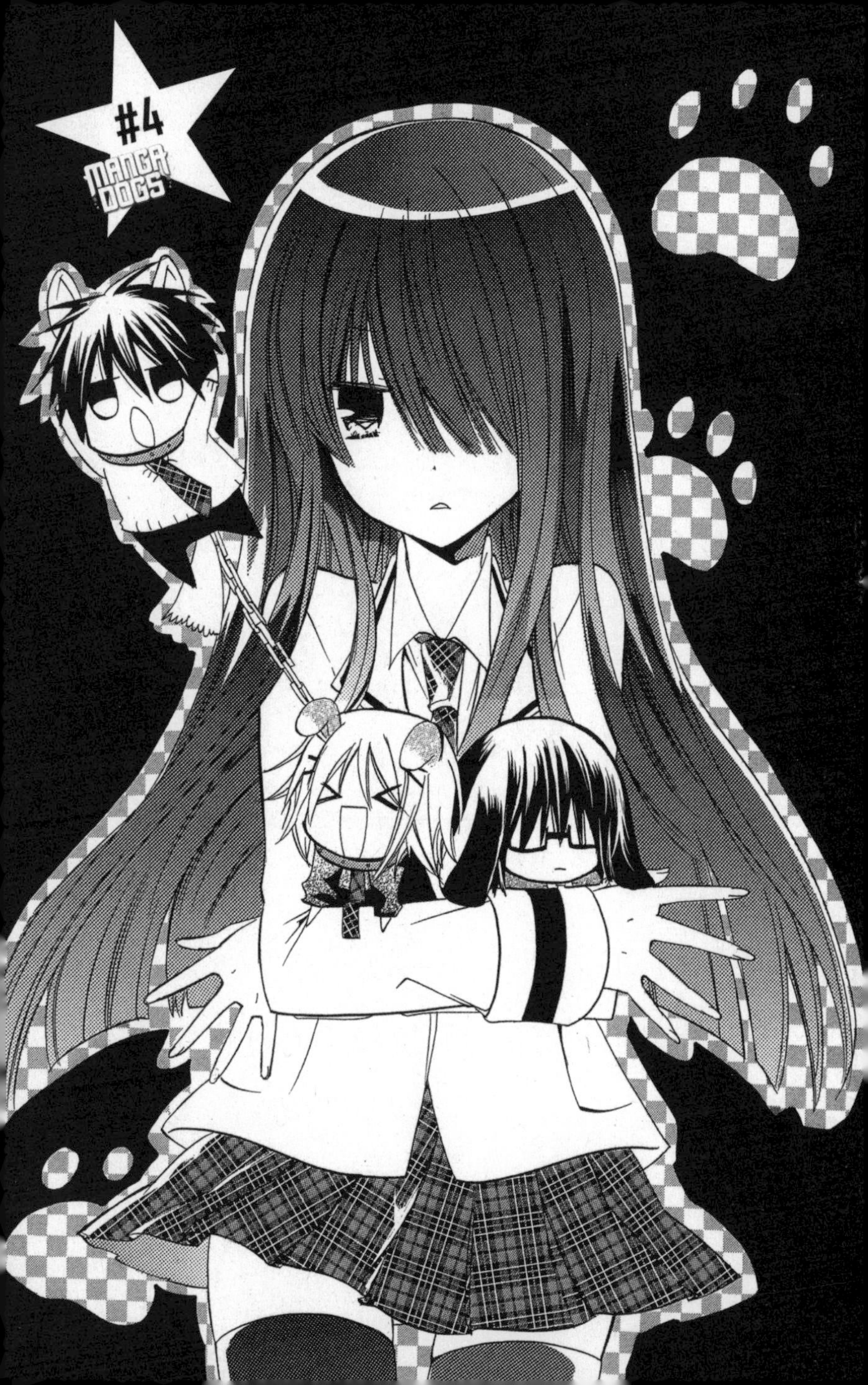
#4
MANGA DOGS

THIS IS
BAD...

IS THIS
BAD.....?

THE
READERS...

...RANKED
YOU
LAST.

YEAH...

LOOK.

P401	Dappled Su
P445	Cosmic
P	Heart
P511	Teach Me ❤ Buddha!
P544	Preview of Next Issue

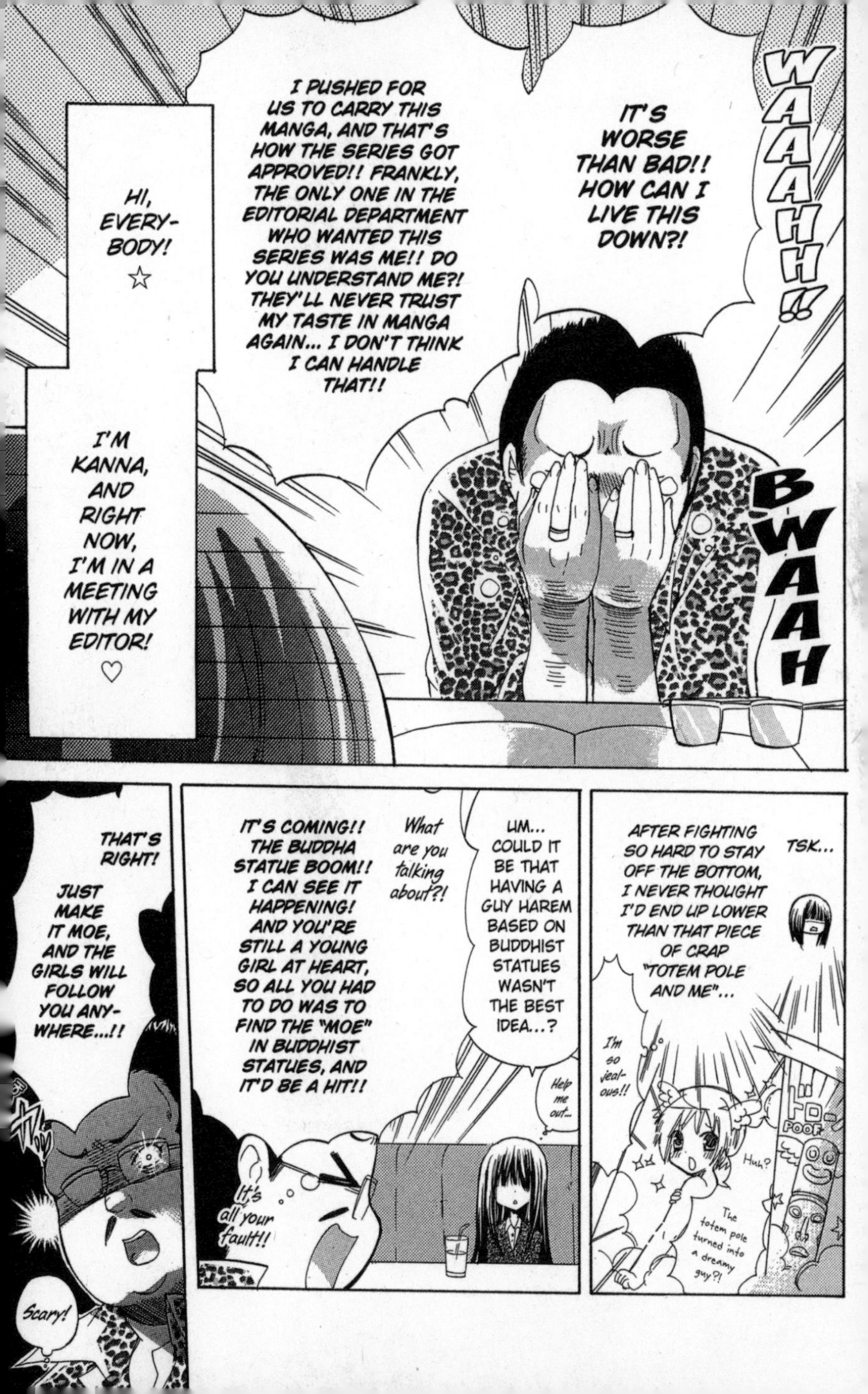
WAAAAHH!!
IT'S WORSE THAN BAD!! HOW CAN I LIVE THIS DOWN?!
BWAAH
I PUSHED FOR US TO CARRY THIS MANGA, AND THAT'S HOW THE SERIES GOT APPROVED!! FRANKLY, THE ONLY ONE IN THE EDITORIAL DEPARTMENT WHO WANTED THIS SERIES WAS ME!! DO YOU UNDERSTAND ME?! THEY'LL NEVER TRUST MY TASTE IN MANGA AGAIN... I DON'T THINK I CAN HANDLE THAT!!
HI, EVERYBODY! ☆
I'M KANNA, AND RIGHT NOW, I'M IN A MEETING WITH MY EDITOR! ♡
TSK...
AFTER FIGHTING SO HARD TO STAY OFF THE BOTTOM, I NEVER THOUGHT I'D END UP LOWER THAN THAT PIECE OF CRAP "TOTEM POLE AND ME"...
I'm so jeal-ous!!
POOF
Huh?
The totem pole turned into a dreamy guy?!
UM... COULD IT BE THAT HAVING A GUY HAREM BASED ON BUDDHIST STATUES WASN'T THE BEST IDEA...?
What are you talking about?!
IT'S COMING!! THE BUDDHA STATUE BOOM!! I CAN SEE IT HAPPENING! AND YOU'RE STILL A YOUNG GIRL AT HEART, SO ALL YOU HAD TO DO WAS TO FIND THE "MOE" IN BUDDHIST STATUES, AND IT'D BE A HIT!!
Help me out...
It's all your fault!!
THAT'S RIGHT!
JUST MAKE IT MOE, AND THE GIRLS WILL FOLLOW YOU ANYWHERE...!!
Scary!

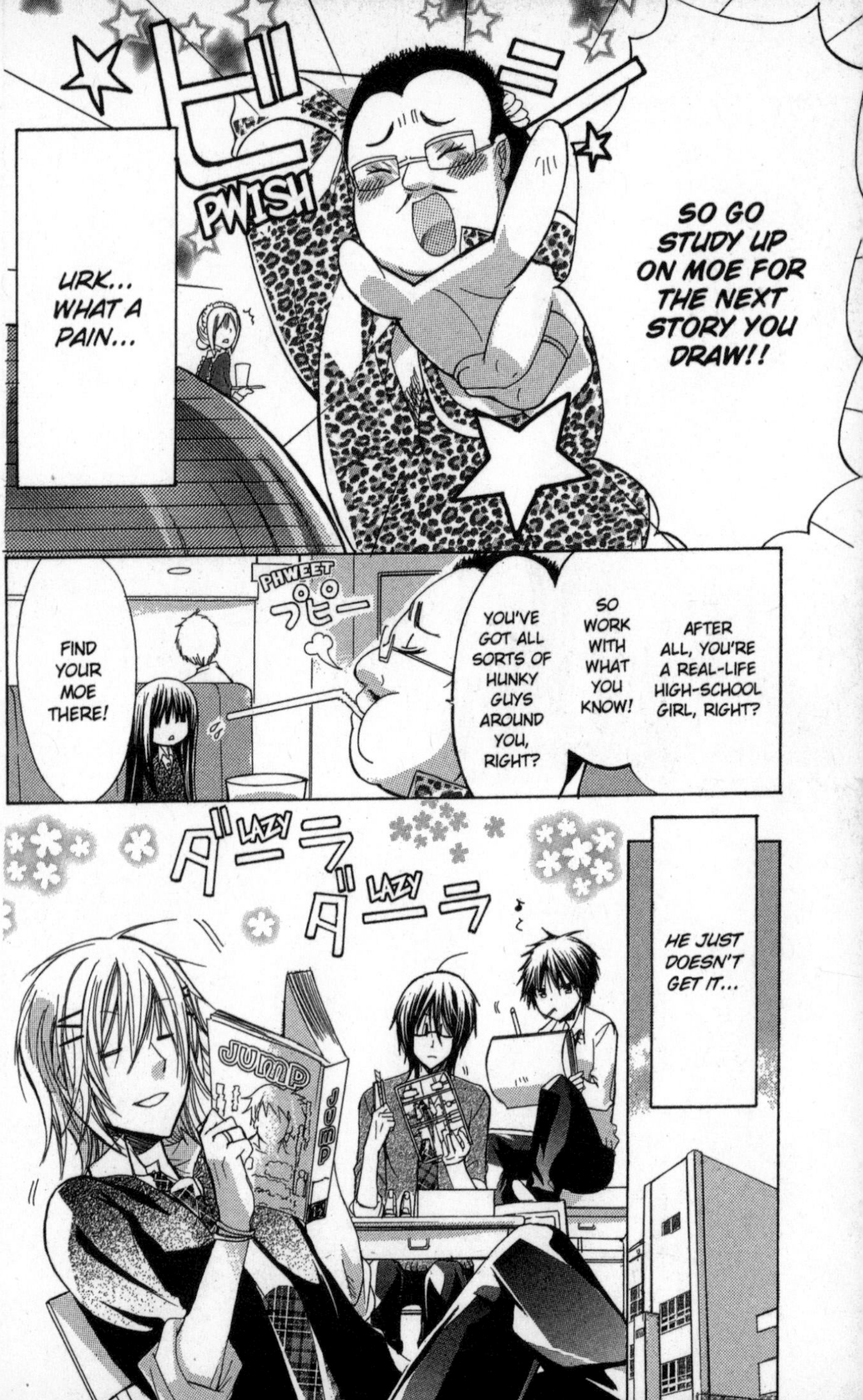
SO GO STUDY UP ON MOE FOR THE NEXT STORY YOU DRAW!!
ビシ
PWISH
URK... WHAT A PAIN...
AFTER ALL, YOU'RE A REAL-LIFE HIGH-SCHOOL GIRL, RIGHT?
SO WORK WITH WHAT YOU KNOW!
YOU'VE GOT ALL SORTS OF HUNKY GUYS AROUND YOU, RIGHT?
PHWEET
プピー
FIND YOUR MOE THERE!
HE JUST DOESN'T GET IT...
ダーラ
LAZY
ダーラ
LAZY

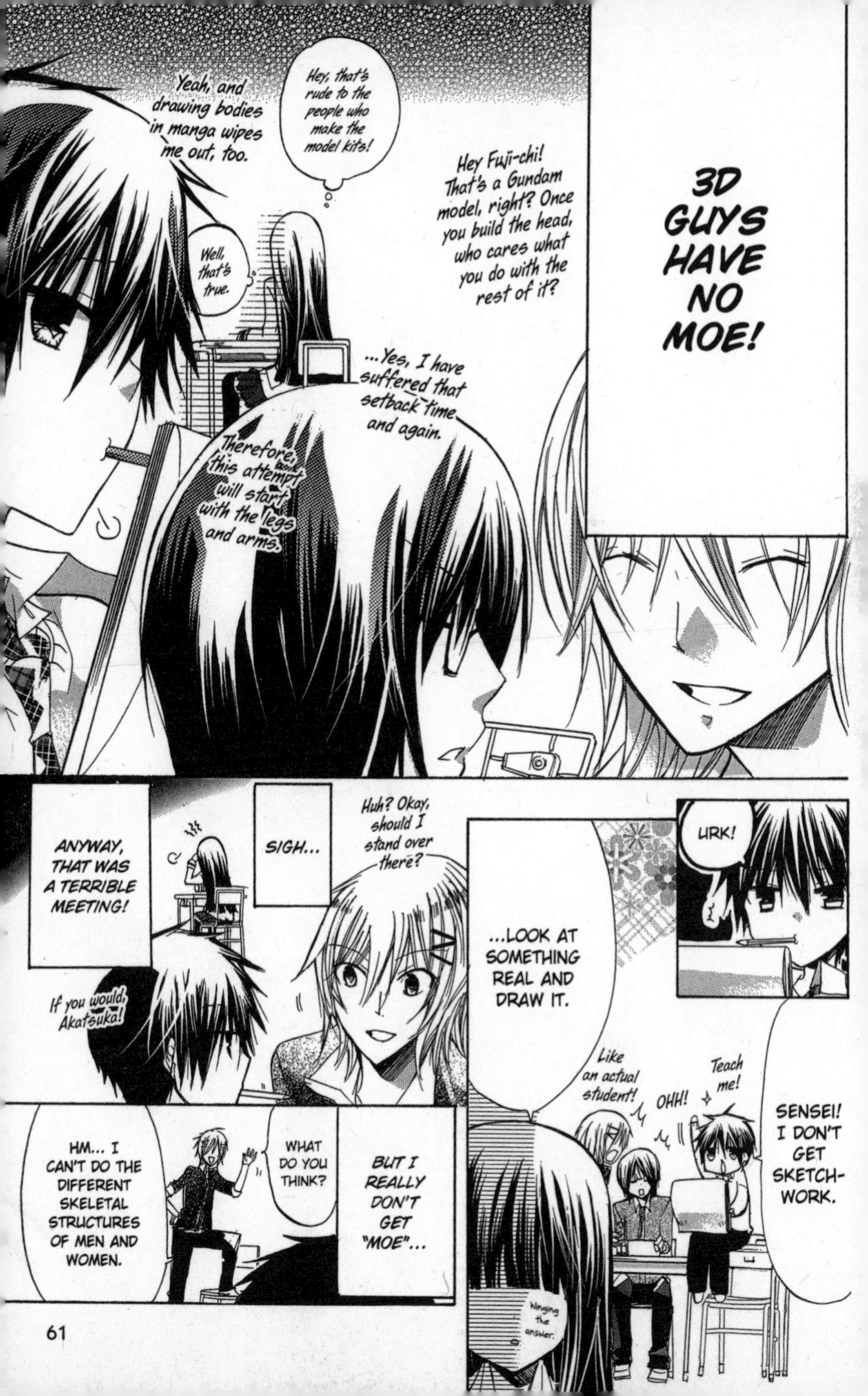
3D GUYS HAVE NO MOE!
Hey Fuji-chi! That's a Gundam model, right? Once you build the head, who cares what you do with the rest of it?
Hey, that's rude to the people who make the model kits!
Yeah, and drawing bodies in manga wipes me out, too.
Well, that's true.
...Yes, I have suffered that setback time and again.
Therefore, this attempt will start with the legs and arms.
URK!
SENSEI! I DON'T GET SKETCH-WORK.
Teach me!
OHH!
Like an actual student!
...LOOK AT SOMETHING REAL AND DRAW IT.
Winging the answer.
Huh? Okay, should I stand over there?
If you would, Akatsuka!
SIGH...
ANYWAY, THAT WAS A TERRIBLE MEETING!
BUT I REALLY DON'T GET "MOE"...
WHAT DO YOU THINK?
HM... I CAN'T DO THE DIFFERENT SKELETAL STRUCTURES OF MEN AND WOMEN.

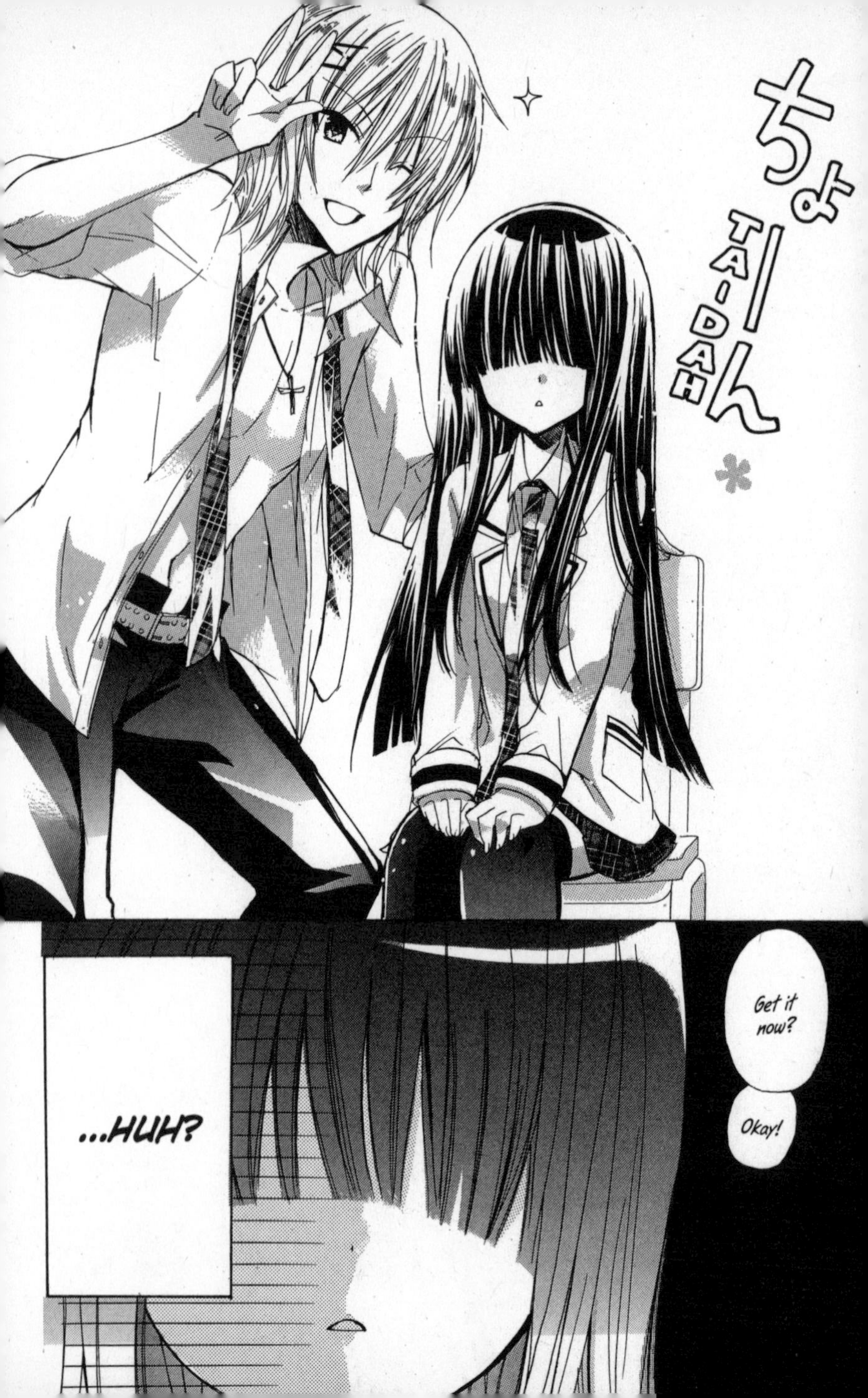
ちょーん
TA-DAH
Get it now?
Okay!
...HUH?

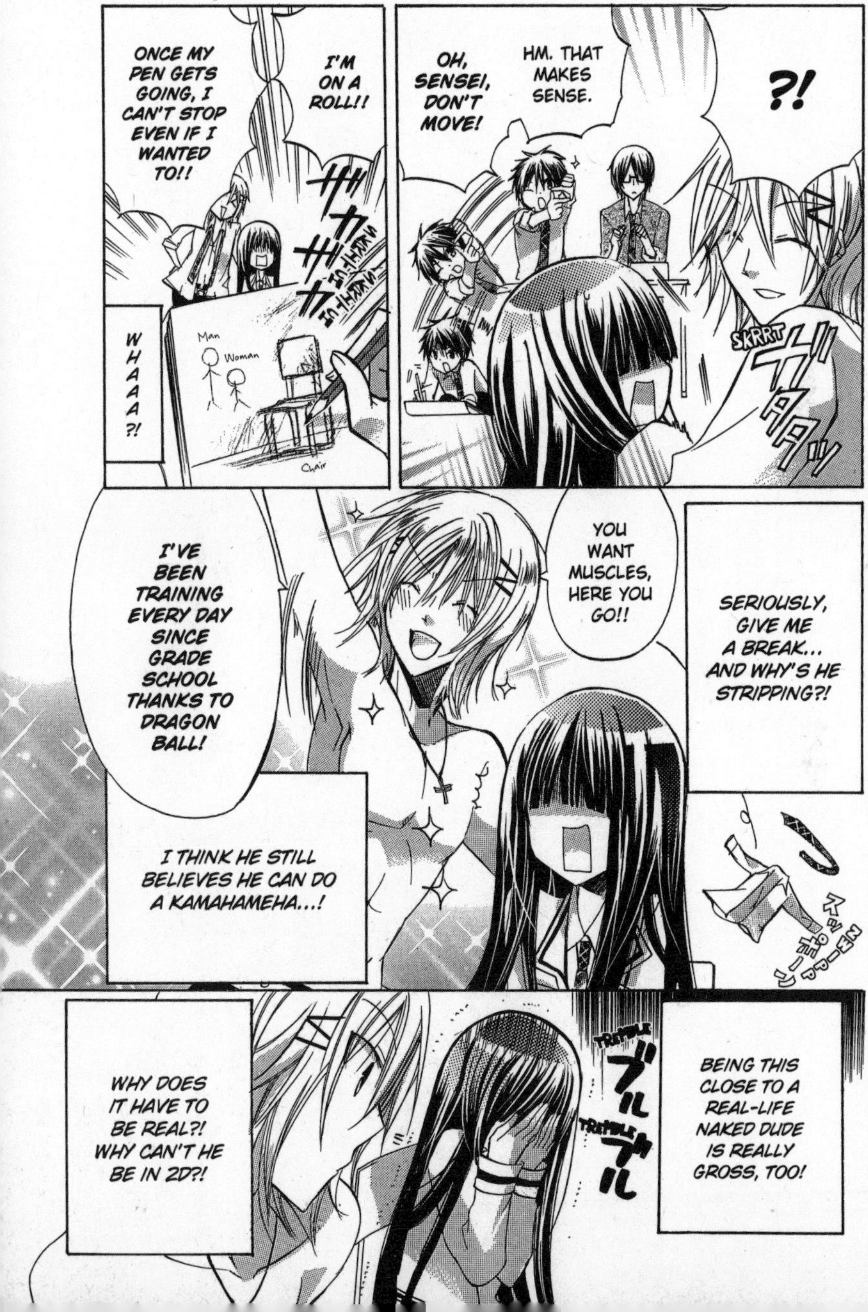
?!
HM. THAT MAKES SENSE.
OH, SENSEI, DON'T MOVE!
SKRRT
I'M ON A ROLL!!
ONCE MY PEN GETS GOING, I CAN'T STOP EVEN IF I WANTED TO!!
WHAAAA?!
Man
Woman
Chair
SERIOUSLY, GIVE ME A BREAK... AND WHY'S HE STRIPPING?!
YOU WANT MUSCLES, HERE YOU GO!!
I'VE BEEN TRAINING EVERY DAY SINCE GRADE SCHOOL THANKS TO DRAGON BALL!
I THINK HE STILL BELIEVES HE CAN DO A KAMAHAMEHA...!
BEING THIS CLOSE TO A REAL-LIFE NAKED DUDE IS REALLY GROSS, TOO!
TREMBLE
TREMBLE
WHY DOES IT HAVE TO BE REAL?! WHY CAN'T HE BE IN 2D?!

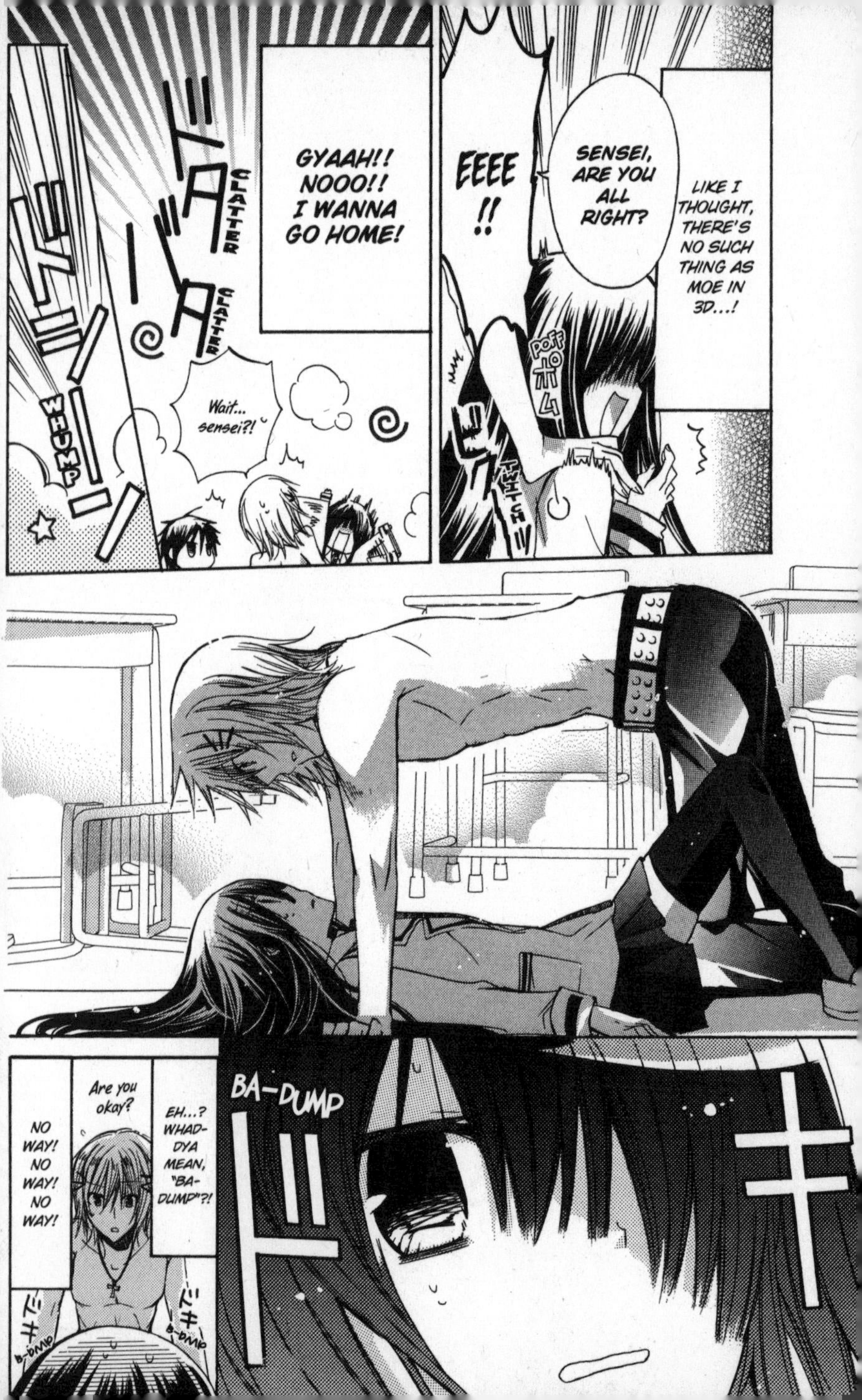
LIKE I THOUGHT, THERE'S NO SUCH THING AS MOE IN 3D...!
SENSEI, ARE YOU ALL RIGHT?
EEEE!!
POFF
TWITCH
GYAAH!! NOOO!! I WANNA GO HOME!
CLATTER
CLATTER
Wait... sensei?!
WHUMP
BA-DUMP
EH...? WHADDYA MEAN, "BA-DUMP"?!
Are you okay?
NO WAY! NO WAY! NO WAY!
B-DMP
B-DMP

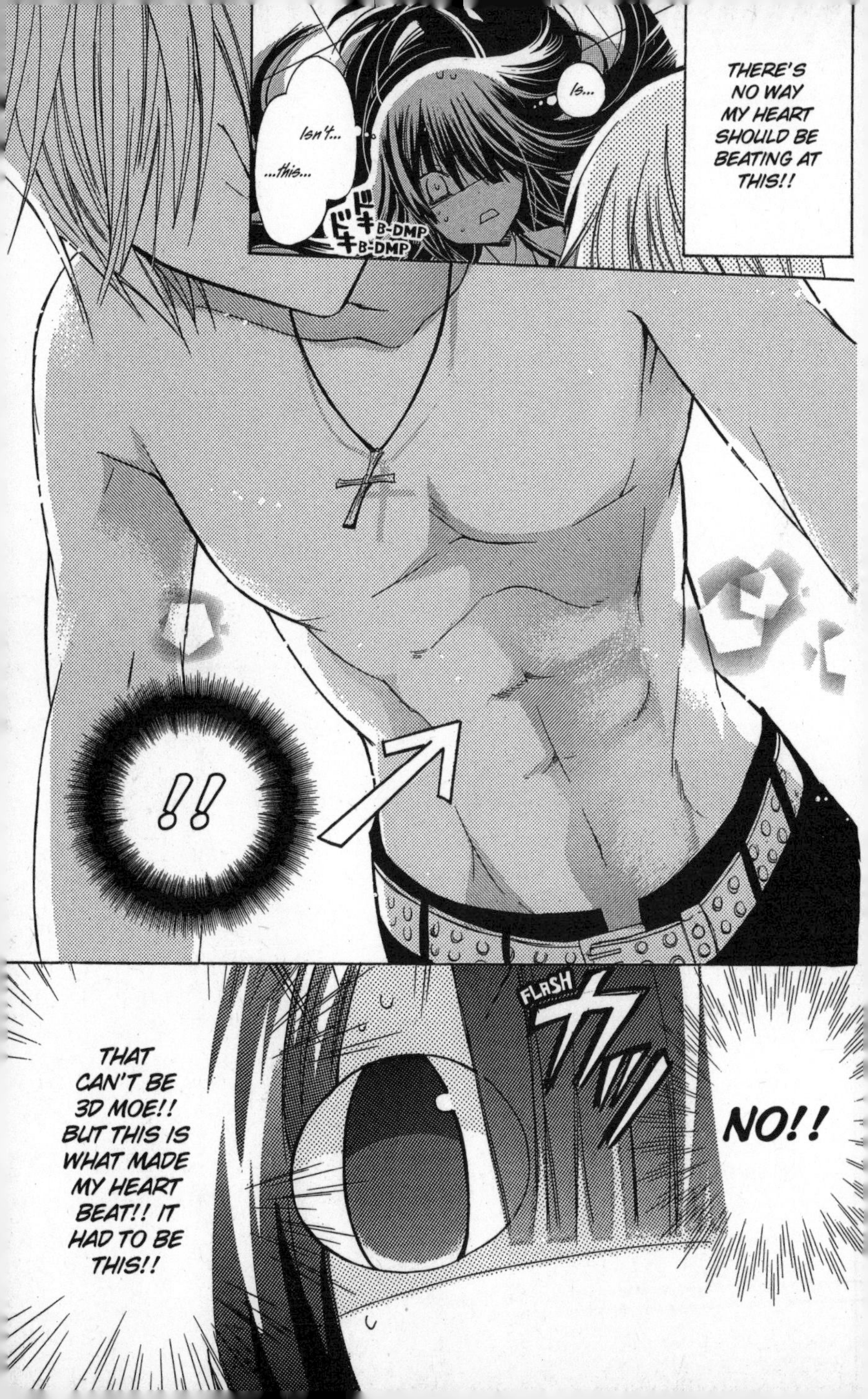
THERE'S NO WAY MY HEART SHOULD BE BEATING AT THIS!!
Is...
Isn't...
...this...
ドキ B-DMP
ドキ B-DMP
!!
NO!!
FLASH
THAT CAN'T BE 3D MOE!! BUT THIS IS WHAT MADE MY HEART BEAT!! IT HAD TO BE THIS!!

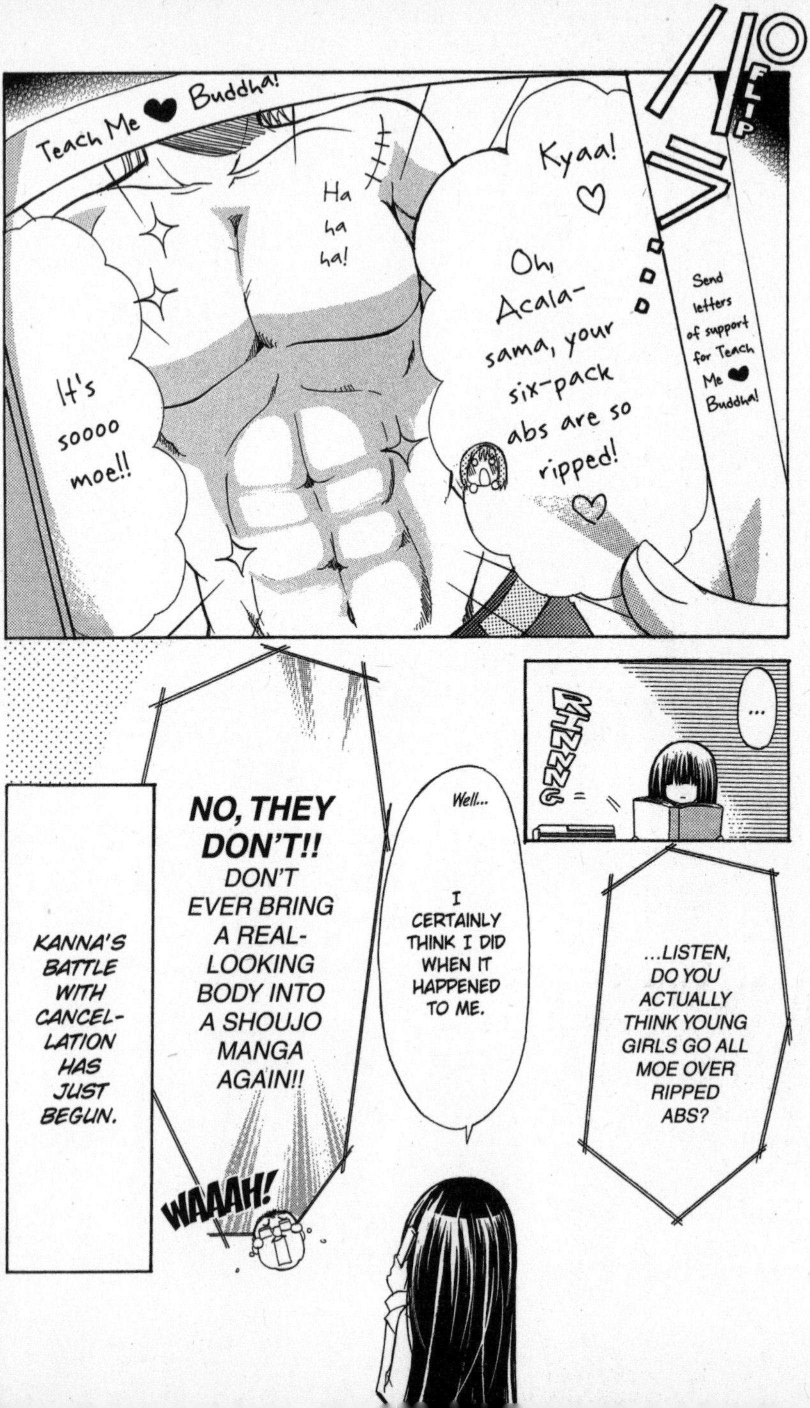
FLIP
Teach Me ♥ Buddha!
Send letters of support for Teach Me ♥ Buddha!
Kyaa! ♡
Oh, Acala-sama, your six-pack abs are so ripped! ♡
Ha ha ha!
It's soooo moe!!
...
DINNNG
...LISTEN, DO YOU ACTUALLY THINK YOUNG GIRLS GO ALL MOE OVER RIPPED ABS?
Well... I CERTAINLY THINK I DID WHEN IT HAPPENED TO ME.
NO, THEY DON'T!! DON'T EVER BRING A REAL-LOOKING BODY INTO A SHOUJO MANGA AGAIN!!
WAAAH!
KANNA'S BATTLE WITH CANCEL-LATION HAS JUST BEGUN.

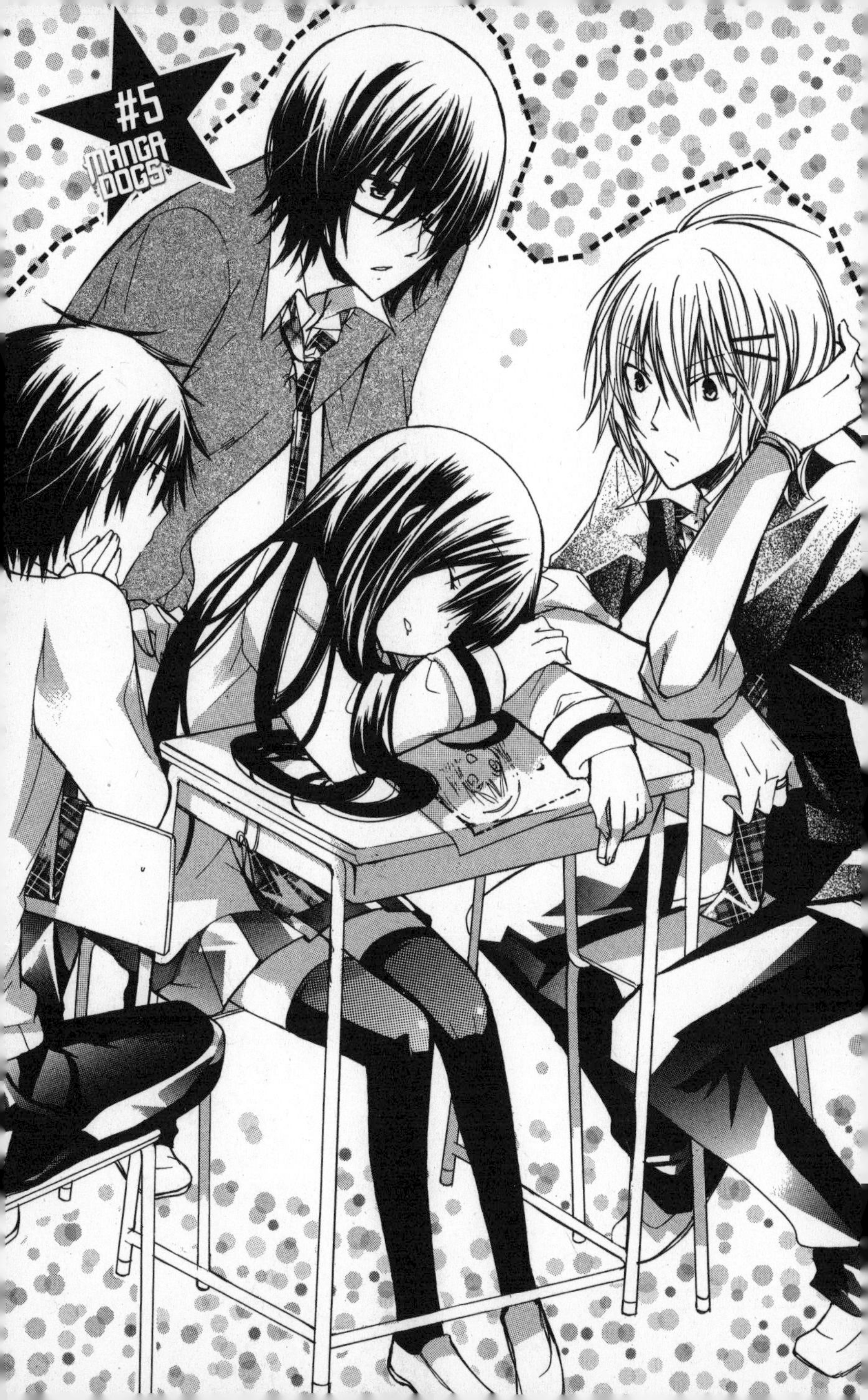
#5
MANGA DOGS

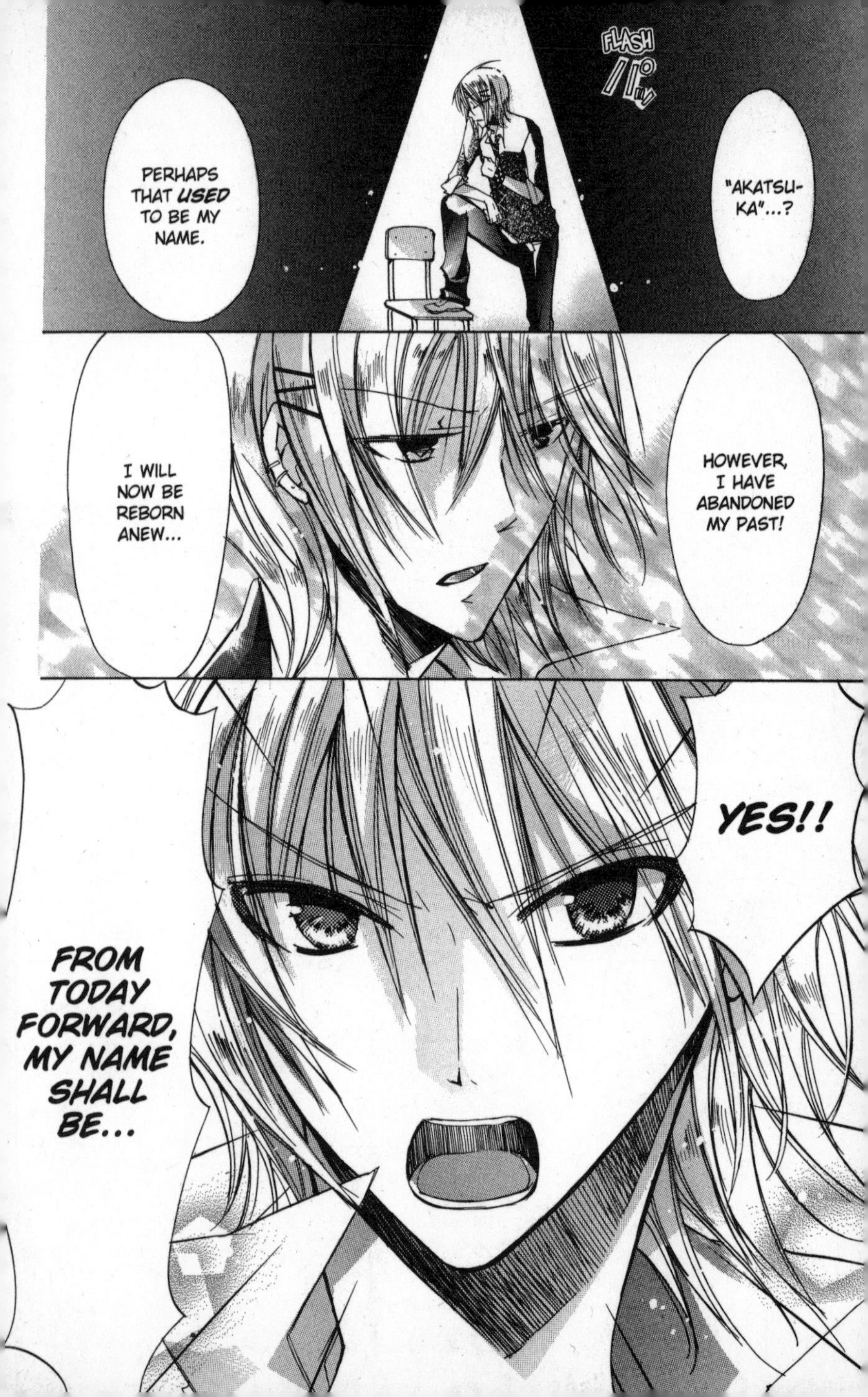
FLASH
"AKATSUKA"...?
PERHAPS THAT *USED* TO BE MY NAME.
HOWEVER, I HAVE ABANDONED MY PAST!
I WILL NOW BE REBORN ANEW...
YES!!
FROM TODAY FORWARD, MY NAME SHALL BE...

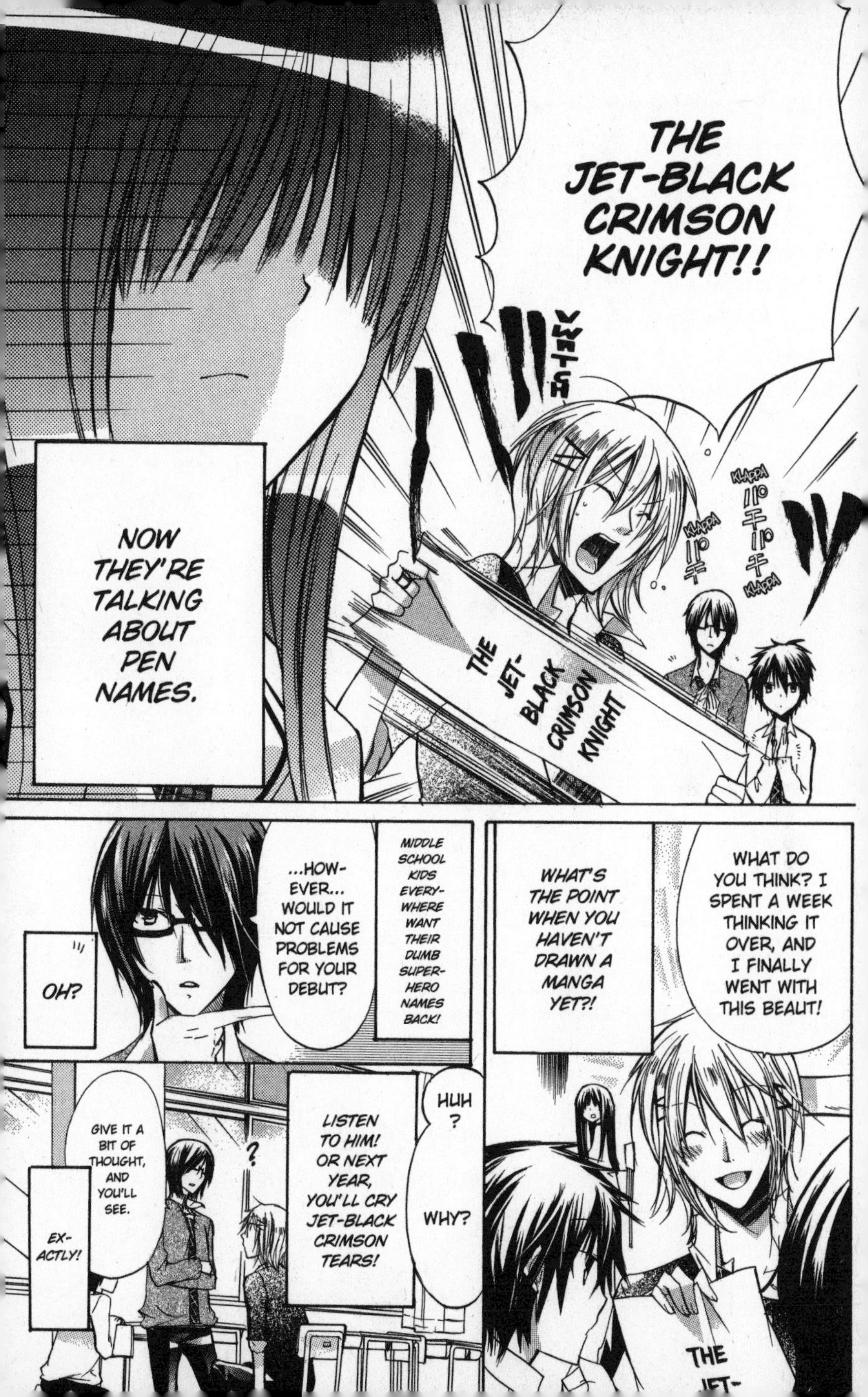
THE JET-BLACK CRIMSON KNIGHT!!
VWATCH
KLAPPA KLAPPA
KLAPPA
THE JET-BLACK CRIMSON KNIGHT
NOW THEY'RE TALKING ABOUT PEN NAMES.
WHAT DO YOU THINK? I SPENT A WEEK THINKING IT OVER, AND I FINALLY WENT WITH THIS BEAUT!
WHAT'S THE POINT WHEN YOU HAVEN'T DRAWN A MANGA YET?!
THE JET-
MIDDLE SCHOOL KIDS EVERYWHERE WANT THEIR DUMB SUPER-HERO NAMES BACK!
...HOW-EVER... WOULD IT NOT CAUSE PROBLEMS FOR YOUR DEBUT?
OH?
HUH? WHY?
LISTEN TO HIM! OR NEXT YEAR, YOU'LL CRY JET-BLACK CRIMSON TEARS!
GIVE IT A BIT OF THOUGHT, AND YOU'LL SEE.
EX-ACTLY!

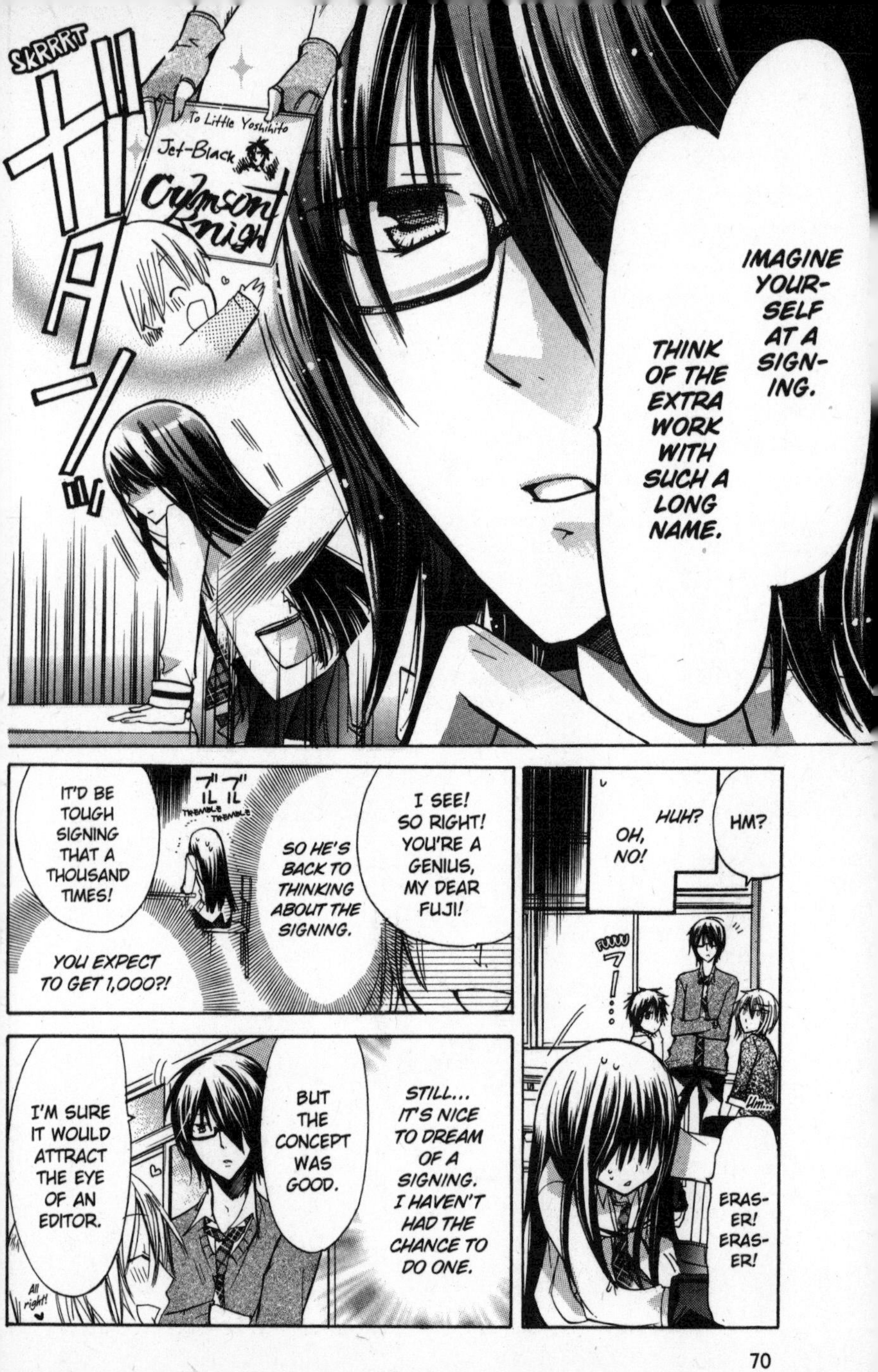
SkRRRT
To Little Yoshihito
Jet-Black Crymson Knight
IMAGINE YOURSELF AT A SIGNING.
THINK OF THE EXTRA WORK WITH SUCH A LONG NAME.
HM?
HUH?
OH, NO!
FUUUU
Um...
ERASER! ERASER!
I SEE! SO RIGHT! YOU'RE A GENIUS, MY DEAR FUJI!
SO HE'S BACK TO THINKING ABOUT THE SIGNING.
IT'D BE TOUGH SIGNING THAT A THOUSAND TIMES!
TREMBLE TREMBLE
YOU EXPECT TO GET 1,000?!
STILL... IT'S NICE TO DREAM OF A SIGNING. I HAVEN'T HAD THE CHANCE TO DO ONE.
BUT THE CONCEPT WAS GOOD.
I'M SURE IT WOULD ATTRACT THE EYE OF AN EDITOR.
All right!

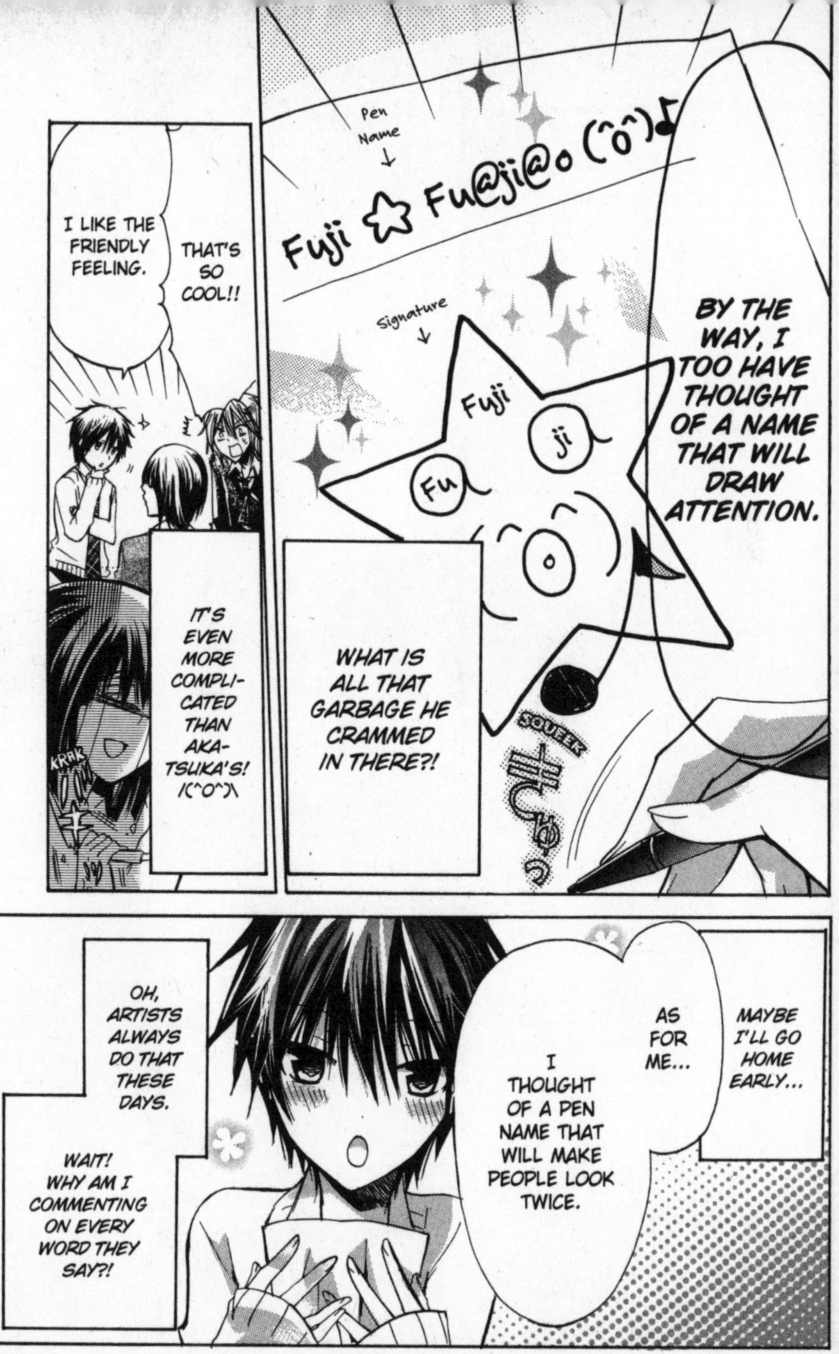
BY THE WAY, I TOO HAVE THOUGHT OF A NAME THAT WILL DRAW ATTENTION.
Pen Name ↓
Fuji ☆ Fu@ji@o (^o^)♪
Signature ↓
Fuji
ji
Fu
WHAT IS ALL THAT GARBAGE HE CRAMMED IN THERE?!
THAT'S SO COOL!!
I LIKE THE FRIENDLY FEELING.
IT'S EVEN MORE COMPLICATED THAN AKA-TSUKA'S! /(^O^)\
KRAK
MAYBE I'LL GO HOME EARLY...
AS FOR ME...
I THOUGHT OF A PEN NAME THAT WILL MAKE PEOPLE LOOK TWICE.
OH, ARTISTS ALWAYS DO THAT THESE DAYS.
WAIT! WHY AM I COMMENTING ON EVERY WORD THEY SAY?!

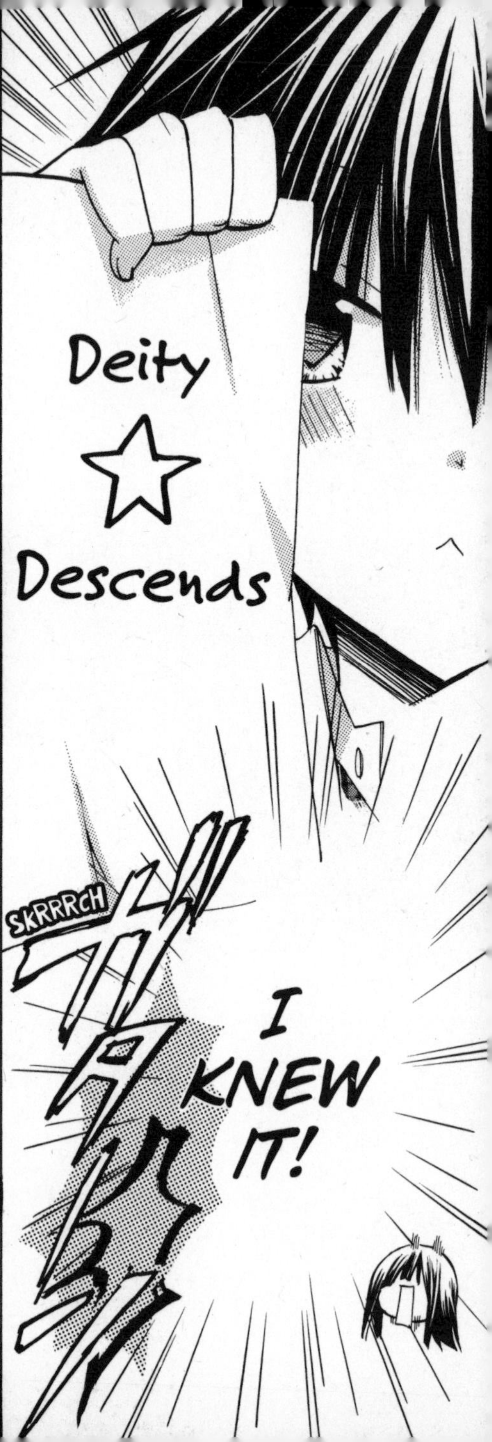
Deity ☆ Descends
SKRRRCH
I KNEW IT!
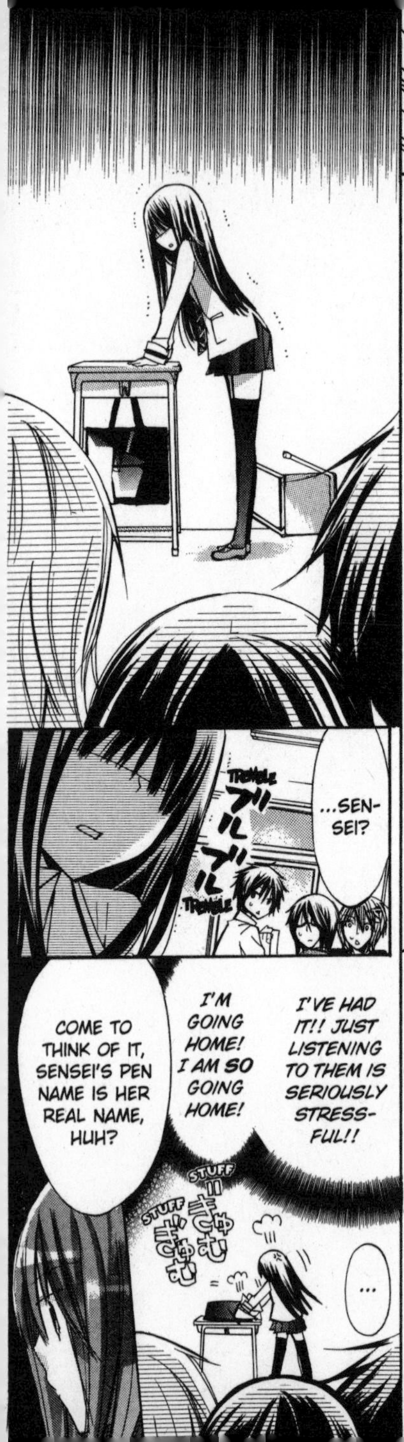
...SEN-SEI?
TREMBLE TREMBLE
I'VE HAD IT!! JUST LISTENING TO THEM IS SERIOUSLY STRESS-FUL!!
I'M GOING HOME! I AM SO GOING HOME!
COME TO THINK OF IT, SENSEI'S PEN NAME IS HER REAL NAME, HUH?
STUFF STUFF
...

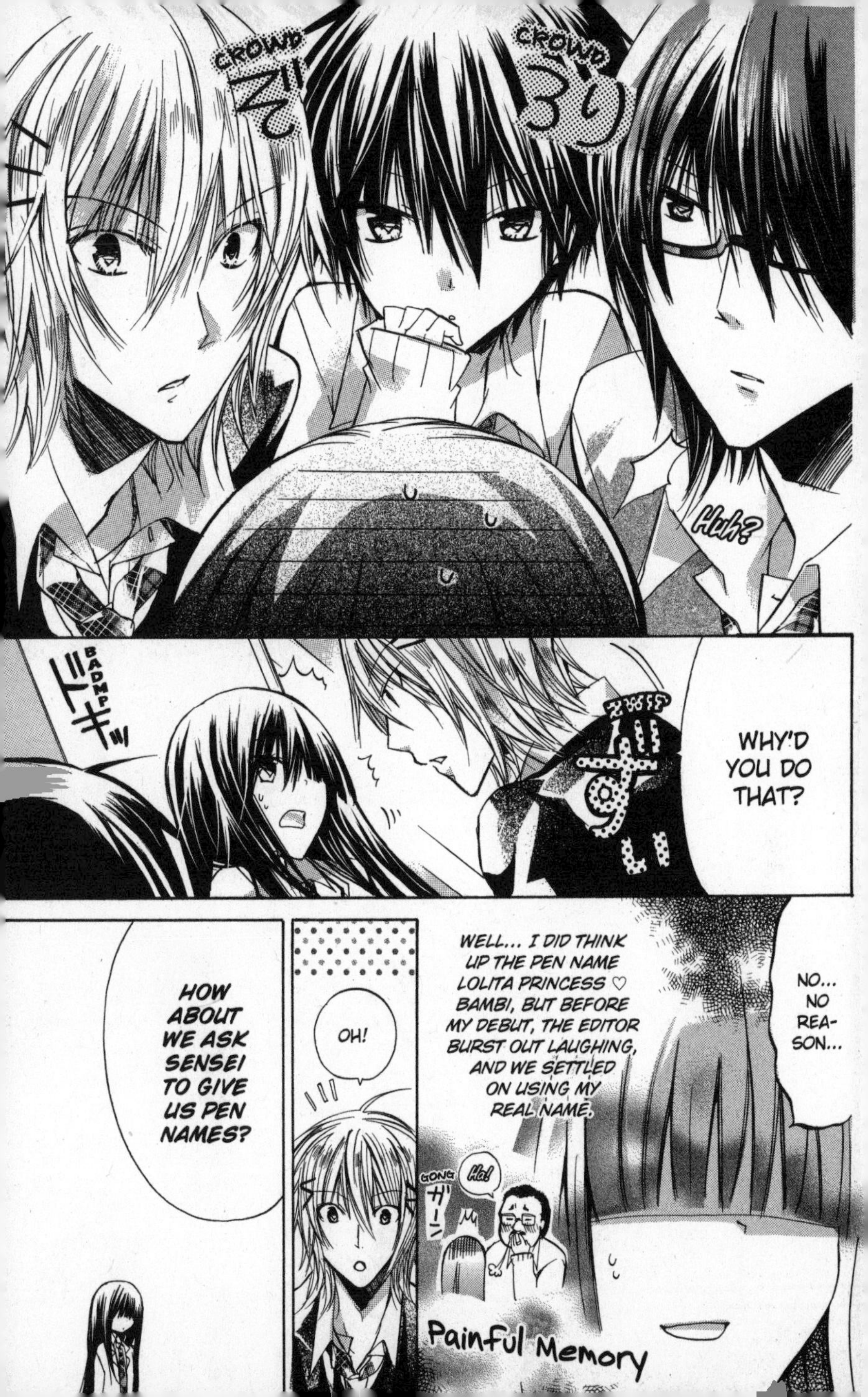
CROWD
CROWD
Huh?
WHY'D YOU DO THAT?
ZWIP
BADMP
NO... NO REA-SON...
WELL... I DID THINK UP THE PEN NAME LOLITA PRINCESS ♡ BAMBI, BUT BEFORE MY DEBUT, THE EDITOR BURST OUT LAUGHING, AND WE SETTLED ON USING MY REAL NAME.
Ha!
GONG
Painful Memory
OH!
HOW ABOUT WE ASK SENSEI TO GIVE US PEN NAMES?

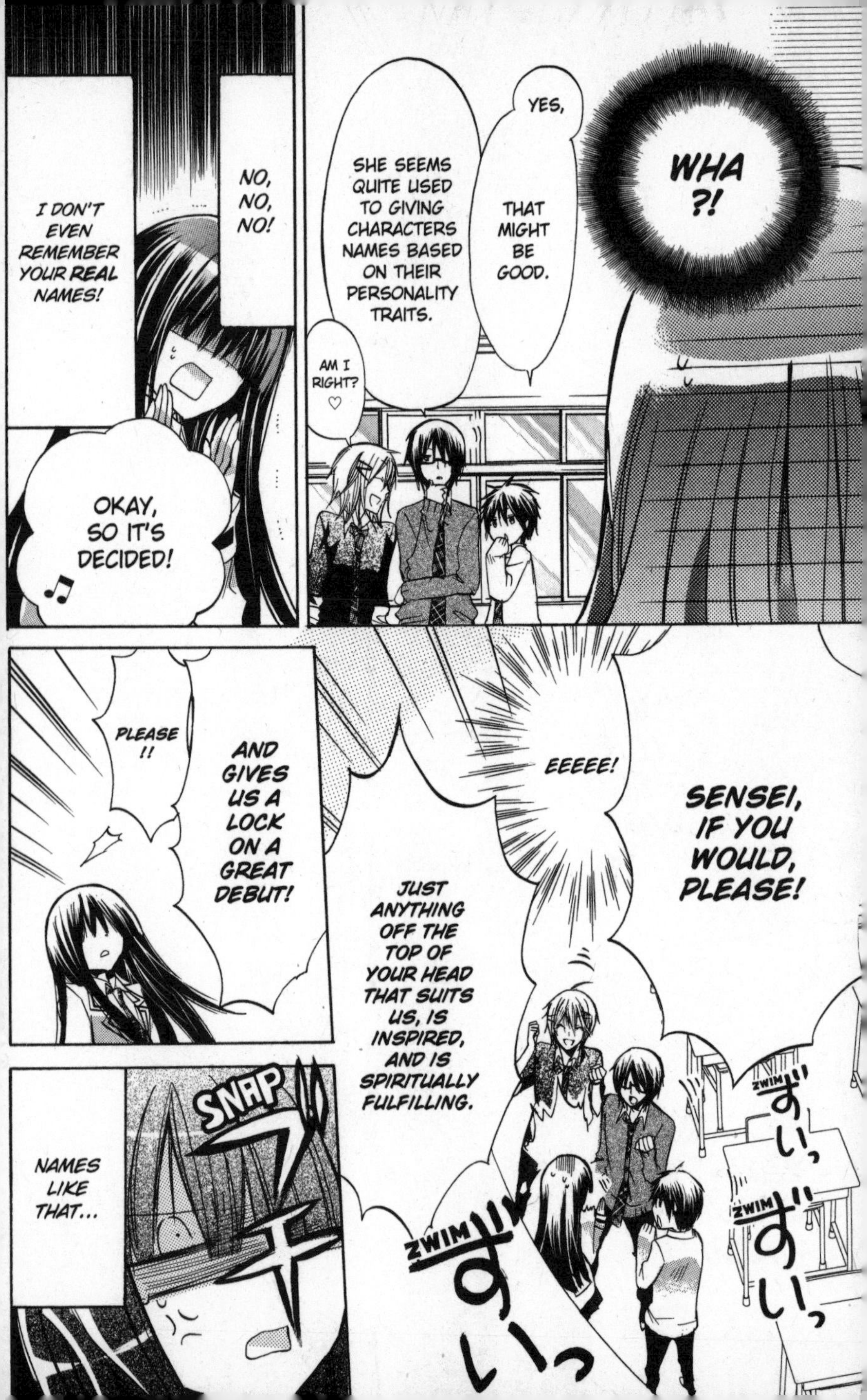
WHA ?!
YES,
THAT MIGHT BE GOOD.
SHE SEEMS QUITE USED TO GIVING CHARACTERS NAMES BASED ON THEIR PERSONALITY TRAITS.
AM I RIGHT? ♡
NO, NO, NO!
I DON'T EVEN REMEMBER YOUR REAL NAMES!
OKAY, SO IT'S DECIDED! ♪
SENSEI, IF YOU WOULD, PLEASE!
EEEEE!
ZWIM ずいっ
ZWIM ずいっ
ZWIM ずいっ
JUST ANYTHING OFF THE TOP OF YOUR HEAD THAT SUITS US, IS INSPIRED, AND IS SPIRITUALLY FULFILLING.
AND GIVES US A LOCK ON A GREAT DEBUT!
PLEASE !!
SNAP
NAMES LIKE THAT...

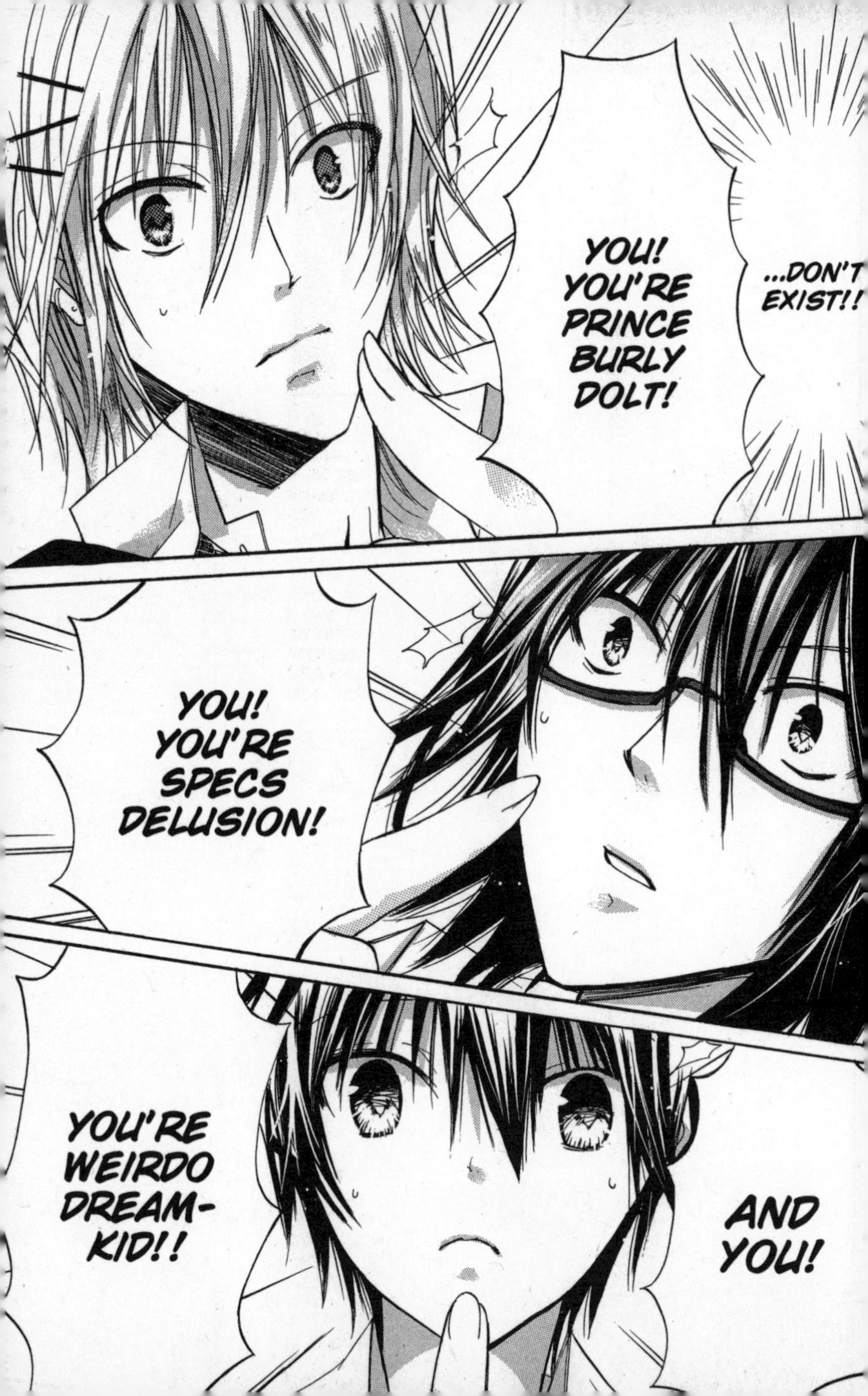
...DON'T EXIST!!
YOU! YOU'RE PRINCE BURLY DOLT!
YOU! YOU'RE SPECS DELUSION!
AND YOU!
YOU'RE WEIRDO DREAM-KID!!

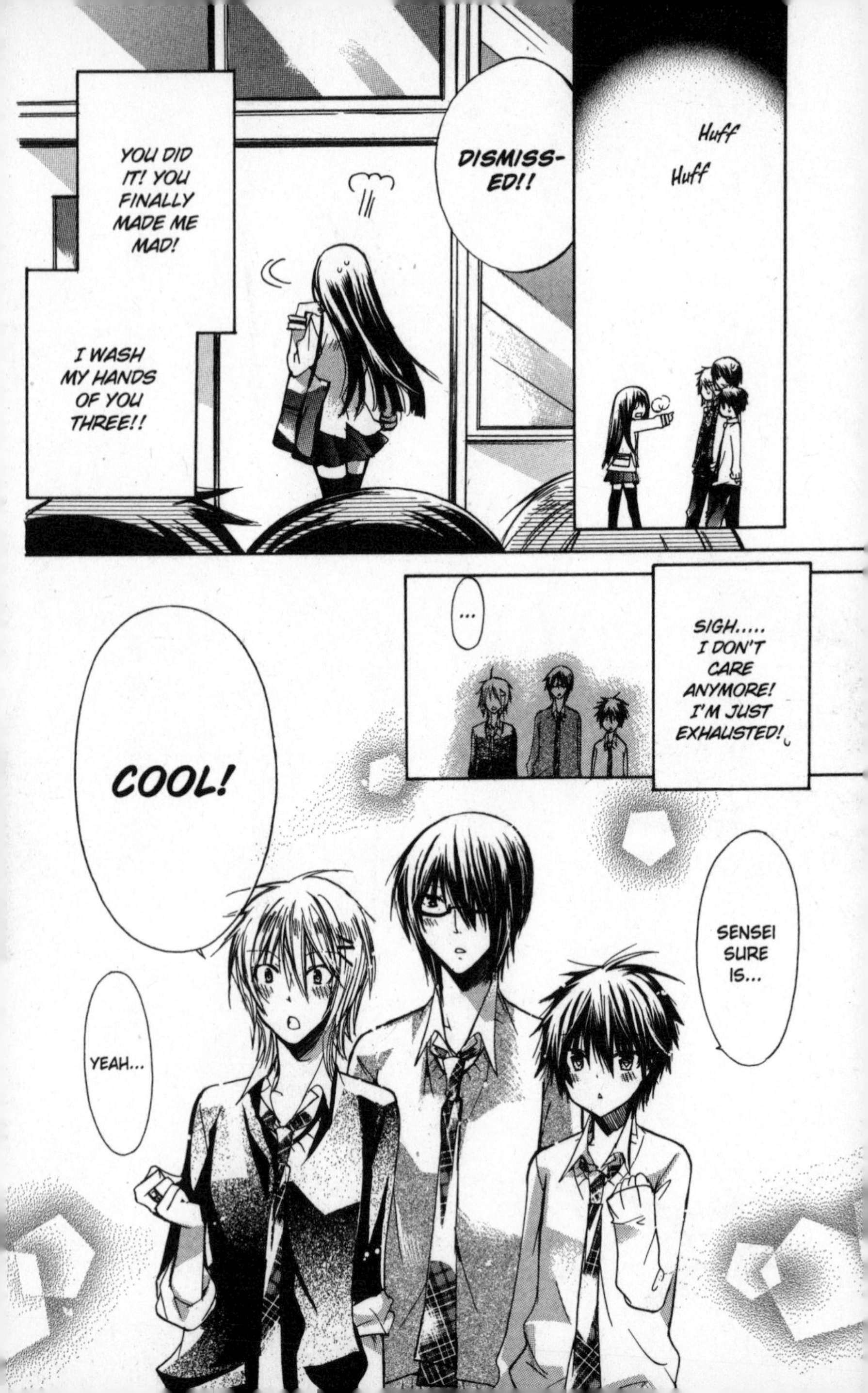
Huff
Huff
DISMISS-ED!!
YOU DID IT! YOU FINALLY MADE ME MAD!
I WASH MY HANDS OF YOU THREE!!
SIGH..... I DON'T CARE ANYMORE! I'M JUST EXHAUSTED!
...
SENSEI SURE IS...
COOL!
YEAH...

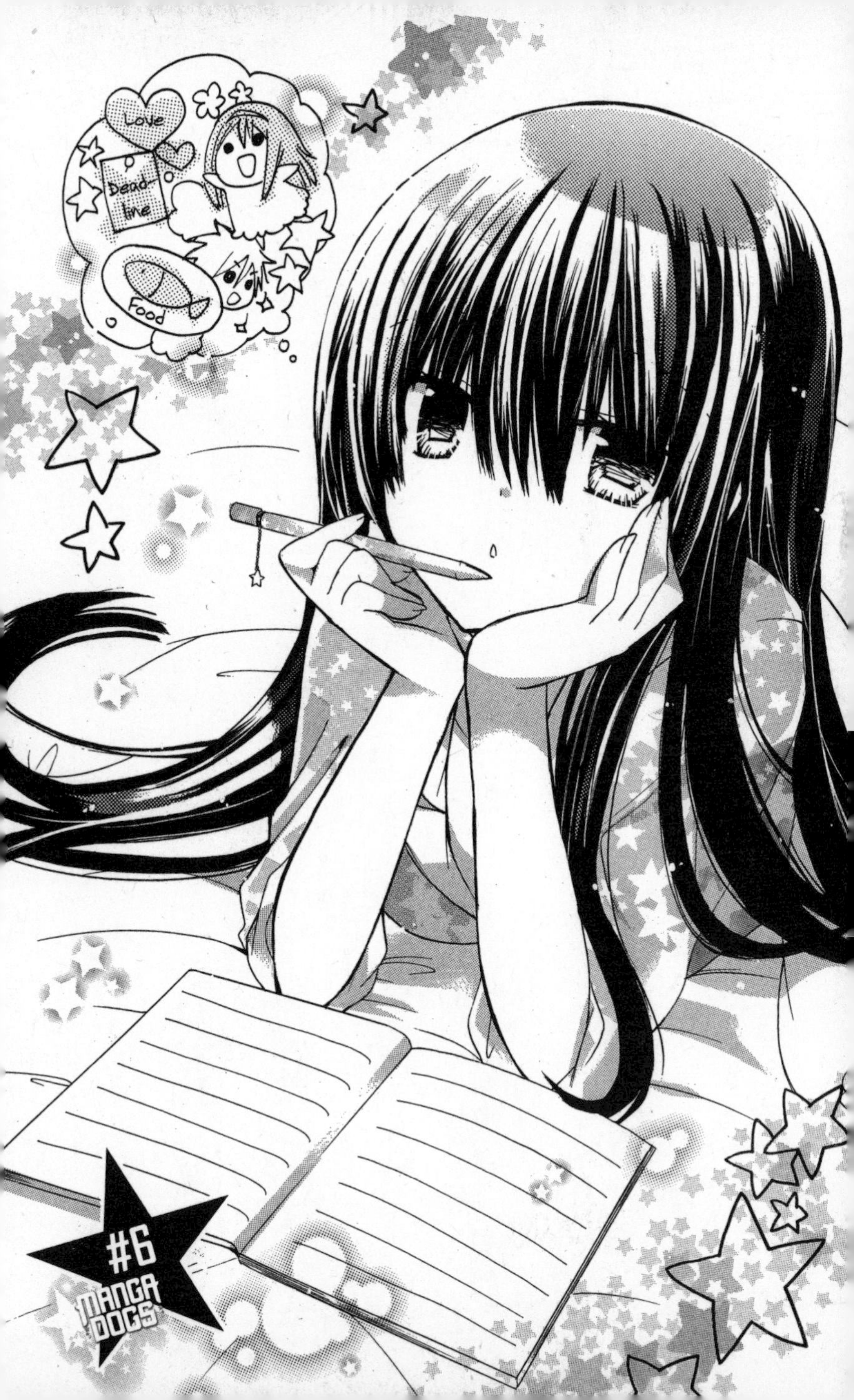
Love
Dead-line
Food
#6
MANGA DOGS

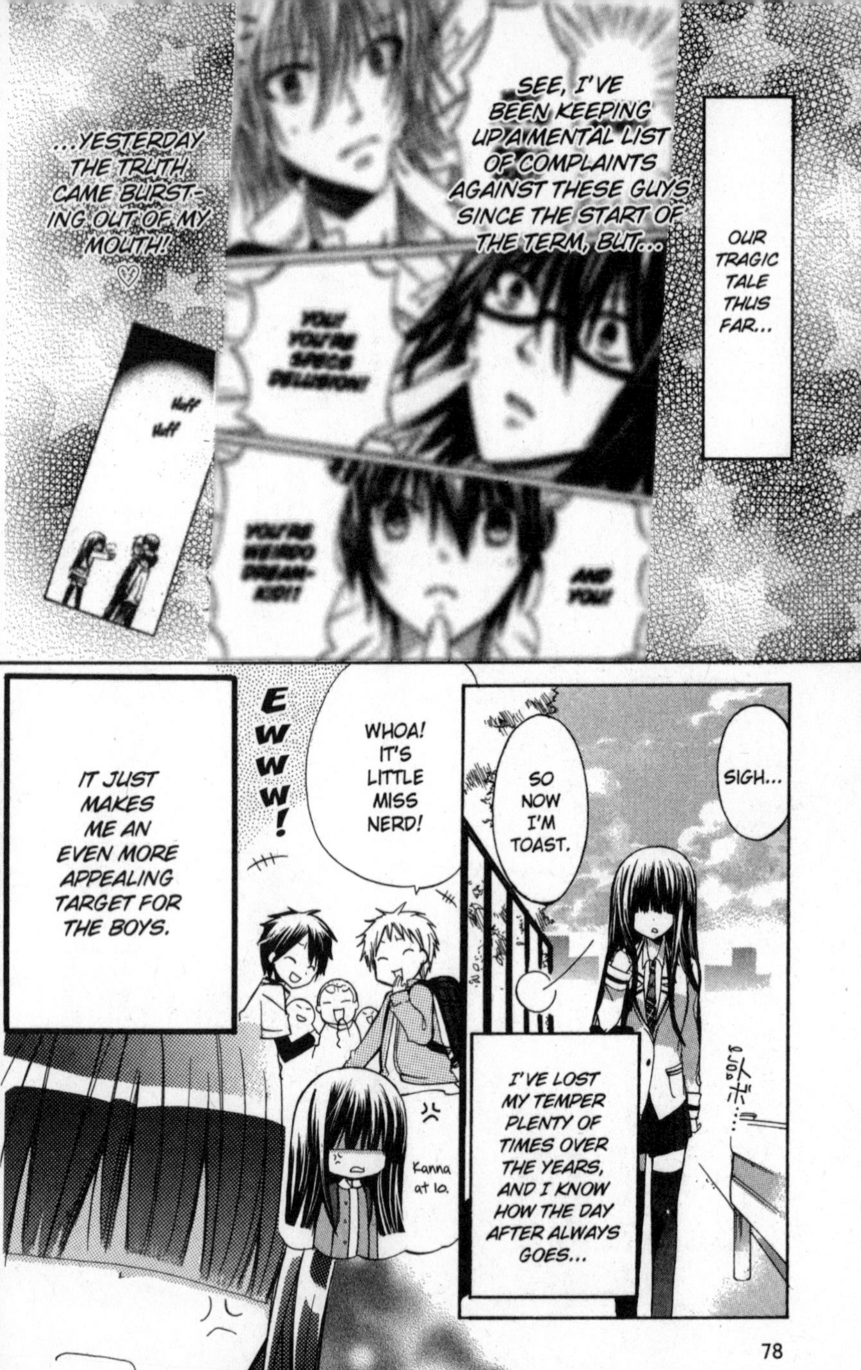
OUR TRAGIC TALE THUS FAR...
SEE, I'VE BEEN KEEPING UP A MENTAL LIST OF COMPLAINTS AGAINST THESE GUYS SINCE THE START OF THE TERM, BUT...
...YESTERDAY THE TRUTH CAME BURSTING OUT OF MY MOUTH! ♡
SIGH...
SO NOW I'M TOAST.
I'VE LOST MY TEMPER PLENTY OF TIMES OVER THE YEARS, AND I KNOW HOW THE DAY AFTER ALWAYS GOES...
WHOA! IT'S LITTLE MISS NERD!
EWWWW!
Kanna at 10.
IT JUST MAKES ME AN EVEN MORE APPEALING TARGET FOR THE BOYS.

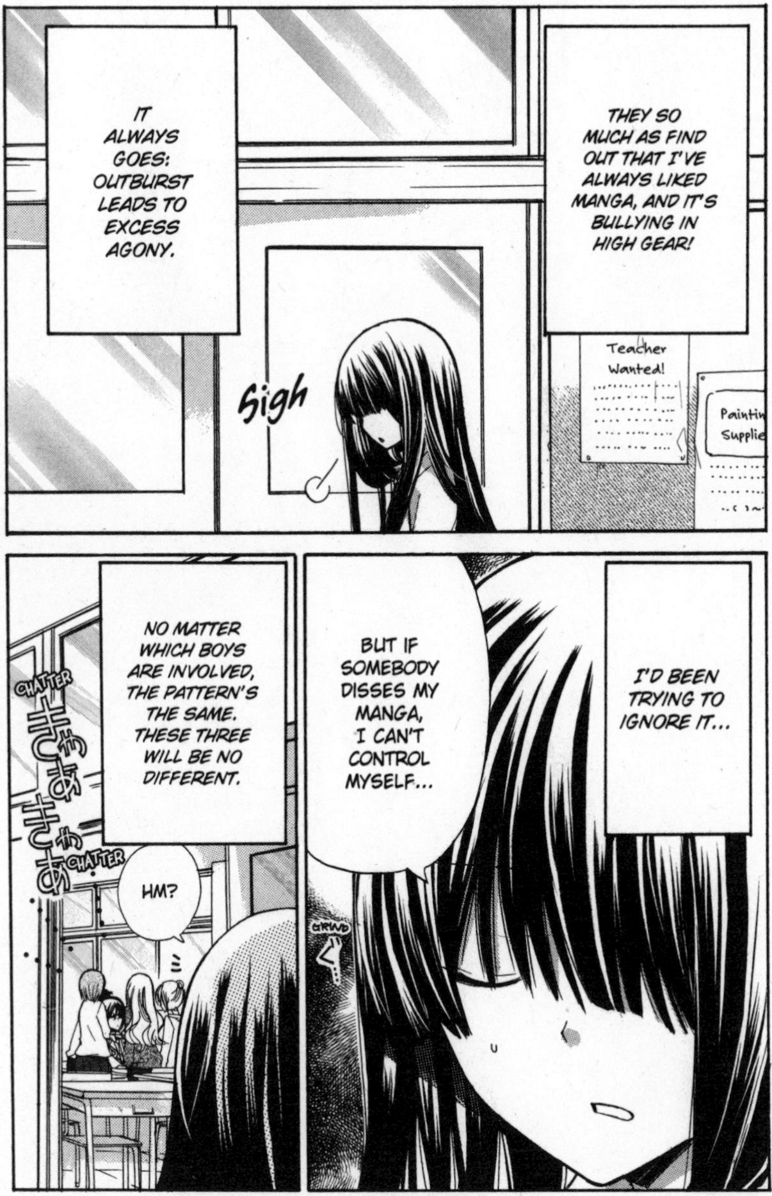
THEY SO MUCH AS FIND OUT THAT I'VE ALWAYS LIKED MANGA, AND IT'S BULLYING IN HIGH GEAR!
Teacher Wanted!
Painting Supplies
Sigh
IT ALWAYS GOES: OUTBURST LEADS TO EXCESS AGONY.
I'D BEEN TRYING TO IGNORE IT...
BUT IF SOMEBODY DISSES MY MANGA, I CAN'T CONTROL MYSELF...
GRIND
NO MATTER WHICH BOYS ARE INVOLVED, THE PATTERN'S THE SAME. THESE THREE WILL BE NO DIFFERENT.
CHATTER
きゃあきゃあ
CHATTER
HM?

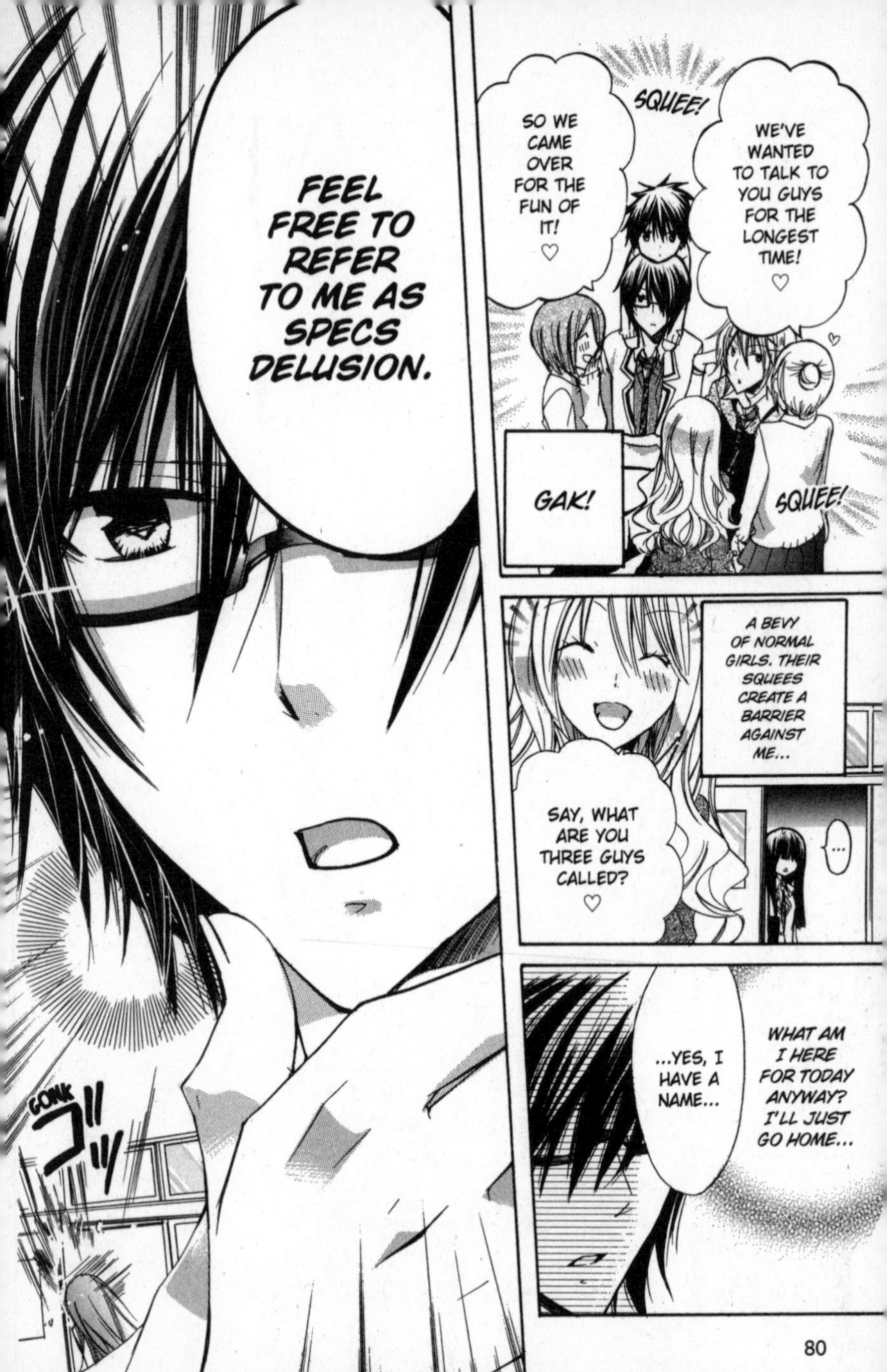
SQUEE!
WE'VE WANTED TO TALK TO YOU GUYS FOR THE LONGEST TIME! ♡
SO WE CAME OVER FOR THE FUN OF IT! ♡
SQUEE!
GAK!
A BEVY OF NORMAL GIRLS. THEIR SQUEES CREATE A BARRIER AGAINST ME...
SAY, WHAT ARE YOU THREE GUYS CALLED? ♡
...
WHAT AM I HERE FOR TODAY ANYWAY? I'LL JUST GO HOME...
...YES, I HAVE A NAME...
FEEL FREE TO REFER TO ME AS SPECS DELUSION.
GONK

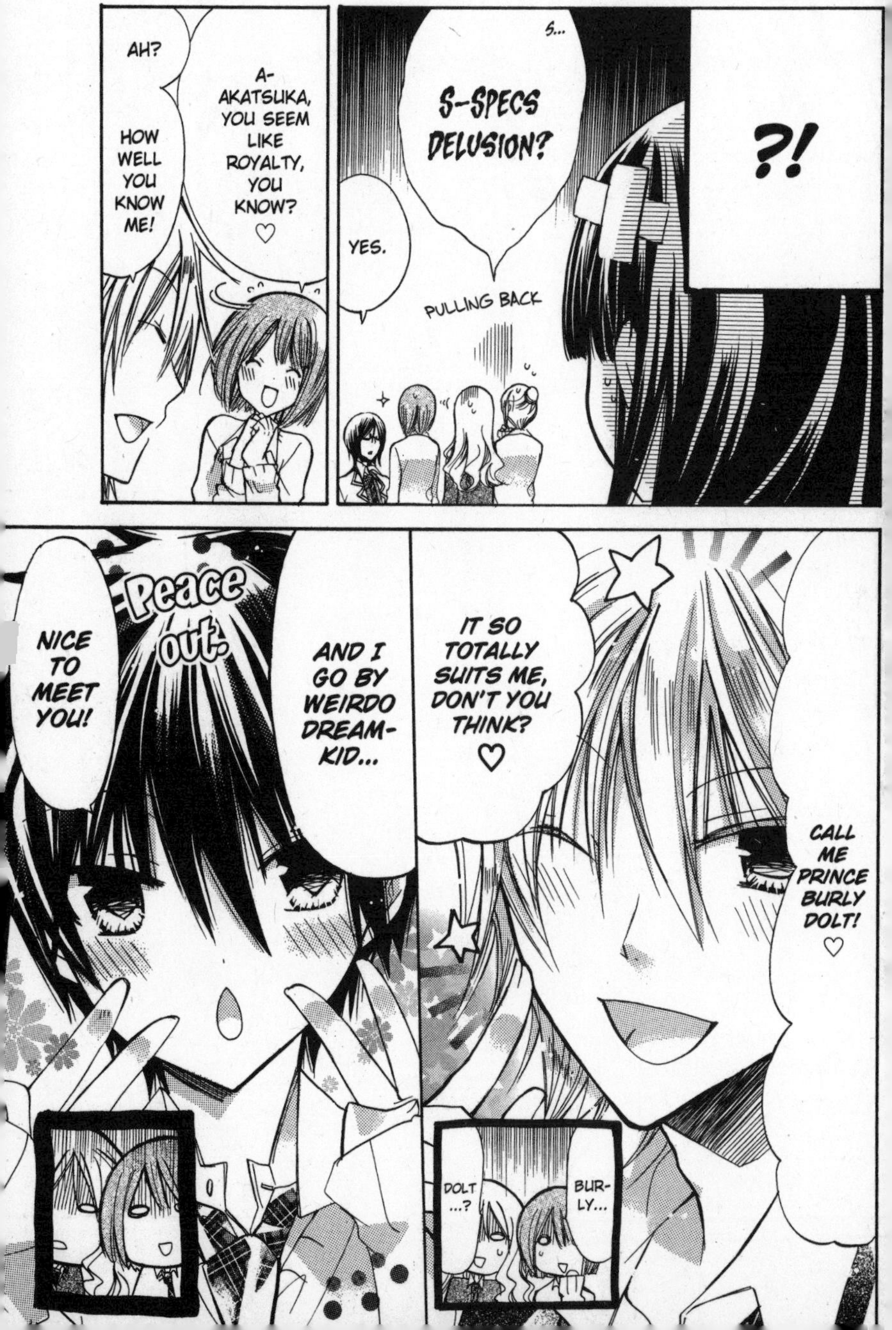
?!
S...
S-SPECS DELUSION?
YES.
PULLING BACK
A-AKATSUKA, YOU SEEM LIKE ROYALTY, YOU KNOW? ♡
AH?
HOW WELL YOU KNOW ME!
CALL ME PRINCE BURLY DOLT! ♡
IT SO TOTALLY SUITS ME, DON'T YOU THINK? ♡
BUR-LY...
DOLT ...?
AND I GO BY WEIRDO DREAM-KID...
Peace out.
NICE TO MEET YOU!

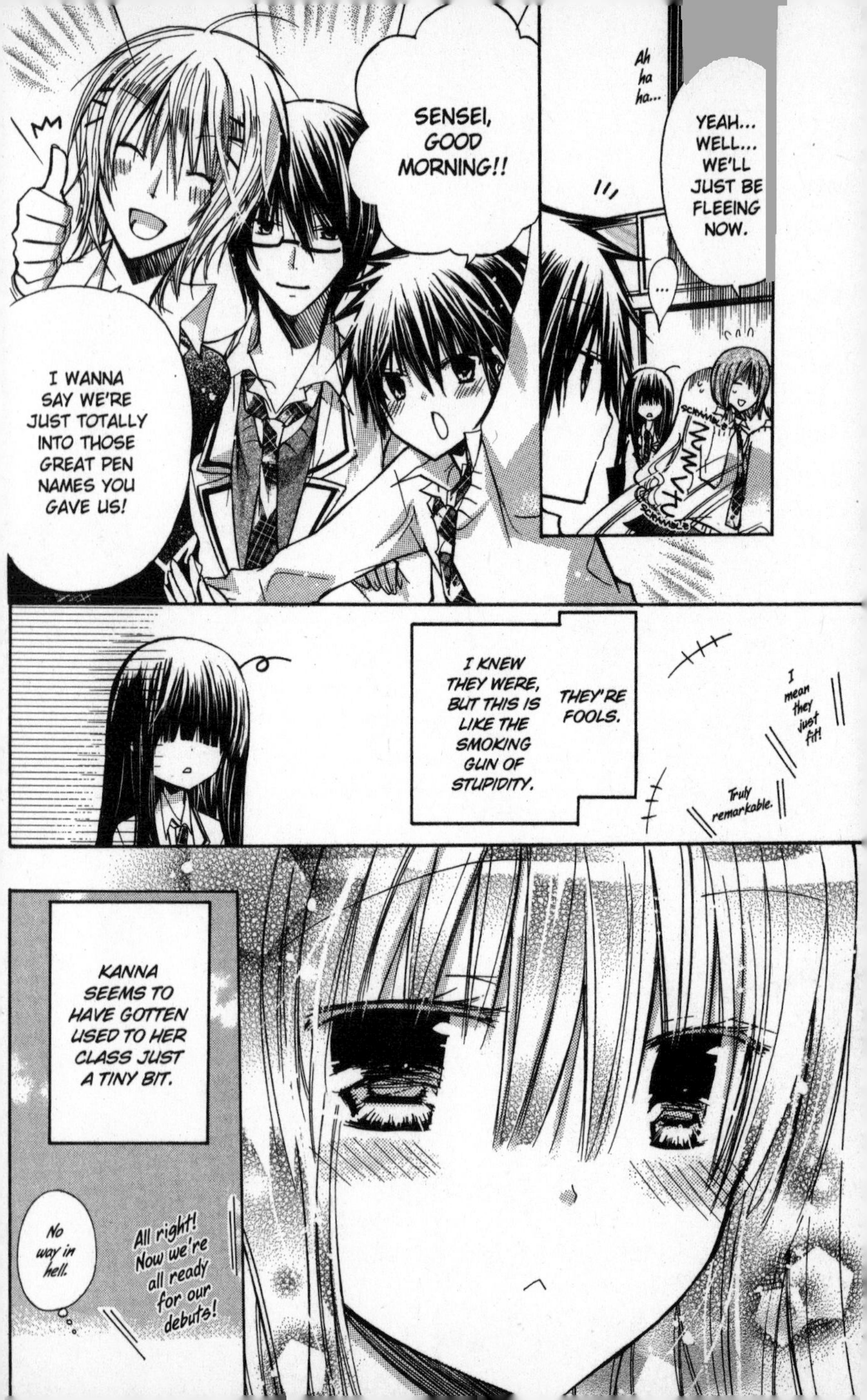
Ah ha ha...
YEAH... WELL... WE'LL JUST BE FLEEING NOW.
...
SCRAMBLE
SCRAMBLE
SENSEI, GOOD MORNING!!
I WANNA SAY WE'RE JUST TOTALLY INTO THOSE GREAT PEN NAMES YOU GAVE US!
I mean they just fit!
Truly remarkable.
THEY'RE FOOLS.
I KNEW THEY WERE, BUT THIS IS LIKE THE SMOKING GUN OF STUPIDITY.
KANNA SEEMS TO HAVE GOTTEN USED TO HER CLASS JUST A TINY BIT.
All right! Now we're all ready for our debuts!
No way in hell.

That manga major is way full of weirdos!

Totally!

...I've been lumped in with them.

MANGA DOGS

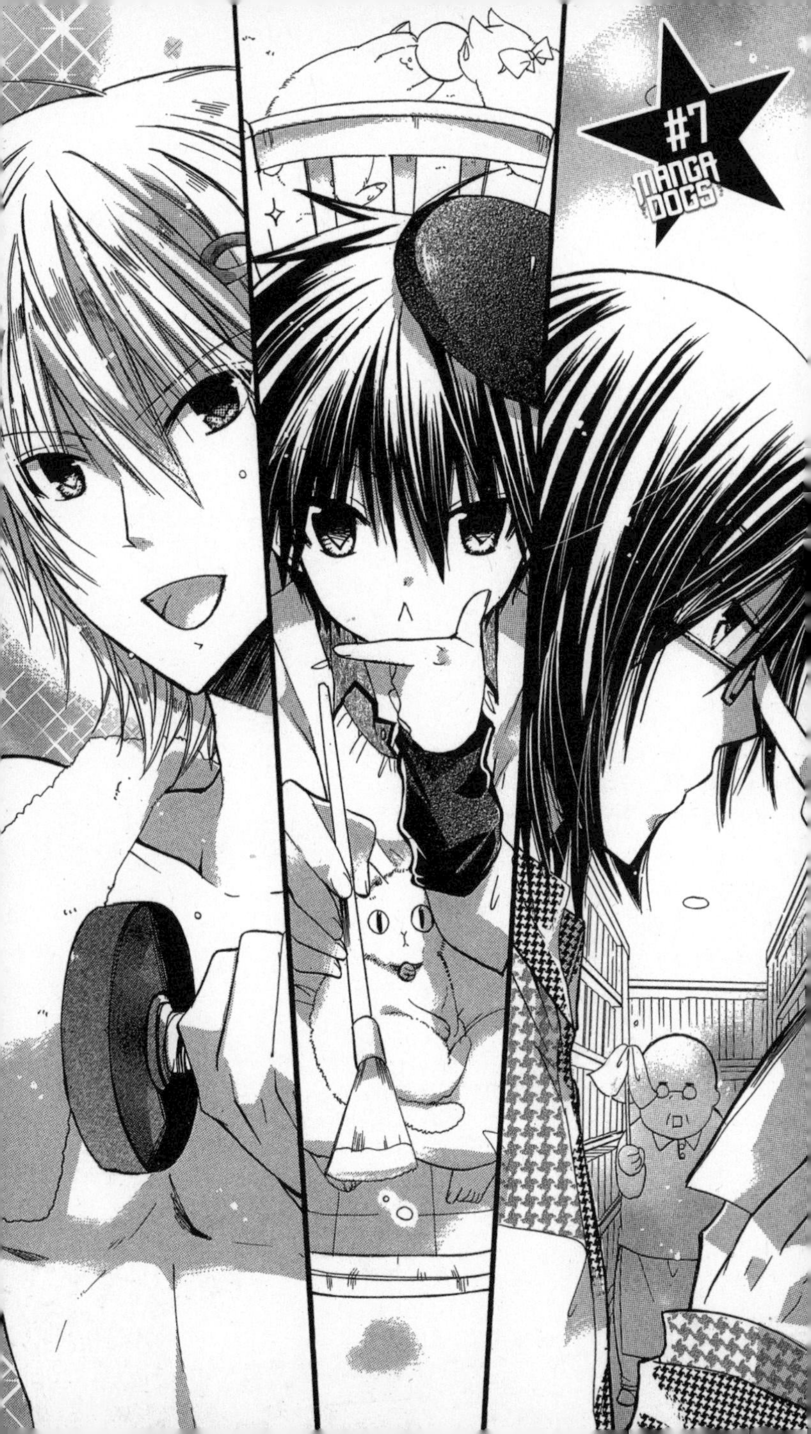
#7
MANGA DOGS

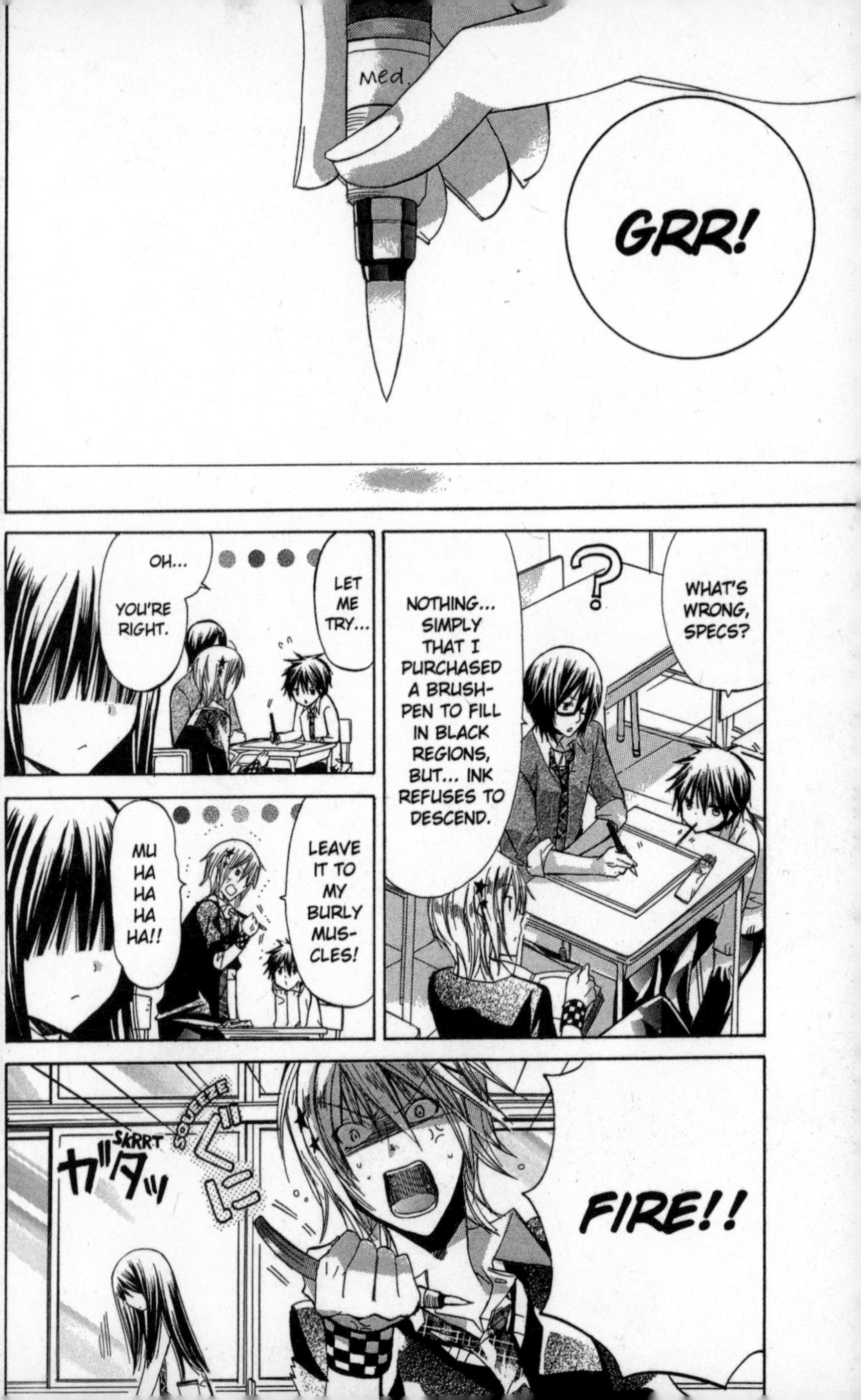
GRR!
Med.
WHAT'S WRONG, SPECS?
?
NOTHING... SIMPLY THAT I PURCHASED A BRUSH-PEN TO FILL IN BLACK REGIONS, BUT... INK REFUSES TO DESCEND.
LET ME TRY...
OH... YOU'RE RIGHT.
LEAVE IT TO MY BURLY MUSCLES!
MU HA HA HA HA!!
FIRE!!
SQUEEZE
SKRRT
ガタッ

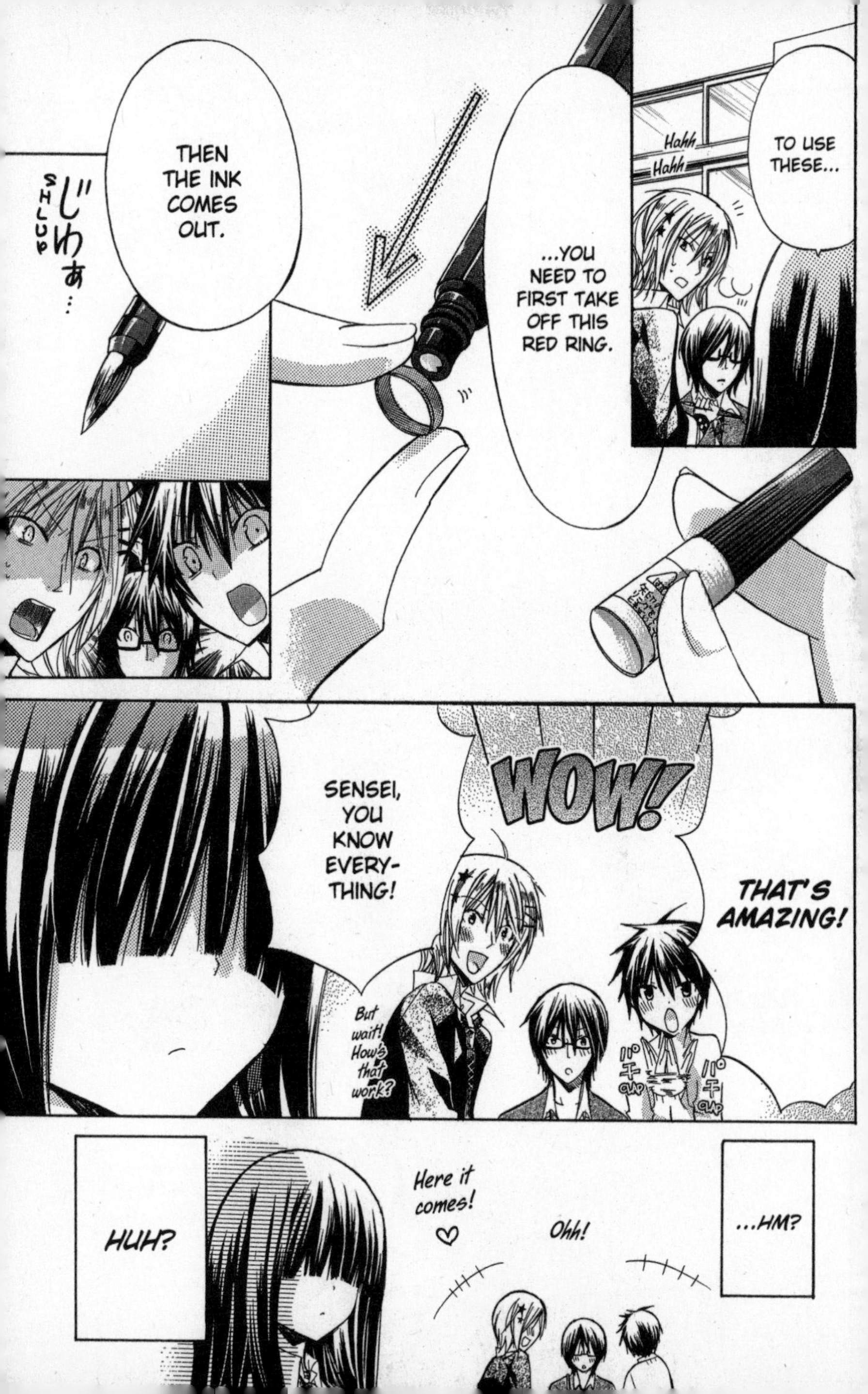
TO USE THESE...
Hahh
Hahh
...YOU NEED TO FIRST TAKE OFF THIS RED RING.
THEN THE INK COMES OUT.
じわぁ…
SHLUP
THAT'S AMAZING!
WOW!
SENSEI, YOU KNOW EVERY-THING!
パチ
CLAP
パチ
CLAP
But wait! How's that work?
...HM?
Ohh!
Here it comes! ♡
HUH?

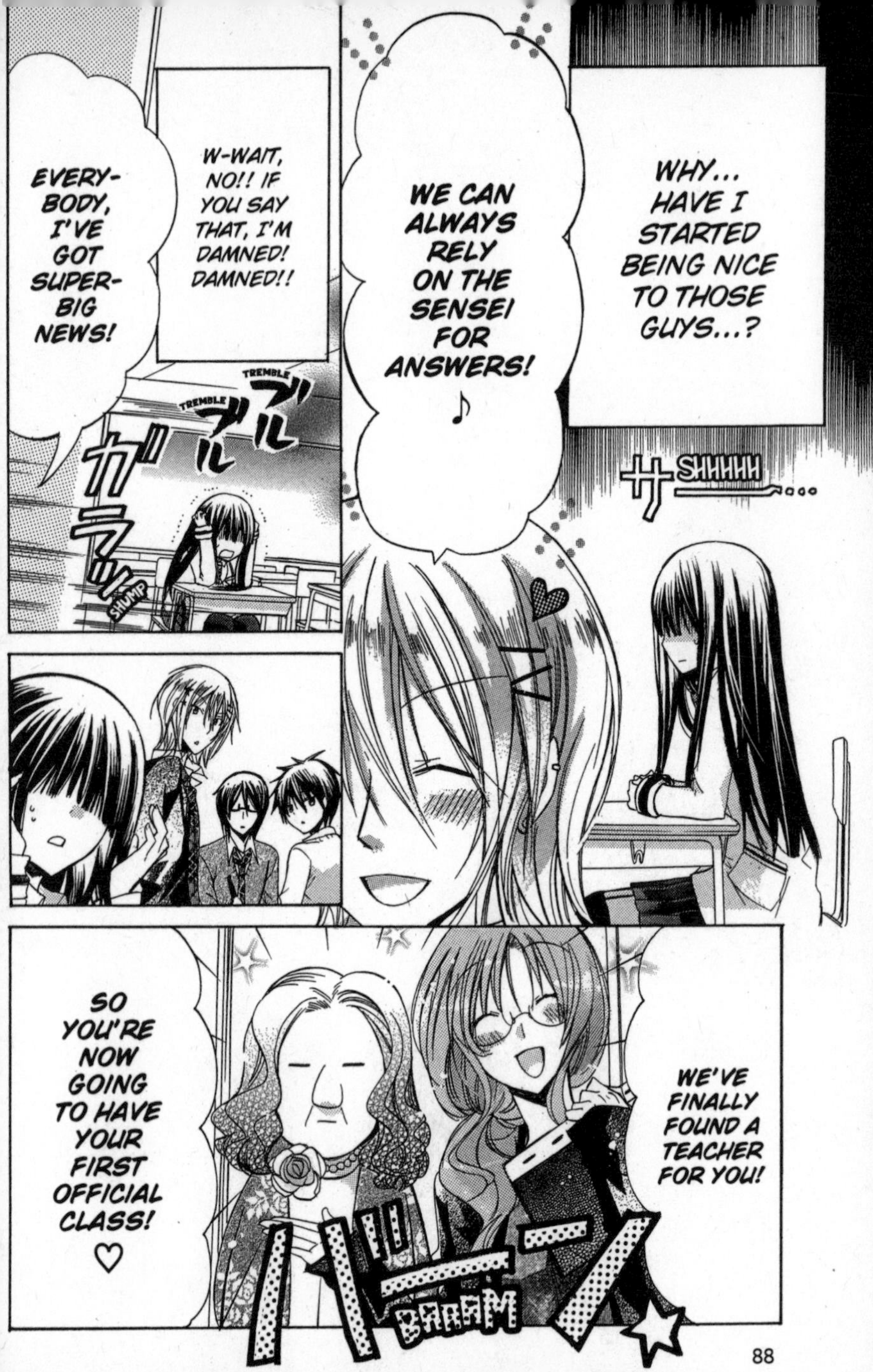
WHY... HAVE I STARTED BEING NICE TO THOSE GUYS...?
WE CAN ALWAYS RELY ON THE SENSEI FOR ANSWERS! ♪
SHHHHH...
W-WAIT, NO!! IF YOU SAY THAT, I'M DAMNED! DAMNED!!
EVERYBODY, I'VE GOT SUPER-BIG NEWS!
TREMBLE
TREMBLE
SHUMP
WE'VE FINALLY FOUND A TEACHER FOR YOU!
SO YOU'RE NOW GOING TO HAVE YOUR FIRST OFFICIAL CLASS! ♡
BRAAM

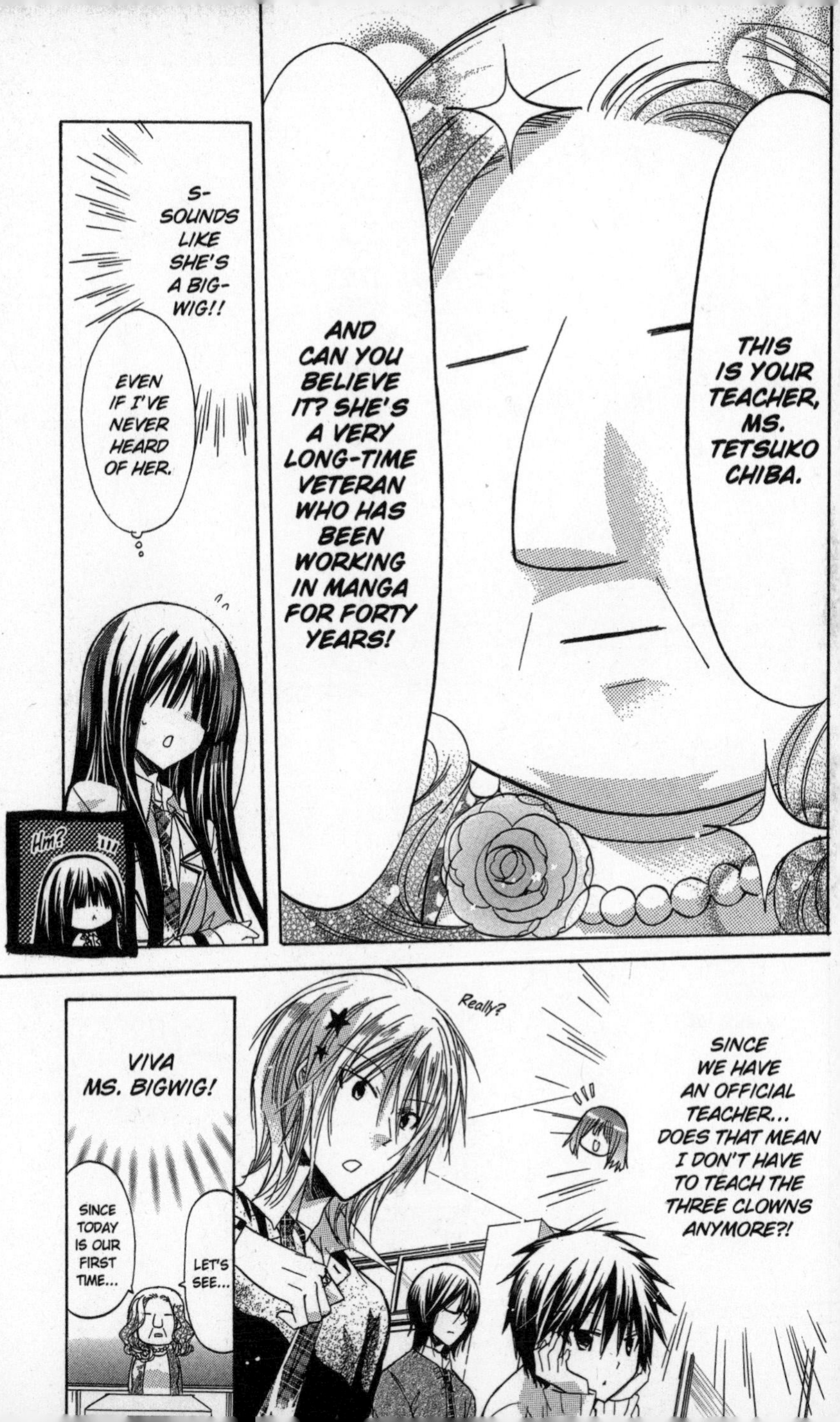
THIS IS YOUR TEACHER, MS. TETSUKO CHIBA.
AND CAN YOU BELIEVE IT? SHE'S A VERY LONG-TIME VETERAN WHO HAS BEEN WORKING IN MANGA FOR FORTY YEARS!
S-SOUNDS LIKE SHE'S A BIG-WIG!!
EVEN IF I'VE NEVER HEARD OF HER.
Hm?
SINCE WE HAVE AN OFFICIAL TEACHER... DOES THAT MEAN I DON'T HAVE TO TEACH THE THREE CLOWNS ANYMORE?!
Really?
VIVA MS. BIGWIG!
LET'S SEE...
SINCE TODAY IS OUR FIRST TIME...

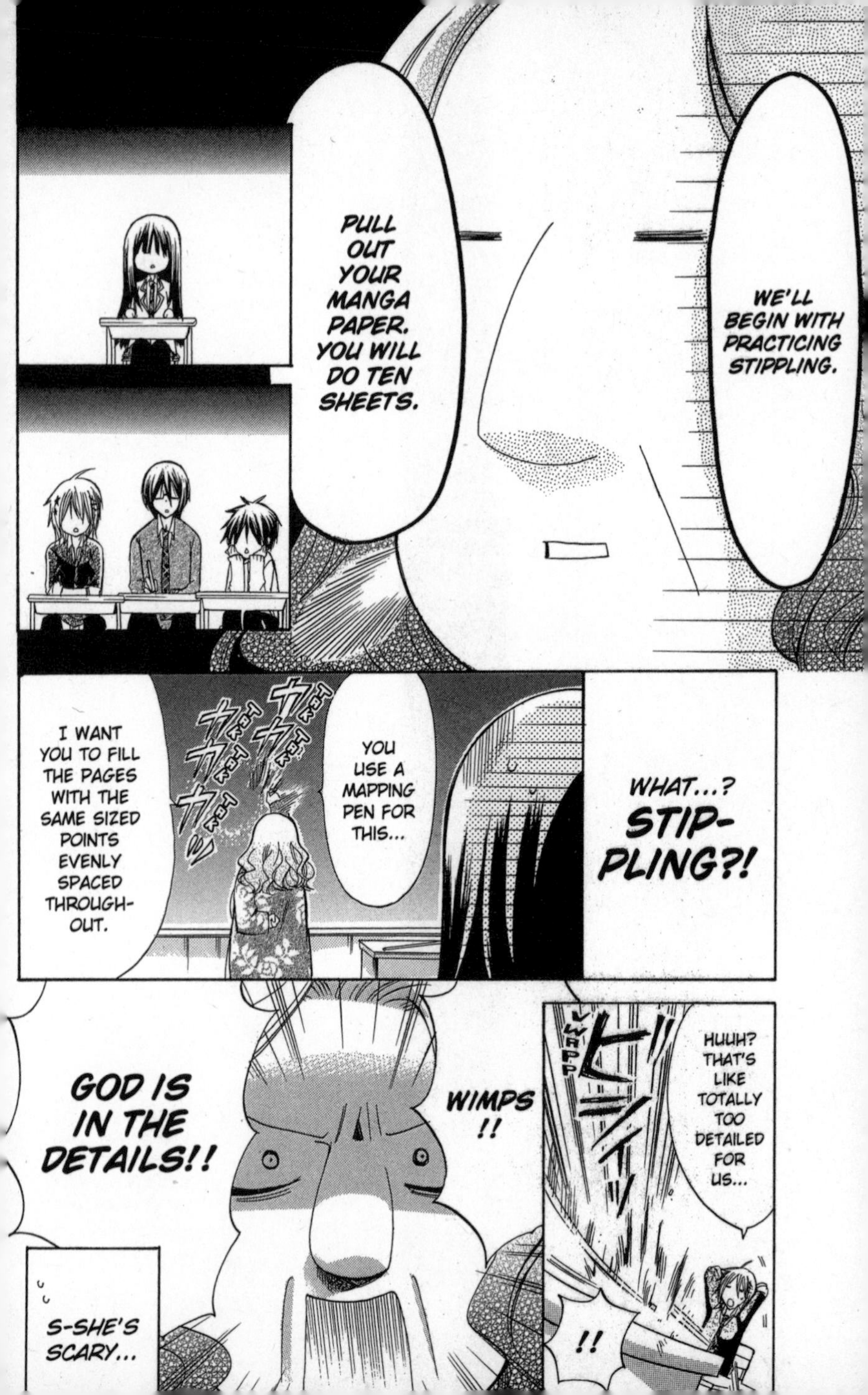
WE'LL BEGIN WITH PRACTICING STIPPLING.
PULL OUT YOUR MANGA PAPER. YOU WILL DO TEN SHEETS.
WHAT...? STIP-PLING?!
YOU USE A MAPPING PEN FOR THIS...
I WANT YOU TO FILL THE PAGES WITH THE SAME SIZED POINTS EVENLY SPACED THROUGH-OUT.
HUUH? THAT'S LIKE TOTALLY TOO DETAILED FOR US...
VWAPP
!!
WIMPS !!
GOD IS IN THE DETAILS!!
S-SHE'S SCARY...

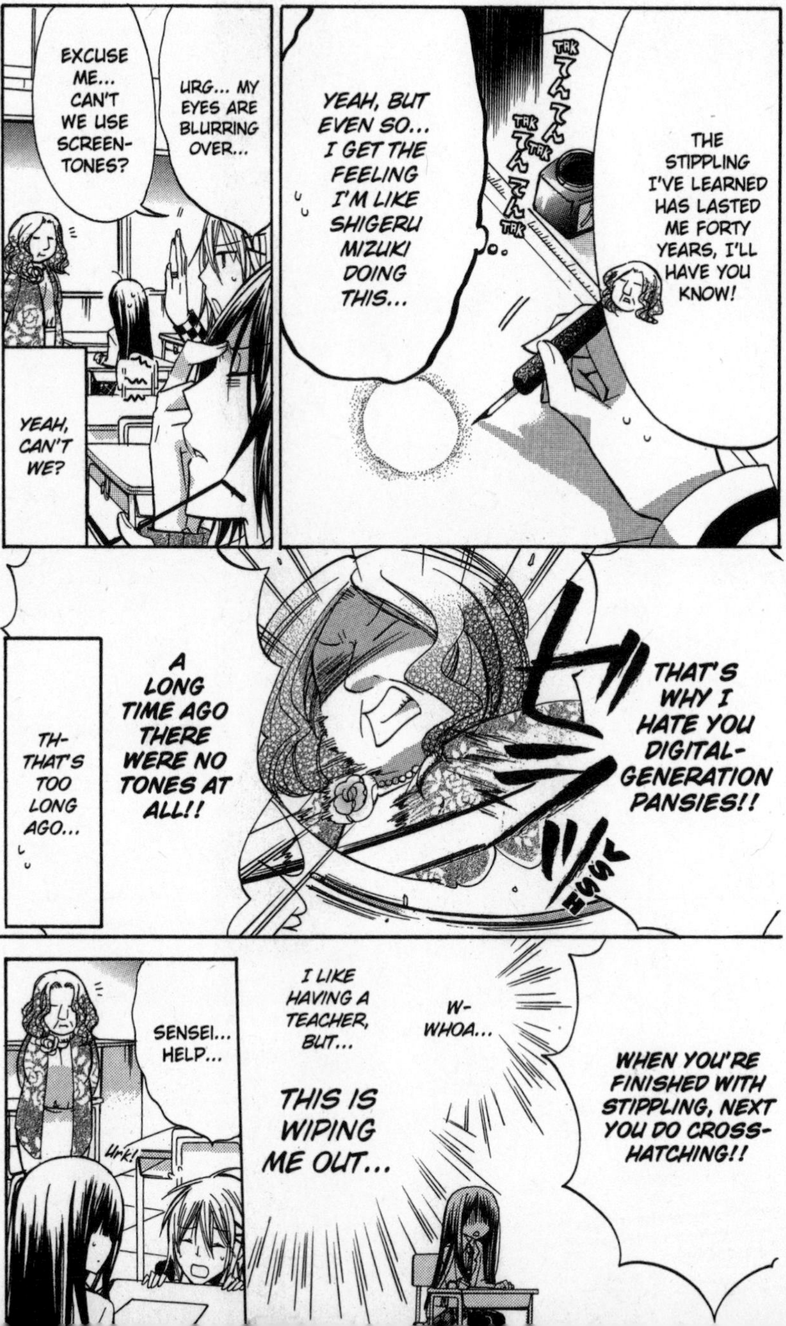
THE STIPPLING I'VE LEARNED HAS LASTED ME FORTY YEARS, I'LL HAVE YOU KNOW!
TAK TAK TAK TAK TAK
YEAH, BUT EVEN SO... I GET THE FEELING I'M LIKE SHIGERU MIZUKI DOING THIS...
URG... MY EYES ARE BLURRING OVER...
EXCUSE ME... CAN'T WE USE SCREEN-TONES?
YEAH, CAN'T WE?
THAT'S WHY I HATE YOU DIGITAL-GENERATION PANSIES!!
HISS
A LONG TIME AGO THERE WERE NO TONES AT ALL!!
TH-THAT'S TOO LONG AGO...
WHEN YOU'RE FINISHED WITH STIPPLING, NEXT YOU DO CROSS-HATCHING!!
W-WHOA...
I LIKE HAVING A TEACHER, BUT...
THIS IS WIPING ME OUT...
SENSEI... HELP...
Urk!

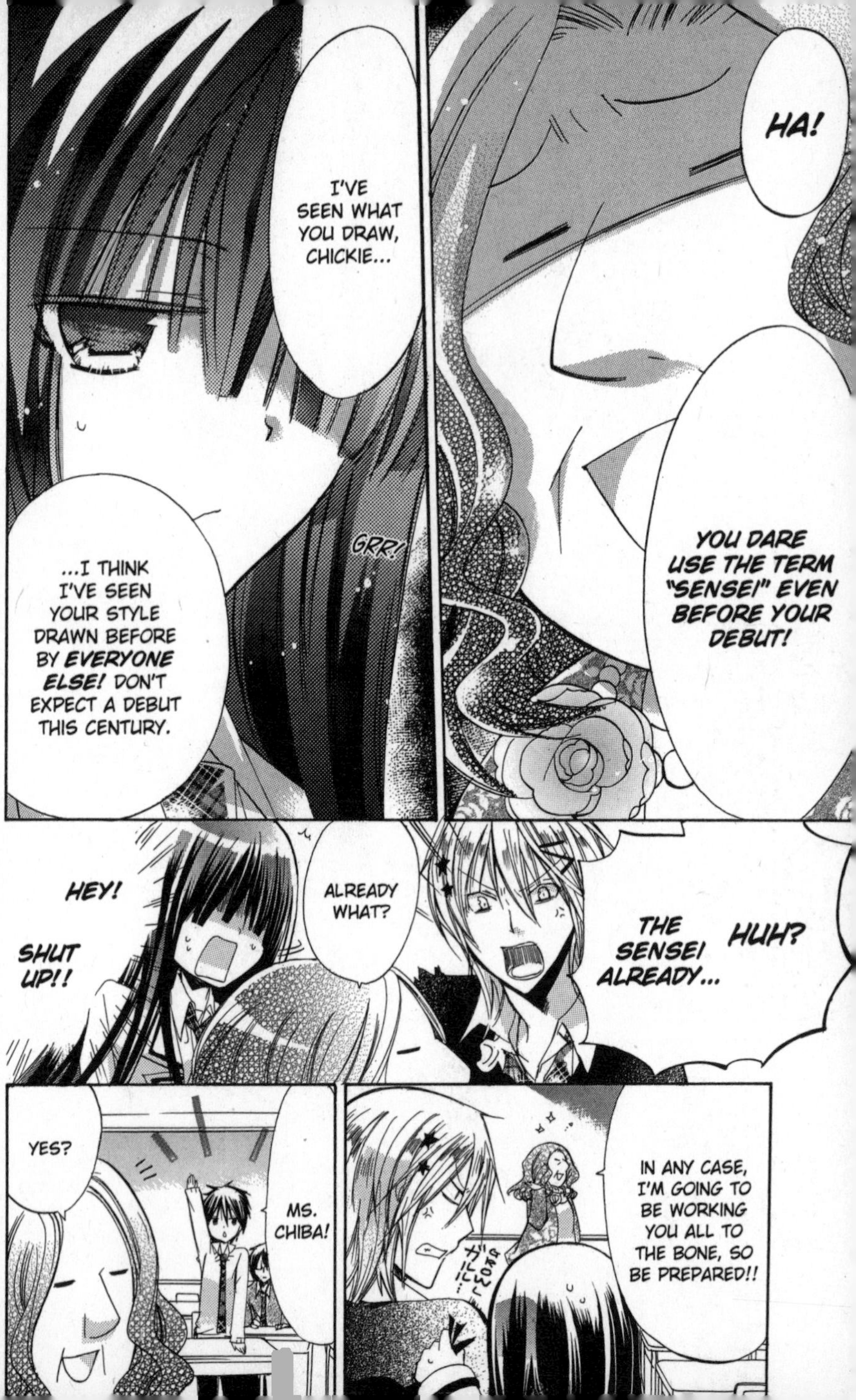
HA!
YOU DARE USE THE TERM "SENSEI" EVEN BEFORE YOUR DEBUT!
I'VE SEEN WHAT YOU DRAW, CHICKIE...
GRR!
...I THINK I'VE SEEN YOUR STYLE DRAWN BEFORE BY EVERYONE ELSE! DON'T EXPECT A DEBUT THIS CENTURY.
HUH?
THE SENSEI ALREADY...
ALREADY WHAT?
HEY!
SHUT UP!!
IN ANY CASE, I'M GOING TO BE WORKING YOU ALL TO THE BONE, SO BE PREPARED!!
GROWL...
MS. CHIBA!
YES?

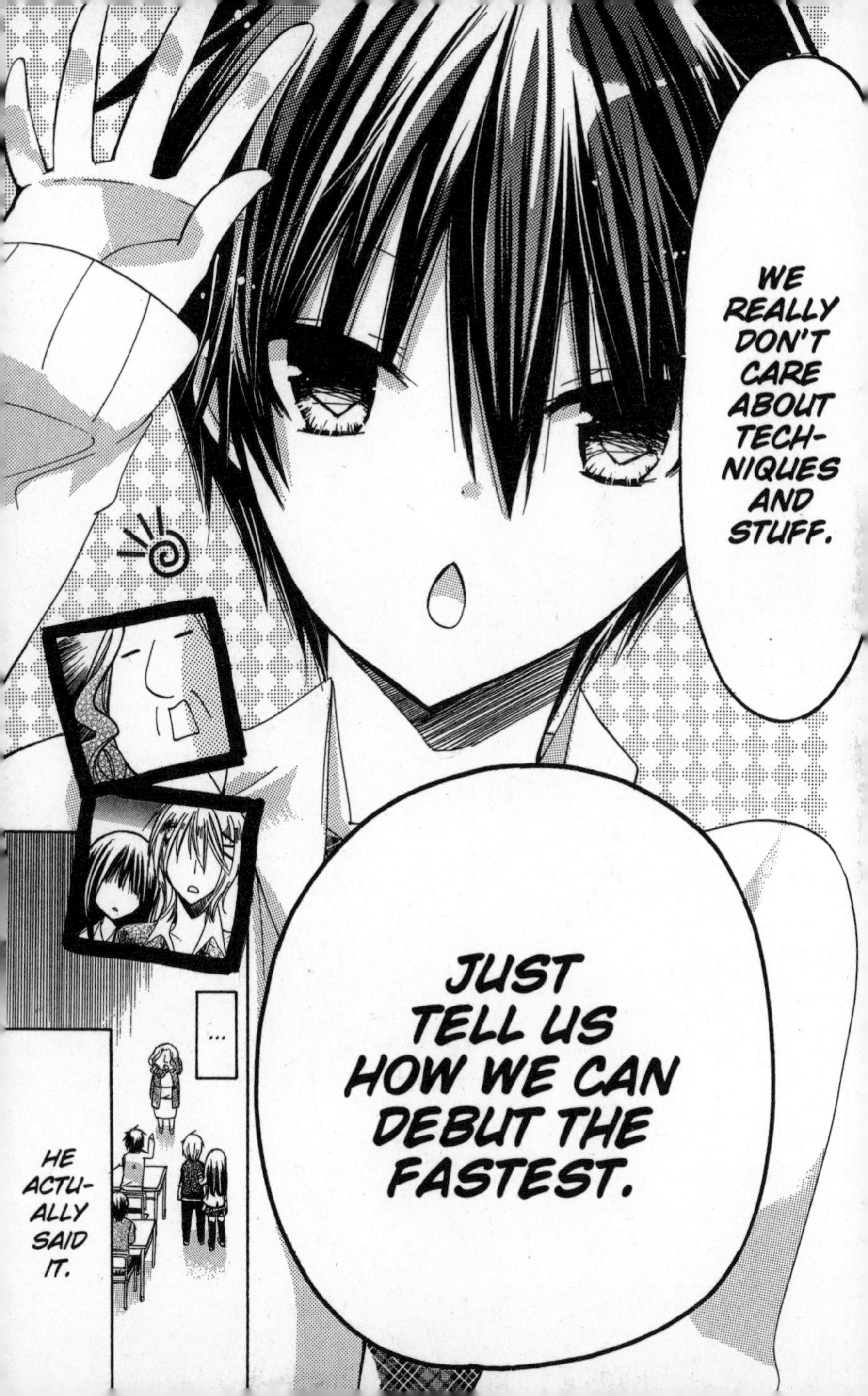
WE REALLY DON'T CARE ABOUT TECH-NIQUES AND STUFF.
JUST TELL US HOW WE CAN DEBUT THE FASTEST.
...
HE ACTU-ALLY SAID IT.

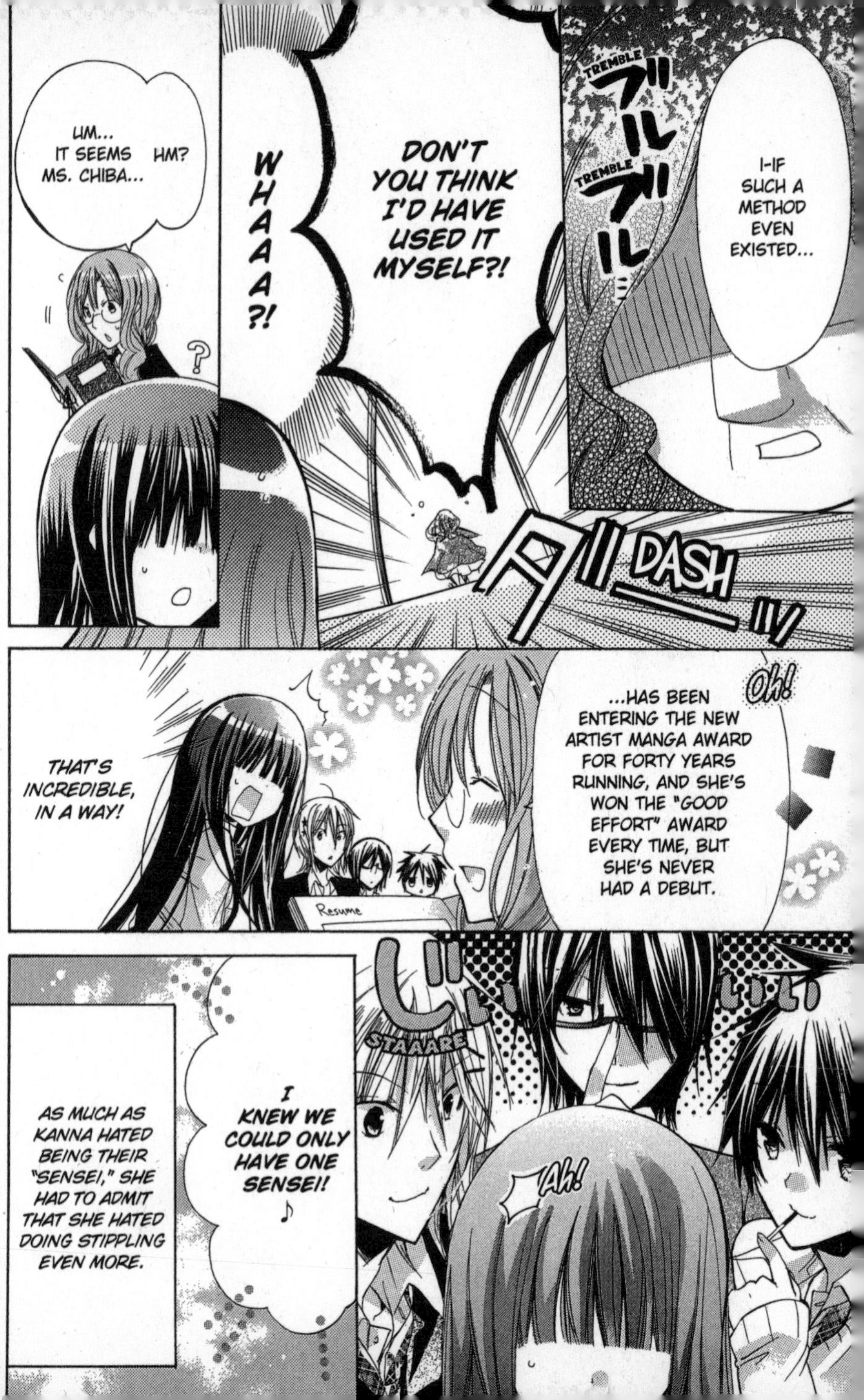

TREMBLE
TREMBLE
I-IF SUCH A METHOD EVEN EXISTED...
DON'T YOU THINK I'D HAVE USED IT MYSELF?!
WHAAAA?!
DASH
HM?
UM... IT SEEMS MS. CHIBA...
Oh!
...HAS BEEN ENTERING THE NEW ARTIST MANGA AWARD FOR FORTY YEARS RUNNING, AND SHE'S WON THE "GOOD EFFORT" AWARD EVERY TIME, BUT SHE'S NEVER HAD A DEBUT.
THAT'S INCREDIBLE, IN A WAY!
Resume
STAAARE
Ah!
I KNEW WE COULD ONLY HAVE ONE SENSEI! ♪
AS MUCH AS KANNA HATED BEING THEIR "SENSEI," SHE HAD TO ADMIT THAT SHE HATED DOING STIPPLING EVEN MORE.

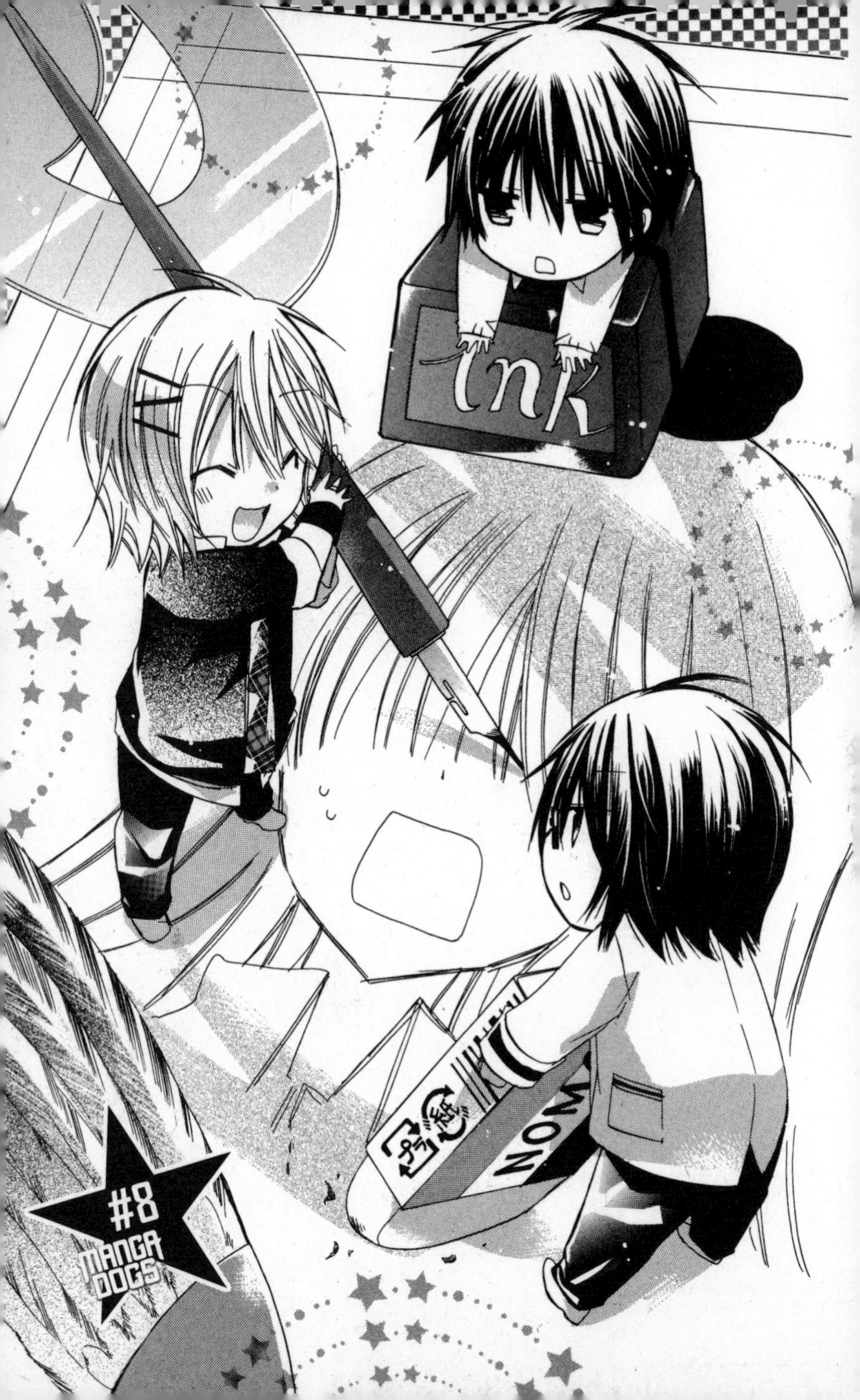
ink
#8
MANGA DOGS

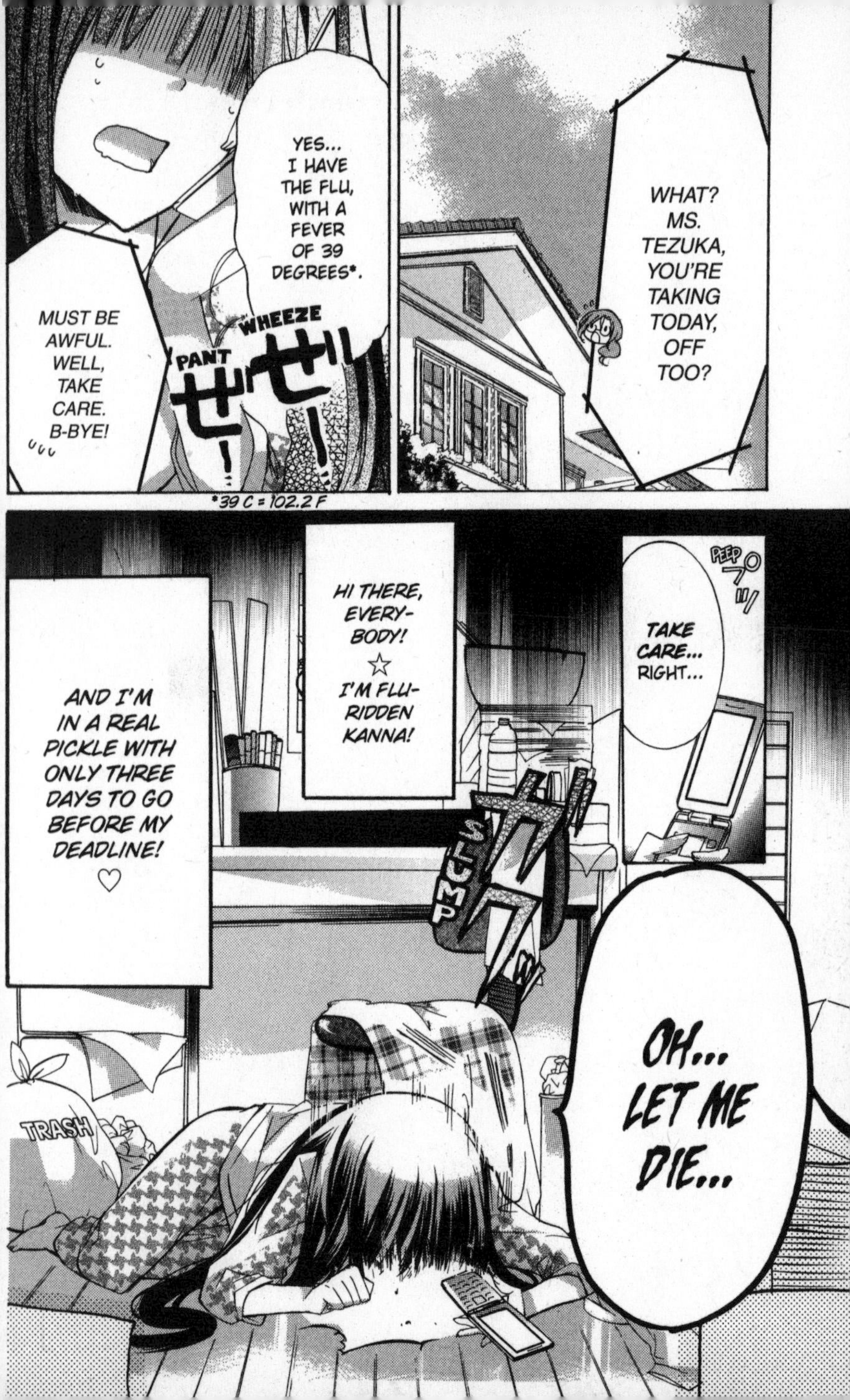
WHAT? MS. TEZUKA, YOU'RE TAKING TODAY, OFF TOO?
YES... I HAVE THE FLU, WITH A FEVER OF 39 DEGREES*.
WHEEZE
PANT
MUST BE AWFUL. WELL, TAKE CARE. B-BYE!
*39 C = 102.2 F
PEEP
TAKE CARE... RIGHT...
HI THERE, EVERY-BODY! ☆ I'M FLU-RIDDEN KANNA!
AND I'M IN A REAL PICKLE WITH ONLY THREE DAYS TO GO BEFORE MY DEADLINE! ♡
SLUMP
OH... LET ME DIE...
TRASH

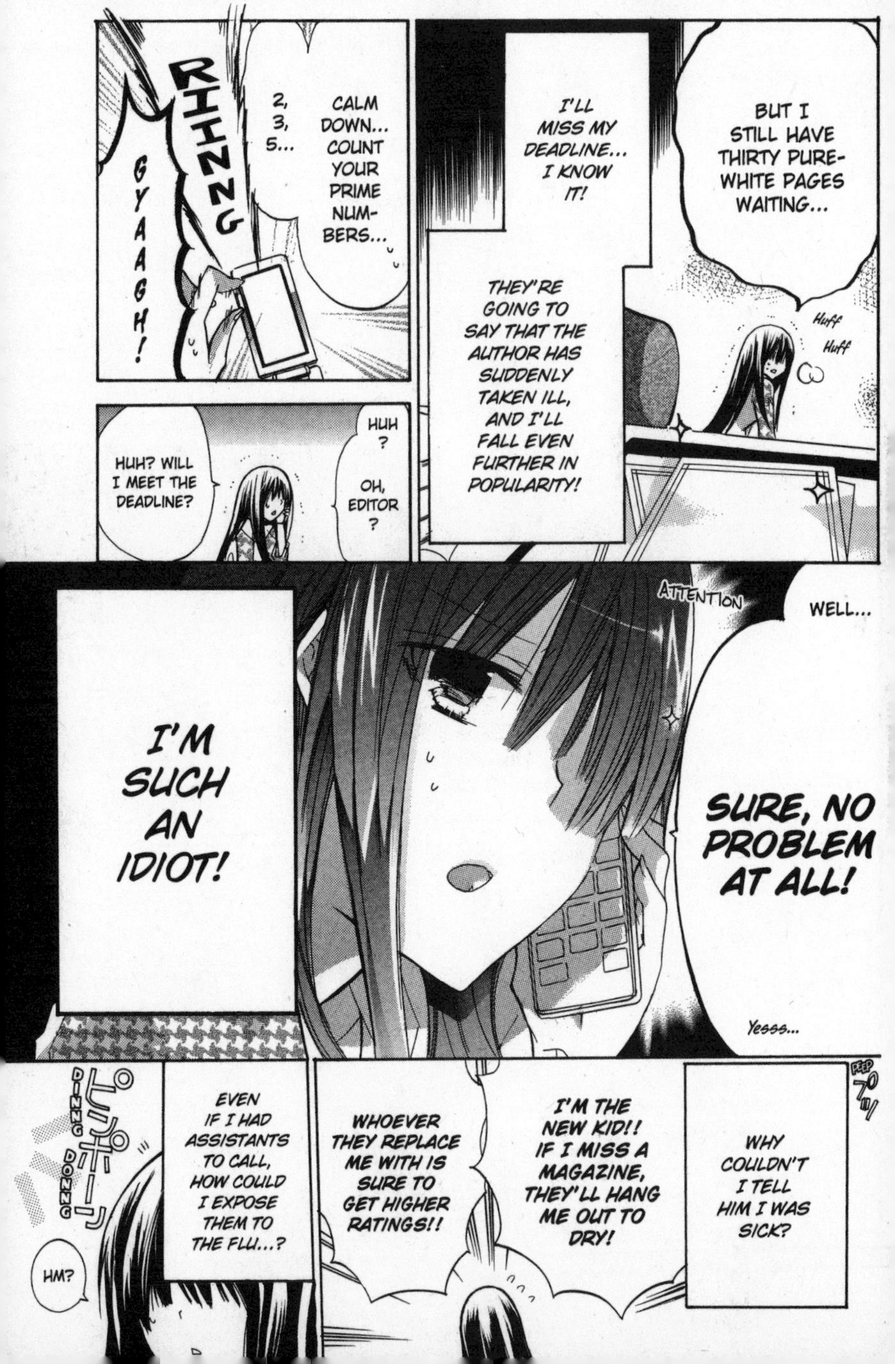
BUT I STILL HAVE THIRTY PURE-WHITE PAGES WAITING...
Huff
Huff
I'LL MISS MY DEADLINE... I KNOW IT!
THEY'RE GOING TO SAY THAT THE AUTHOR HAS SUDDENLY TAKEN ILL, AND I'LL FALL EVEN FURTHER IN POPULARITY!
CALM DOWN... COUNT YOUR PRIME NUMBERS...
2, 3, 5...
RIIINNG
GYAAAGH!
HUH?
OH, EDITOR?
HUH? WILL I MEET THE DEADLINE?
WELL...
ATTENTION
SURE, NO PROBLEM AT ALL!
Yesss...
I'M SUCH AN IDIOT!
PEEP
WHY COULDN'T I TELL HIM I WAS SICK?
I'M THE NEW KID!! IF I MISS A MAGAZINE, THEY'LL HANG ME OUT TO DRY!
WHOEVER THEY REPLACE ME WITH IS SURE TO GET HIGHER RATINGS!!
EVEN IF I HAD ASSISTANTS TO CALL, HOW COULD I EXPOSE THEM TO THE FLU...?
DING DONG
HM?

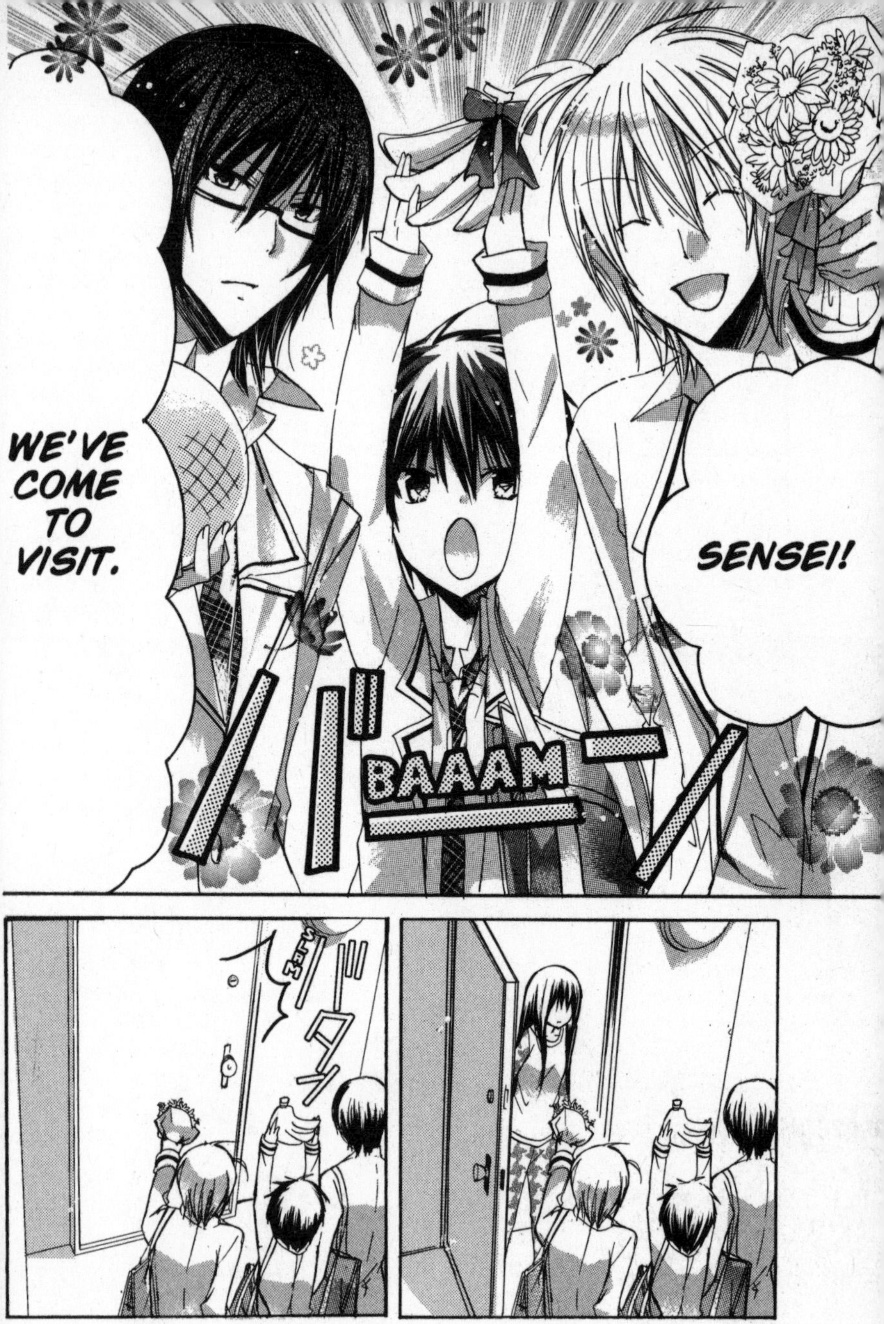
SENSEI!
WE'VE COME TO VISIT.
BAAAM
SLAM

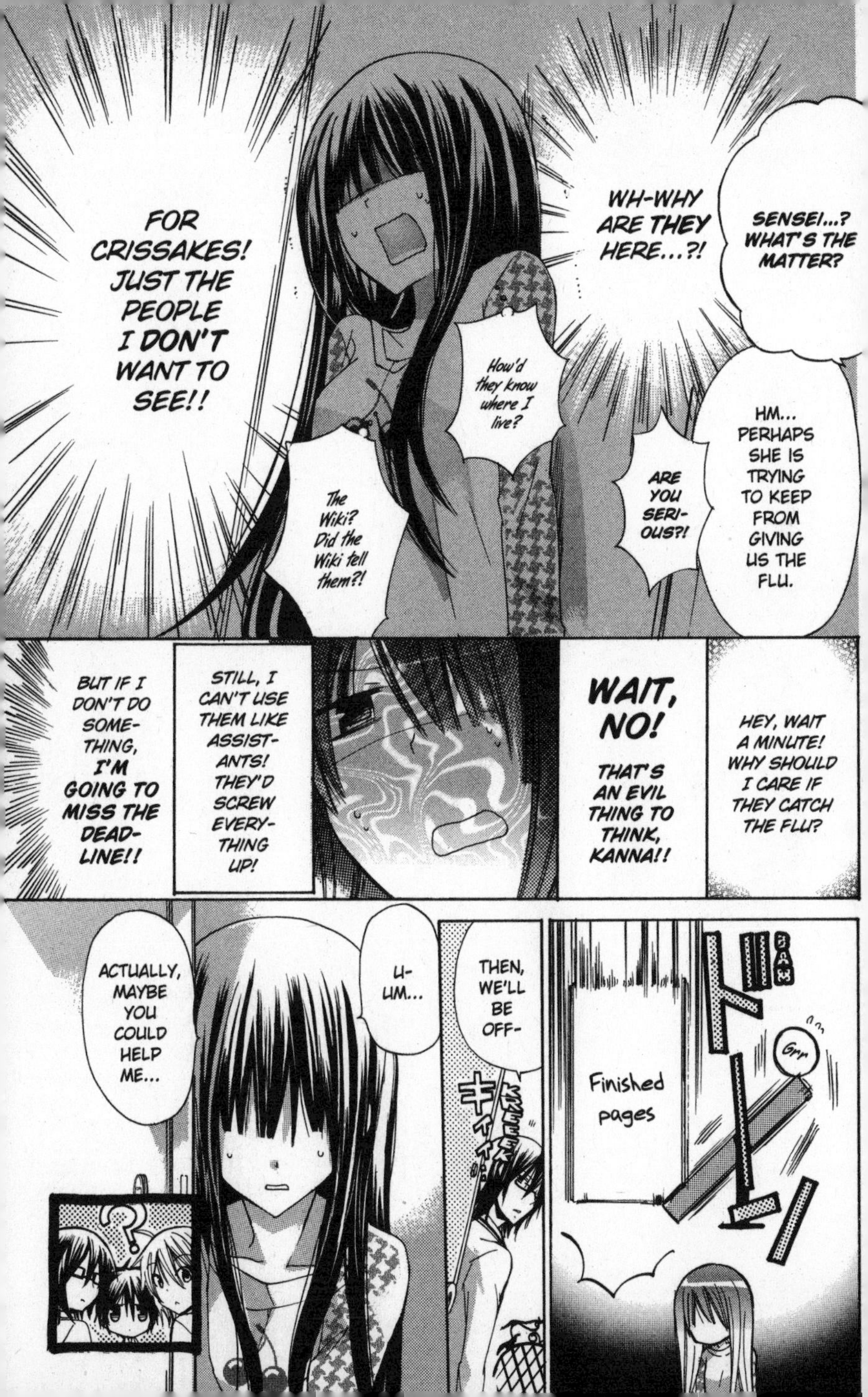
SENSEI...? WHAT'S THE MATTER?
WH-WHY ARE THEY HERE...?!
HM... PERHAPS SHE IS TRYING TO KEEP FROM GIVING US THE FLU.
ARE YOU SERI-OUS?!
How'd they know where I live?
FOR CRISSAKES! JUST THE PEOPLE I DON'T WANT TO SEE!!
The Wiki? Did the Wiki tell them?!
HEY, WAIT A MINUTE! WHY SHOULD I CARE IF THEY CATCH THE FLU?
WAIT, NO!
THAT'S AN EVIL THING TO THINK, KANNA!!
STILL, I CAN'T USE THEM LIKE ASSIST-ANTS! THEY'D SCREW EVERY-THING UP!
BUT IF I DON'T DO SOME-THING, I'M GOING TO MISS THE DEAD-LINE!!
BAM
Grr
Finished pages
THEN, WE'LL BE OFF-
KREEEK
U-UM...
ACTUALLY, MAYBE YOU COULD HELP ME...
?

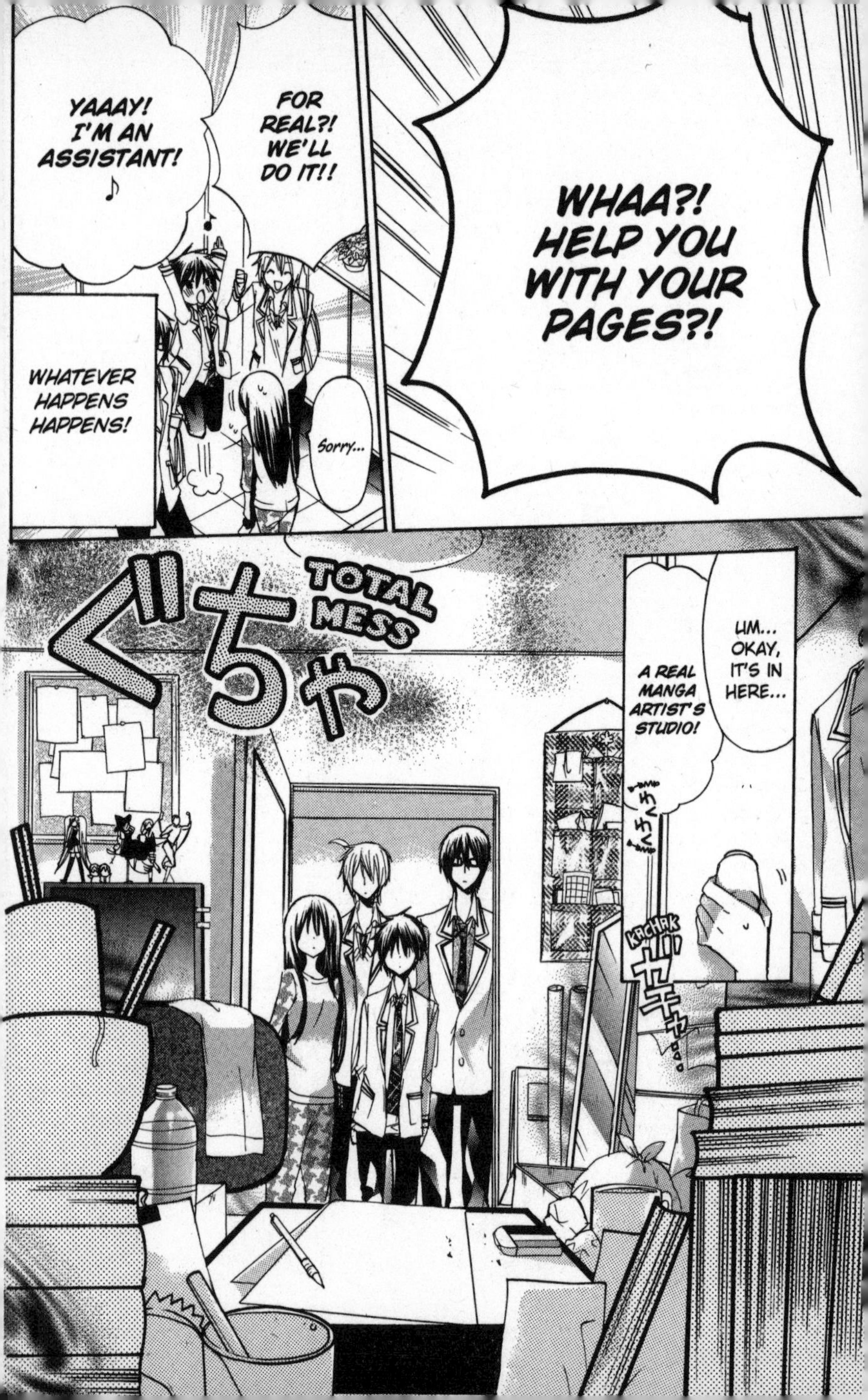
WHAA?! HELP YOU WITH YOUR PAGES?!
FOR REAL?! WE'LL DO IT!!
YAAAY! I'M AN ASSISTANT! ♪
Sorry...
WHATEVER HAPPENS HAPPENS!
UM... OKAY, IT'S IN HERE...
A REAL MANGA ARTIST'S STUDIO!
KACHAK
ぐちゃ
TOTAL MESS

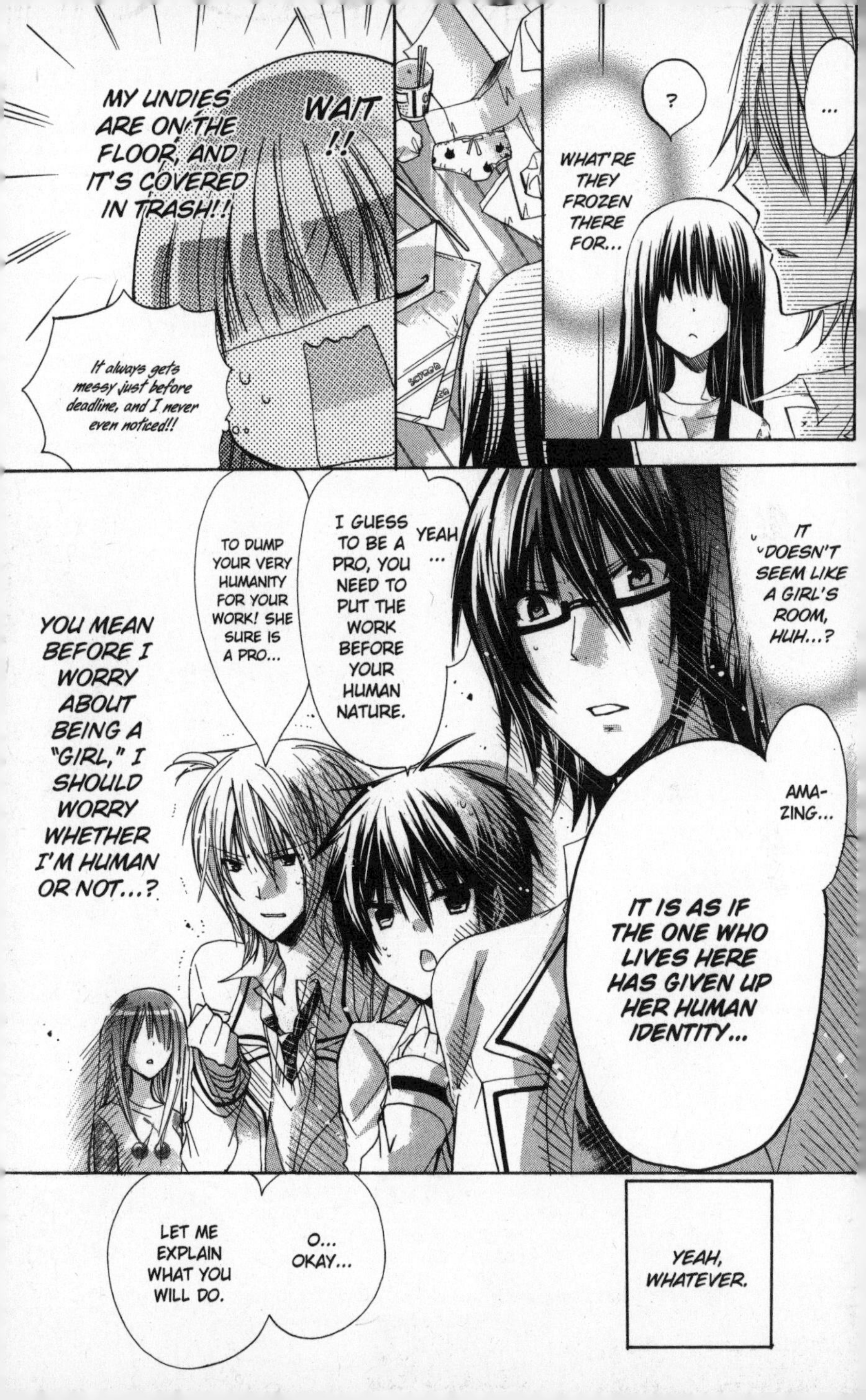
...
?
WHAT'RE THEY FROZEN THERE FOR...
WAIT!!
MY UNDIES ARE ON THE FLOOR, AND IT'S COVERED IN TRASH!!
It always gets messy just before deadline, and I never even noticed!!
IT DOESN'T SEEM LIKE A GIRL'S ROOM, HUH...?
AMA-ZING...
IT IS AS IF THE ONE WHO LIVES HERE HAS GIVEN UP HER HUMAN IDENTITY...
YEAH...
I GUESS TO BE A PRO, YOU NEED TO PUT THE WORK BEFORE YOUR HUMAN NATURE.
TO DUMP YOUR VERY HUMANITY FOR YOUR WORK! SHE SURE IS A PRO...
YOU MEAN BEFORE I WORRY ABOUT BEING A "GIRL," I SHOULD WORRY WHETHER I'M HUMAN OR NOT...?
YEAH, WHATEVER.
O... OKAY...
LET ME EXPLAIN WHAT YOU WILL DO.

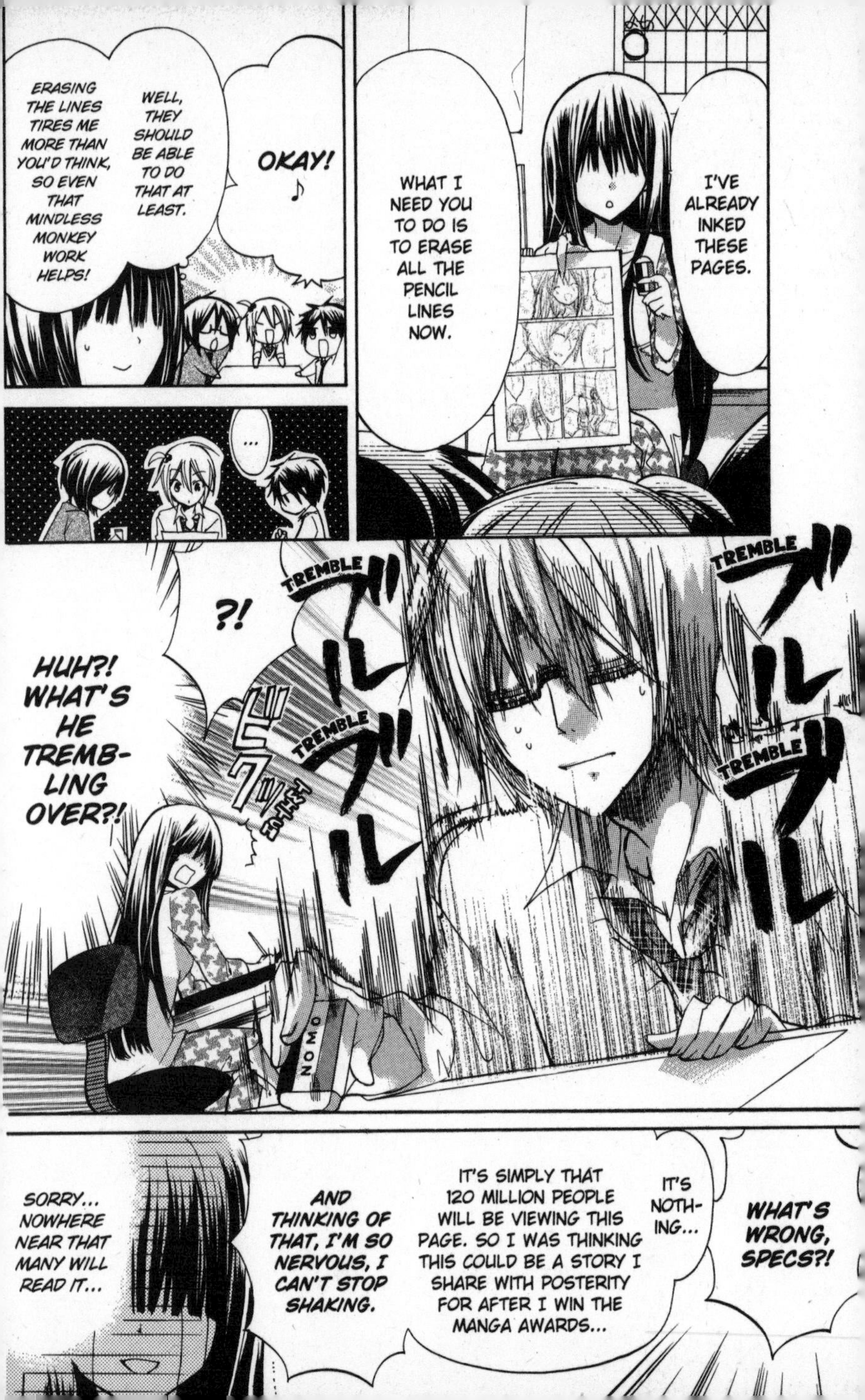
I'VE ALREADY INKED THESE PAGES.
WHAT I NEED YOU TO DO IS TO ERASE ALL THE PENCIL LINES NOW.
OKAY! ♪
WELL, THEY SHOULD BE ABLE TO DO THAT AT LEAST.
ERASING THE LINES TIRES ME MORE THAN YOU'D THINK, SO EVEN THAT MINDLESS MONKEY WORK HELPS!
...
TREMBLE
TREMBLE
TREMBLE
TREMBLE
?!
TWITCH
HUH?! WHAT'S HE TREMB-LING OVER?!
WHAT'S WRONG, SPECS?!
IT'S NOTHING...
IT'S SIMPLY THAT 120 MILLION PEOPLE WILL BE VIEWING THIS PAGE. SO I WAS THINKING THIS COULD BE A STORY I SHARE WITH POSTERITY FOR AFTER I WIN THE MANGA AWARDS...
AND THINKING OF THAT, I'M SO NERVOUS, I CAN'T STOP SHAKING.
SORRY... NOWHERE NEAR THAT MANY WILL READ IT...

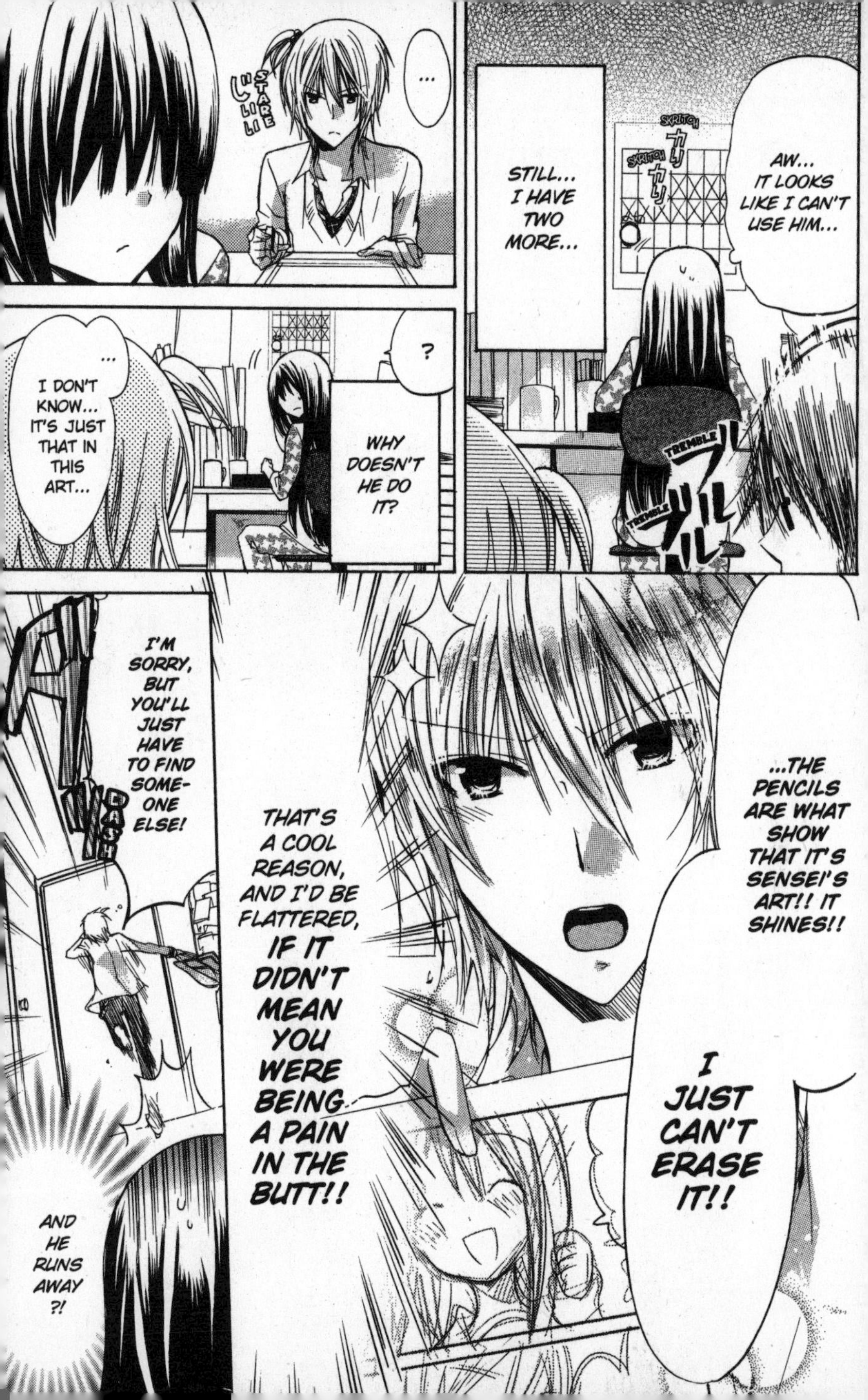
AW... IT LOOKS LIKE I CAN'T USE HIM...
SKRITCH
SKRITCH
STILL... I HAVE TWO MORE...
TREMBLE
TREMBLE
STARE
...
?
WHY DOESN'T HE DO IT?
... I DON'T KNOW... IT'S JUST THAT IN THIS ART...
...THE PENCILS ARE WHAT SHOW THAT IT'S SENSEI'S ART!! IT SHINES!!
I JUST CAN'T ERASE IT!!
THAT'S A COOL REASON, AND I'D BE FLATTERED, IF IT DIDN'T MEAN YOU WERE BEING A PAIN IN THE BUTT!!
I'M SORRY, BUT YOU'LL JUST HAVE TO FIND SOME-ONE ELSE!
DASH
AND HE RUNS AWAY?!

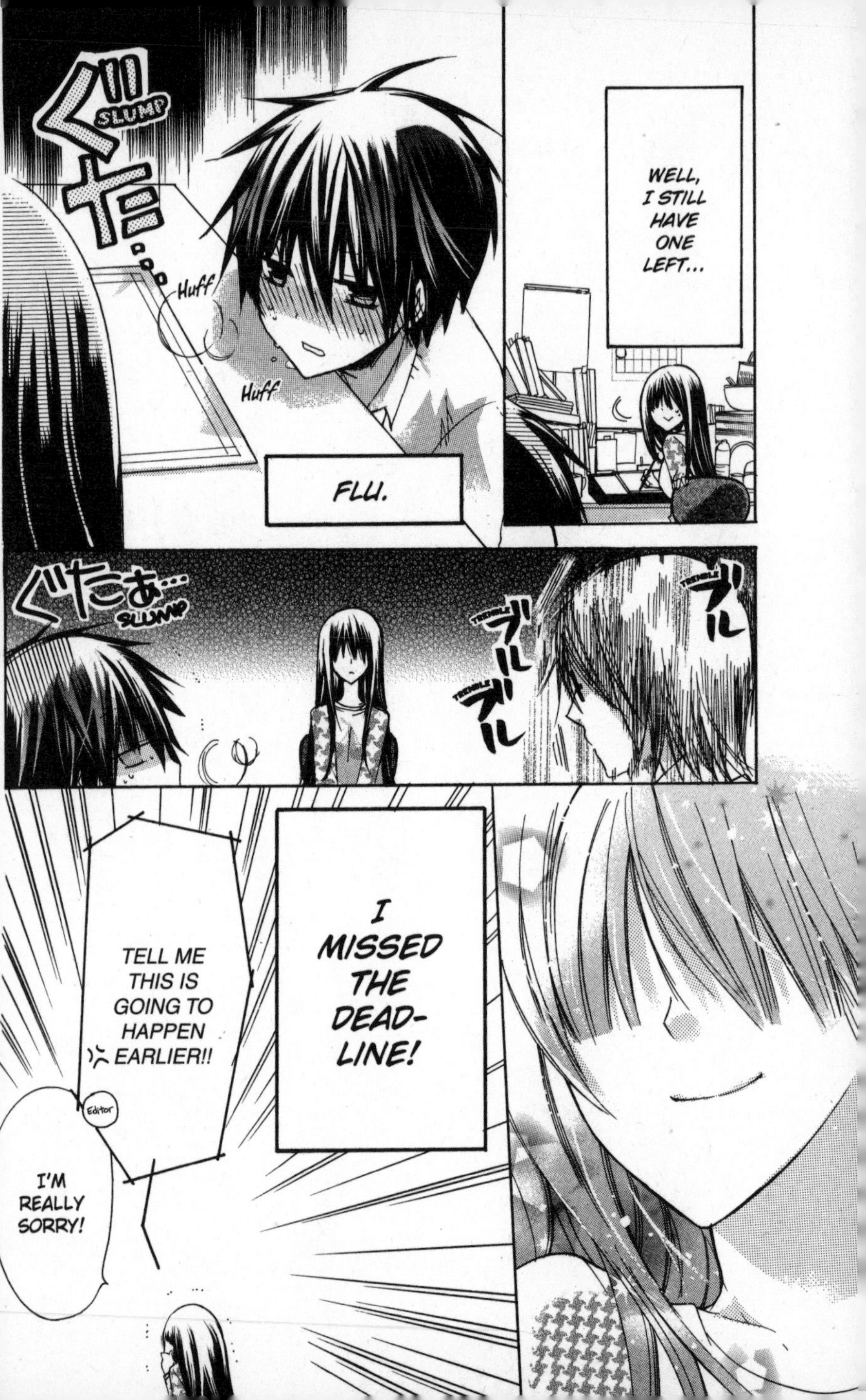
WELL, I STILL HAVE ONE LEFT...
SLUMP
Huff
Huff
FLU.
TREMBLE
ブル
TREMBLE
ブル
TREMBLE
ブル
ぐたぁ…
SLUMP
I MISSED THE DEAD-LINE!
TELL ME THIS IS GOING TO HAPPEN EARLIER!!
Editor
I'M REALLY SORRY!

You know,
I think the
pencil lines
actually do
look better...

Naw...
It's just my
imagination.

MANGA DOGS

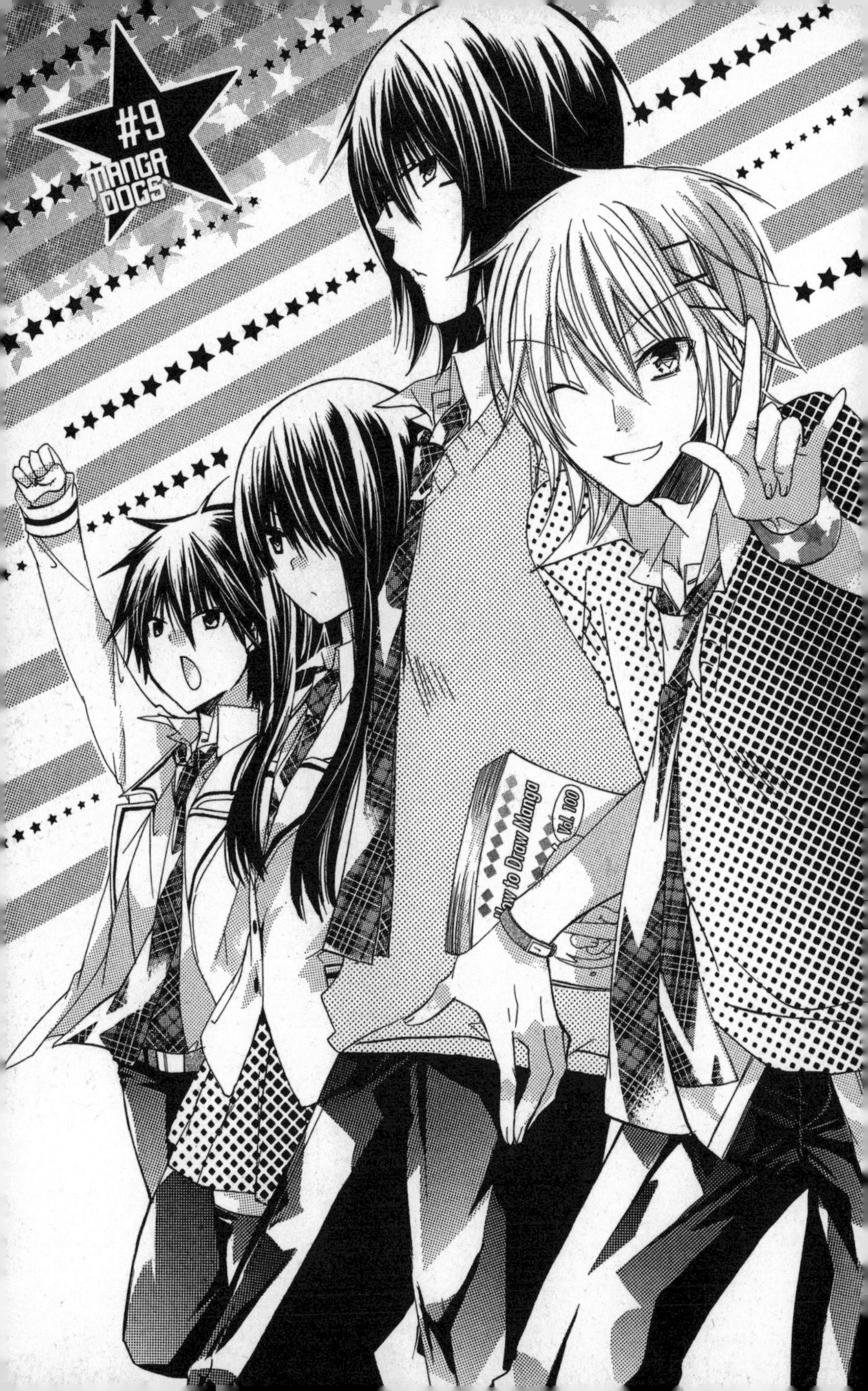
#9
MANGA DOGS
How to Draw Manga
Vol. 100

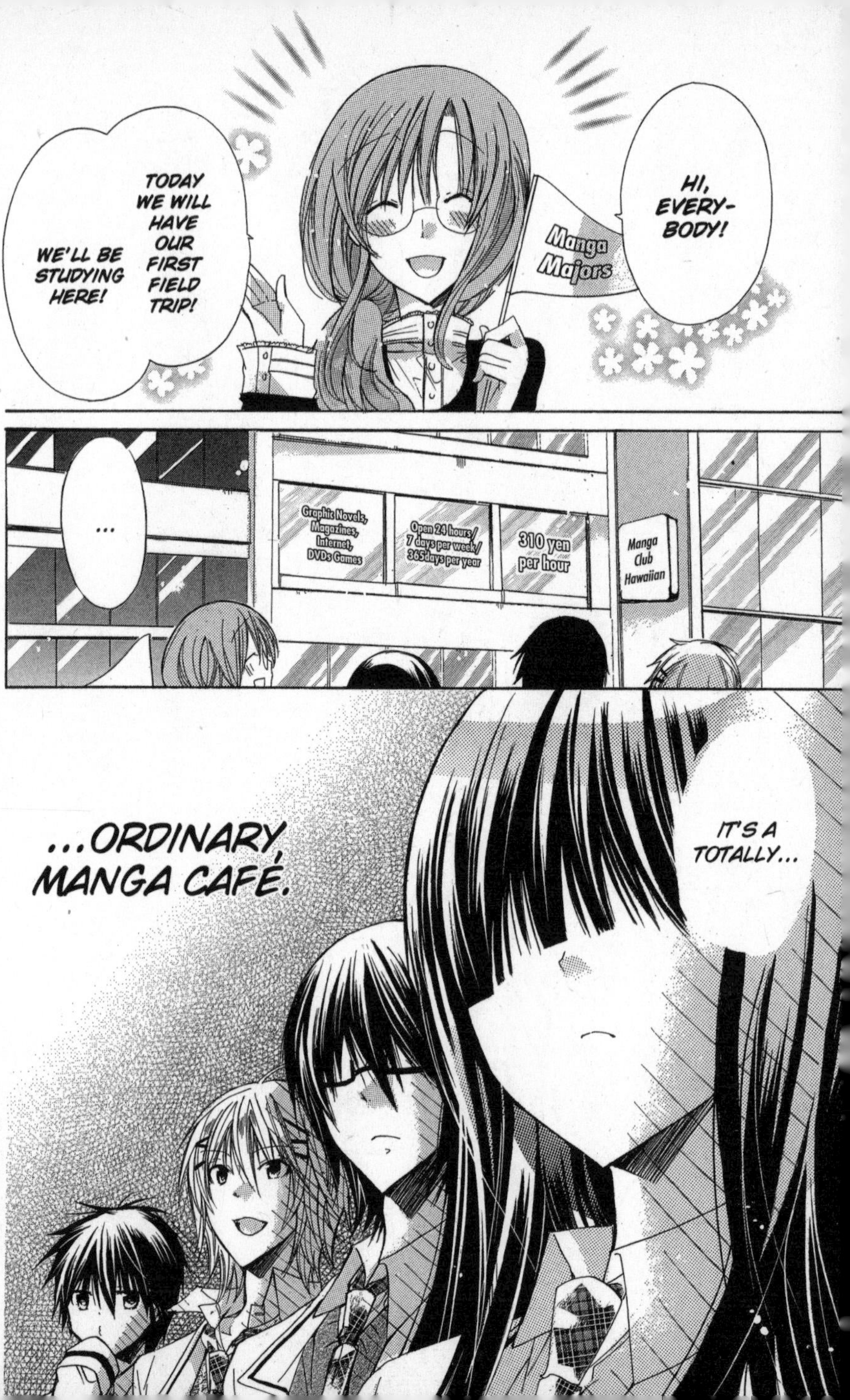
HI, EVERY-BODY!
Manga Majors
TODAY WE WILL HAVE OUR FIRST FIELD TRIP!
WE'LL BE STUDYING HERE!
Manga Club Hawaiian
310 yen per hour
Open 24 hours/ 7 days per week/ 365days per year
Graphic Novels, Magazines, Internet, DVDs Games
...
IT'S A TOTALLY...
...ORDINARY, MANGA CAFÉ.

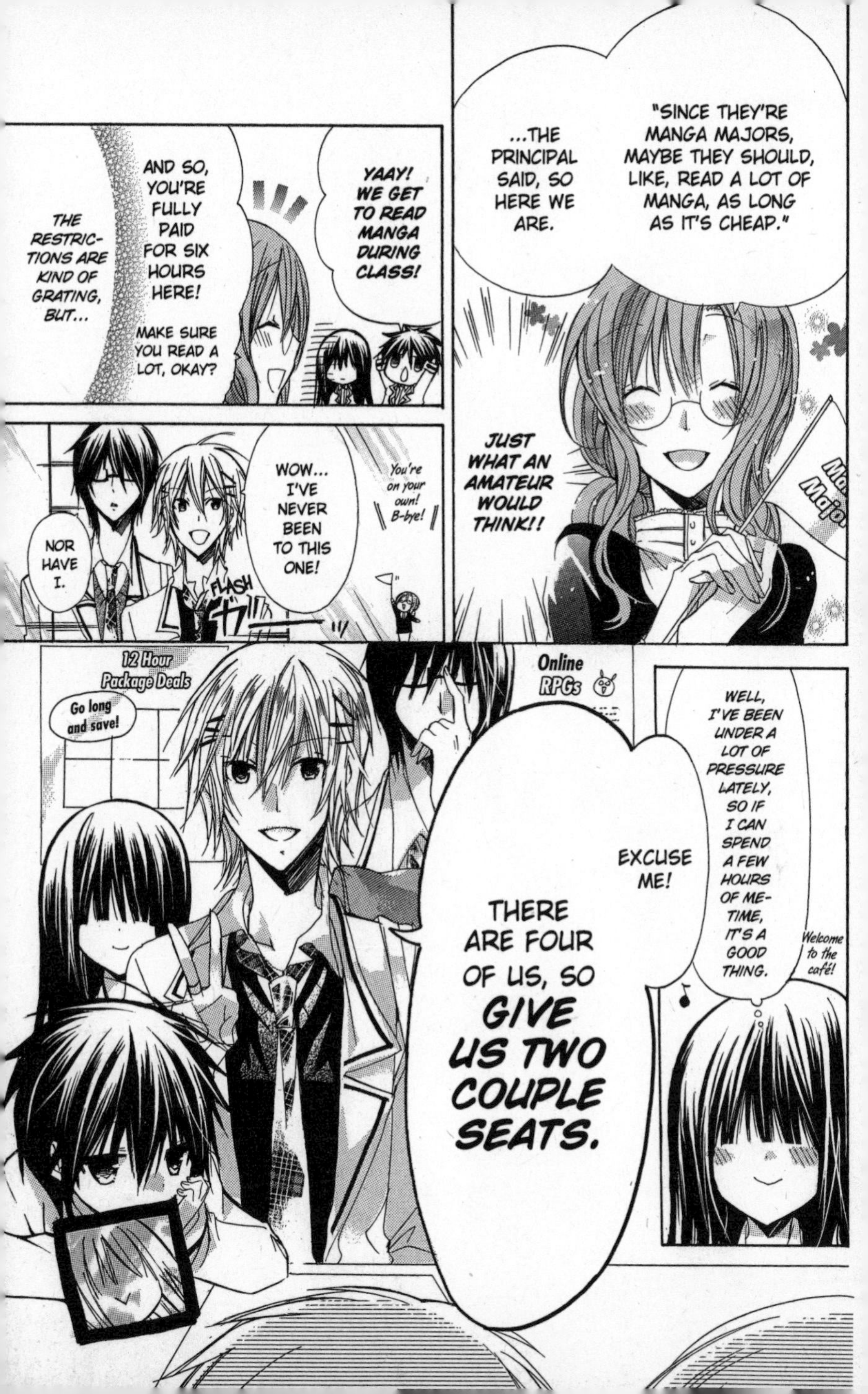
"SINCE THEY'RE MANGA MAJORS, MAYBE THEY SHOULD, LIKE, READ A LOT OF MANGA, AS LONG AS IT'S CHEAP."
...THE PRINCIPAL SAID, SO HERE WE ARE.
JUST WHAT AN AMATEUR WOULD THINK!!
YAAY! WE GET TO READ MANGA DURING CLASS!
AND SO, YOU'RE FULLY PAID FOR SIX HOURS HERE!
MAKE SURE YOU READ A LOT, OKAY?
THE RESTRICTIONS ARE KIND OF GRATING, BUT...
You're on your own! B-bye!
WOW... I'VE NEVER BEEN TO THIS ONE!
FLASH
NOR HAVE I.
Welcome to the café!
WELL, I'VE BEEN UNDER A LOT OF PRESSURE LATELY, SO IF I CAN SPEND A FEW HOURS OF ME-TIME, IT'S A GOOD THING.
EXCUSE ME!
THERE ARE FOUR OF US, SO GIVE US TWO COUPLE SEATS.
Online RPGs
12 Hour Package Deals
Go long and save!

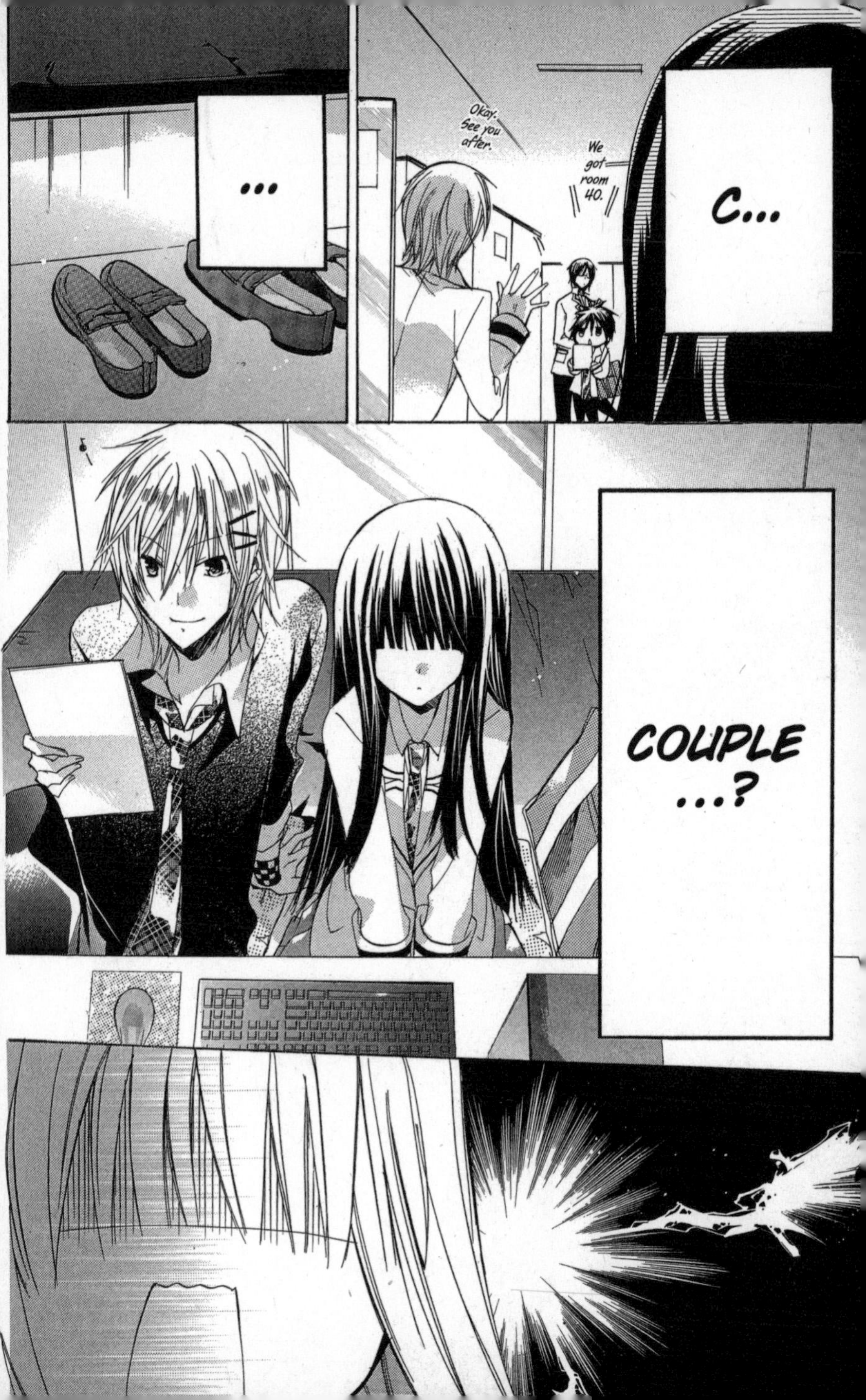
C...
We got room 40.
Okay. See you after.
...
COUPLE ...?

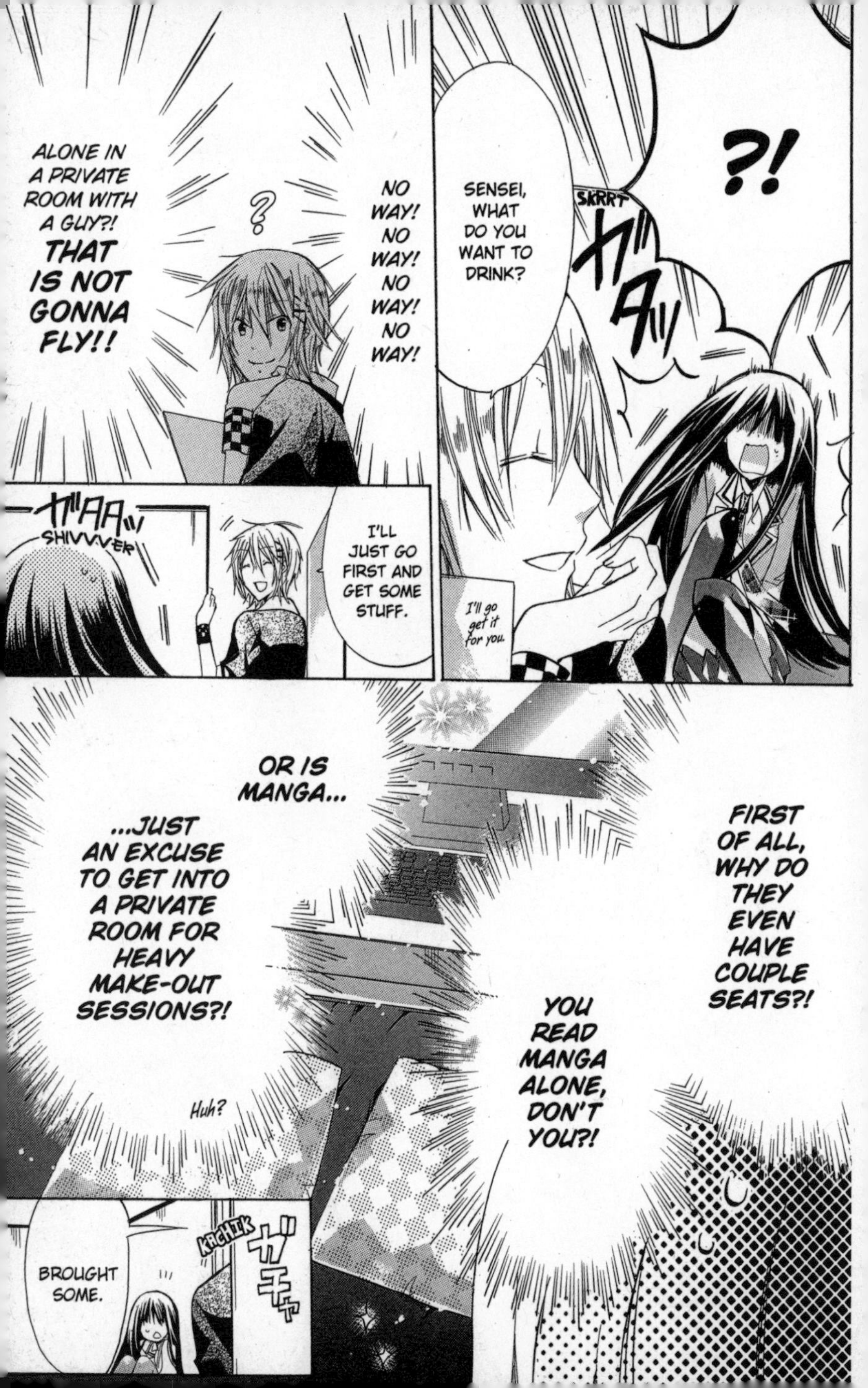
?!
SENSEI, WHAT DO YOU WANT TO DRINK?
SKRRT
I'll go get it for you.
NO WAY! NO WAY! NO WAY! NO WAY!
?
ALONE IN A PRIVATE ROOM WITH A GUY?! THAT IS NOT GONNA FLY!!
I'LL JUST GO FIRST AND GET SOME STUFF.
SHIVVVVER
FIRST OF ALL, WHY DO THEY EVEN HAVE COUPLE SEATS?!
YOU READ MANGA ALONE, DON'T YOU?!
OR IS MANGA...
...JUST AN EXCUSE TO GET INTO A PRIVATE ROOM FOR HEAVY MAKE-OUT SESSIONS?!
Huh?
KACHIK
BROUGHT SOME.

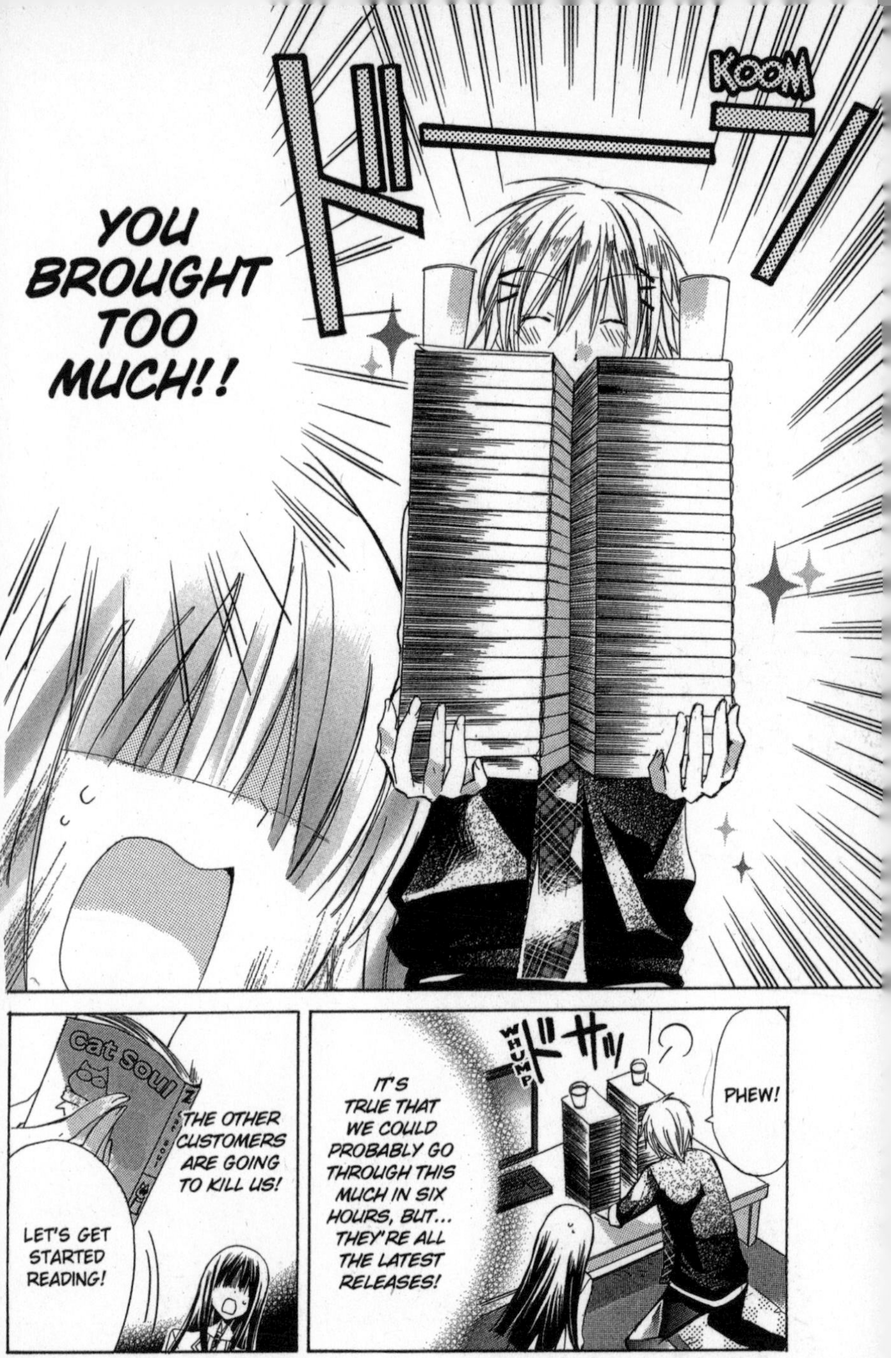
KOOM
YOU BROUGHT TOO MUCH!!
PHEW!
WHUMP
IT'S TRUE THAT WE COULD PROBABLY GO THROUGH THIS MUCH IN SIX HOURS, BUT... THEY'RE ALL THE LATEST RELEASES!
THE OTHER CUSTOMERS ARE GOING TO KILL US!
Cat Soul
LET'S GET STARTED READING!

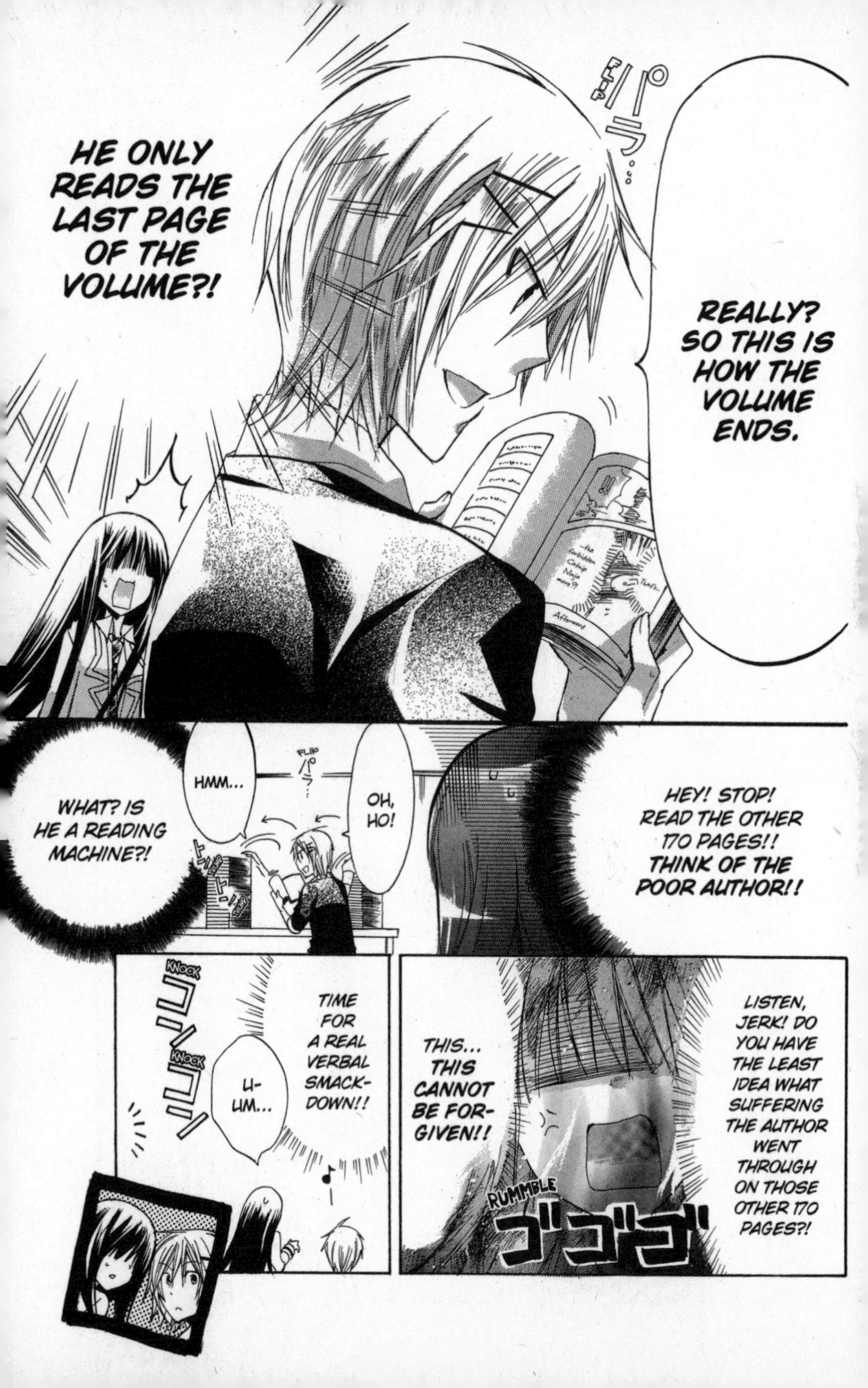
FLIP
パラ…
REALLY? SO THIS IS HOW THE VOLUME ENDS.
HE ONLY READS THE LAST PAGE OF THE VOLUME?!
Afterword
HEY! STOP! READ THE OTHER 170 PAGES!! THINK OF THE POOR AUTHOR!!
OH, HO!
FLIP
パラ…
HMM...
THUMP
THUMP
WHAT? IS HE A READING MACHINE?!
LISTEN, JERK! DO YOU HAVE THE LEAST IDEA WHAT SUFFERING THE AUTHOR WENT THROUGH ON THOSE OTHER 170 PAGES?!
THIS... THIS CANNOT BE FORGIVEN!!
RUMMBLE
ゴゴゴ
TIME FOR A REAL VERBAL SMACK-DOWN!!
U-UM...
KNOCK
コン
KNOCK
コン

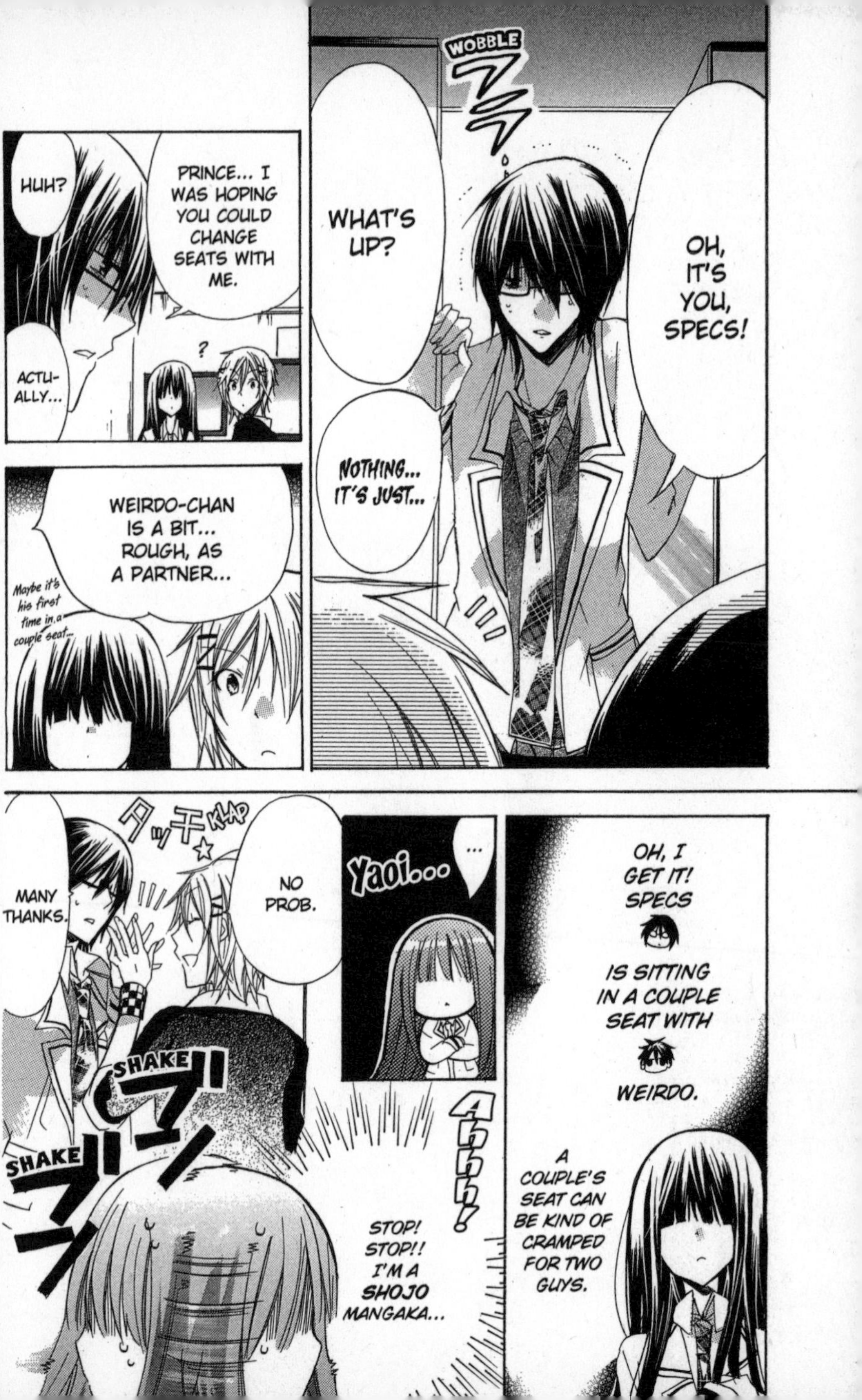
WOBBLE
OH, IT'S YOU, SPECS!
WHAT'S UP?
NOTHING... IT'S JUST...
PRINCE... I WAS HOPING YOU COULD CHANGE SEATS WITH ME.
HUH?
?
ACTUALLY...
WEIRDO-CHAN IS A BIT... ROUGH, AS A PARTNER...
Maybe it's his first time in a couple seat...
OH, I GET IT! SPECS IS SITTING IN A COUPLE SEAT WITH WEIRDO.
A COUPLE'S SEAT CAN BE KIND OF CRAMPED FOR TWO GUYS.
...
Yaoi...
KLAP
NO PROB.
MANY THANKS.
Ahhh!
STOP! STOP!! I'M A SHOJO MANGAKA...
SHAKE
SHAKE

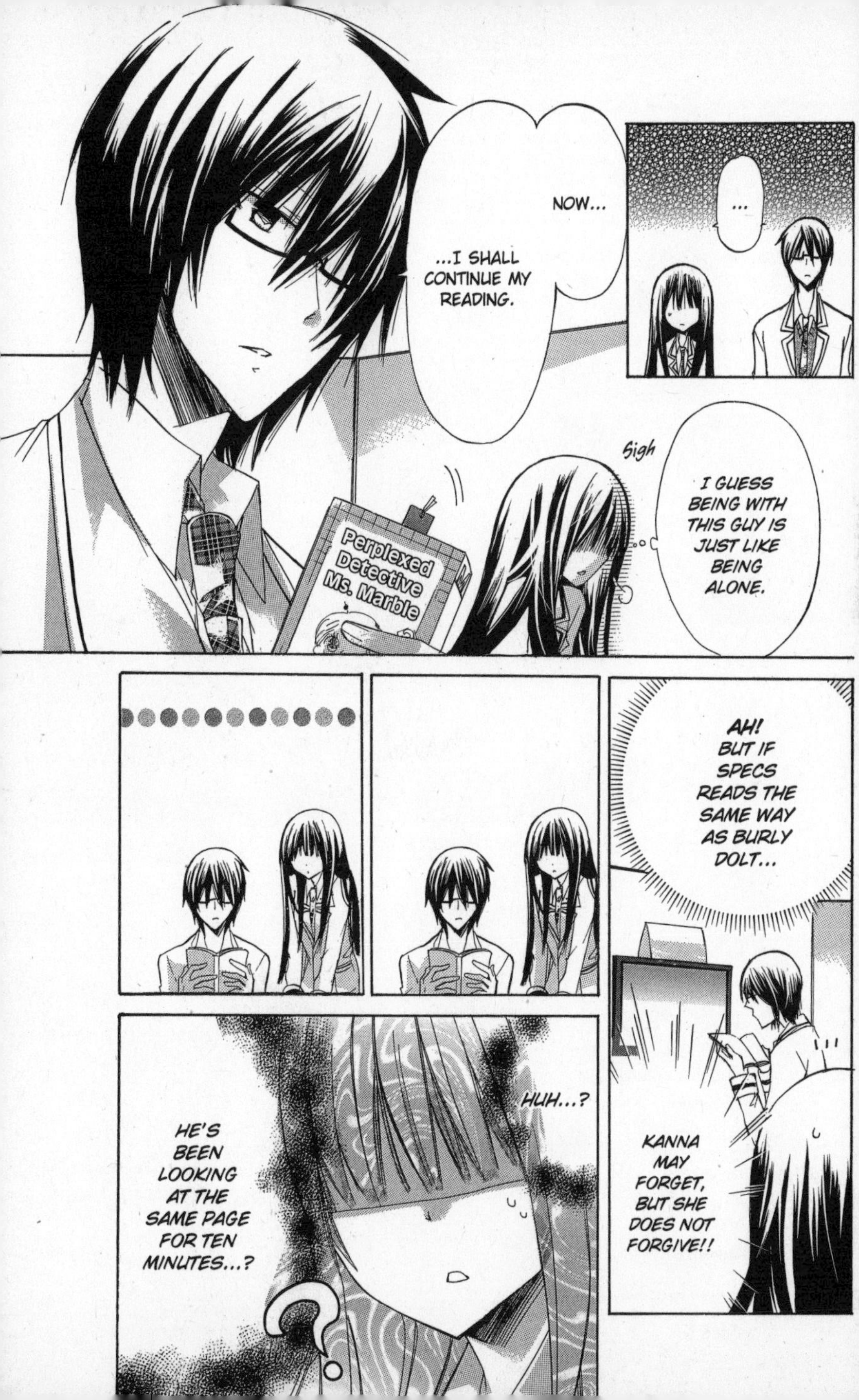
...
NOW...
...I SHALL CONTINUE MY READING.
Perplexed Detective Ms. Marble
Sigh
I GUESS BEING WITH THIS GUY IS JUST LIKE BEING ALONE.
AH! BUT IF SPECS READS THE SAME WAY AS BURLY DOLT...
KANNA MAY FORGET, BUT SHE DOES NOT FORGIVE!!
HUH...?
HE'S BEEN LOOKING AT THE SAME PAGE FOR TEN MINUTES...?

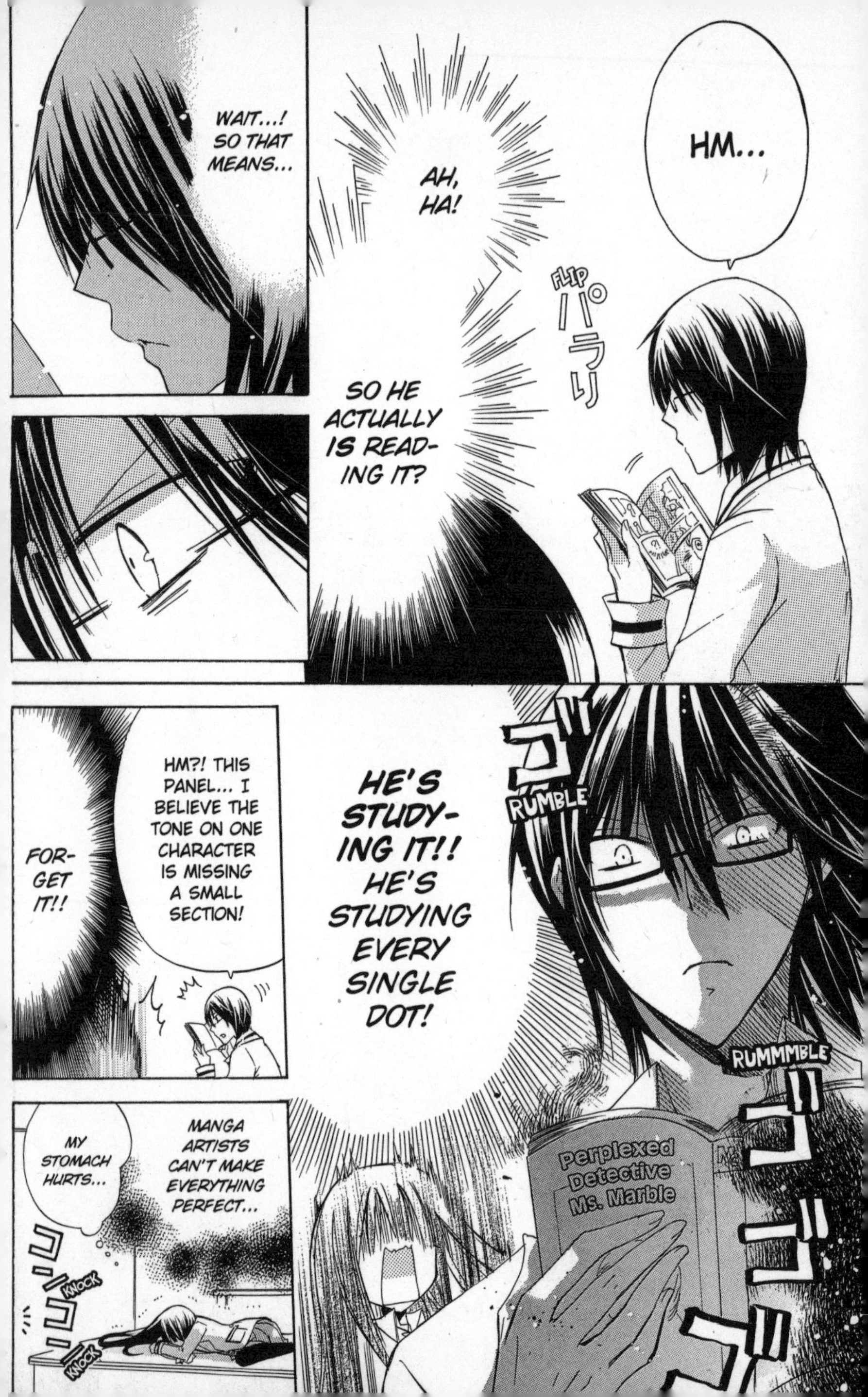
HM...
FLIP
パラリ
AH, HA!
SO HE ACTUALLY IS READING IT?
WAIT...! SO THAT MEANS...
RUMBLE
HE'S STUDYING IT!! HE'S STUDYING EVERY SINGLE DOT!
RUMMMBLE
Perplexed Detective Ms. Marble
HM?! THIS PANEL... I BELIEVE THE TONE ON ONE CHARACTER IS MISSING A SMALL SECTION!
FOR-GET IT!!
MANGA ARTISTS CAN'T MAKE EVERYTHING PERFECT...
MY STOMACH HURTS...
KNOCK
KNOCK

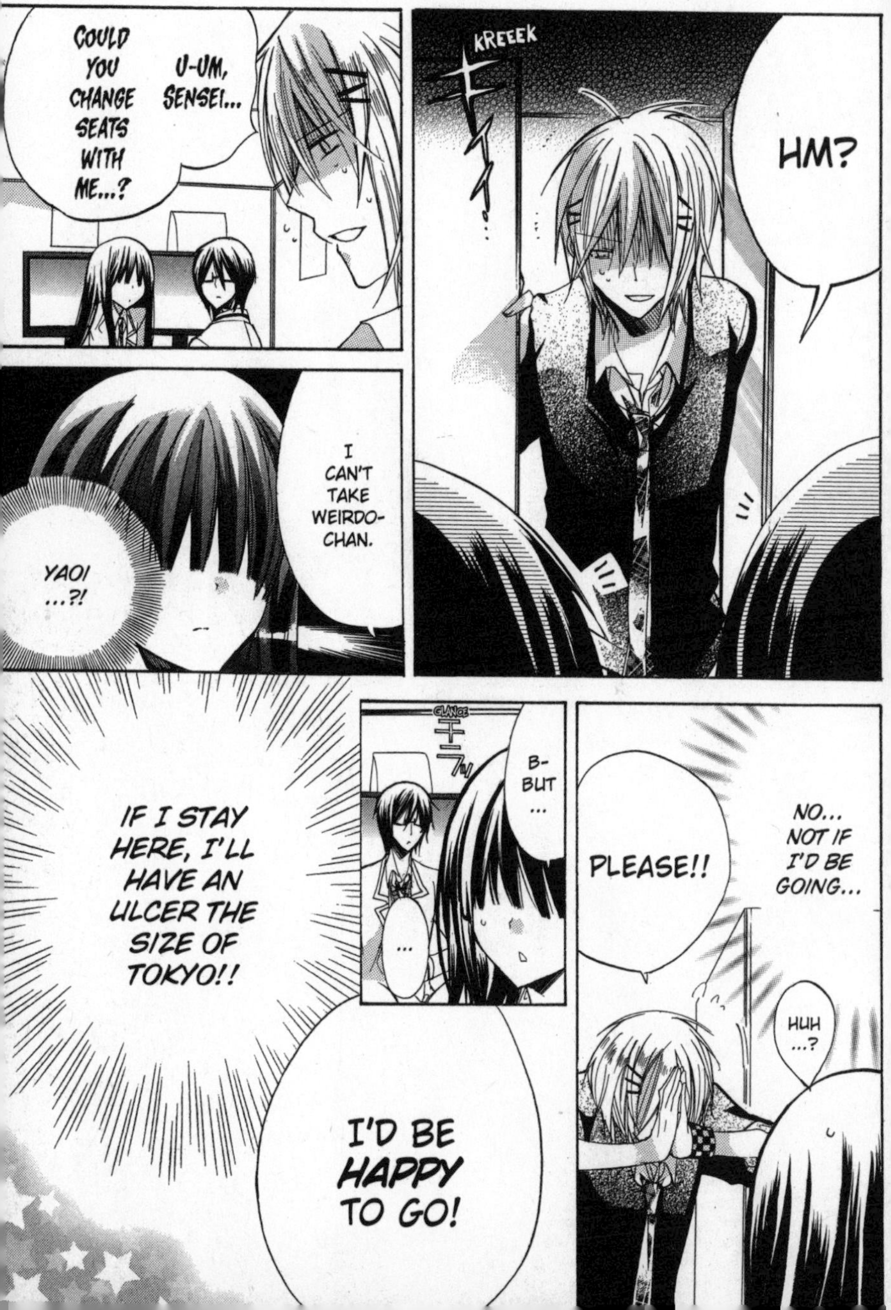
KREEEK
HM?
U-UM, SENSEI...
COULD YOU CHANGE SEATS WITH ME...?
I CAN'T TAKE WEIRDO-CHAN.
YAOI ...?!
NO... NOT IF I'D BE GOING...
PLEASE!!
HUH ...?
GLANCE
B-BUT ...
...
I'D BE HAPPY TO GO!
IF I STAY HERE, I'LL HAVE AN ULCER THE SIZE OF TOKYO!!

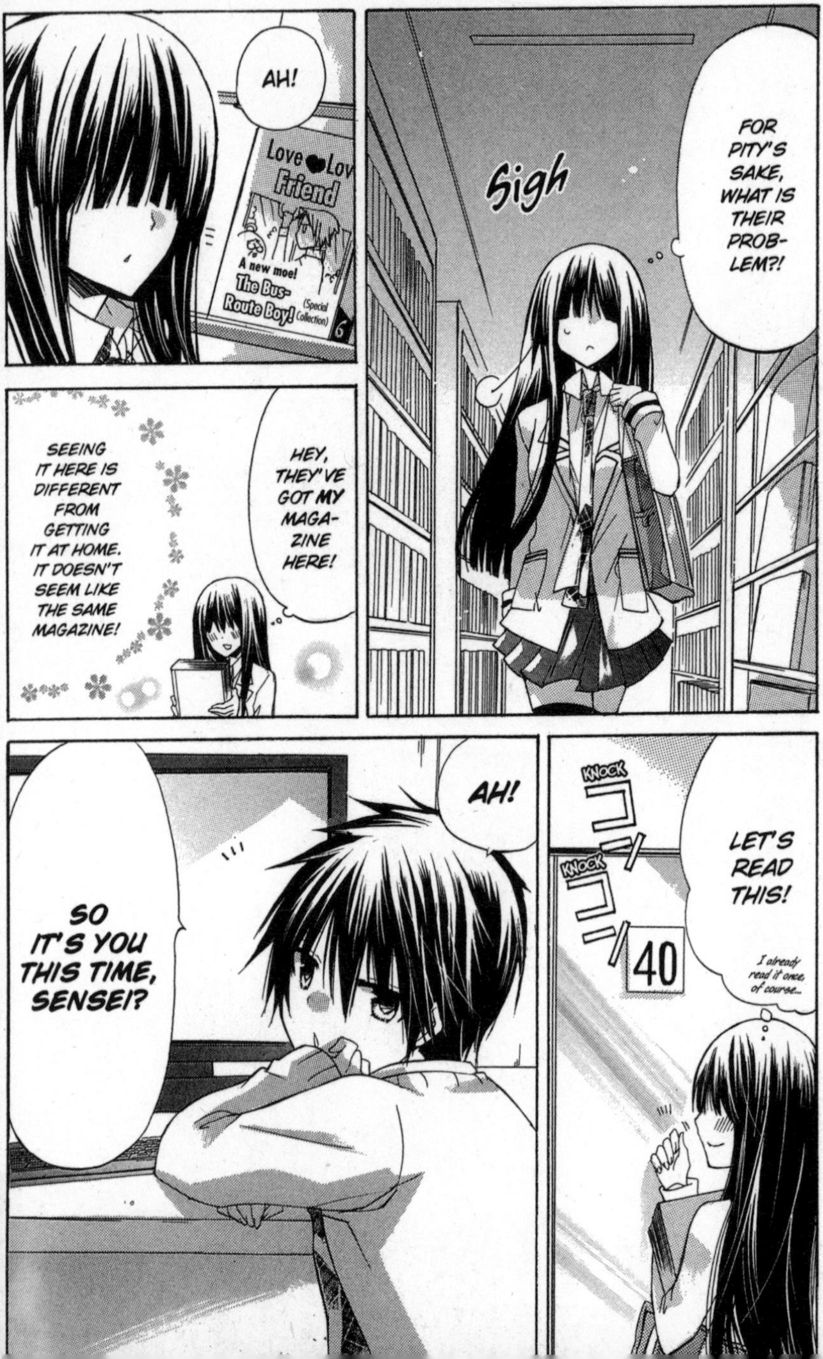
Sigh
FOR PITY'S SAKE, WHAT IS THEIR PROB-LEM?!
AH!
Love Lov
Friend
A new moe!
The Bus-Route Boy!
(Special Collection)
6
HEY, THEY'VE GOT MY MAGA-ZINE HERE!
SEEING IT HERE IS DIFFERENT FROM GETTING IT AT HOME. IT DOESN'T SEEM LIKE THE SAME MAGAZINE!
KNOCK
KNOCK
LET'S READ THIS!
40
I already read it once, of course...
AH!
SO IT'S YOU THIS TIME, SENSEI?

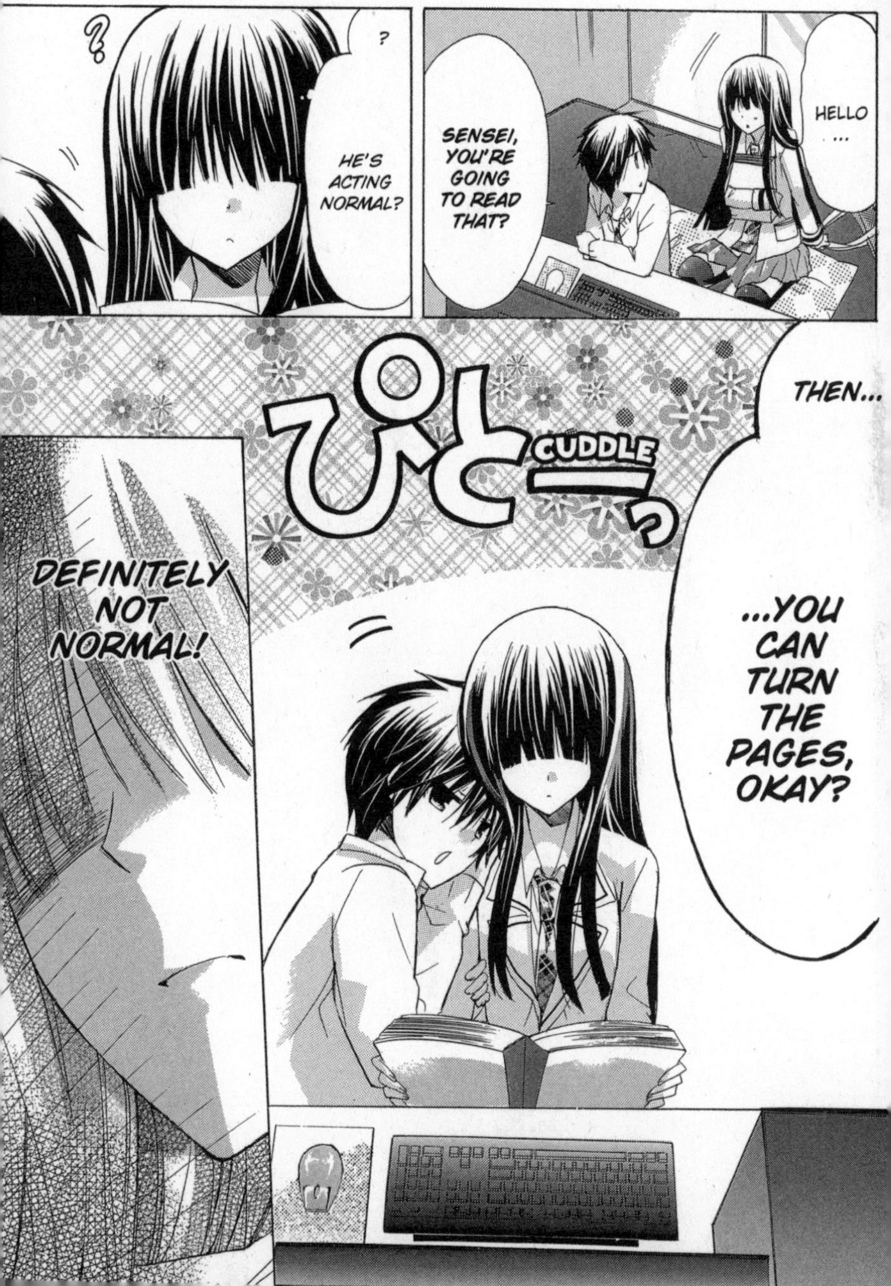
HELLO ...
SENSEI, YOU'RE GOING TO READ THAT?
?
HE'S ACTING NORMAL?
THEN...
ぴとーっ
CUDDLE
...YOU CAN TURN THE PAGES, OKAY?
DEFINITELY NOT NORMAL!

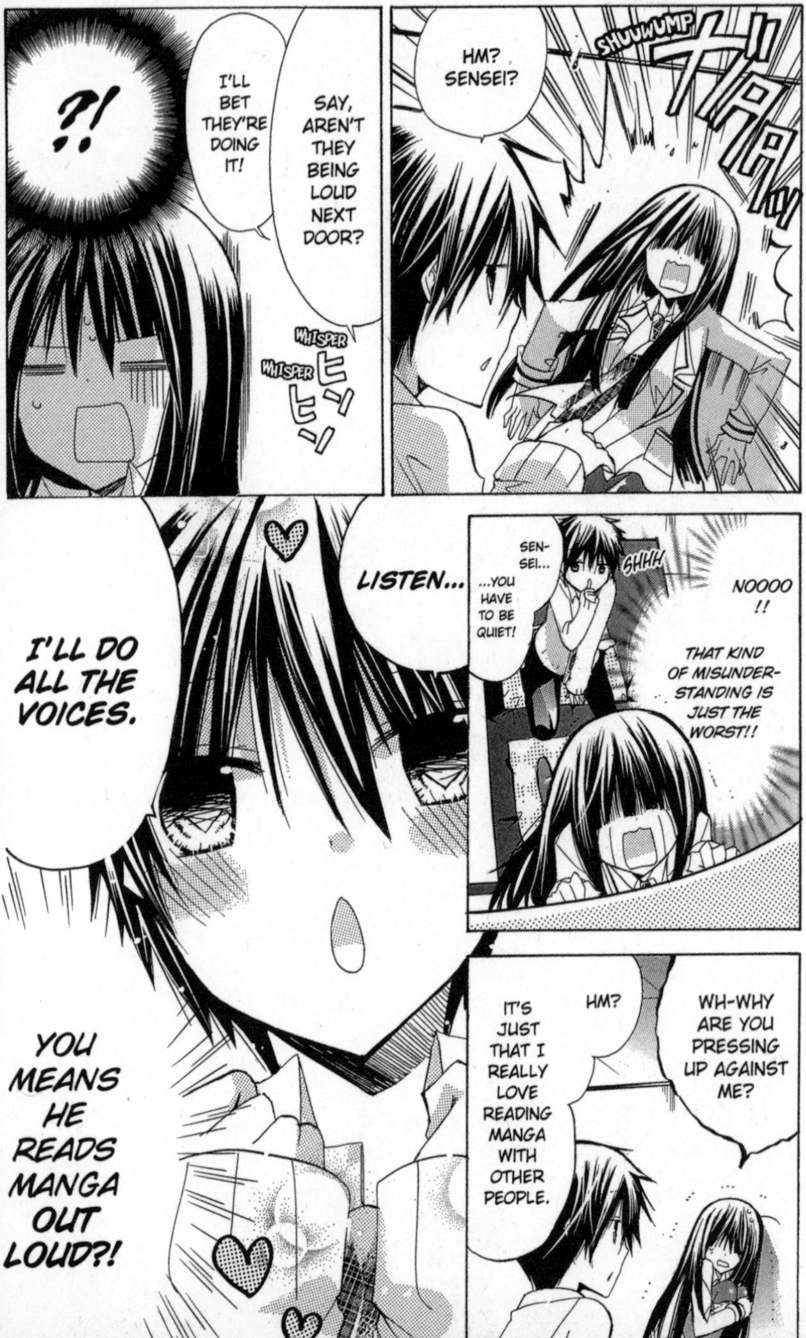
SHUUWUMP
HM? SENSEI?
SAY, AREN'T THEY BEING LOUD NEXT DOOR?
I'LL BET THEY'RE DOING IT!
WHISPER
WHISPER
?!
SEN-SEI...
...YOU HAVE TO BE QUIET!
SHHH
NOOOO!!
THAT KIND OF MISUNDER-STANDING IS JUST THE WORST!!
WH-WHY ARE YOU PRESSING UP AGAINST ME?
HM?
IT'S JUST THAT I REALLY LOVE READING MANGA WITH OTHER PEOPLE.
LISTEN...
I'LL DO ALL THE VOICES.
YOU MEANS HE READS MANGA OUT LOUD?!

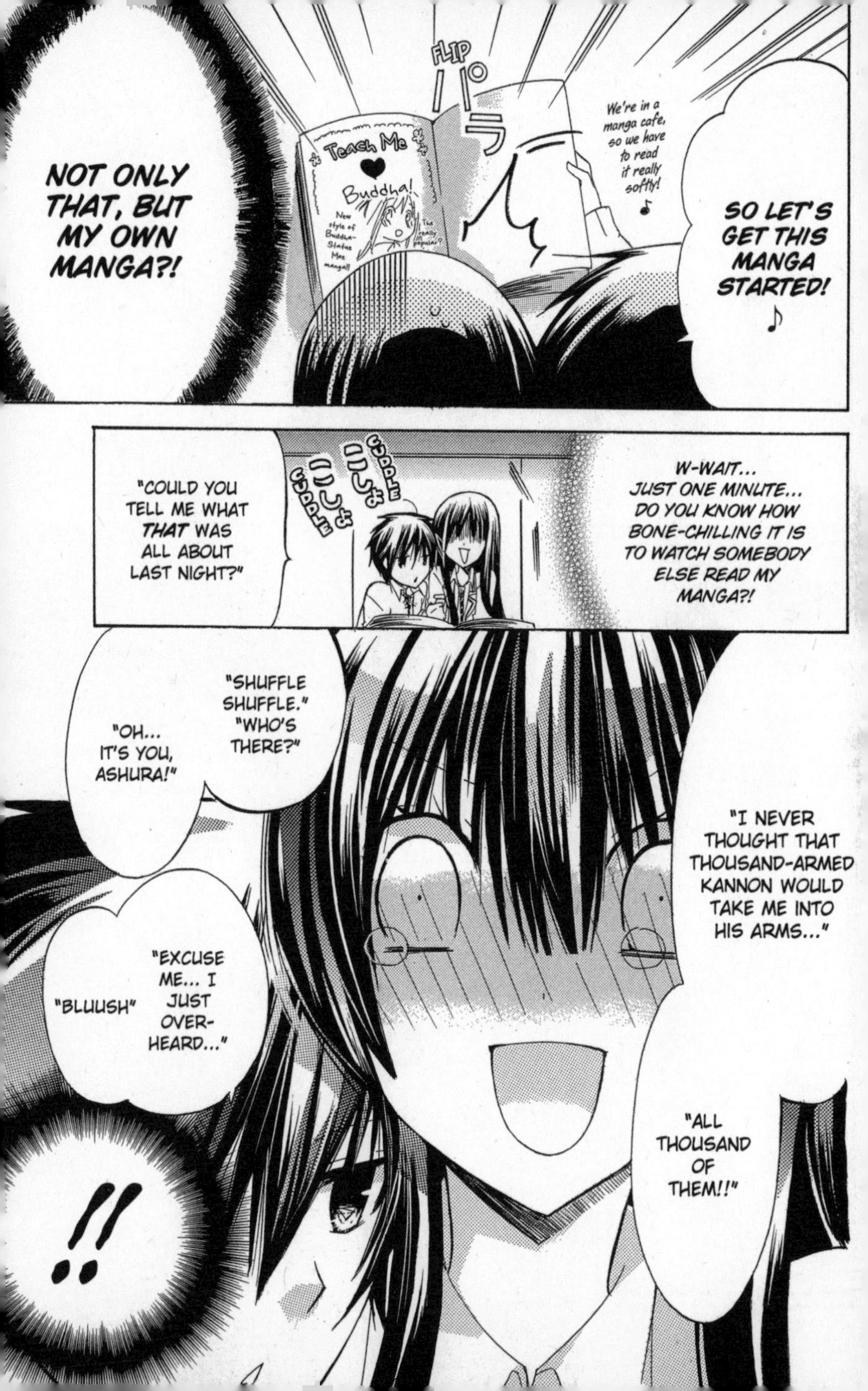
SO LET'S GET THIS MANGA STARTED! ♪
We're in a manga cafe, so we have to read it really softly! ♪
FLIP
パラ
Teach Me ♥ Buddha!
New style of Buddha-Statue Moe manga!!
The really popular?
NOT ONLY THAT, BUT MY OWN MANGA?!
W-WAIT... JUST ONE MINUTE... DO YOU KNOW HOW BONE-CHILLING IT IS TO WATCH SOMEBODY ELSE READ MY MANGA?!
CUDDLE
CUDDLE
"COULD YOU TELL ME WHAT *THAT* WAS ALL ABOUT LAST NIGHT?"
"I NEVER THOUGHT THAT THOUSAND-ARMED KANNON WOULD TAKE ME INTO HIS ARMS..."
"ALL THOUSAND OF THEM!!"
"SHUFFLE SHUFFLE." "WHO'S THERE?"
"OH... IT'S YOU, ASHURA!"
"EXCUSE ME... I JUST OVER-HEARD..."
"BLUUSH"
!!

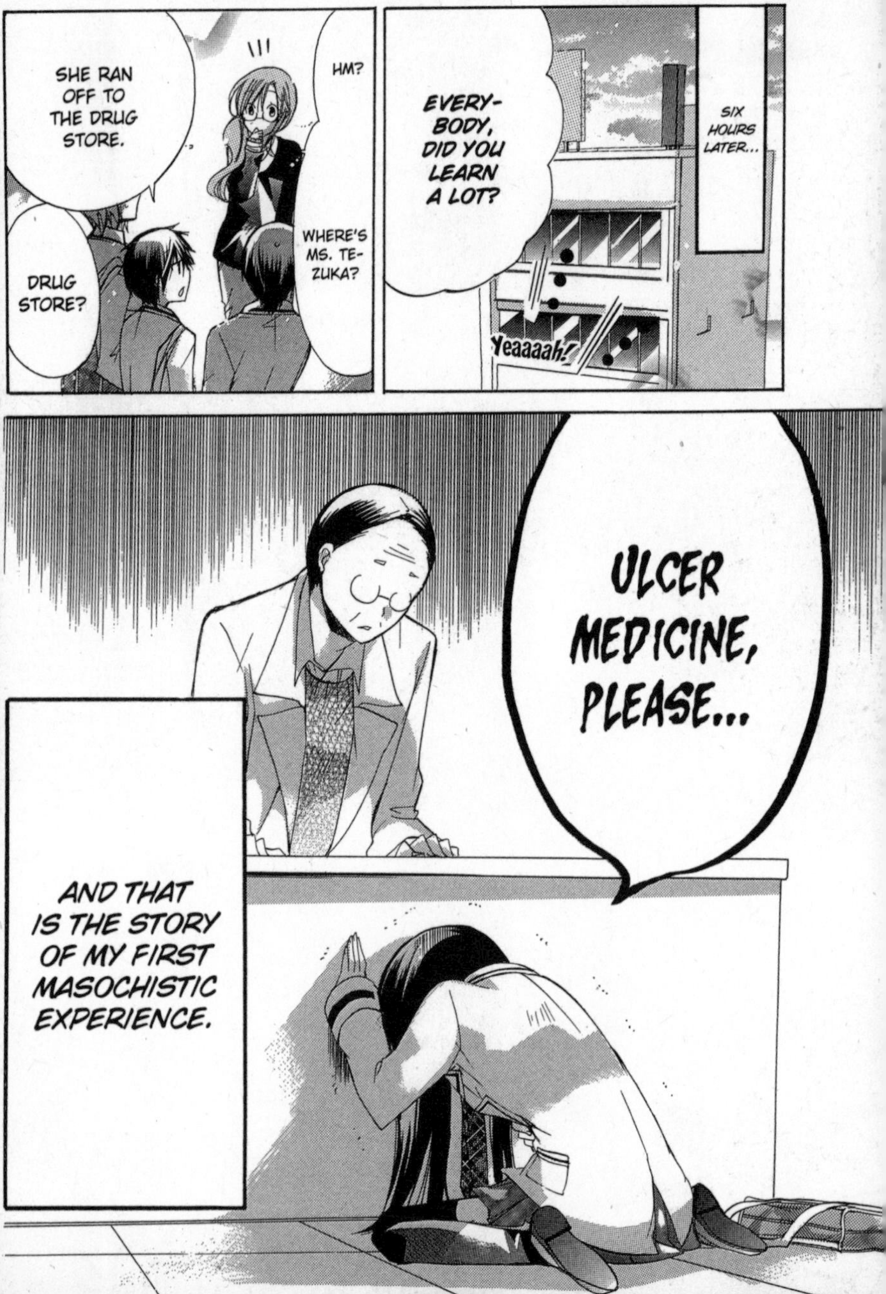
SIX HOURS LATER...
EVERY-BODY, DID YOU LEARN A LOT?
Yeaaaah!
HM?
WHERE'S MS. TE-ZUKA?
SHE RAN OFF TO THE DRUG STORE.
DRUG STORE?
ULCER MEDICINE, PLEASE...
AND THAT IS THE STORY OF MY FIRST MASOCHISTIC EXPERIENCE.

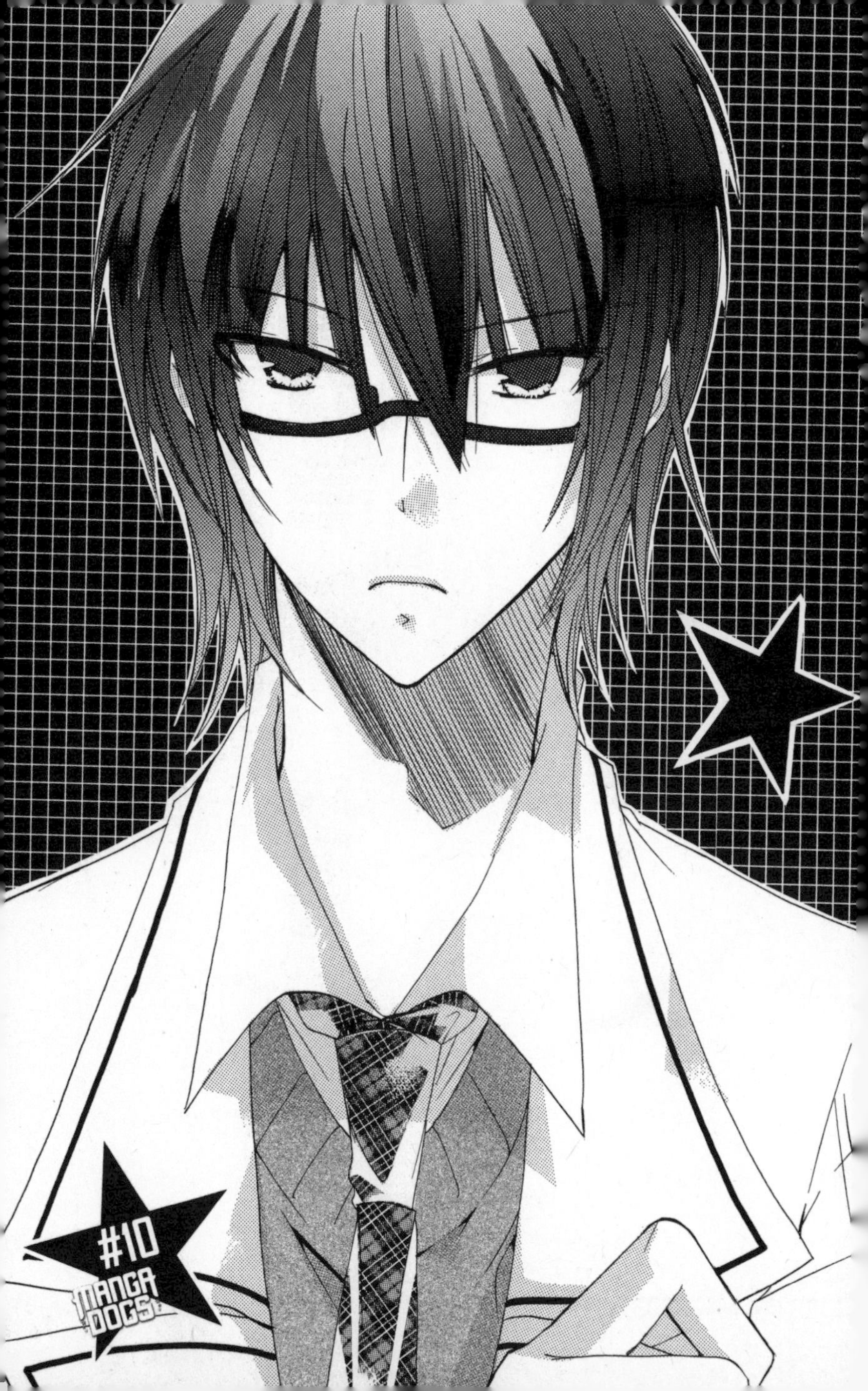
#10
MANGA DOGS

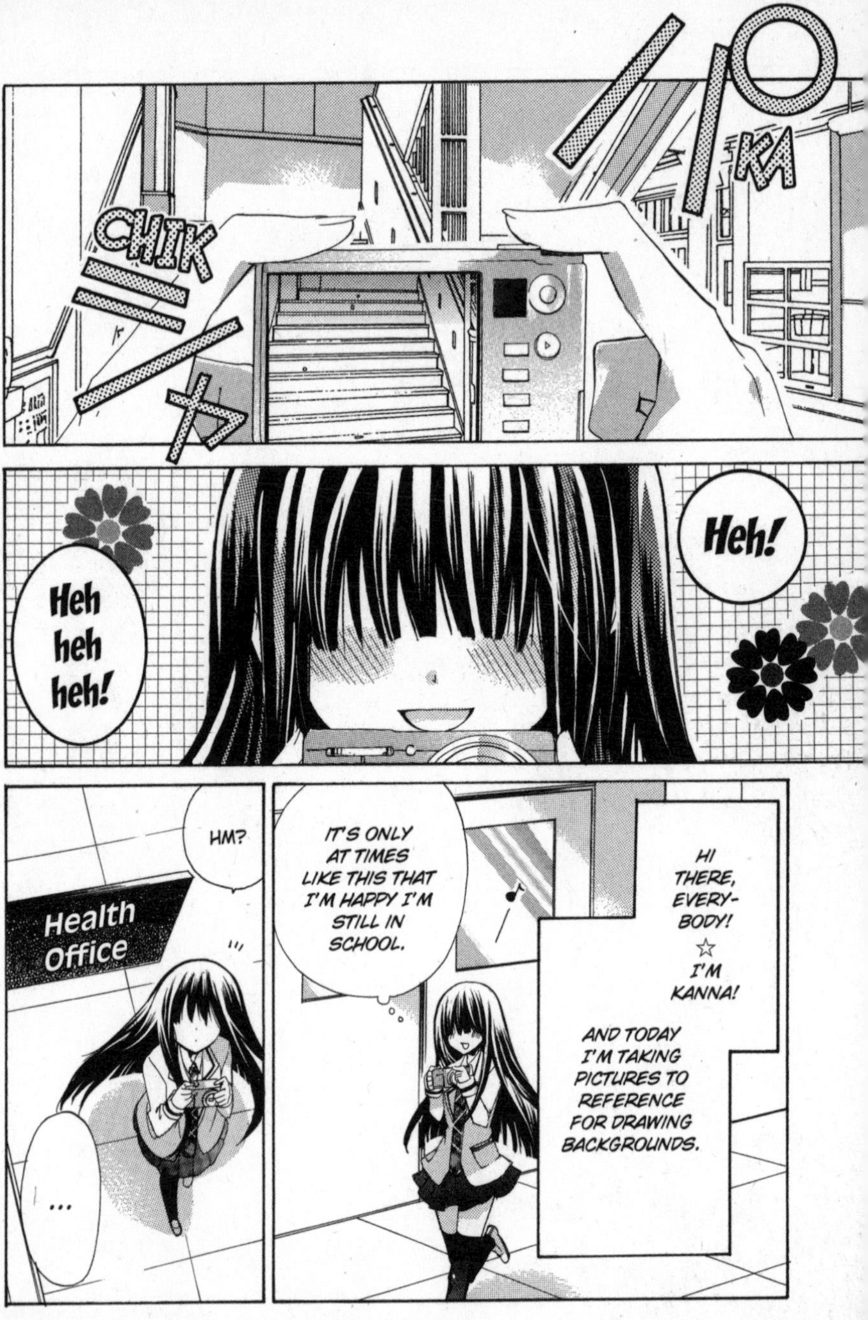
KA
CHIK
Heh!
Heh heh heh!
HI THERE, EVERY-BODY! ☆ I'M KANNA!
AND TODAY I'M TAKING PICTURES TO REFERENCE FOR DRAWING BACKGROUNDS.
IT'S ONLY AT TIMES LIKE THIS THAT I'M HAPPY I'M STILL IN SCHOOL.
HM?
Health Office
...

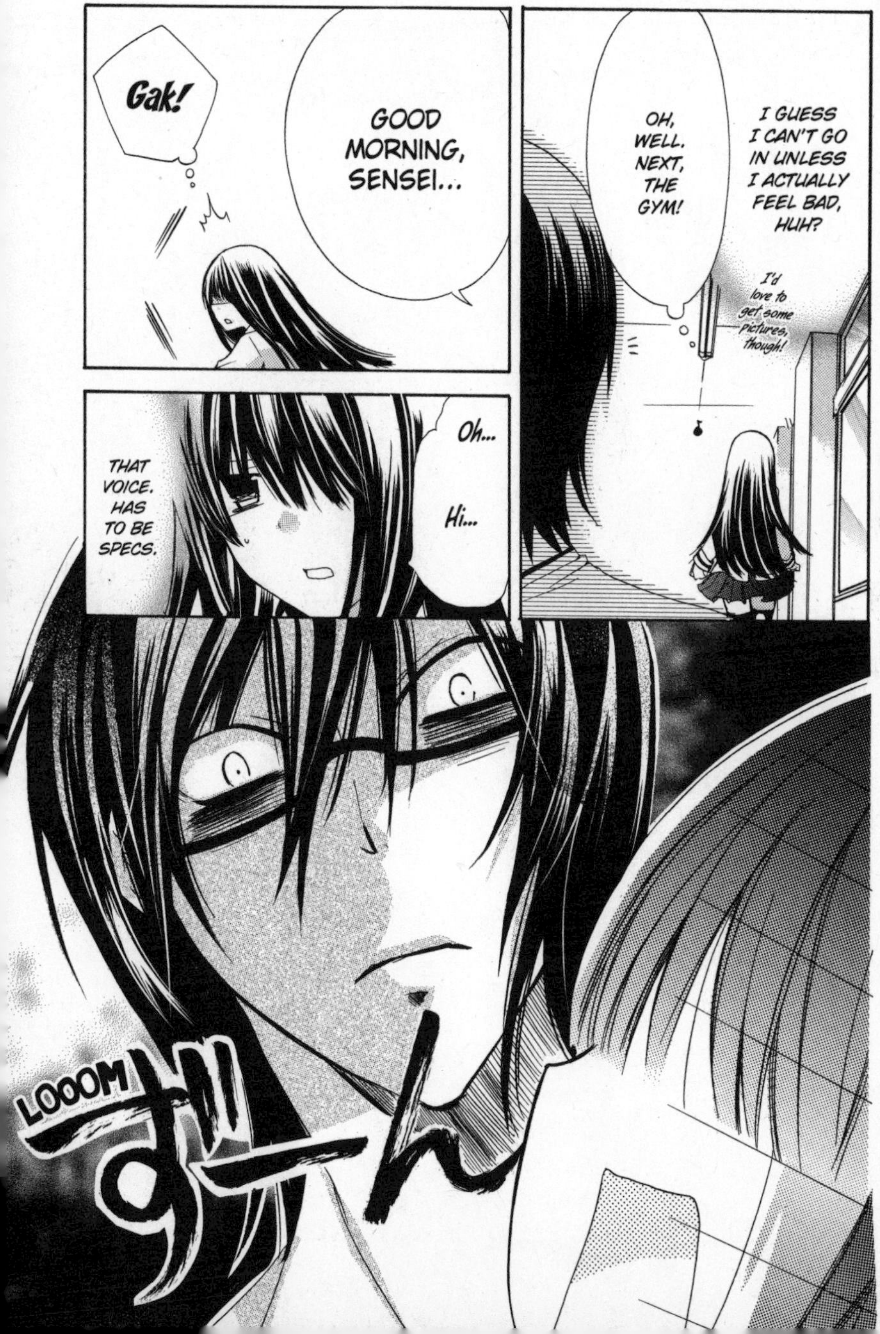
I GUESS I CAN'T GO IN UNLESS I ACTUALLY FEEL BAD, HUH?
OH, WELL. NEXT, THE GYM!
I'd love to get some pictures, though!
GOOD MORNING, SENSEI...
Gak!
Oh...
Hi...
THAT VOICE. HAS TO BE SPECS.
LOOOM

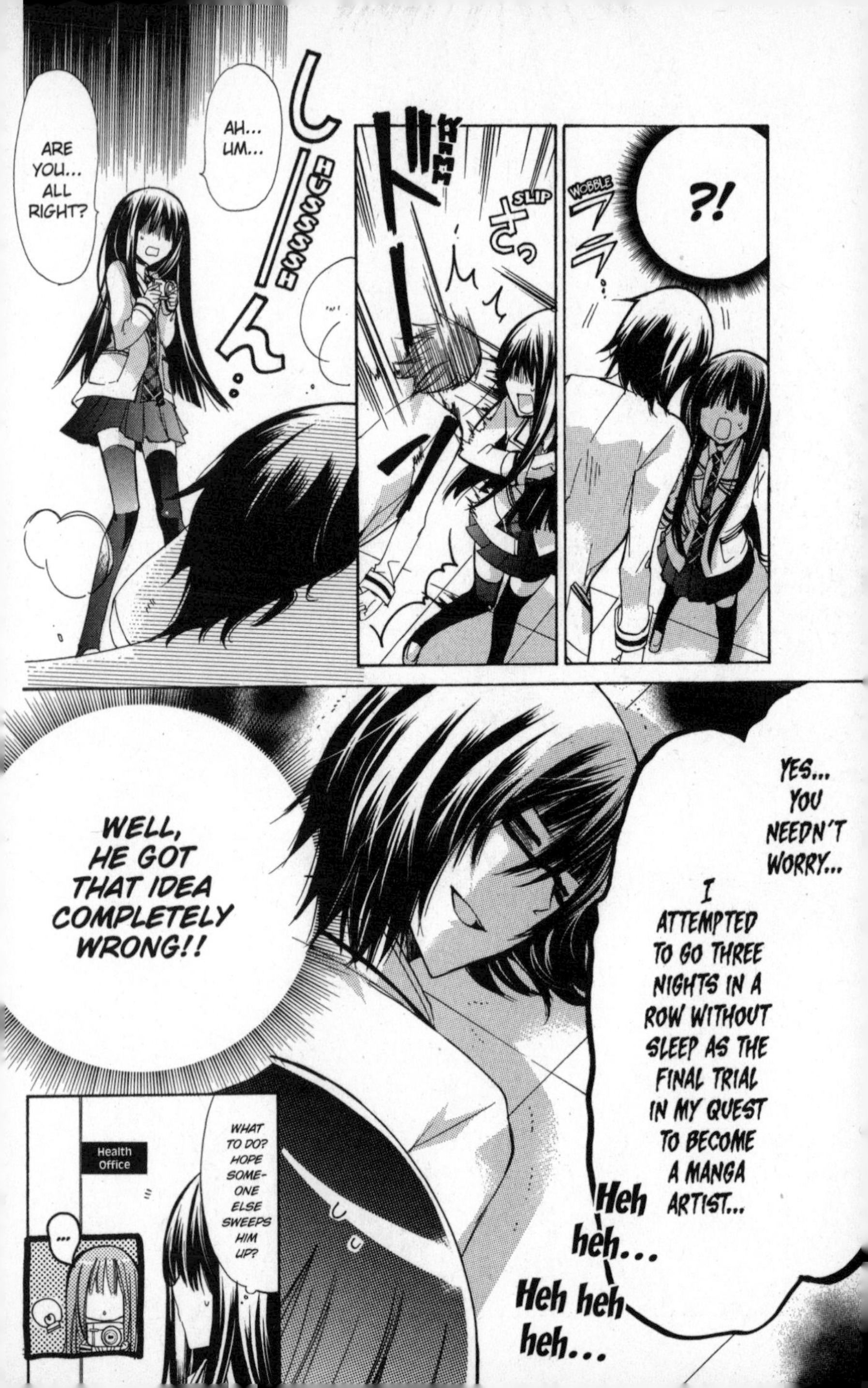
?!
WOBBLE
SLIP
WHAM
HUSSSSSH
AH... UM...
ARE YOU... ALL RIGHT?
YES... YOU NEEDN'T WORRY...
I ATTEMPTED TO GO THREE NIGHTS IN A ROW WITHOUT SLEEP AS THE FINAL TRIAL IN MY QUEST TO BECOME A MANGA ARTIST...
Heh heh...
Heh heh heh...
WELL, HE GOT THAT IDEA COMPLETELY WRONG!!
Health Office
WHAT TO DO? HOPE SOME-ONE ELSE SWEEPS HIM UP?
...

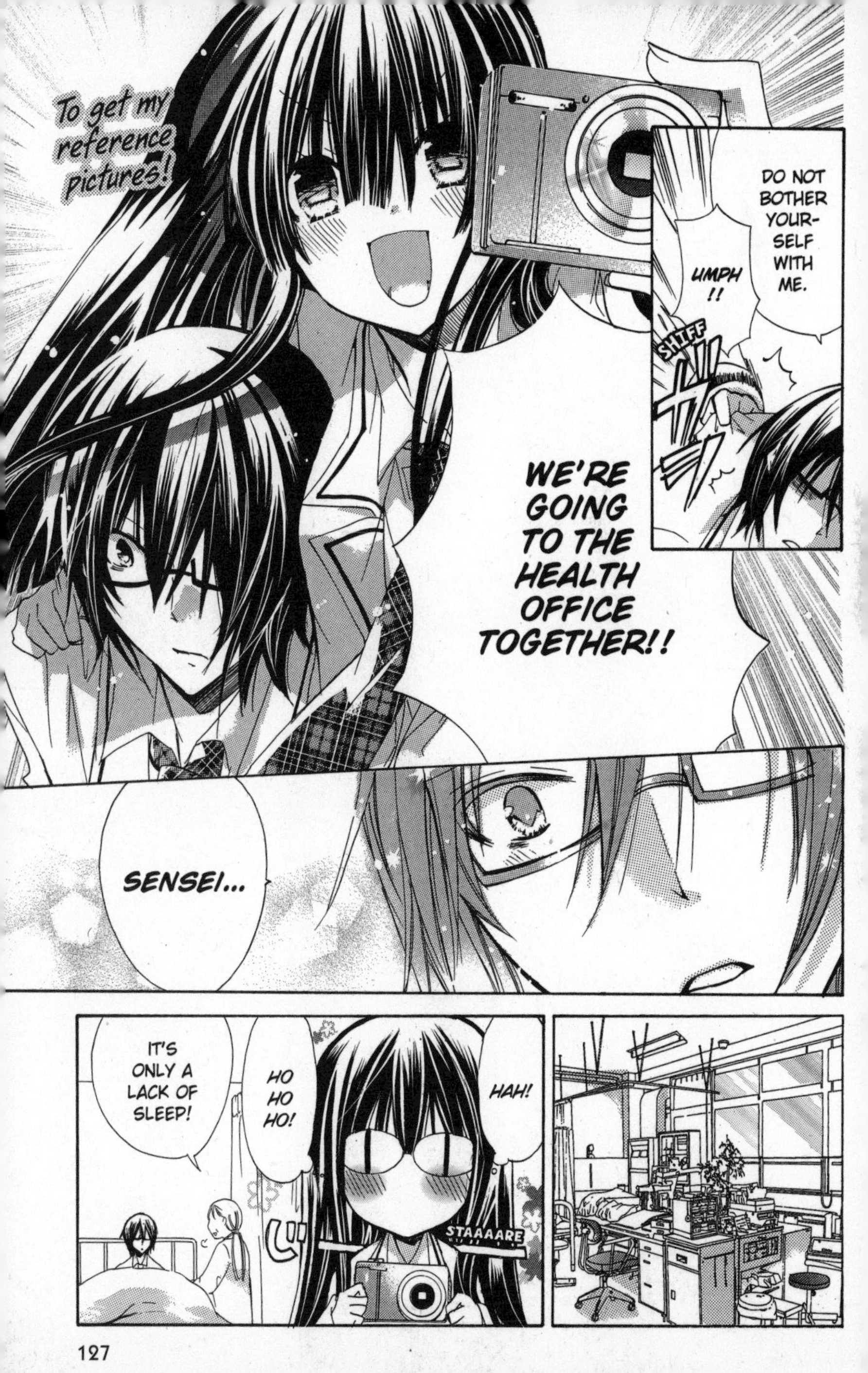
DO NOT BOTHER YOURSELF WITH ME.
UMPH!!
SHIFF
WE'RE GOING TO THE HEALTH OFFICE TOGETHER!!
To get my reference pictures!
SENSEI...
HAH!
HO HO HO!
IT'S ONLY A LACK OF SLEEP!
STAAAARE

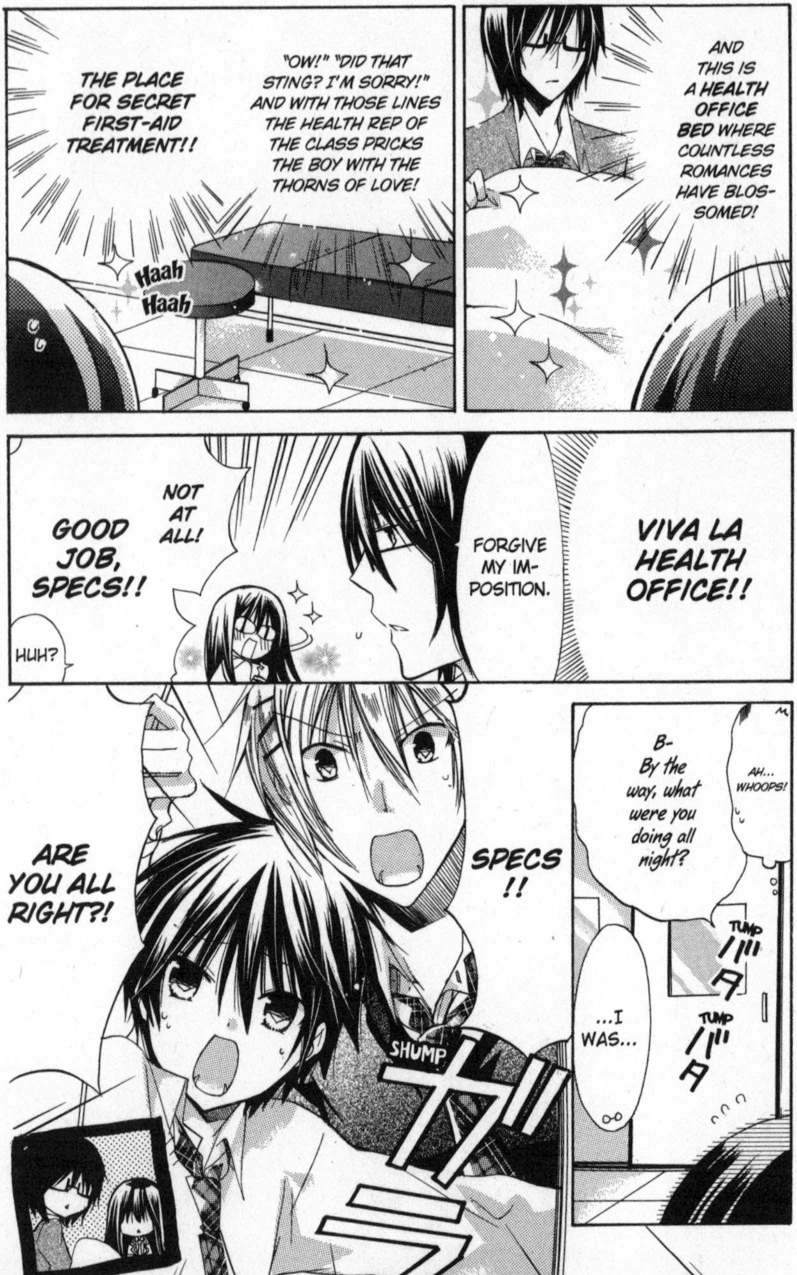
AND THIS IS A HEALTH OFFICE BED WHERE COUNTLESS ROMANCES HAVE BLOSSOMED!
"OW!" "DID THAT STING? I'M SORRY!" AND WITH THOSE LINES THE HEALTH REP OF THE CLASS PRICKS THE BOY WITH THE THORNS OF LOVE!
THE PLACE FOR SECRET FIRST-AID TREATMENT!!
Haah Haah
VIVA LA HEALTH OFFICE!!
FORGIVE MY IMPOSITION.
NOT AT ALL!
GOOD JOB, SPECS!!
HUH?
AH... WHOOPS!
B- By the way, what were you doing all night?
TUMP
TUMP
...I WAS...
SPECS!!
ARE YOU ALL RIGHT?!
SHUMP

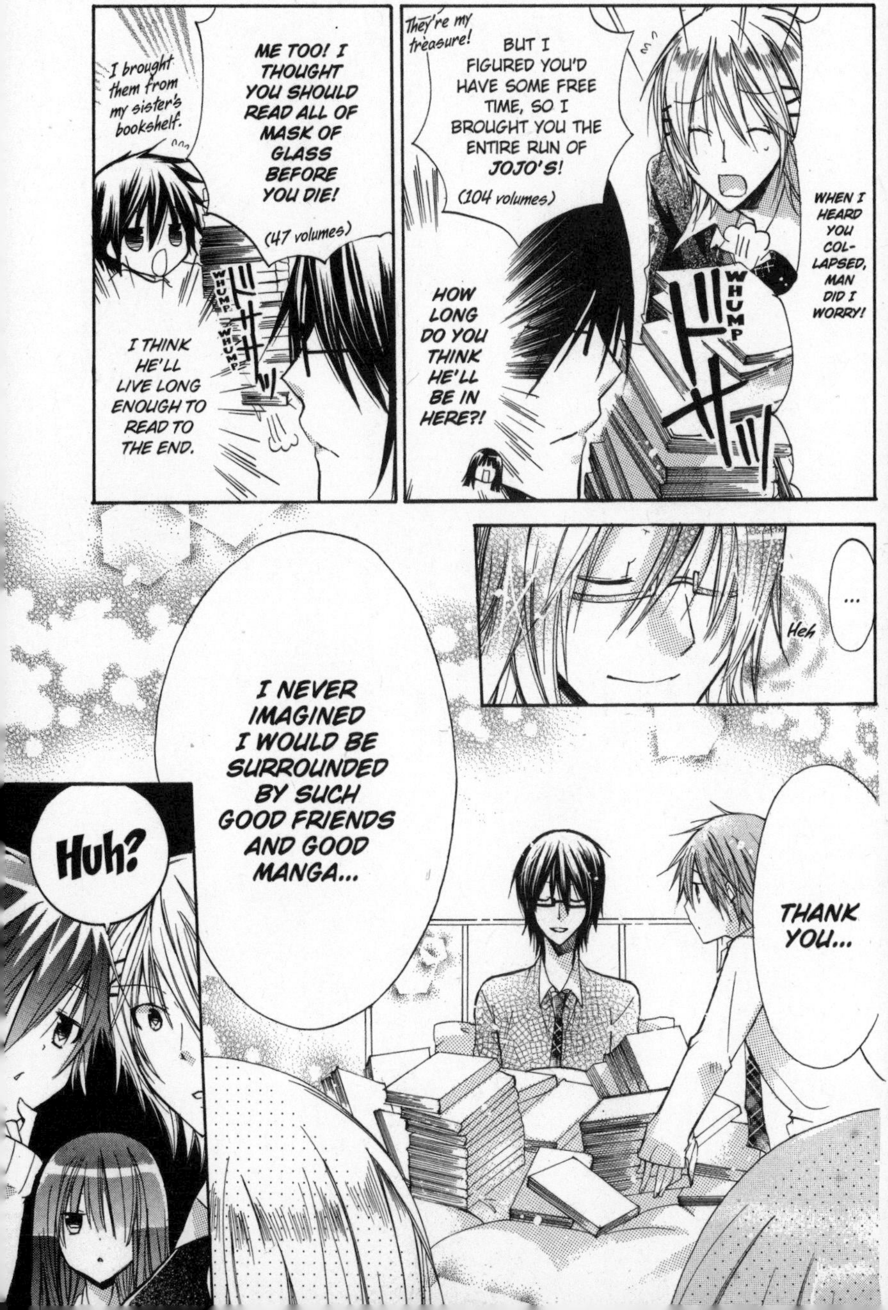
WHEN I HEARD YOU COL-LAPSED, MAN DID I WORRY!
BUT I FIGURED YOU'D HAVE SOME FREE TIME, SO I BROUGHT YOU THE ENTIRE RUN OF JOJO'S!
(104 volumes)
They're my treasure!
WHUMP
HOW LONG DO YOU THINK HE'LL BE IN HERE?!
ME TOO! I THOUGHT YOU SHOULD READ ALL OF MASK OF GLASS BEFORE YOU DIE!
(47 volumes)
I brought them from my sister's bookshelf.
WHUMP
WHUMP
I THINK HE'LL LIVE LONG ENOUGH TO READ TO THE END.
...
Heh
THANK YOU...
I NEVER IMAGINED I WOULD BE SURROUNDED BY SUCH GOOD FRIENDS AND GOOD MANGA...
Huh?

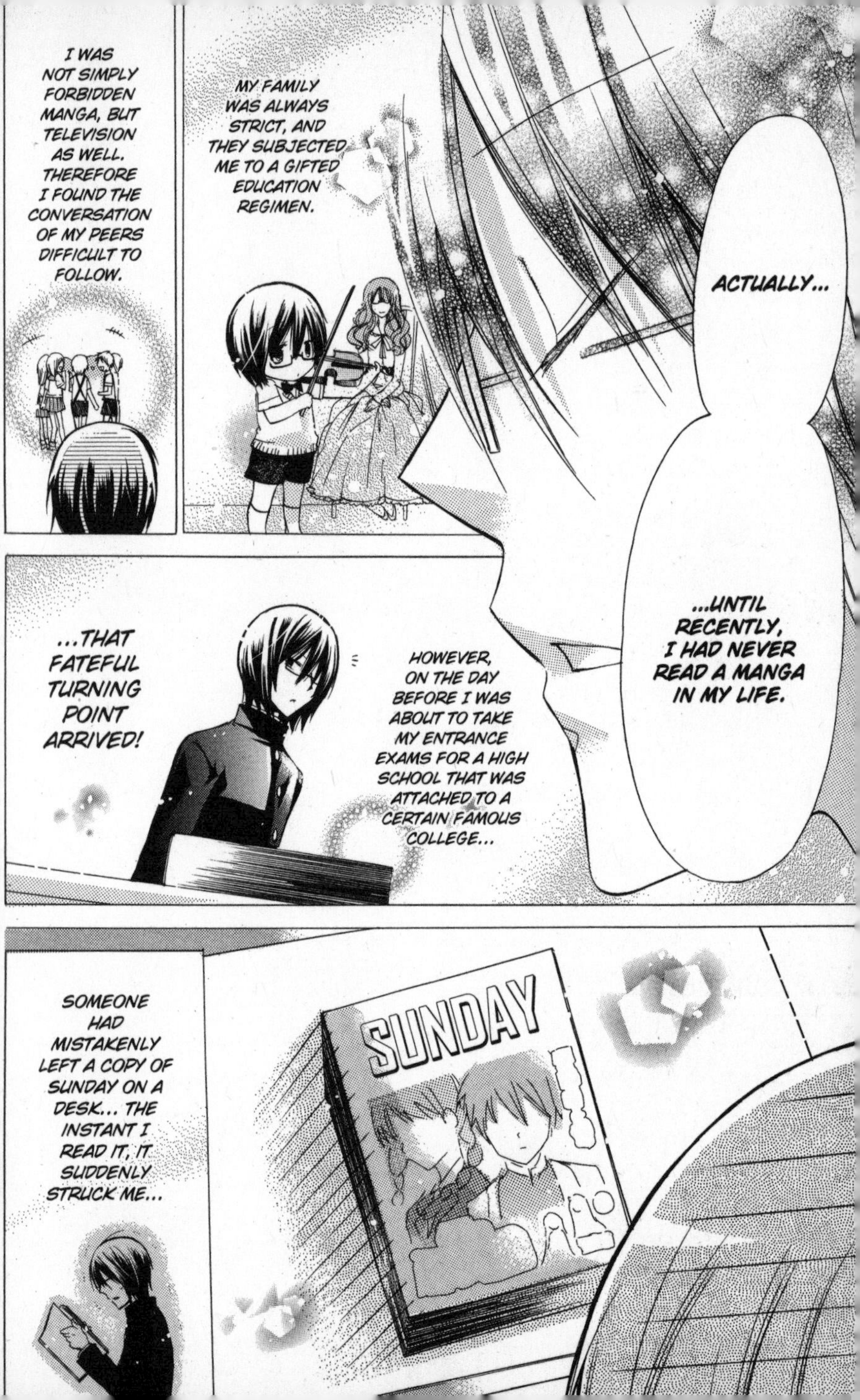
ACTUALLY...
...UNTIL RECENTLY, I HAD NEVER READ A MANGA IN MY LIFE.
MY FAMILY WAS ALWAYS STRICT, AND THEY SUBJECTED ME TO A GIFTED EDUCATION REGIMEN.
I WAS NOT SIMPLY FORBIDDEN MANGA, BUT TELEVISION AS WELL. THEREFORE I FOUND THE CONVERSATION OF MY PEERS DIFFICULT TO FOLLOW.
HOWEVER, ON THE DAY BEFORE I WAS ABOUT TO TAKE MY ENTRANCE EXAMS FOR A HIGH SCHOOL THAT WAS ATTACHED TO A CERTAIN FAMOUS COLLEGE...
...THAT FATEFUL TURNING POINT ARRIVED!
SUNDAY
SOMEONE HAD MISTAKENLY LEFT A COPY OF SUNDAY ON A DESK... THE INSTANT I READ IT, IT SUDDENLY STRUCK ME...

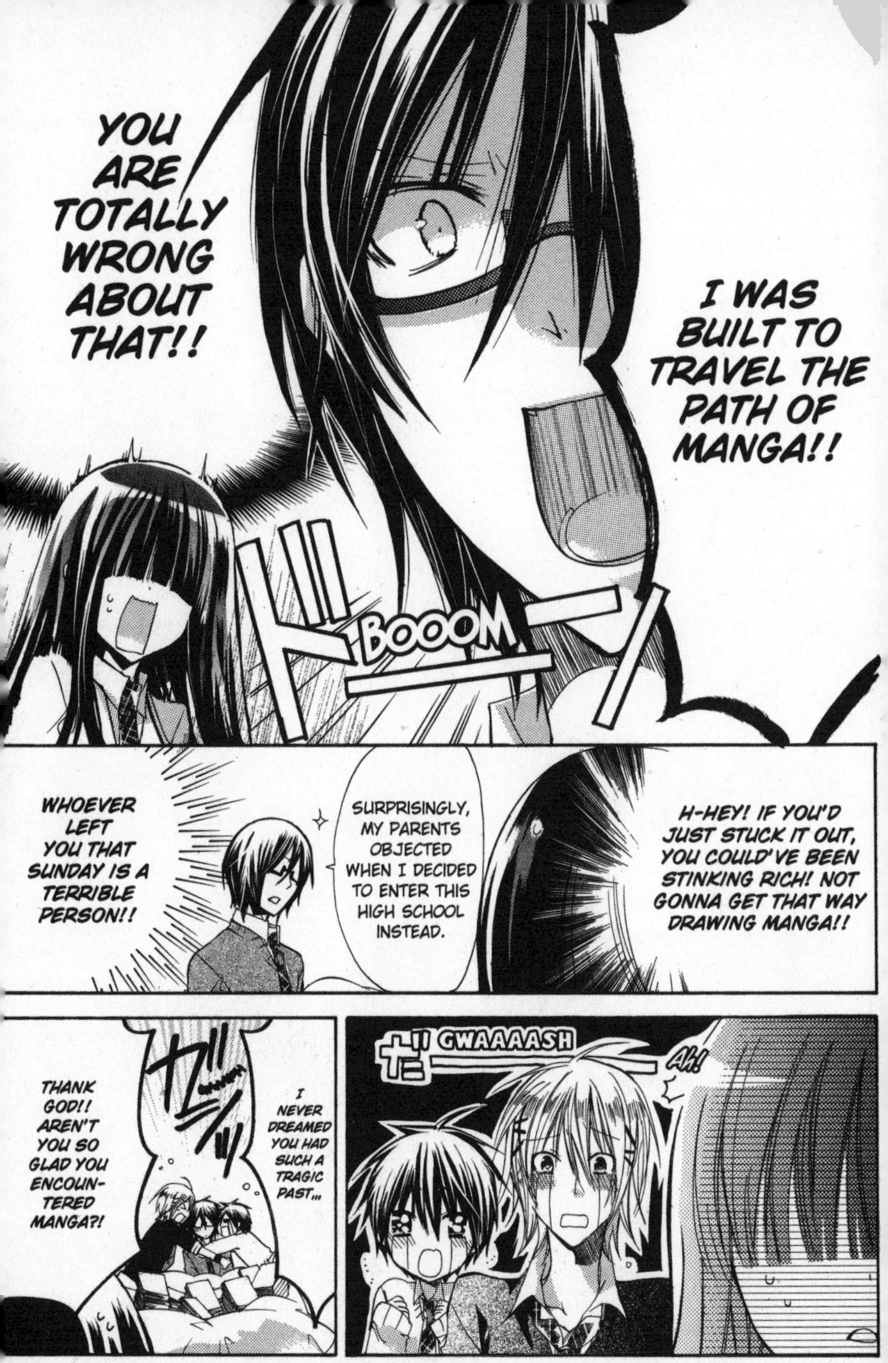
YOU ARE TOTALLY WRONG ABOUT THAT!!
I WAS BUILT TO TRAVEL THE PATH OF MANGA!!
BOOOM
H-HEY! IF YOU'D JUST STUCK IT OUT, YOU COULD'VE BEEN STINKING RICH! NOT GONNA GET THAT WAY DRAWING MANGA!!
SURPRISINGLY, MY PARENTS OBJECTED WHEN I DECIDED TO ENTER THIS HIGH SCHOOL INSTEAD.
WHOEVER LEFT YOU THAT SUNDAY IS A TERRIBLE PERSON!!
GWAAAASH
AH!
I NEVER DREAMED YOU HAD SUCH A TRAGIC PAST...
THANK GOD!! AREN'T YOU SO GLAD YOU ENCOUN-TERED MANGA?!

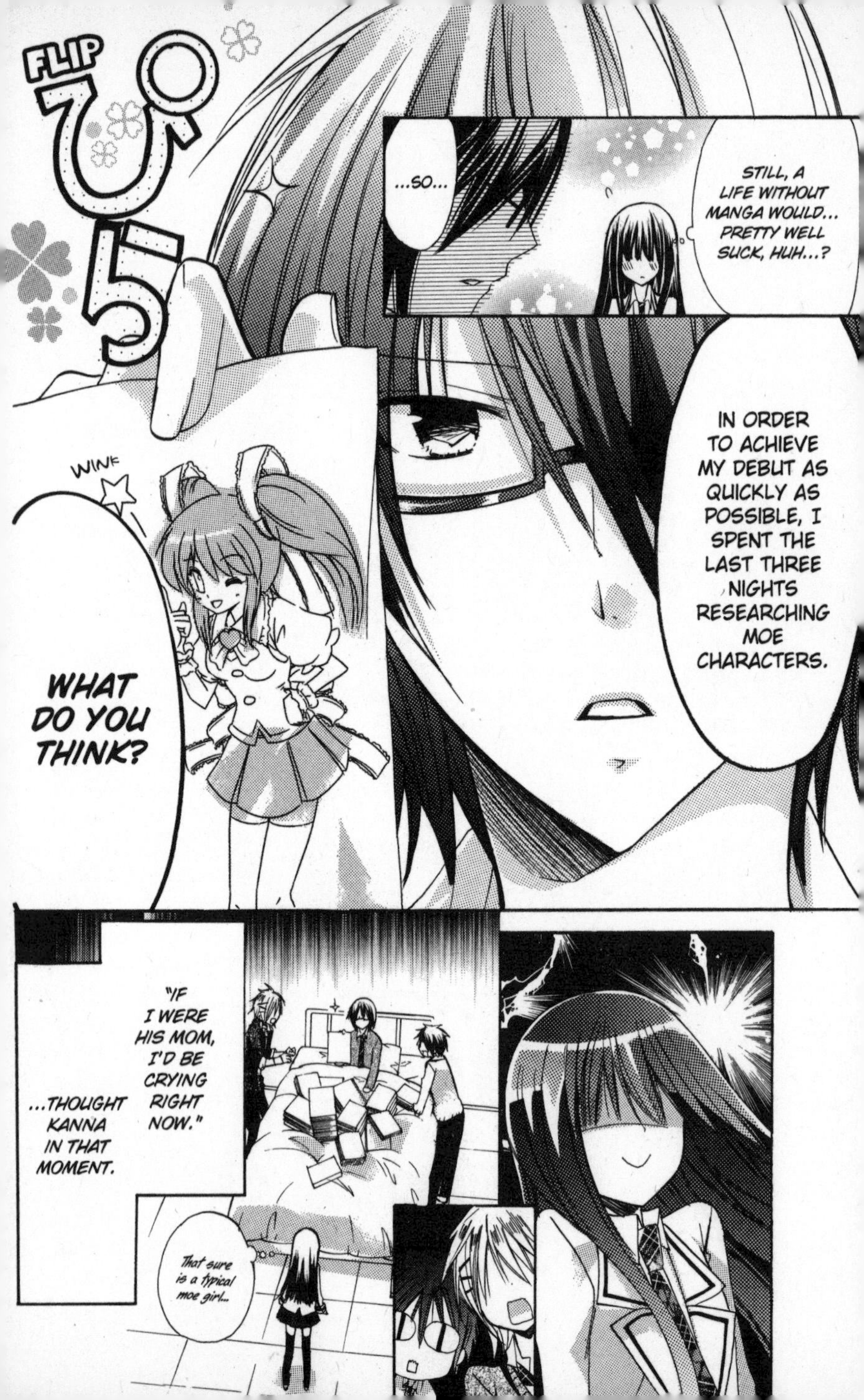
FLIP 5
STILL, A LIFE WITHOUT MANGA WOULD... PRETTY WELL SUCK, HUH...?
...SO...
IN ORDER TO ACHIEVE MY DEBUT AS QUICKLY AS POSSIBLE, I SPENT THE LAST THREE NIGHTS RESEARCHING MOE CHARACTERS.
WINK
WHAT DO YOU THINK?
"IF I WERE HIS MOM, I'D BE CRYING RIGHT NOW."
...THOUGHT KANNA IN THAT MOMENT.
That sure is a typical moe girl...

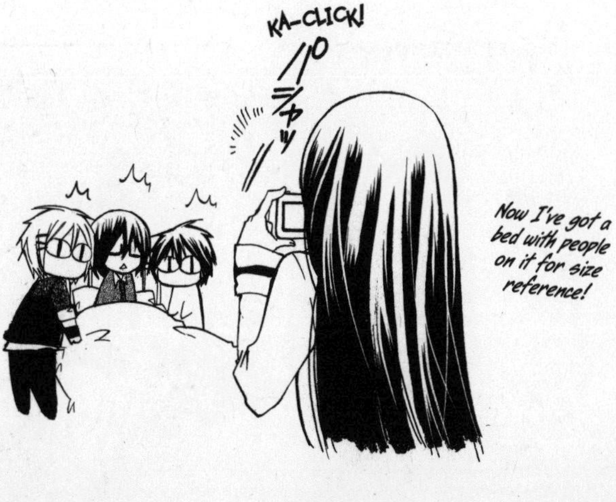
KA-CLICK!
パシャッ
Now I've got a bed with people on it for size reference!

MANGA DOGS

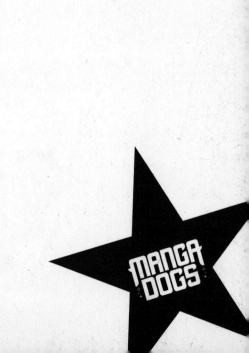

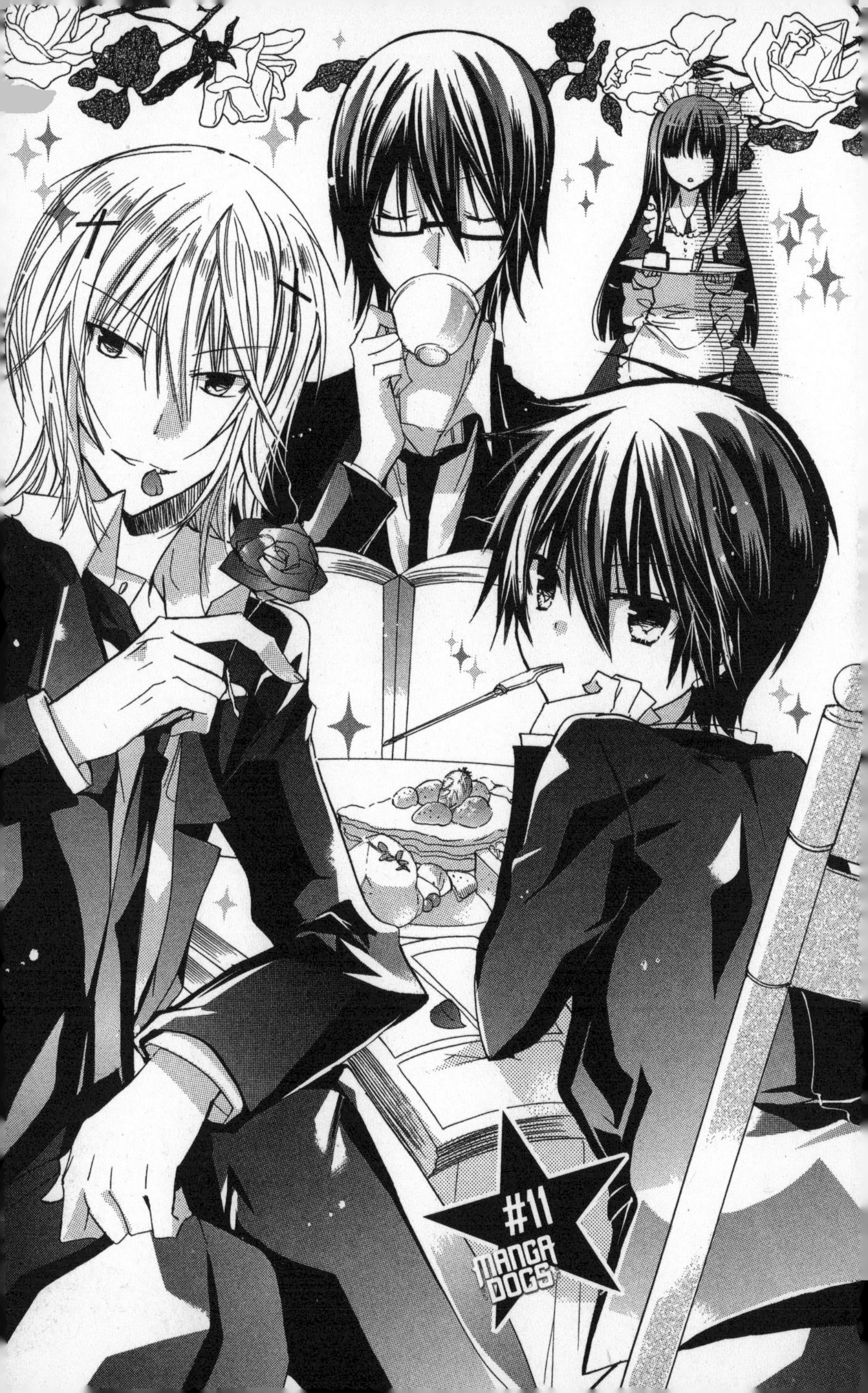
#11
MANGA DOGS

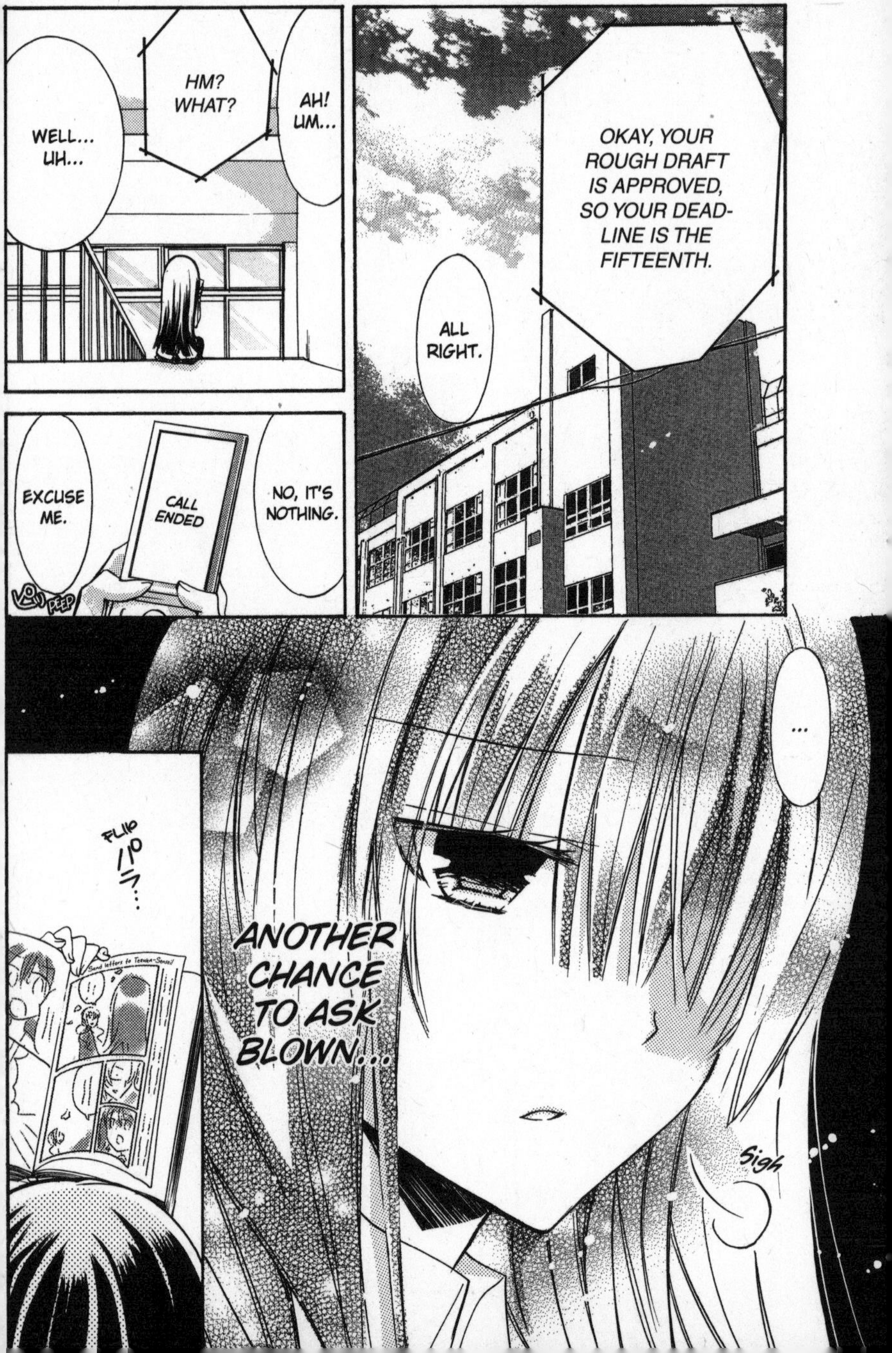
OKAY, YOUR ROUGH DRAFT IS APPROVED, SO YOUR DEAD-LINE IS THE FIFTEENTH.
ALL RIGHT.
AH! UM...
HM? WHAT?
WELL... UH...
NO, IT'S NOTHING.
CALL ENDED
EXCUSE ME.
PEEP
...
ANOTHER CHANCE TO ASK BLOWN...
Sigh
FLIP
Send letters to Tezuka-Sensei!

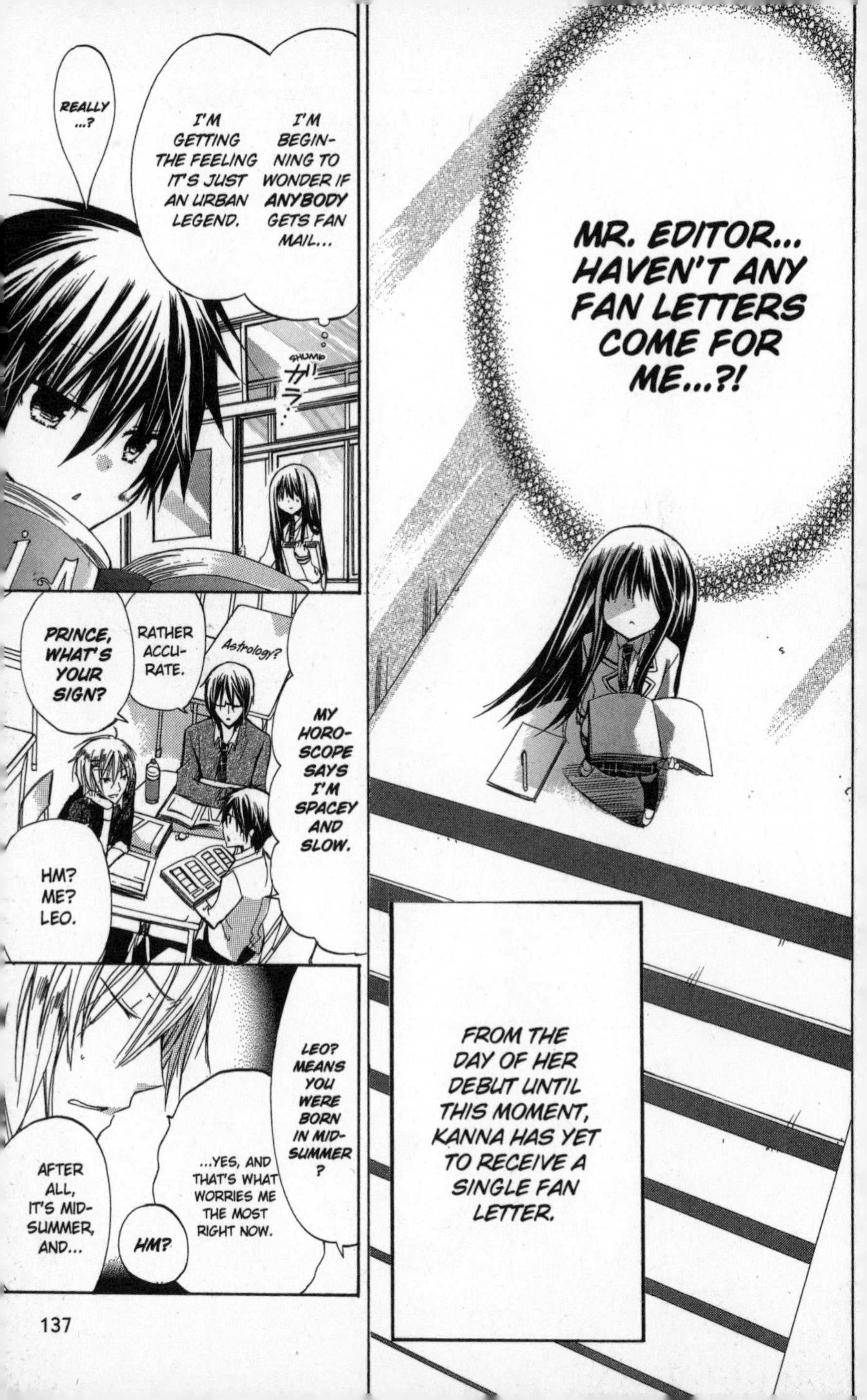
MR. EDITOR... HAVEN'T ANY FAN LETTERS COME FOR ME...?!
FROM THE DAY OF HER DEBUT UNTIL THIS MOMENT, KANNA HAS YET TO RECEIVE A SINGLE FAN LETTER.
I'M BEGINNING TO WONDER IF ANYBODY GETS FAN MAIL...
I'M GETTING THE FEELING IT'S JUST AN URBAN LEGEND.
REALLY ...?
SHUMP
MY HOROSCOPE SAYS I'M SPACEY AND SLOW.
Astrology?
RATHER ACCURATE.
PRINCE, WHAT'S YOUR SIGN?
HM? ME? LEO.
LEO? MEANS YOU WERE BORN IN MIDSUMMER?
...YES, AND THAT'S WHAT WORRIES ME THE MOST RIGHT NOW.
HM?
AFTER ALL, IT'S MIDSUMMER, AND...

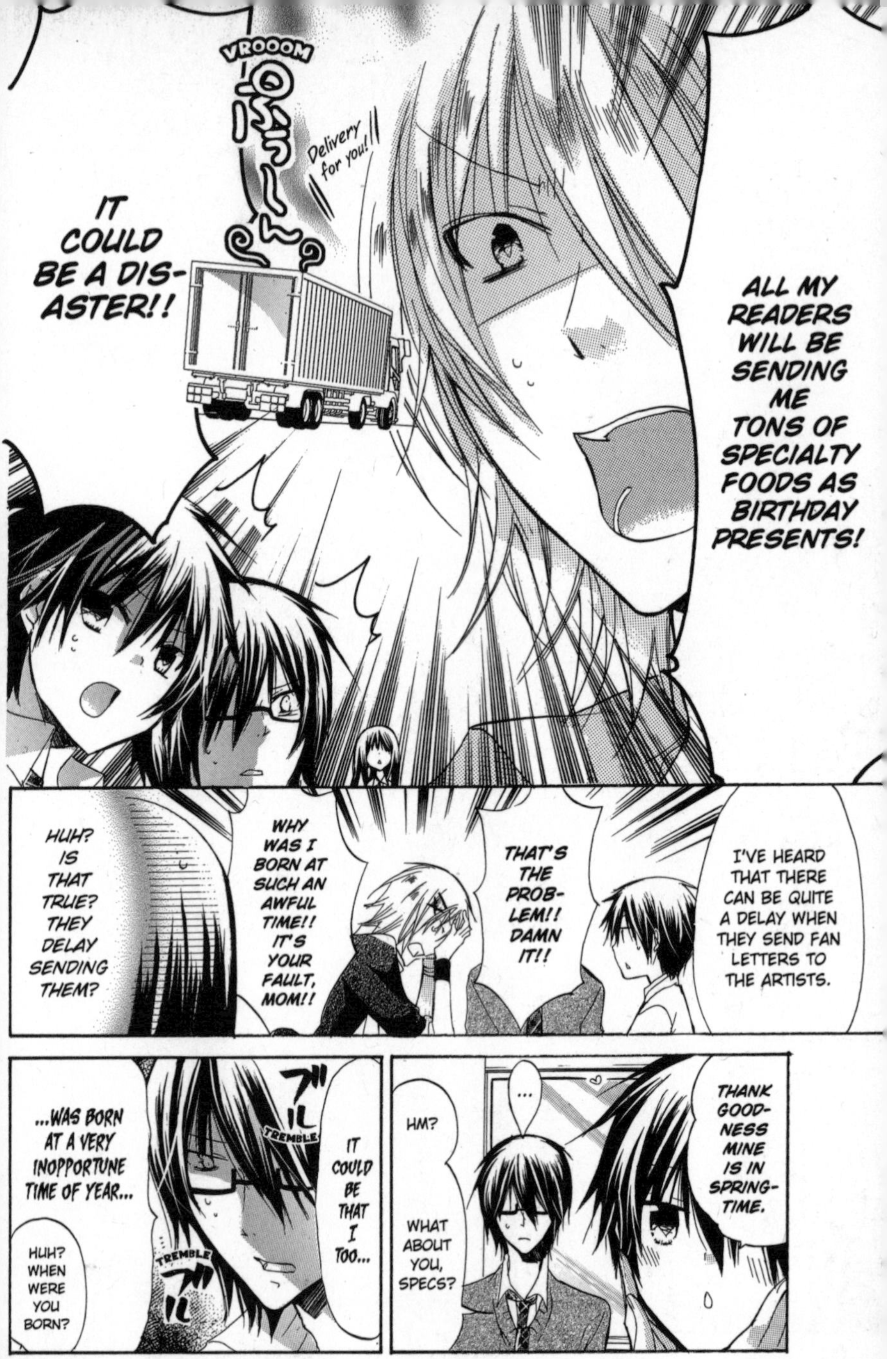
ALL MY READERS WILL BE SENDING ME TONS OF SPECIALTY FOODS AS BIRTHDAY PRESENTS!
IT COULD BE A DIS-ASTER!!
Delivery for you!
VROOOM
I'VE HEARD THAT THERE CAN BE QUITE A DELAY WHEN THEY SEND FAN LETTERS TO THE ARTISTS.
THAT'S THE PROB-LEM!! DAMN IT!!
WHY WAS I BORN AT SUCH AN AWFUL TIME!! IT'S YOUR FAULT, MOM!!
HUH? IS THAT TRUE? THEY DELAY SENDING THEM?
THANK GOOD-NESS MINE IS IN SPRING-TIME.
...
HM?
WHAT ABOUT YOU, SPECS?
TREMBLE
IT COULD BE THAT I TOO...
...WAS BORN AT A VERY INOPPORTUNE TIME OF YEAR...
TREMBLE
HUH? WHEN WERE YOU BORN?

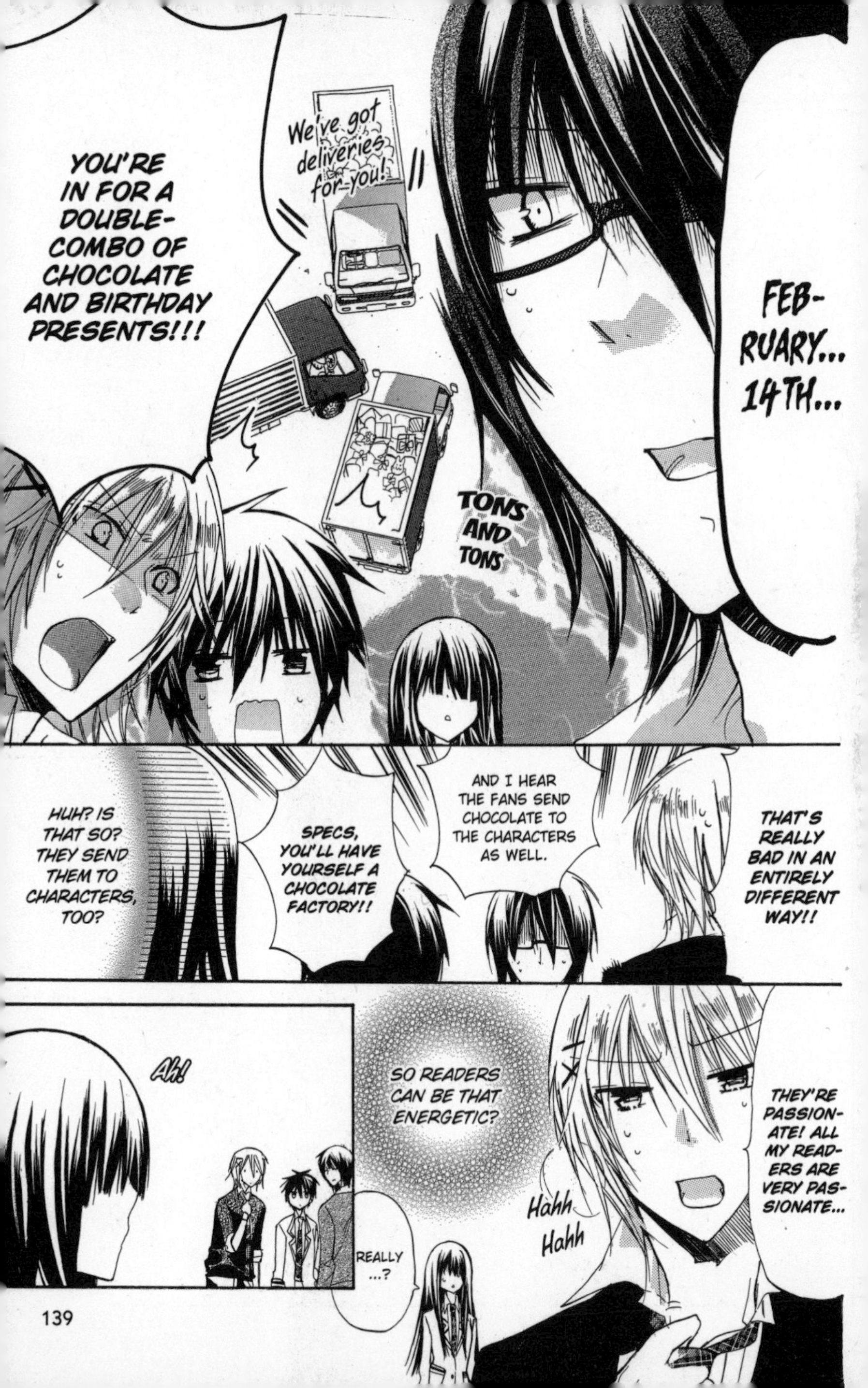
FEB-RUARY... 14TH...
We've got deliveries for you!
YOU'RE IN FOR A DOUBLE-COMBO OF CHOCOLATE AND BIRTHDAY PRESENTS!!!
TONS AND TONS
THAT'S REALLY BAD IN AN ENTIRELY DIFFERENT WAY!!
AND I HEAR THE FANS SEND CHOCOLATE TO THE CHARACTERS AS WELL.
SPECS, YOU'LL HAVE YOURSELF A CHOCOLATE FACTORY!!
HUH? IS THAT SO? THEY SEND THEM TO CHARACTERS, TOO?
THEY'RE PASSION-ATE! ALL MY READ-ERS ARE VERY PAS-SIONATE...
Hahh Hahh
SO READERS CAN BE THAT ENERGETIC?
REALLY ...?
Ah!

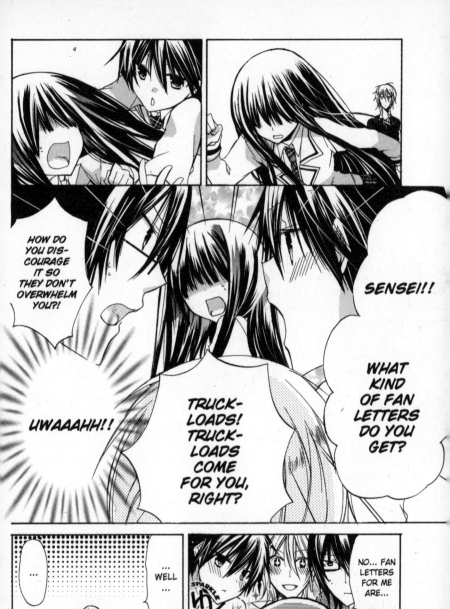

SENSEI!!
WHAT KIND OF FAN LETTERS DO YOU GET?
TRUCK-LOADS! TRUCK-LOADS COME FOR YOU, RIGHT?
HOW DO YOU DIS-COURAGE IT SO THEY DON'T OVERWHELM YOU?!
UWAAAHH!!
NO... FAN LETTERS FOR ME ARE...
SPARKLE
... WELL ...
...

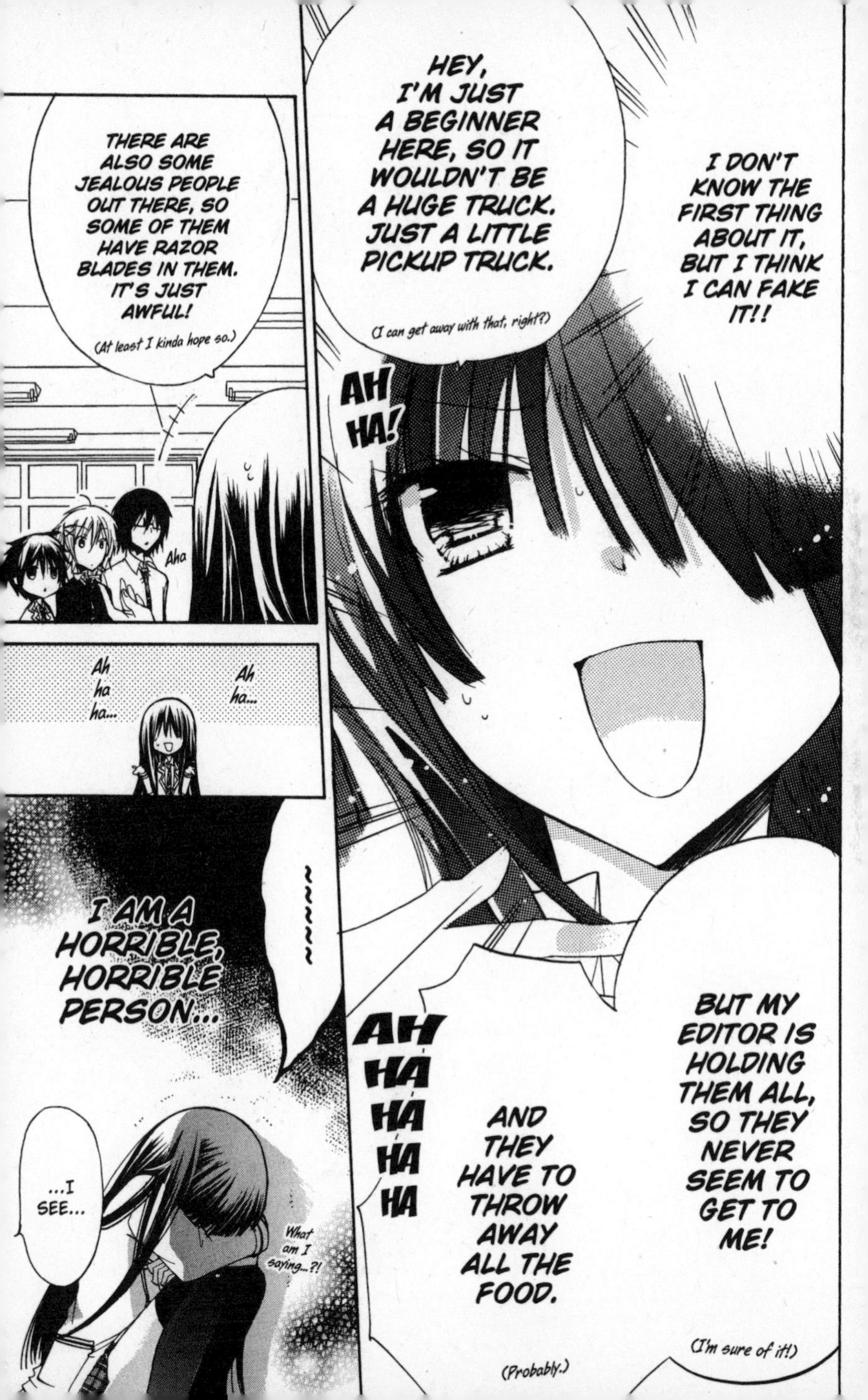
I DON'T KNOW THE FIRST THING ABOUT IT, BUT I THINK I CAN FAKE IT!!
HEY, I'M JUST A BEGINNER HERE, SO IT WOULDN'T BE A HUGE TRUCK. JUST A LITTLE PICKUP TRUCK.
(I can get away with that, right?)
AH HA!
BUT MY EDITOR IS HOLDING THEM ALL, SO THEY NEVER SEEM TO GET TO ME!
(I'm sure of it!)
AND THEY HAVE TO THROW AWAY ALL THE FOOD.
(Probably.)
AH HA HA HA HA
THERE ARE ALSO SOME JEALOUS PEOPLE OUT THERE, SO SOME OF THEM HAVE RAZOR BLADES IN THEM. IT'S JUST AWFUL!
(At least I kinda hope so.)
Aha
Ah ha...
Ah ha ha...
I AM A HORRIBLE, HORRIBLE PERSON...
...I SEE...
What am I saying...?!

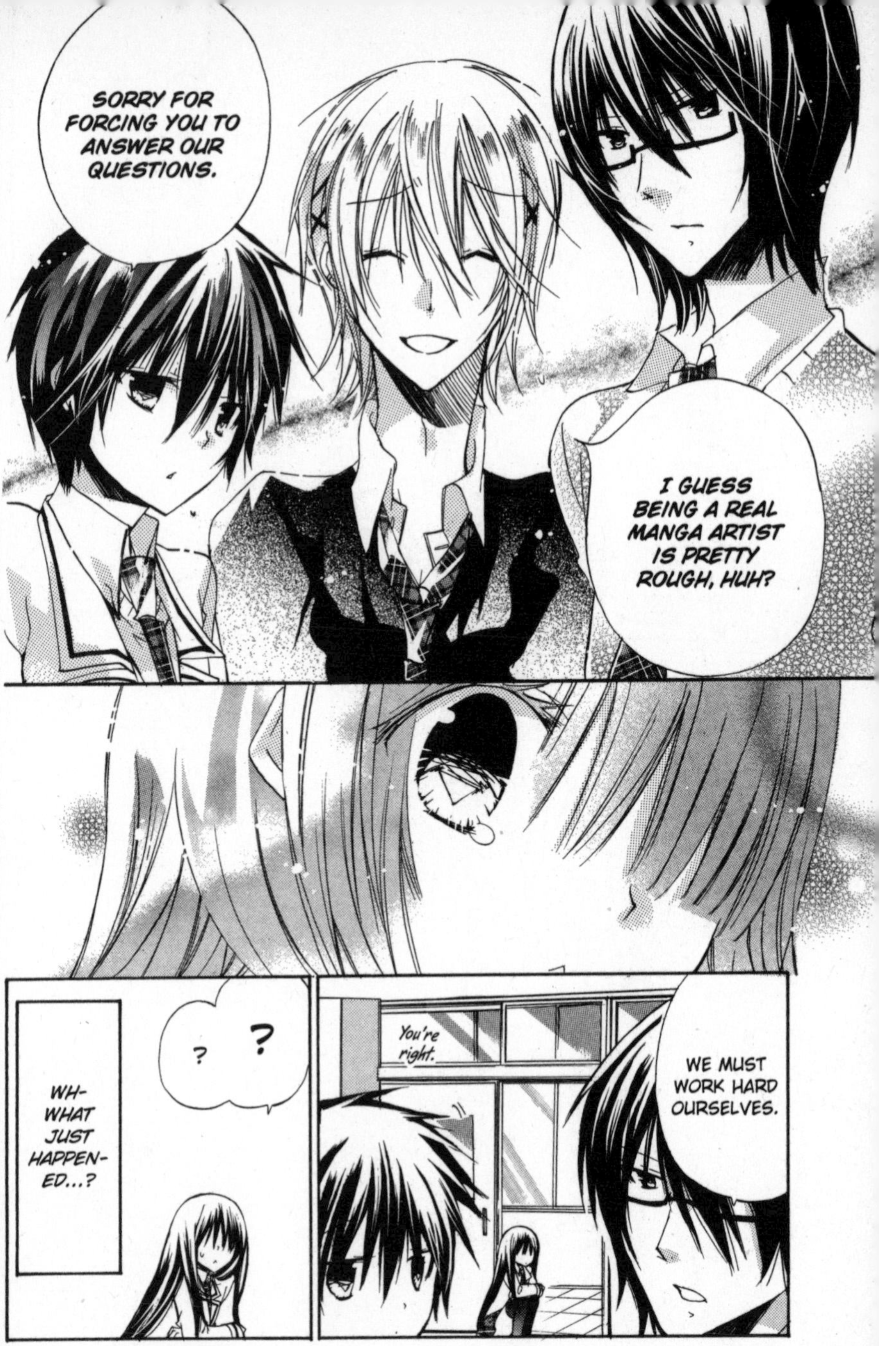

SORRY FOR FORCING YOU TO ANSWER OUR QUESTIONS.
I GUESS BEING A REAL MANGA ARTIST IS PRETTY ROUGH, HUH?
WE MUST WORK HARD OURSELVES.
You're right.
? ?
WH-WHAT JUST HAPPEN-ED...?

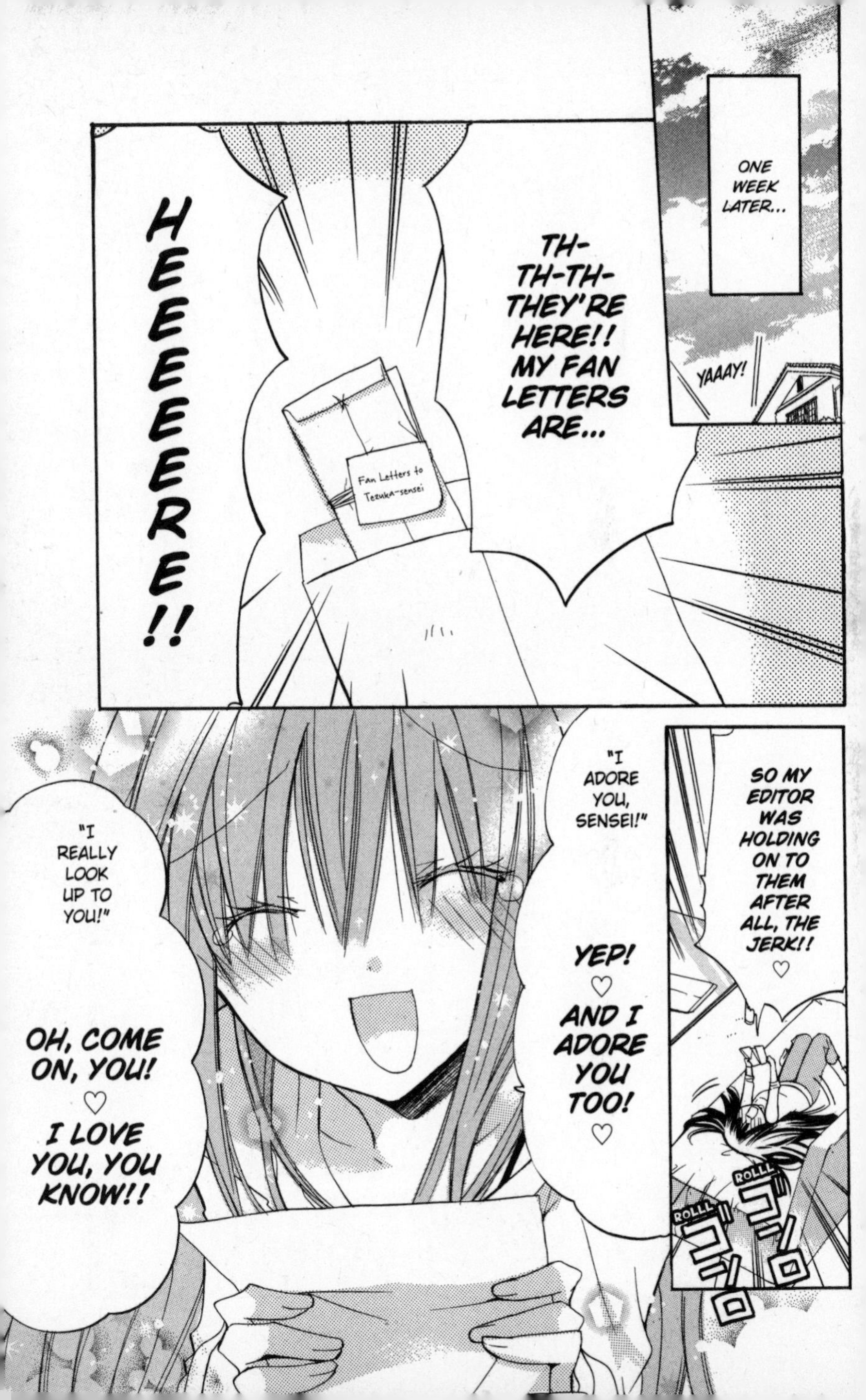
ONE WEEK LATER...
YAAAY!
TH-TH-TH-THEY'RE HERE!! MY FAN LETTERS ARE...
HEEEEEEERE!!
Fan Letters to Tezuka-sensei
SO MY EDITOR WAS HOLDING ON TO THEM AFTER ALL, THE JERK!! ♡
ROLLL
ROLLL
"I ADORE YOU, SENSEI!"
YEP! ♡ AND I ADORE YOU TOO! ♡
"I REALLY LOOK UP TO YOU!"
OH, COME ON, YOU! ♡ I LOVE YOU, YOU KNOW!!

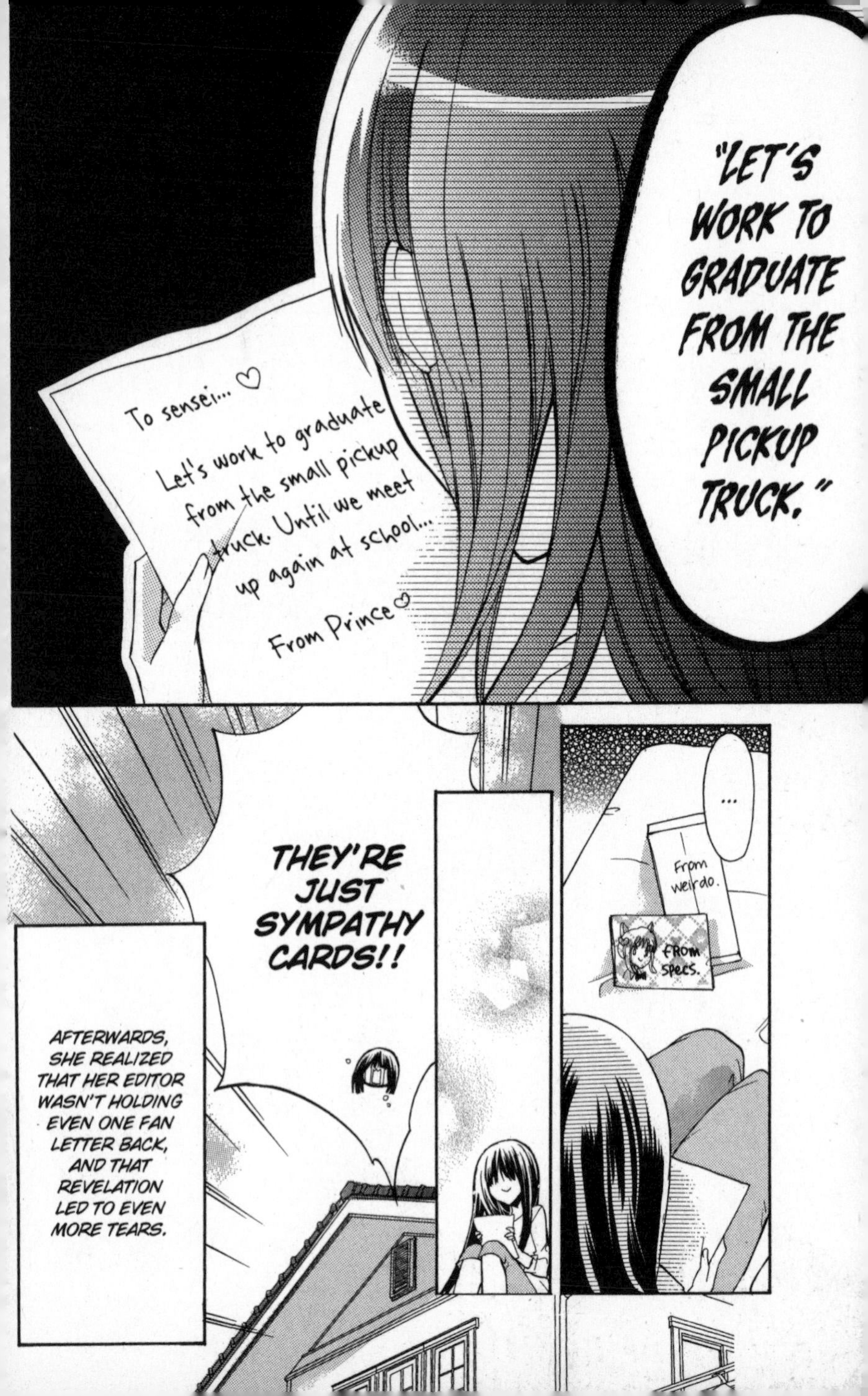
"LET'S WORK TO GRADUATE FROM THE SMALL PICKUP TRUCK."
To sensei... ♡
Let's work to graduate from the small pickup truck. Until we meet up again at school...
From Prince ♡
...
From weirdo.
FROM specs.
THEY'RE JUST SYMPATHY CARDS!!
AFTERWARDS, SHE REALIZED THAT HER EDITOR WASN'T HOLDING EVEN ONE FAN LETTER BACK, AND THAT REVELATION LED TO EVEN MORE TEARS.

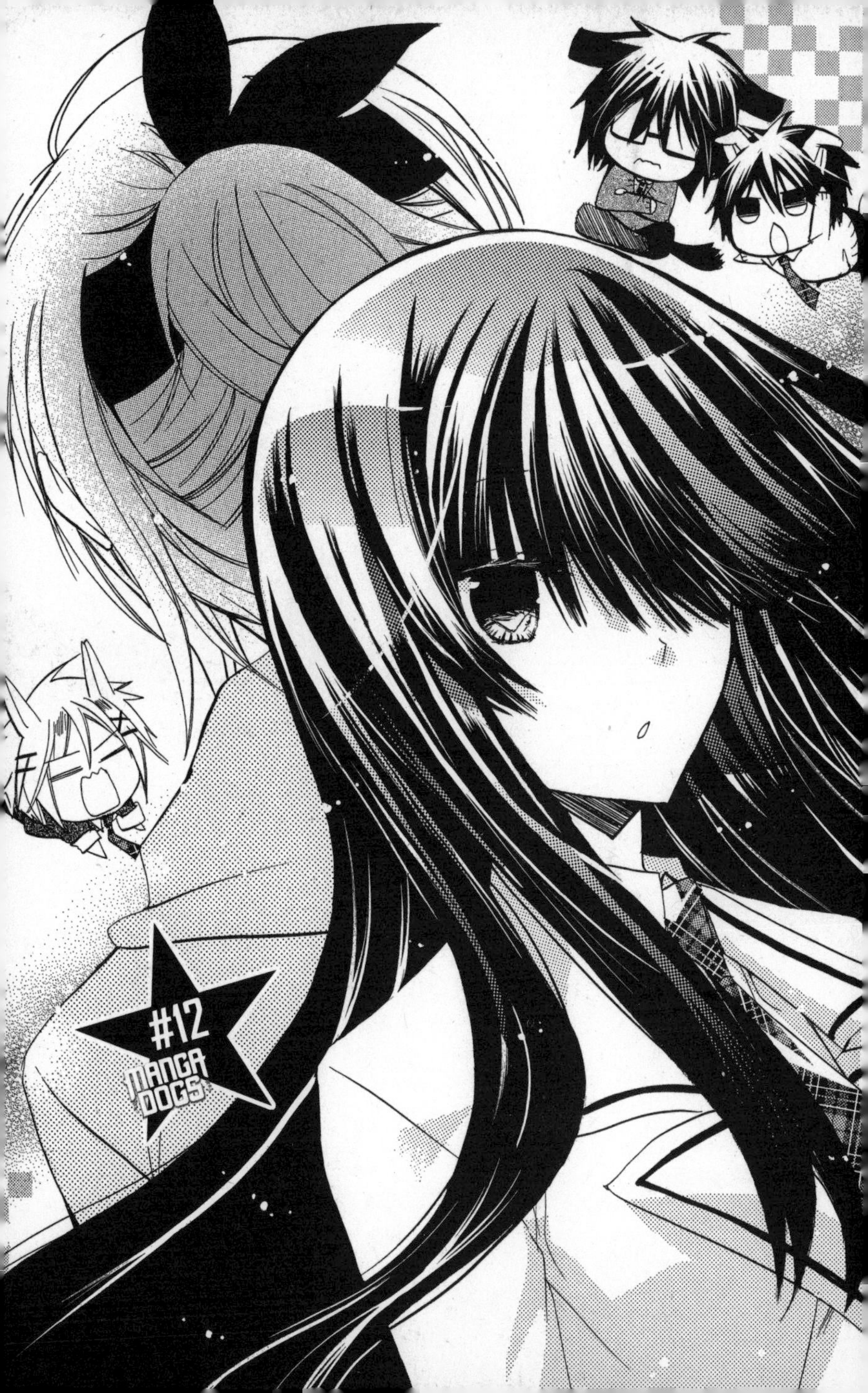
#12
MANGA DOGS

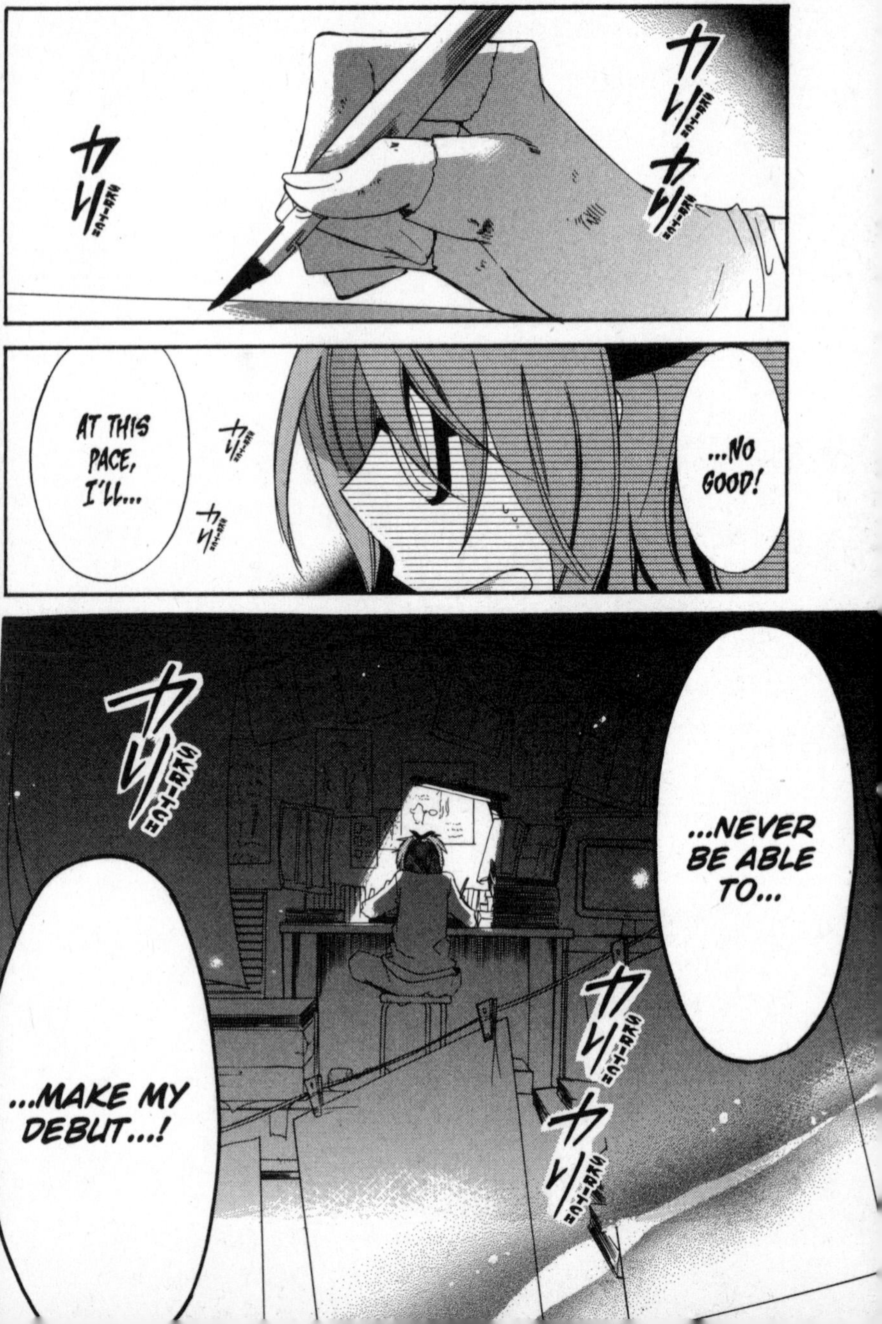

カリ SKRITCH
カリ SKRITCH
カリ SKRITCH
...NO GOOD!
カリ SKRITCH
カリ SKRITCH
AT THIS PACE, I'LL...
...NEVER BE ABLE TO...
カリ SKRITCH
カリ SKRITCH
カリ SKRITCH
...MAKE MY DEBUT...!

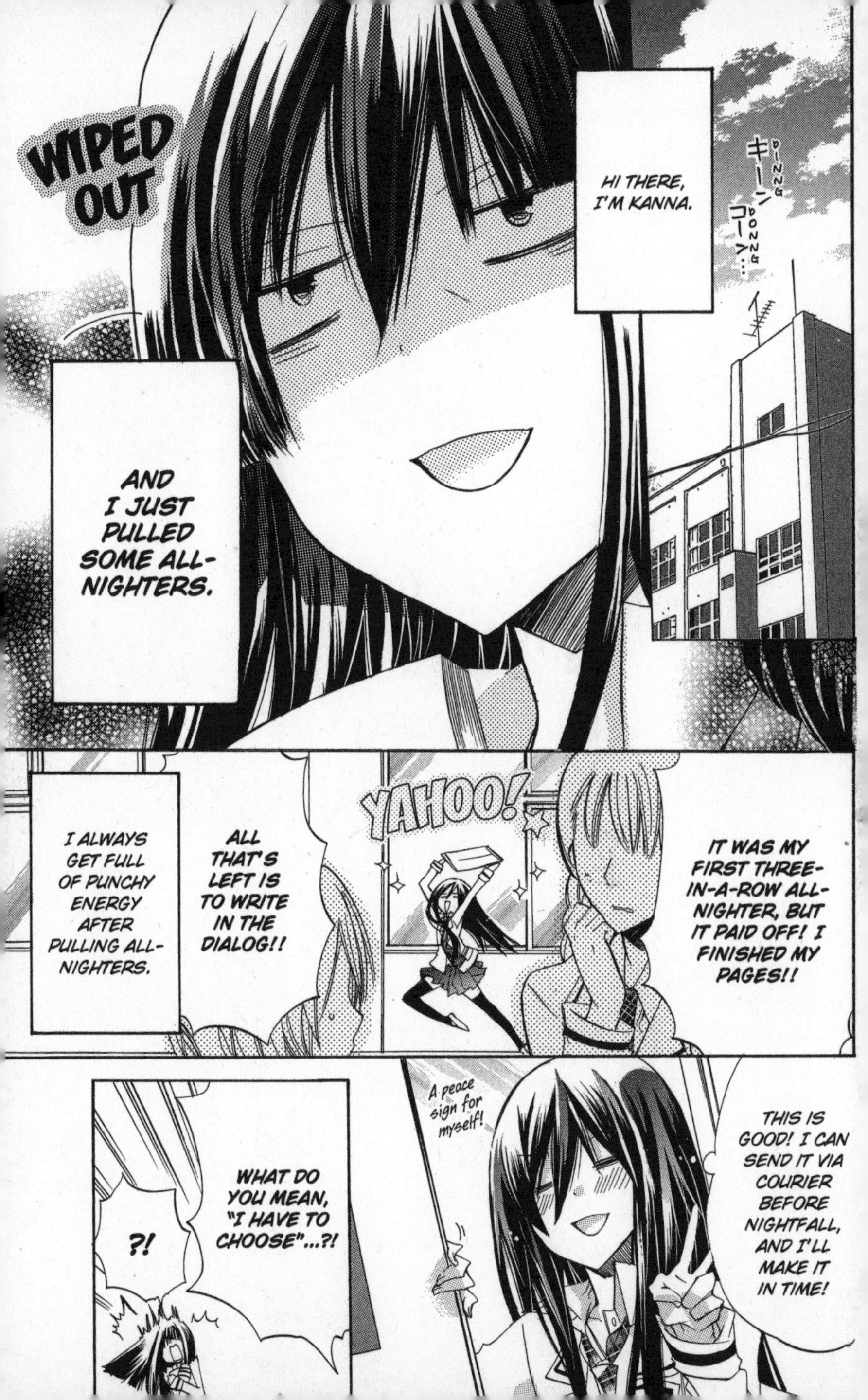
キーン DINNG
コーン… DONNG
HI THERE, I'M KANNA.
WIPED OUT
AND I JUST PULLED SOME ALL-NIGHTERS.
IT WAS MY FIRST THREE-IN-A-ROW ALL-NIGHTER, BUT IT PAID OFF! I FINISHED MY PAGES!!
YAHOO!
ALL THAT'S LEFT IS TO WRITE IN THE DIALOG!!
I ALWAYS GET FULL OF PUNCHY ENERGY AFTER PULLING ALL-NIGHTERS.
THIS IS GOOD! I CAN SEND IT VIA COURIER BEFORE NIGHTFALL, AND I'LL MAKE IT IN TIME!
A peace sign for myself!
WHAT DO YOU MEAN, "I HAVE TO CHOOSE"...?!
?!

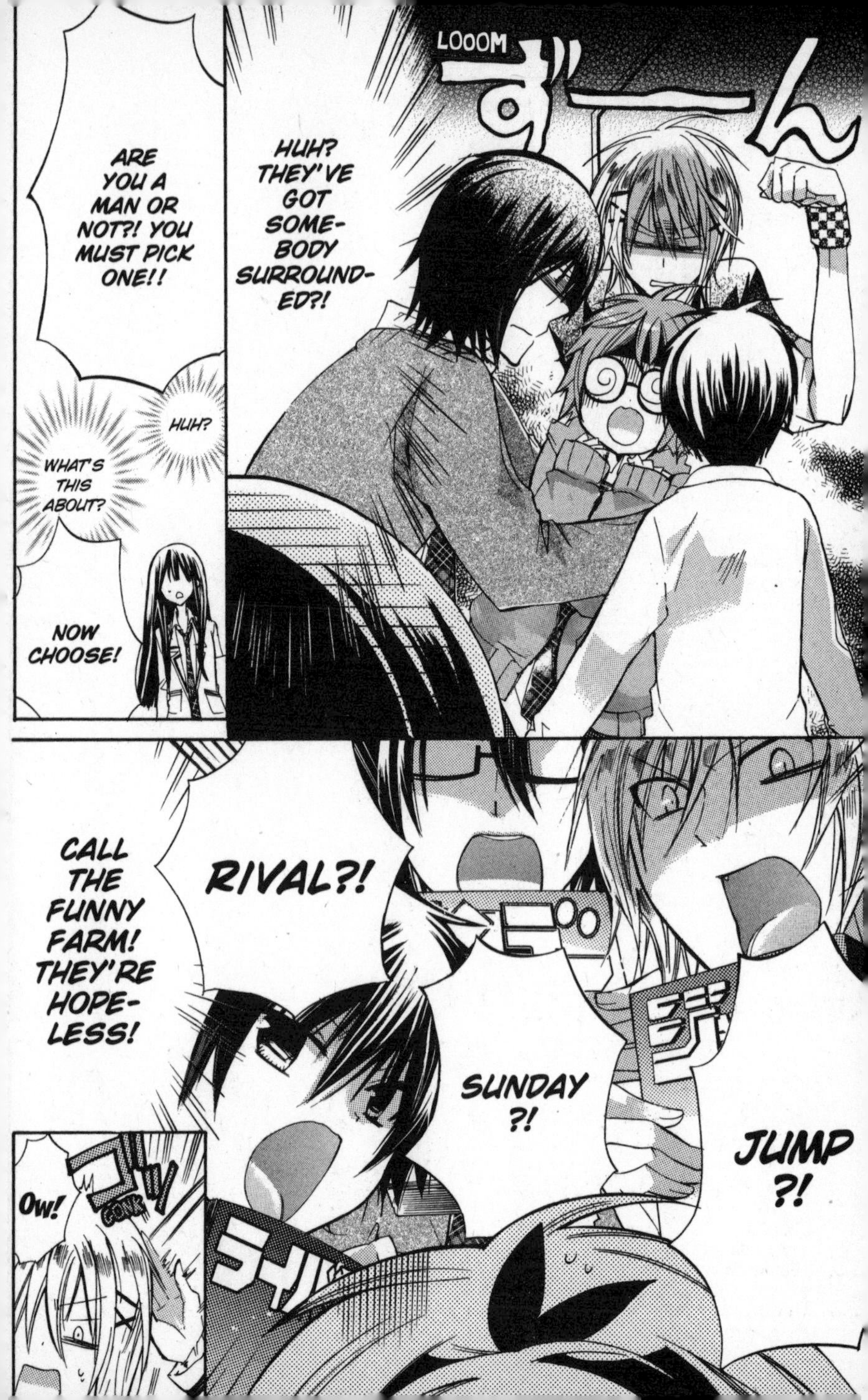
LOOOM
HUH? THEY'VE GOT SOME-BODY SURROUND-ED?!
ARE YOU A MAN OR NOT?! YOU MUST PICK ONE!!
HUH?
WHAT'S THIS ABOUT?
NOW CHOOSE!
RIVAL?!
SUNDAY ?!
JUMP ?!
CALL THE FUNNY FARM! THEY'RE HOPE-LESS!
GONK
Ow!

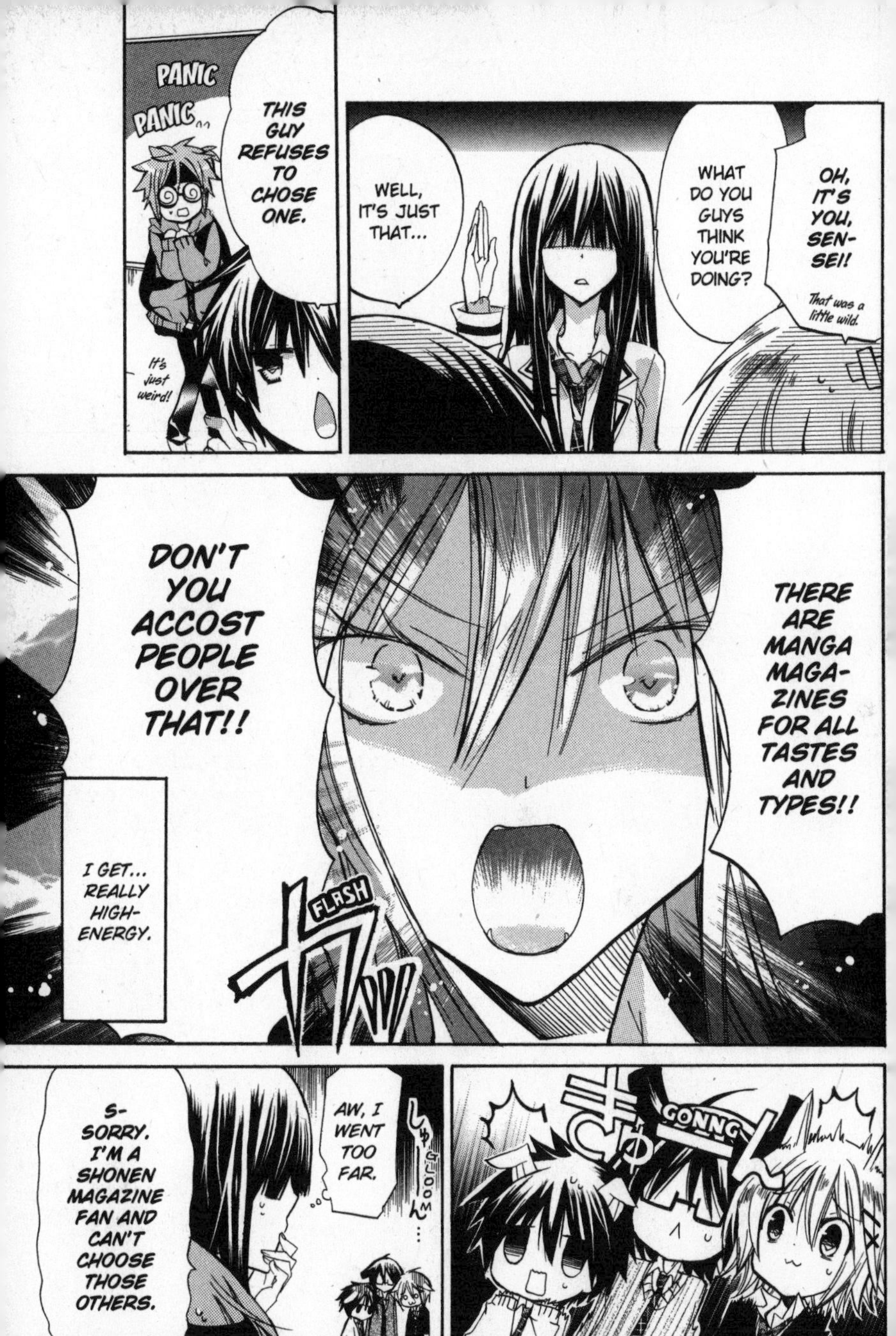
OH, IT'S YOU, SENSEI!
That was a little wild.
WHAT DO YOU GUYS THINK YOU'RE DOING?
WELL, IT'S JUST THAT...
THIS GUY REFUSES TO CHOSE ONE.
PANIC
PANIC
It's just weird!
THERE ARE MANGA MAGAZINES FOR ALL TASTES AND TYPES!!
DON'T YOU ACCOST PEOPLE OVER THAT!!
FLASH
I GET... REALLY HIGH-ENERGY.
GONNG
AW, I WENT TOO FAR.
S-SORRY. I'M A SHONEN MAGAZINE FAN AND CAN'T CHOOSE THOSE OTHERS.

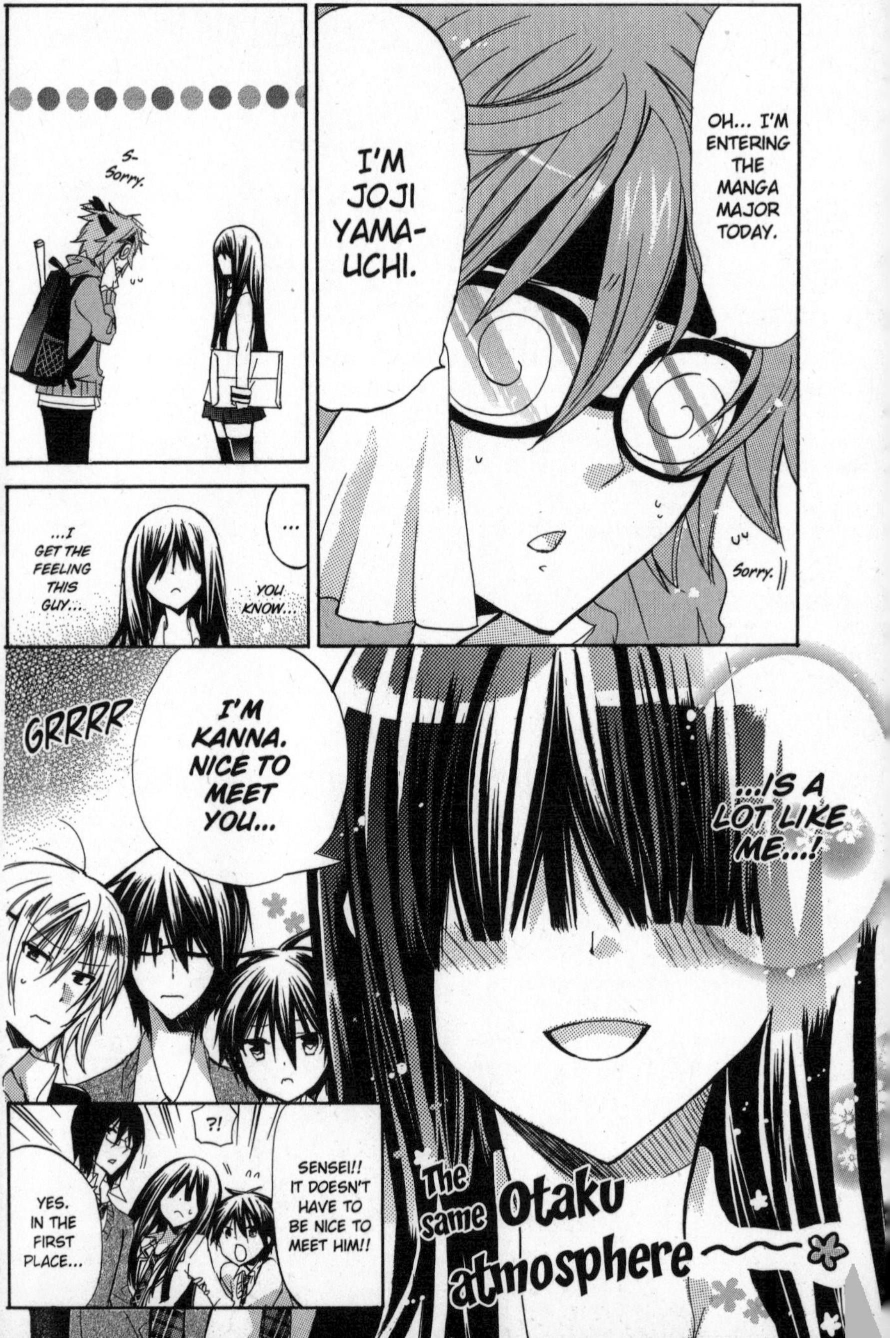
OH... I'M ENTERING THE MANGA MAJOR TODAY.
I'M JOJI YAMA-UCHI.
Sorry.
S-Sorry.
...
YOU KNOW...
...I GET THE FEELING THIS GUY...
...IS A LOT LIKE ME...!
The same Otaku atmosphere
I'M KANNA. NICE TO MEET YOU...
GRRRR
SENSEI!! IT DOESN'T HAVE TO BE NICE TO MEET HIM!!
?!
YES. IN THE FIRST PLACE...

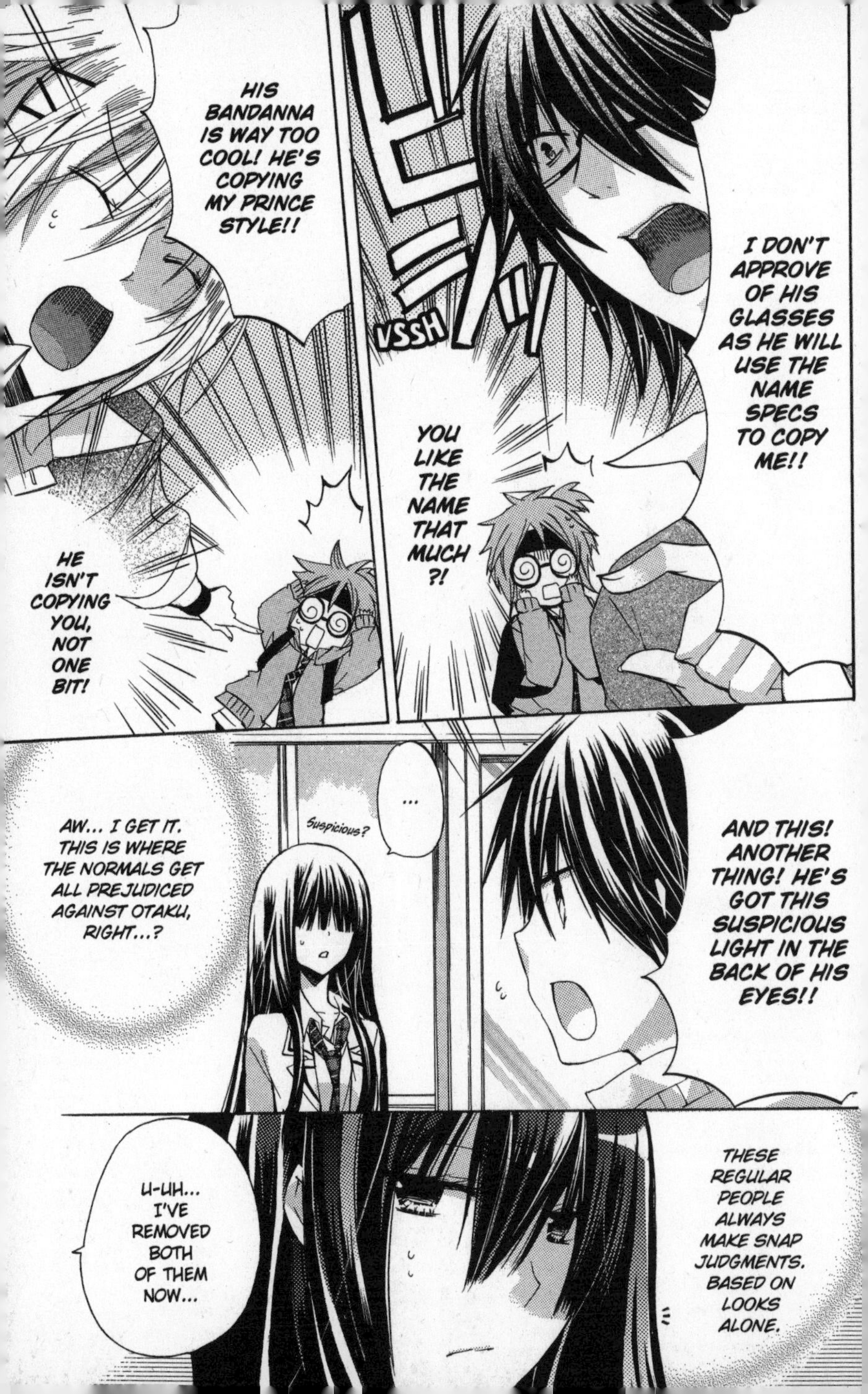
I DON'T APPROVE OF HIS GLASSES AS HE WILL USE THE NAME SPECS TO COPY ME!!
VSSH
YOU LIKE THE NAME THAT MUCH?!
HIS BANDANNA IS WAY TOO COOL! HE'S COPYING MY PRINCE STYLE!!
HE ISN'T COPYING YOU, NOT ONE BIT!
AND THIS! ANOTHER THING! HE'S GOT THIS SUSPICIOUS LIGHT IN THE BACK OF HIS EYES!!
...
Suspicious?
AW... I GET IT. THIS IS WHERE THE NORMALS GET ALL PREJUDICED AGAINST OTAKU, RIGHT...?
THESE REGULAR PEOPLE ALWAYS MAKE SNAP JUDGMENTS. BASED ON LOOKS ALONE.
U-UH... I'VE REMOVED BOTH OF THEM NOW...

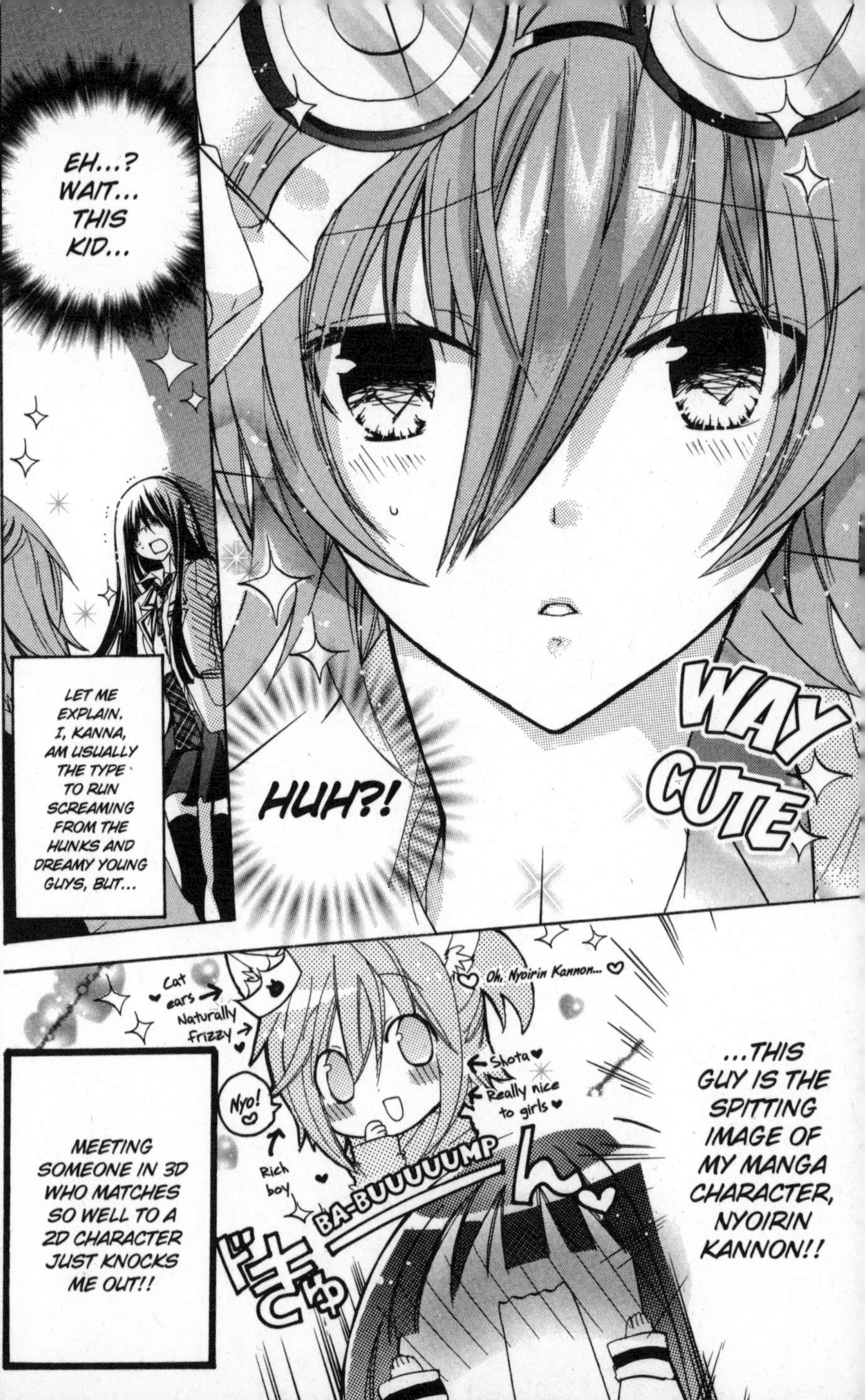
HUH?!
WAY CUTE
EH...? WAIT... THIS KID...
LET ME EXPLAIN. I, KANNA, AM USUALLY THE TYPE TO RUN SCREAMING FROM THE HUNKS AND DREAMY YOUNG GUYS, BUT...
...THIS GUY IS THE SPITTING IMAGE OF MY MANGA CHARACTER, NYOIRIN KANNON!!
Oh, Nyoirin Kannon...
Cat ears
Naturally frizzy
Shota
Really nice to girls
Nyo!
Rich boy
BA-BUUUUUMP
MEETING SOMEONE IN 3D WHO MATCHES SO WELL TO A 2D CHARACTER JUST KNOCKS ME OUT!!

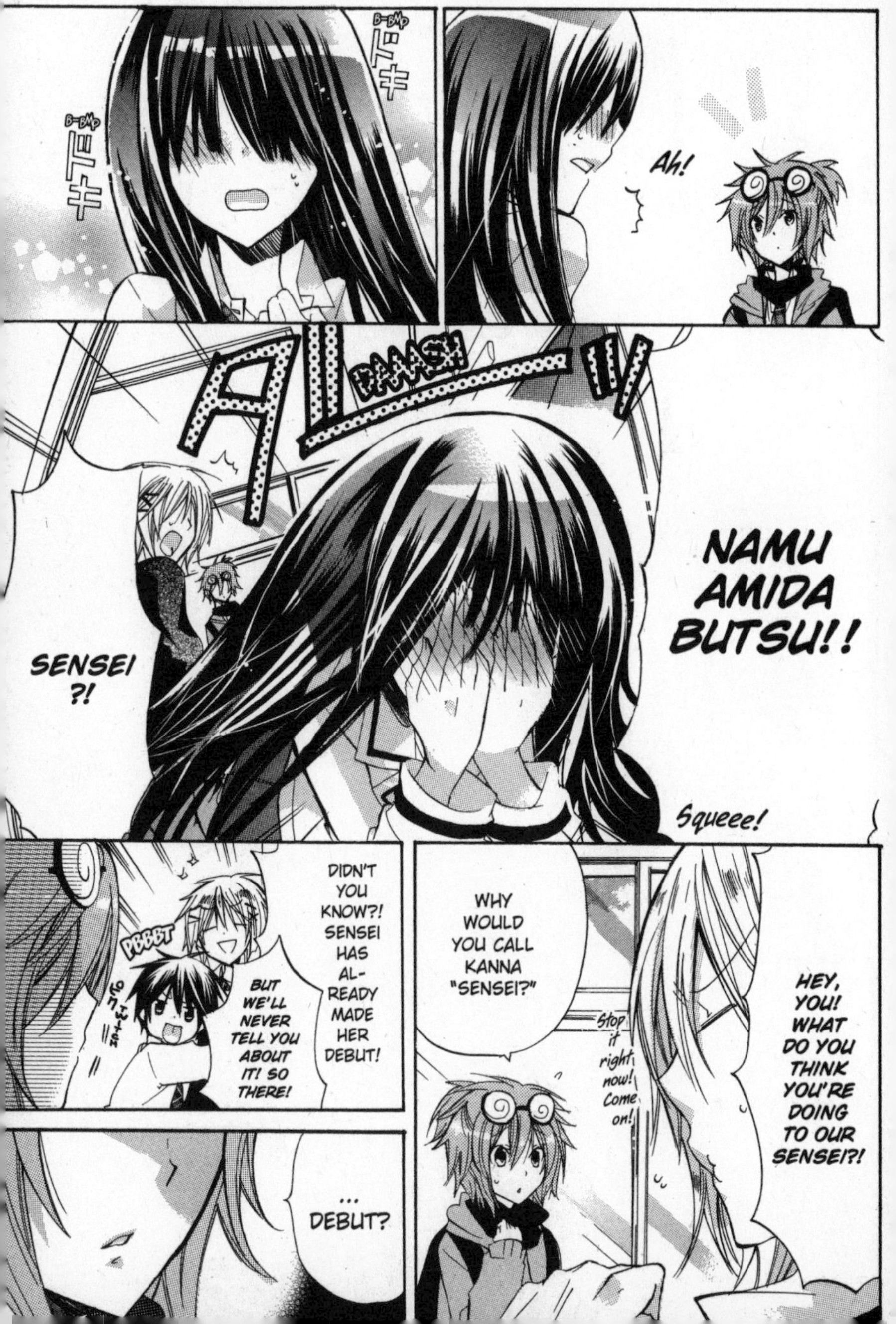
Ah!
B-BMP
B-BMP
DAASH!
NAMU AMIDA BUTSU!!
SENSEI ?!
Squeee!
HEY, YOU! WHAT DO YOU THINK YOU'RE DOING TO OUR SENSEI?!
Stop it right now! Come on!
WHY WOULD YOU CALL KANNA "SENSEI?"
DIDN'T YOU KNOW?! SENSEI HAS AL-READY MADE HER DEBUT!
BUT WE'LL NEVER TELL YOU ABOUT IT! SO THERE!
PBBBT
... DEBUT?

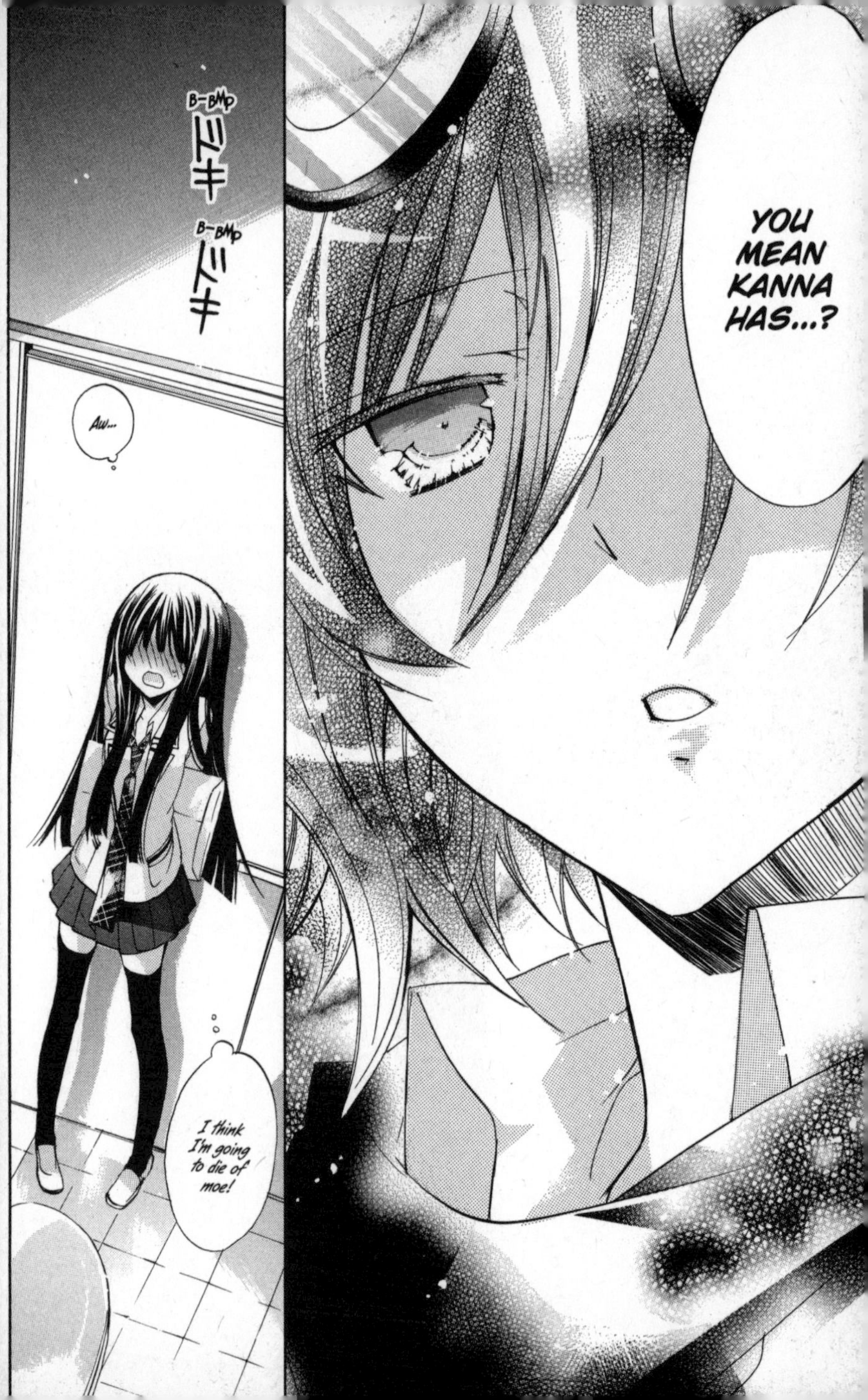
YOU MEAN KANNA HAS...?
B-BMP
ドキ
B-BMP
ドキ
Aw...
I think I'm going to die of moe!

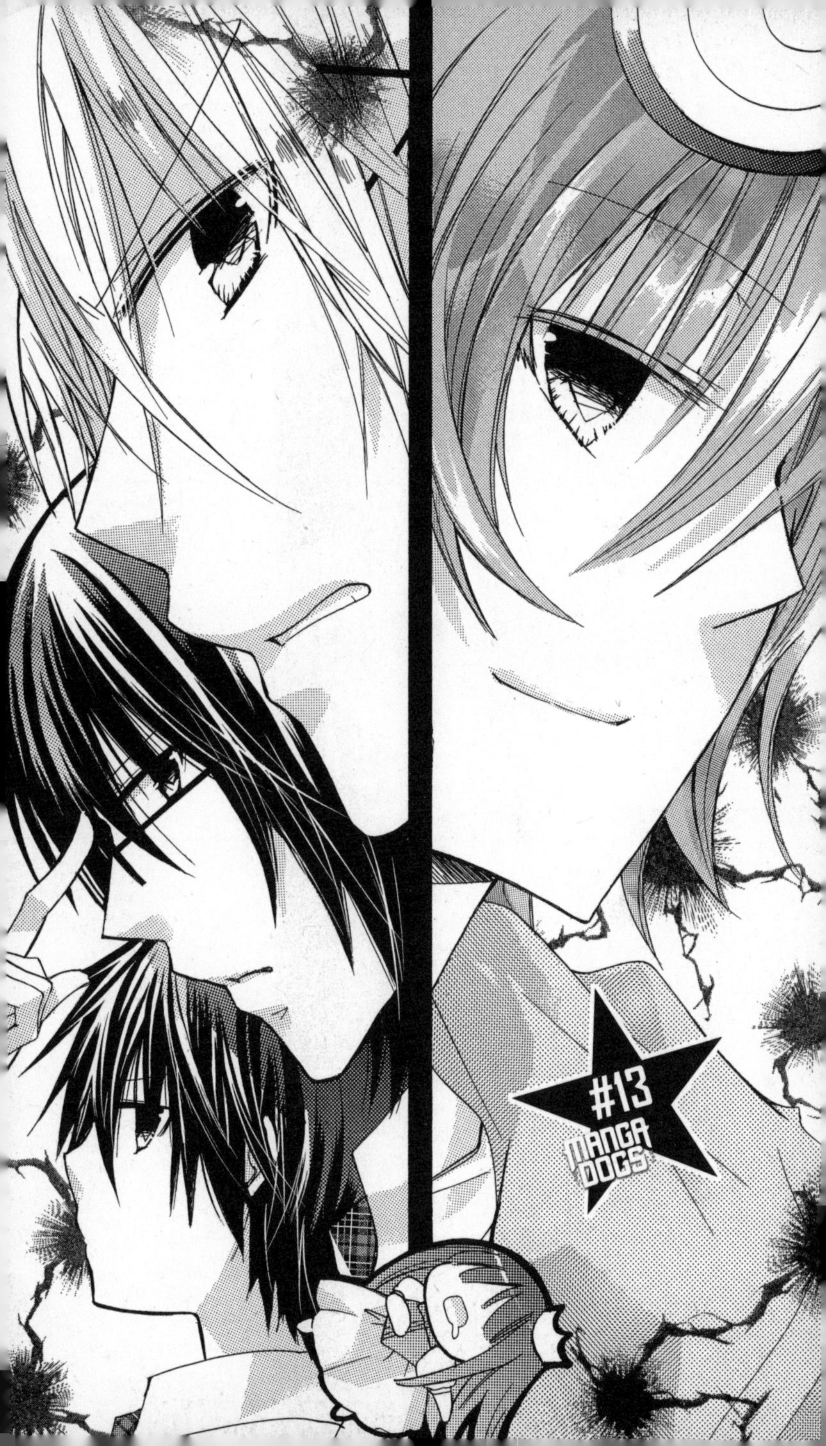
#13
MANGA DOGS

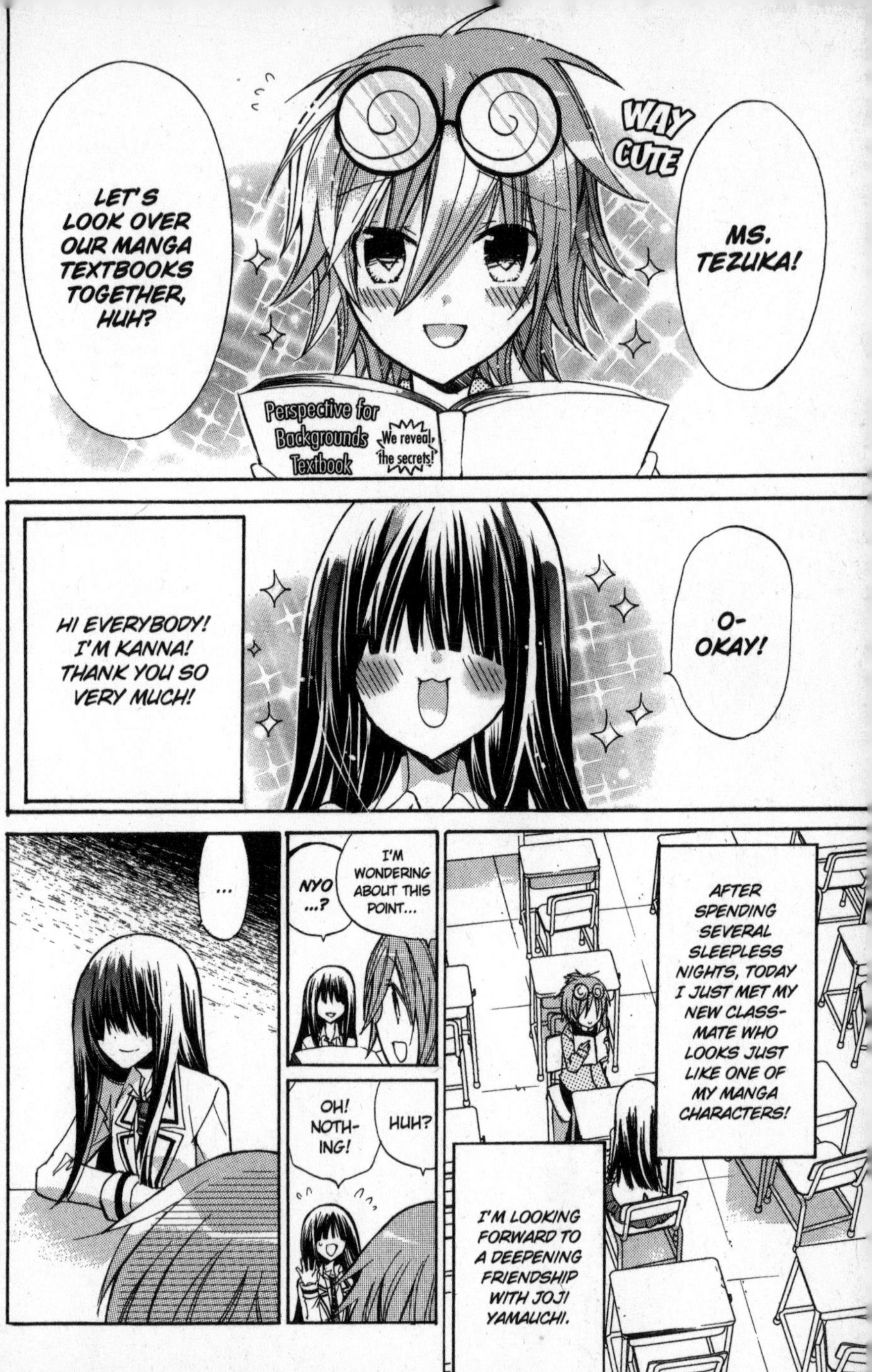
WAY CUTE
MS. TEZUKA!
LET'S LOOK OVER OUR MANGA TEXTBOOKS TOGETHER, HUH?
Perspective for Backgrounds Textbook
We reveal the secrets!
O-OKAY!
HI EVERYBODY! I'M KANNA! THANK YOU SO VERY MUCH!
AFTER SPENDING SEVERAL SLEEPLESS NIGHTS, TODAY I JUST MET MY NEW CLASS-MATE WHO LOOKS JUST LIKE ONE OF MY MANGA CHARACTERS!
I'M LOOKING FORWARD TO A DEEPENING FRIENDSHIP WITH JOJI YAMAUCHI.
I'M WONDERING ABOUT THIS POINT...
NYO ...?
HUH?
OH! NOTH-ING!
...

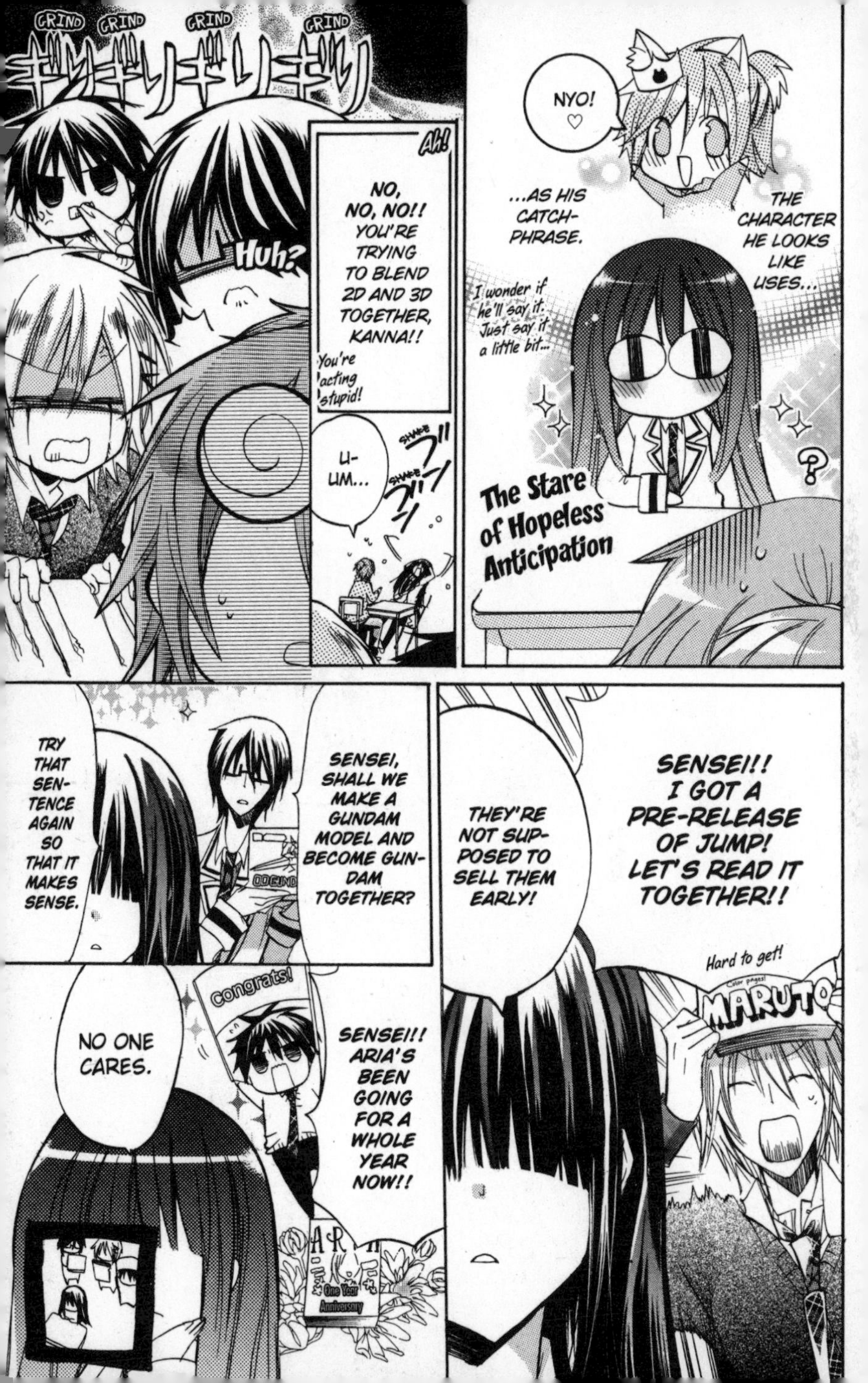
THE CHARACTER HE LOOKS LIKE USES...
NYO! ♡
...AS HIS CATCH-PHRASE.
I wonder if he'll say it. Just say it a little bit...
?
The Stare of Hopeless Anticipation
Ah!
NO, NO, NO!! YOU'RE TRYING TO BLEND 2D AND 3D TOGETHER, KANNA!!
You're acting stupid!
SHAKE
SHAKE
U-UM...
GRIND GRIND GRIND GRIND
Huh?
SENSEI!!! I GOT A PRE-RELEASE OF JUMP! LET'S READ IT TOGETHER!!
THEY'RE NOT SUP-POSED TO SELL THEM EARLY!
Hard to get!
Color pages!
MARUTO
SENSEI, SHALL WE MAKE A GUNDAM MODEL AND BECOME GUN-DAM TOGETHER?
TRY THAT SEN-TENCE AGAIN SO THAT IT MAKES SENSE.
SENSEI!! ARIA'S BEEN GOING FOR A WHOLE YEAR NOW!!
congrats!
ARIA
One Year Anniversary
NO ONE CARES.

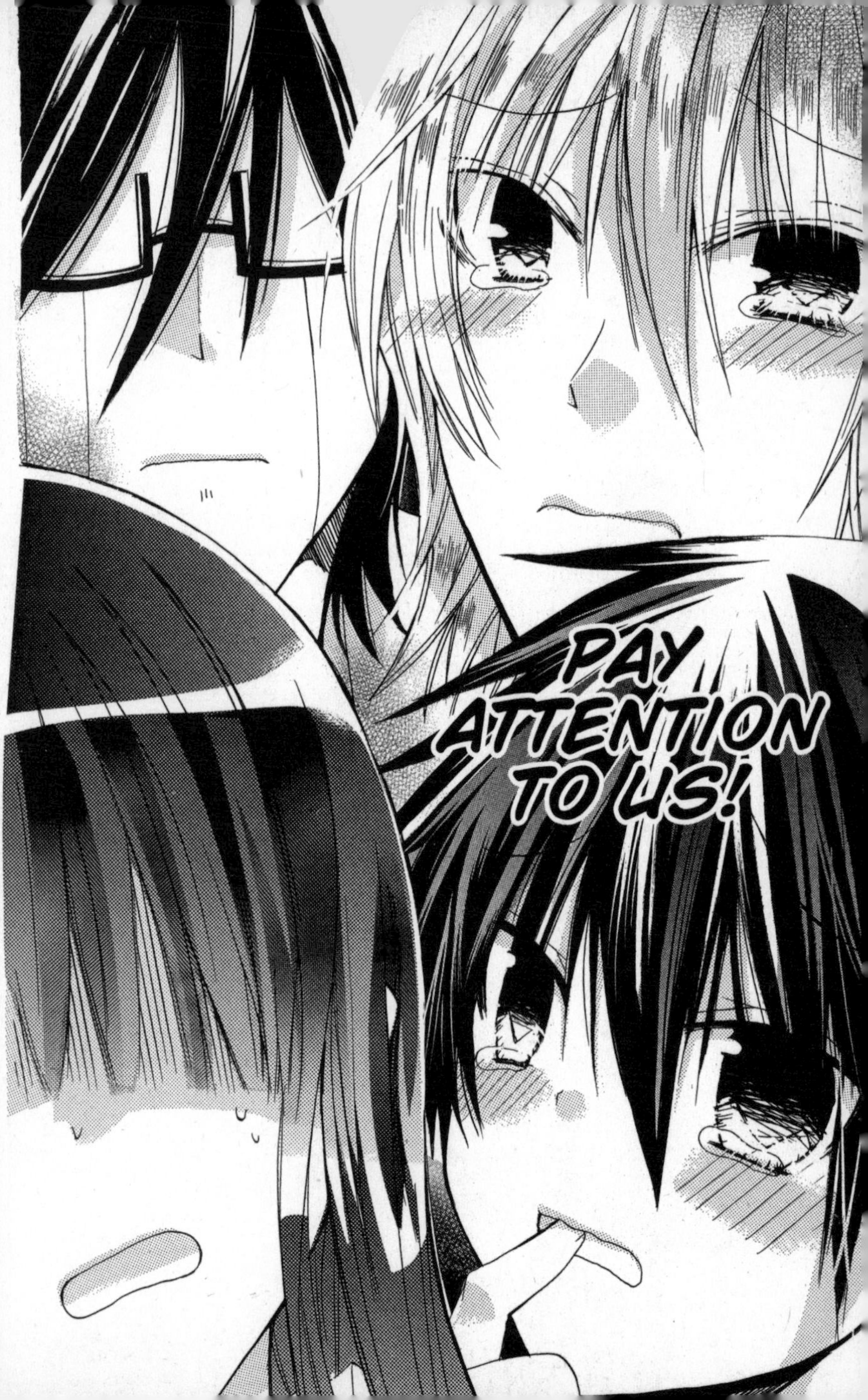
PAY ATTENTION TO US!

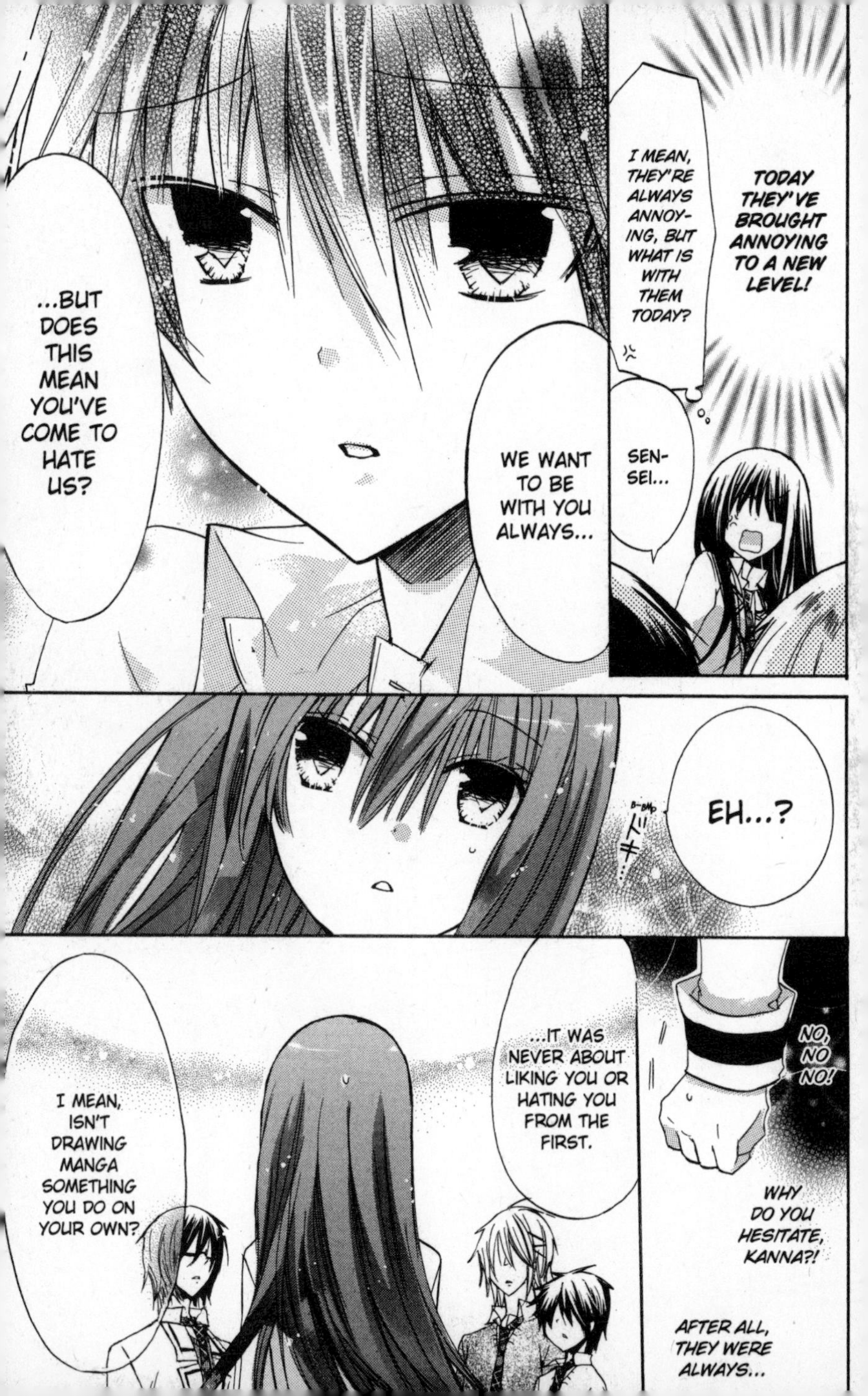
TODAY THEY'VE BROUGHT ANNOYING TO A NEW LEVEL!
I MEAN, THEY'RE ALWAYS ANNOYING, BUT WHAT IS WITH THEM TODAY?
SEN-SEI...
WE WANT TO BE WITH YOU ALWAYS...
...BUT DOES THIS MEAN YOU'VE COME TO HATE US?
EH...?
B-BMP
NO, NO NO!
WHY DO YOU HESITATE, KANNA?!
AFTER ALL, THEY WERE ALWAYS...
...IT WAS NEVER ABOUT LIKING YOU OR HATING YOU FROM THE FIRST.
I MEAN, ISN'T DRAWING MANGA SOMETHING YOU DO ON YOUR OWN?

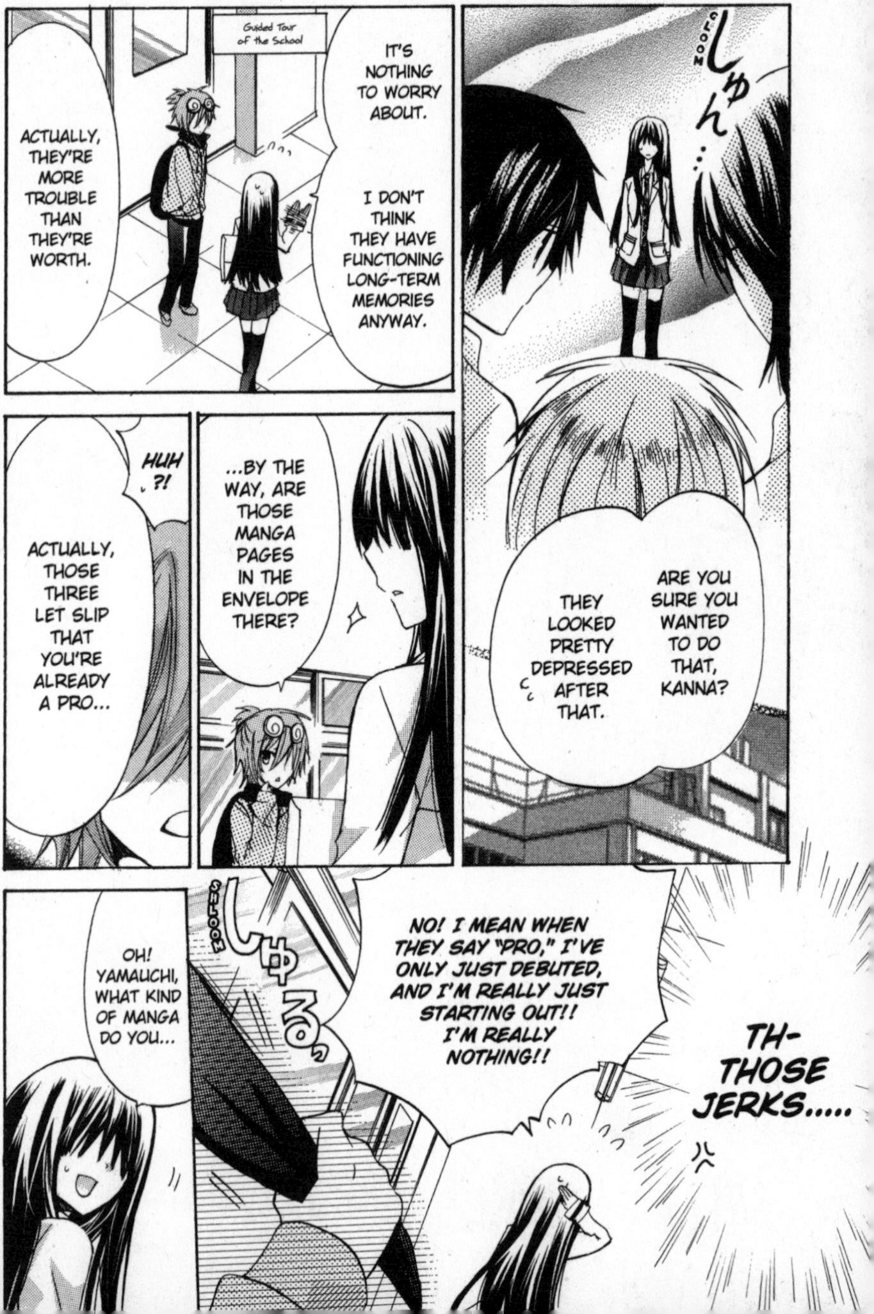
GLOOM
しゅん…
ARE YOU SURE YOU WANTED TO DO THAT, KANNA?
THEY LOOKED PRETTY DEPRESSED AFTER THAT.
Guided Tour of the School
IT'S NOTHING TO WORRY ABOUT.
I DON'T THINK THEY HAVE FUNCTIONING LONG-TERM MEMORIES ANYWAY.
ACTUALLY, THEY'RE MORE TROUBLE THAN THEY'RE WORTH.
...BY THE WAY, ARE THOSE MANGA PAGES IN THE ENVELOPE THERE?
HUH?!
ACTUALLY, THOSE THREE LET SLIP THAT YOU'RE ALREADY A PRO...
TH- THOSE JERKS.....
NO! I MEAN WHEN THEY SAY "PRO," I'VE ONLY JUST DEBUTED, AND I'M REALLY JUST STARTING OUT!! I'M REALLY NOTHING!!
SHLOOM
しゅるっ
OH! YAMAUCHI, WHAT KIND OF MANGA DO YOU...

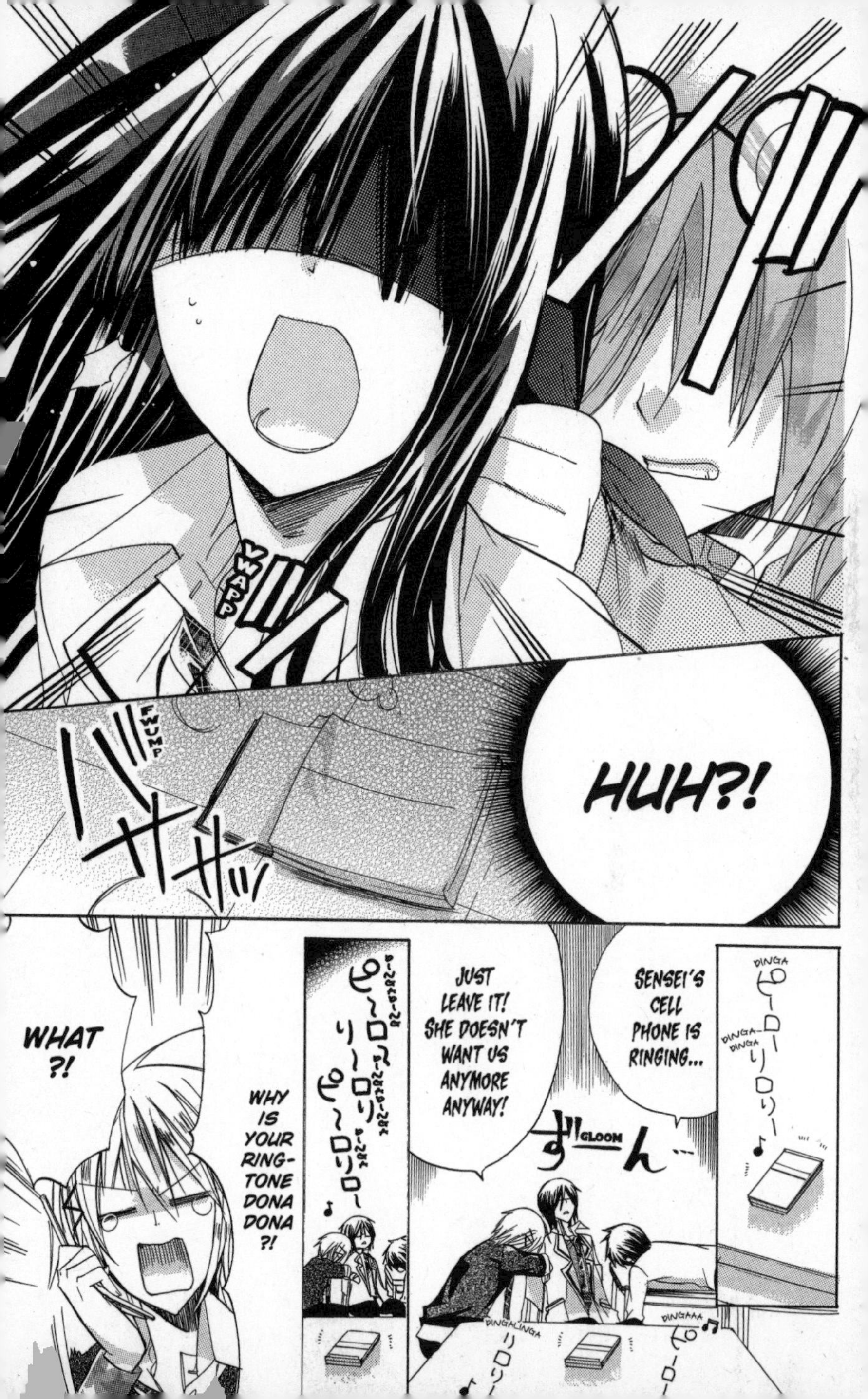
VWAPP
HUH?!
FWUMP
DINGA
DINGA-DINGA
SENSEI'S CELL PHONE IS RINGING...
JUST LEAVE IT! SHE DOESN'T WANT US ANYMORE ANYWAY!
GLOOM
DINGAAA
DINGALINGA
WHY IS YOUR RING-TONE DONA DONA?!
WHAT?!

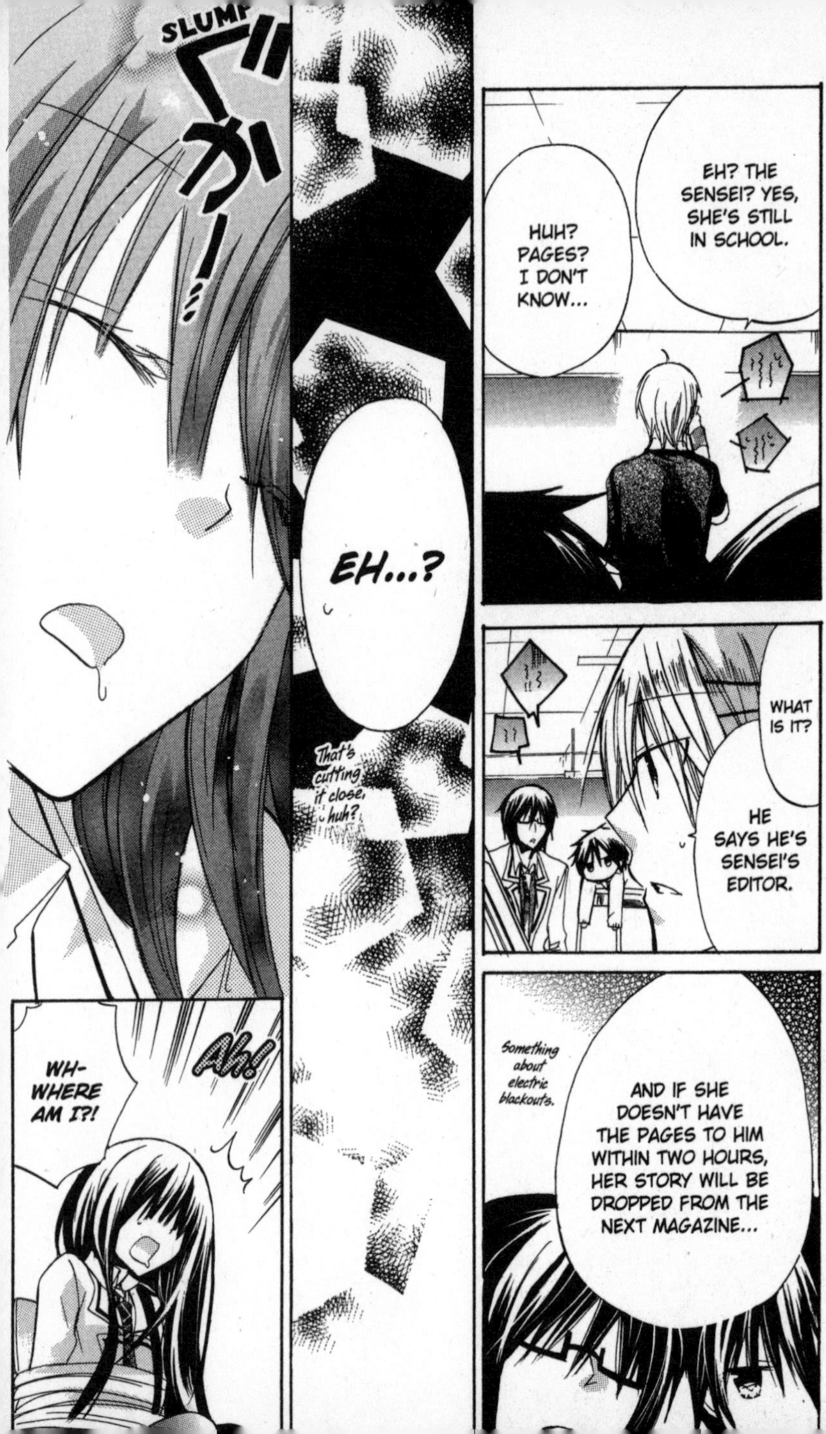
EH? THE SENSEI? YES, SHE'S STILL IN SCHOOL.
HUH? PAGES? I DON'T KNOW...
WHAT IS IT?
HE SAYS HE'S SENSEI'S EDITOR.
AND IF SHE DOESN'T HAVE THE PAGES TO HIM WITHIN TWO HOURS, HER STORY WILL BE DROPPED FROM THE NEXT MAGAZINE...
Something about electric blackouts.
EH...?
That's cutting it close, huh?
SLUMP
Ah!
WH- WHERE AM I?!

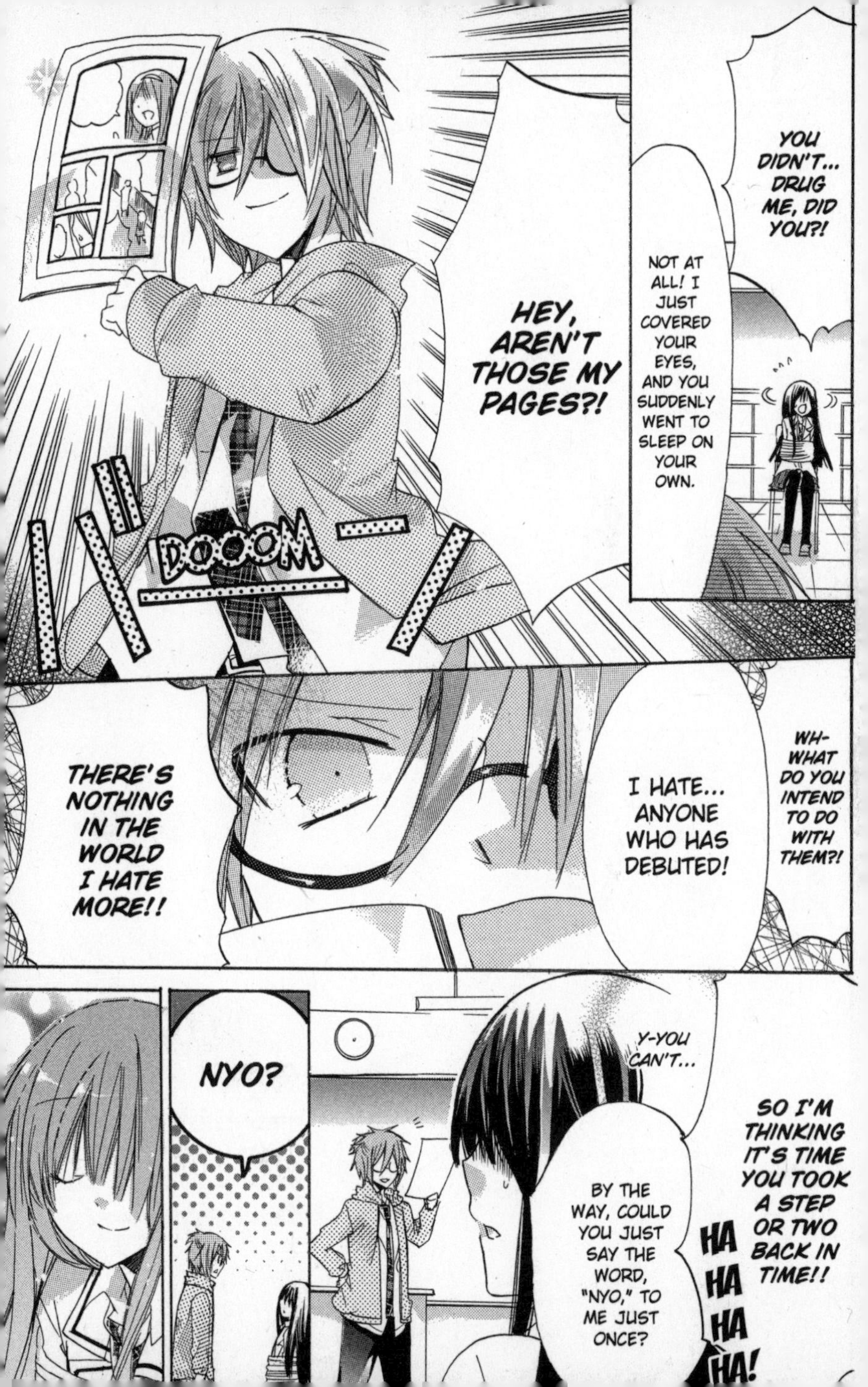
YOU DIDN'T... DRUG ME, DID YOU?!
NOT AT ALL! I JUST COVERED YOUR EYES, AND YOU SUDDENLY WENT TO SLEEP ON YOUR OWN.
HEY, AREN'T THOSE MY PAGES?!
DOOOM
WH-WHAT DO YOU INTEND TO DO WITH THEM?!
I HATE... ANYONE WHO HAS DEBUTED!
THERE'S NOTHING IN THE WORLD I HATE MORE!!
SO I'M THINKING IT'S TIME YOU TOOK A STEP OR TWO BACK IN TIME!!
HA HA HA HA!
Y-YOU CAN'T...
BY THE WAY, COULD YOU JUST SAY THE WORD, "NYO," TO ME JUST ONCE?
NYO?

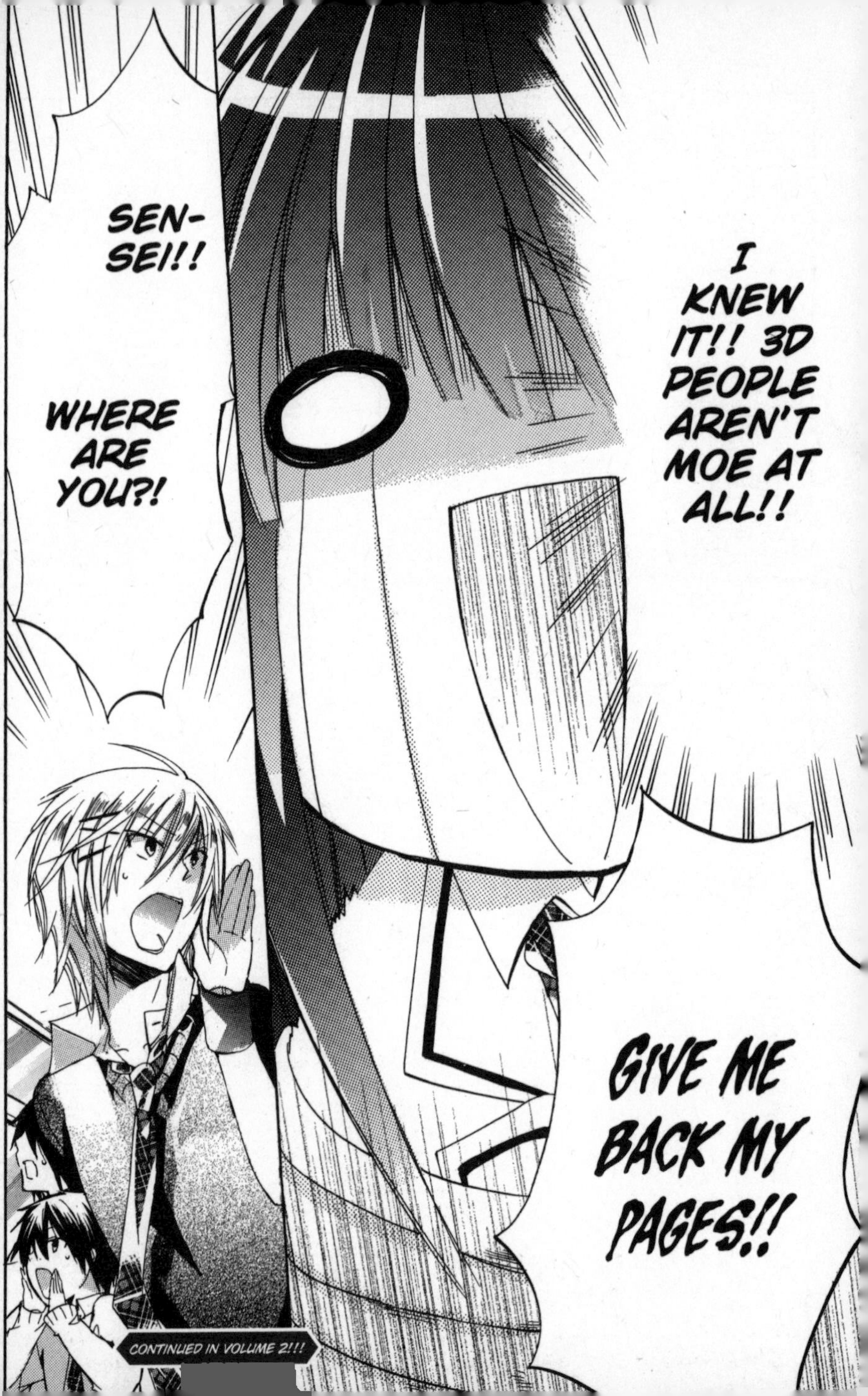
I KNEW IT!! 3D PEOPLE AREN'T MOE AT ALL!!
GIVE ME BACK MY PAGES!!
SEN-SEI!!
WHERE ARE YOU?!
CONTINUED IN VOLUME 2!!!

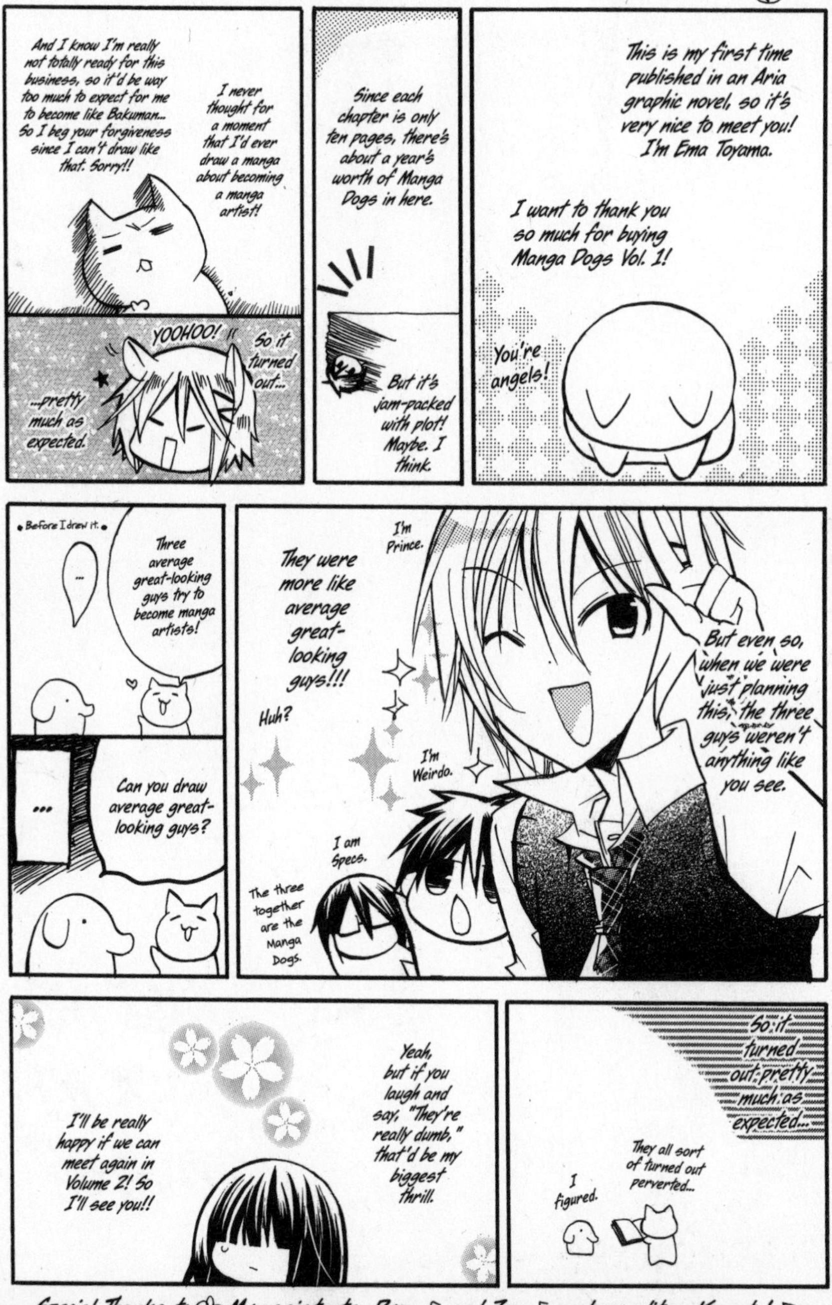
This is my first time published in an Aria graphic novel, so it's very nice to meet you! I'm Ema Toyama.
I want to thank you so much for buying Manga Dogs Vol. 1!
You're angels!
Since each chapter is only ten pages, there's about a year's worth of Manga Dogs in here.
But it's jam-packed with plot! Maybe. I think.
I never thought for a moment that I'd ever draw a manga about becoming a manga artist!
And I know I'm really not totally ready for this business, so it'd be way too much to expect for me to become like Bakuman... So I beg your forgiveness since I can't draw like that. Sorry!!
So it turned out...
YOOHOO!
...pretty much as expected.
But even so, when we were just planning this, the three guys weren't anything like you see.
They were more like average great-looking guys!!!
Huh?
I'm Prince.
I'm Weirdo.
I am Specs.
The three together are the Manga Dogs.
Before I drew it.
Three average great-looking guys try to become manga artists!
...
Can you draw average great-looking guys?
...
So it turned out pretty much as expected...
They all sort of turned out perverted...
I figured.
Yeah, but if you laugh and say, "They're really dumb," that'd be my biggest thrill.
I'll be really happy if we can meet again in Volume 2! So I'll see you!!

Special Thanks to ✿ My assistants, Ryou ♪ and Zou ♪ and my editor, K-moto! ♪

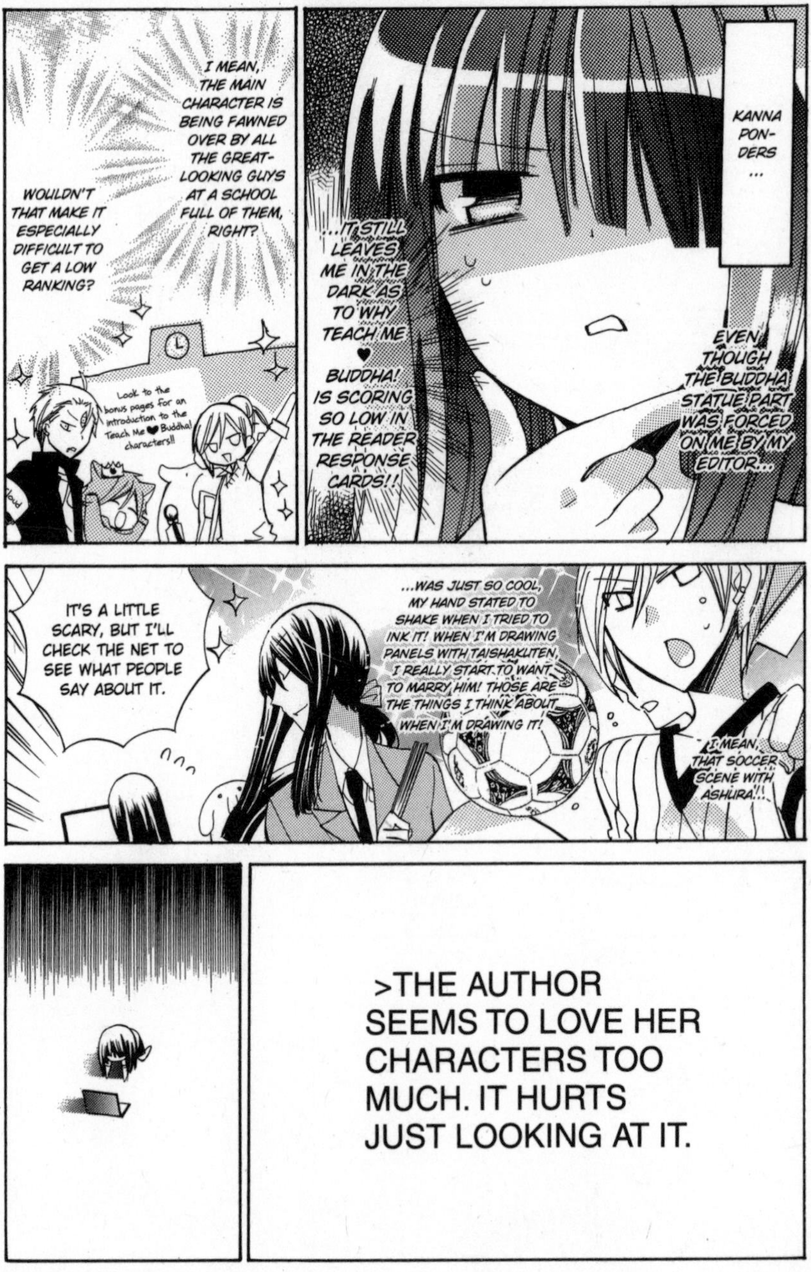
KANNA PONDERS...
EVEN THOUGH THE BUDDHA STATUE PART WAS FORCED ON ME BY MY EDITOR...
...IT STILL LEAVES ME IN THE DARK AS TO WHY TEACH ME ♥ BUDDHA! IS SCORING SO LOW IN THE READER RESPONSE CARDS!!
I MEAN, THE MAIN CHARACTER IS BEING FAWNED OVER BY ALL THE GREAT-LOOKING GUYS AT A SCHOOL FULL OF THEM, RIGHT?
WOULDN'T THAT MAKE IT ESPECIALLY DIFFICULT TO GET A LOW RANKING?
Look to the bonus pages for an introduction to the Teach Me ♥ Buddha! characters!!
I MEAN, THAT SOCCER SCENE WITH ASHURA!!
...WAS JUST SO COOL, MY HAND STATED TO SHAKE WHEN I TRIED TO INK IT! WHEN I'M DRAWING PANELS WITH TAISHAKUTEN, I REALLY START TO WANT TO MARRY HIM! THOSE ARE THE THINGS I THINK ABOUT WHEN I'M DRAWING IT!
IT'S A LITTLE SCARY, BUT I'LL CHECK THE NET TO SEE WHAT PEOPLE SAY ABOUT IT.
>THE AUTHOR SEEMS TO LOVE HER CHARACTERS TOO MUCH. IT HURTS JUST LOOKING AT IT.

KANNA'S ANGST ②

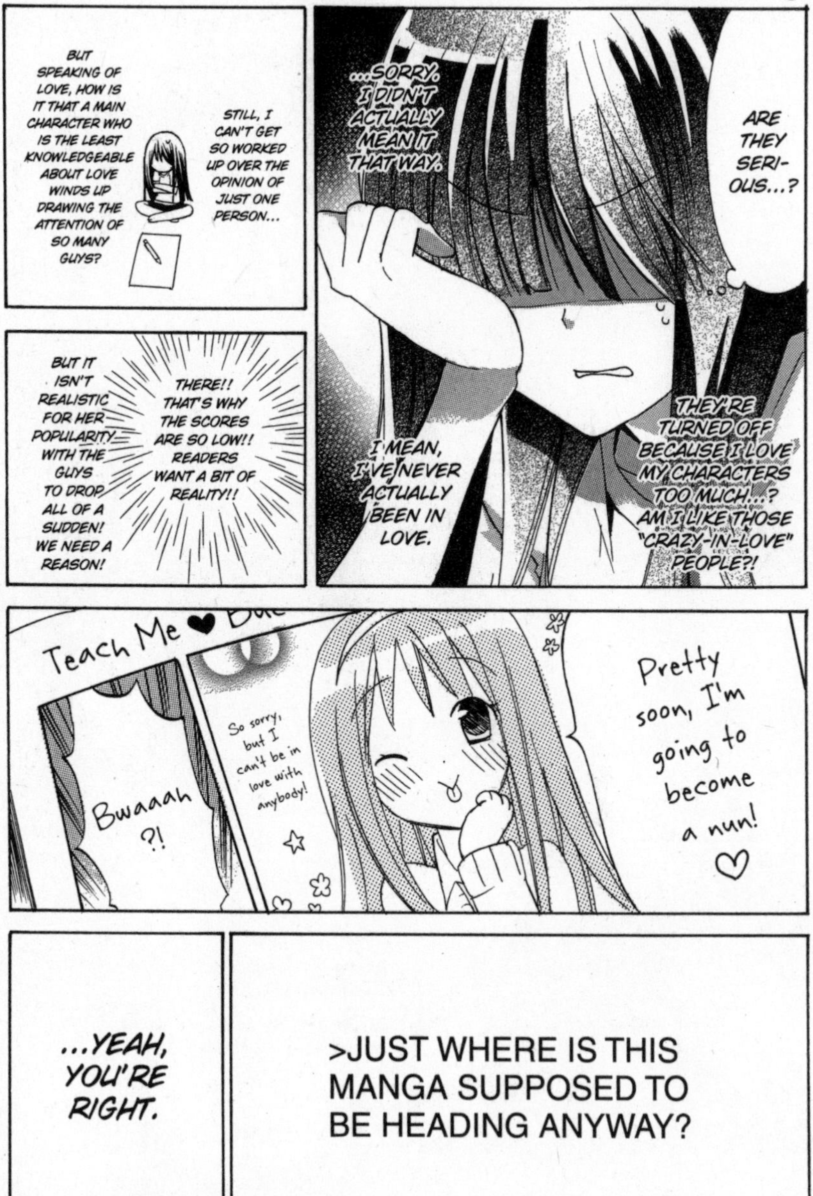
ARE THEY SERI-OUS...?
...SORRY. I DIDN'T ACTUALLY MEAN IT THAT WAY.
THEY'RE TURNED OFF BECAUSE I LOVE MY CHARACTERS TOO MUCH...? AM I LIKE THOSE "CRAZY-IN-LOVE" PEOPLE?!
I MEAN, I'VE NEVER ACTUALLY BEEN IN LOVE.
STILL, I CAN'T GET SO WORKED UP OVER THE OPINION OF JUST ONE PERSON...
BUT SPEAKING OF LOVE, HOW IS IT THAT A MAIN CHARACTER WHO IS THE LEAST KNOWLEDGEABLE ABOUT LOVE WINDS UP DRAWING THE ATTENTION OF SO MANY GUYS?
THERE!! THAT'S WHY THE SCORES ARE SO LOW!! READERS WANT A BIT OF REALITY!!
BUT IT ISN'T REALISTIC FOR HER POPULARITY WITH THE GUYS TO DROP ALL OF A SUDDEN! WE NEED A REASON!
Pretty soon, I'm going to become a nun! ♡
Teach Me ♥
So sorry, but I can't be in love with anybody!
Bwaaah ?!
>JUST WHERE IS THIS MANGA SUPPOSED TO BE HEADING ANYWAY?
...YEAH, YOU'RE RIGHT.

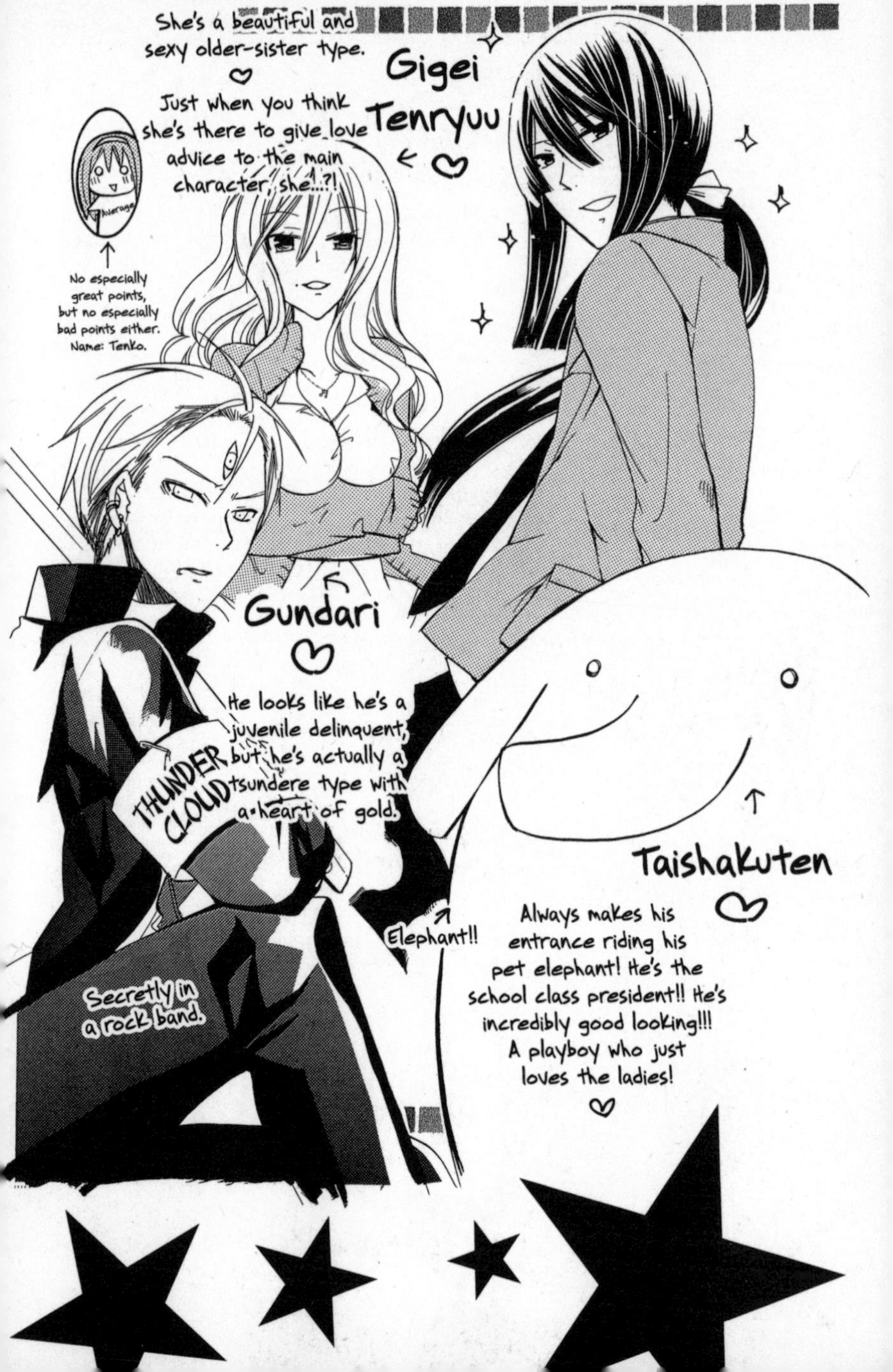
Gigei Tenryuu
She's a beautiful and sexy older-sister type.
Just when you think she's there to give love advice to the main character, she...?!
Average
No especially great points, but no especially bad points either. Name: Tenko.
Gundari
He looks like he's a juvenile delinquent, but he's actually a tsundere type with a heart of gold.
THUNDER CLOUD
Secretly in a rock band.
Taishakuten
Always makes his entrance riding his pet elephant! He's the school class president!! He's incredibly good looking!!! A playboy who just loves the ladies!
Elephant!!

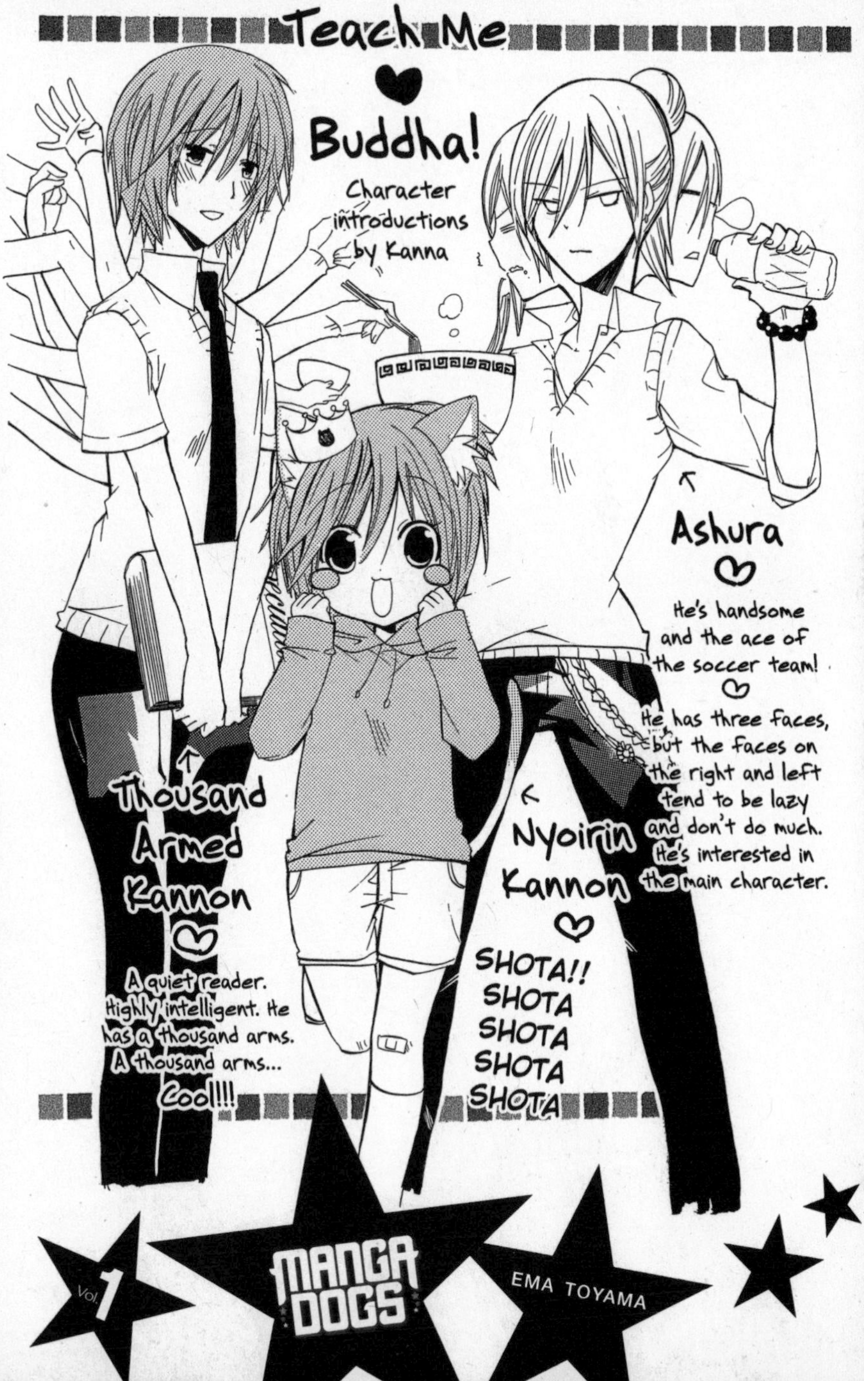
Teach Me ♥ Buddha!
Character introductions by Kanna
Ashura ♡
He's handsome and the ace of the soccer team! ♡
He has three faces, but the faces on the right and left tend to be lazy and don't do much. He's interested in the main character.
Nyoirin Kannon ♡
SHOTA!! SHOTA SHOTA SHOTA SHOTA
Thousand Armed Kannon ♡
A quiet reader. Highly intelligent. He has a thousand arms. A thousand arms... Cool!!!
Vol. 1
MANGA DOGS
EMA TOYAMA

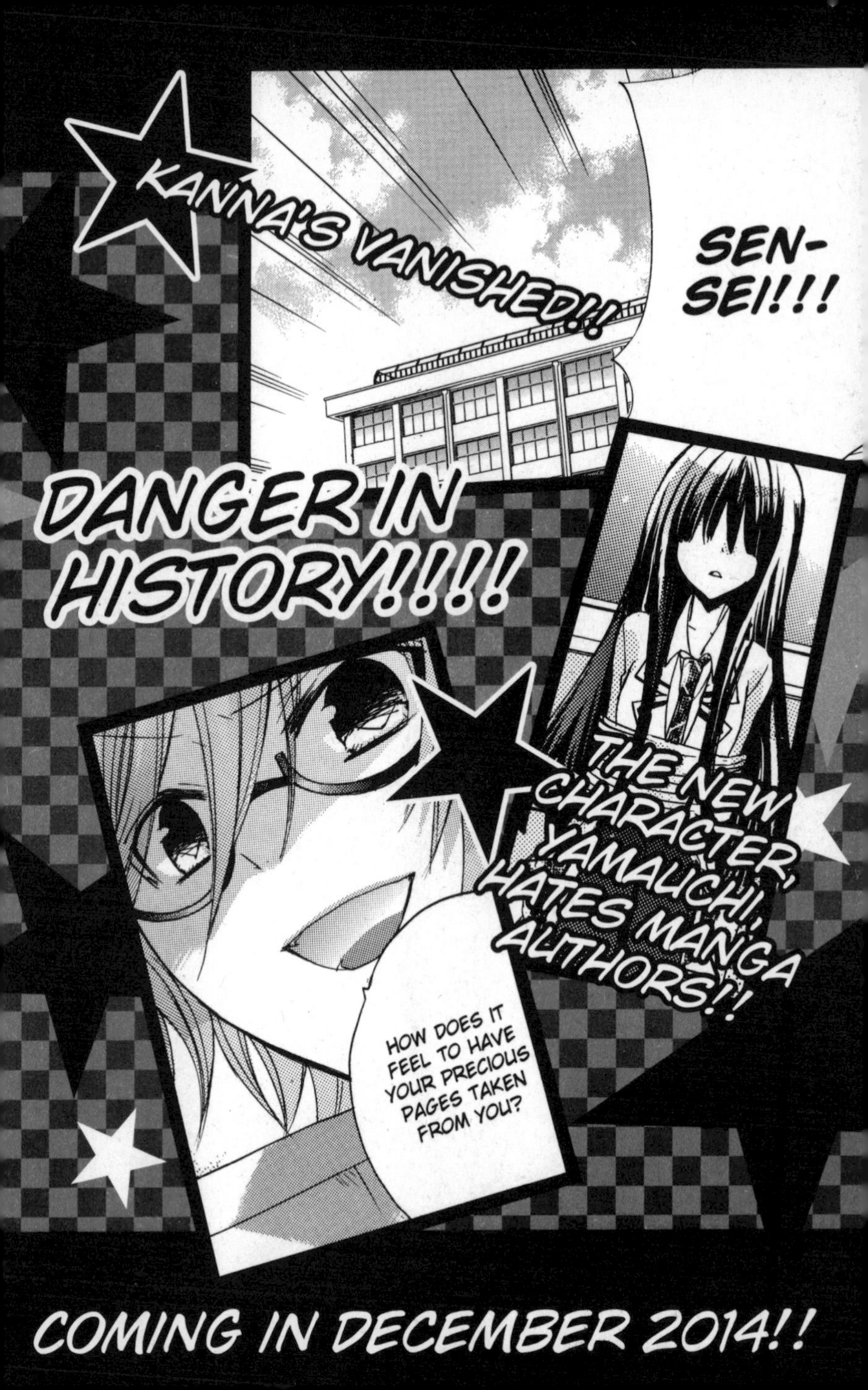
SEN-SEI!!!
KANNA'S VANISHED!!
DANGER IN HISTORY!!!!
THE NEW CHARACTER, YAMAUCHI, HATES MANGA AUTHORS!!
HOW DOES IT FEEL TO HAVE YOUR PRECIOUS PAGES TAKEN FROM YOU?
COMING IN DECEMBER 2014!!

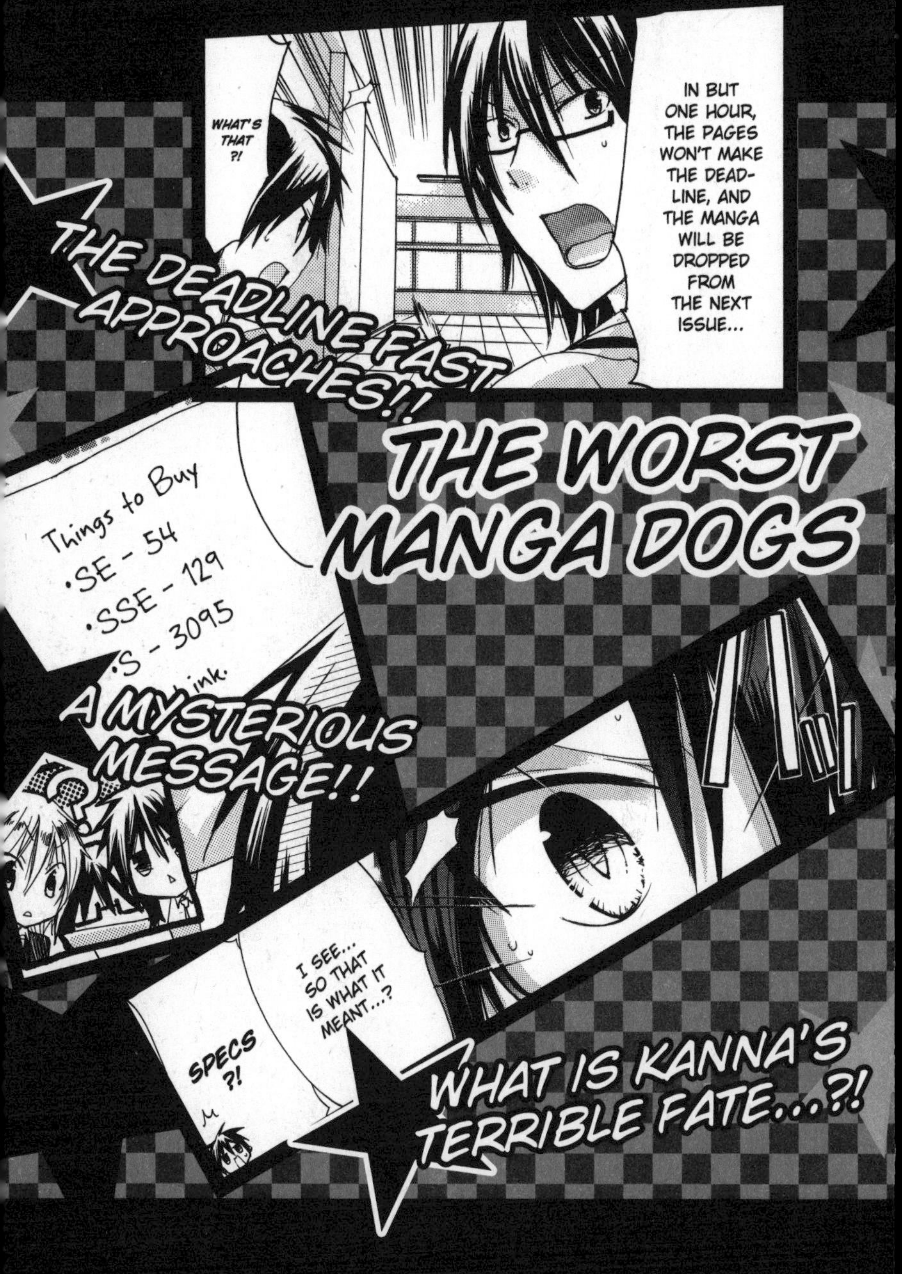

IN BUT ONE HOUR, THE PAGES WON'T MAKE THE DEAD-LINE, AND THE MANGA WILL BE DROPPED FROM THE NEXT ISSUE...
WHAT'S THAT ?!
THE DEADLINE FAST APPROACHES!!
THE WORST MANGA DOGS
Things to Buy
•SE - 54
•SSE - 129
•S - 3095
ink.
A MYSTERIOUS MESSAGE!!
I SEE... SO THAT IS WHAT IT MEANT...?
SPECS ?!
WHAT IS KANNA'S TERRIBLE FATE...?!

MANGA DOGS VOLUME 2

Translation Notes

Japanese is a tricky language for most Westerners, and translation is often more art than science. For your edification and reading pleasure, here are notes on some of the places where we could have gone in a different direction with our translation of the work, or where a Japanese cultural reference is used.

General Note:
Although one can elect to send one's child to a private school, most Japanese send their children to public schools. In elementary school and middle school, the location of one's home determines which school one enters, but it's different for high school. Many Japanese high schools have specialties or majors, so a student may commute a long time to attend a school that has a major the student is interested in studying. This is the story of a high school that has recently established a manga major.

Tokiwa High School (page 4)
"Tokiwa" is a reference to Tokiwa-sou, an apartment building where the "God of Manga" Osamu Tezuka worked, and that later became a gathering place for up-and-coming manga talent. Because of the concentration of great artists, Tokiwa-sou became famous in the 1950s and early '60s as a Mecca for manga. Most of the names of characters in this manga are based on names of residents of Tokiwa-sou.

Tezuka (page 5)
Kanna's last name is taken from the famous manga artist Osamu Tezuka, also called the God of Manga, because he not only created top-selling manga and anime *Astro Boy,* but also went on to establish styles in every genre and demographic of manga that persist to this day, including shonen and shojo as well as manga with more adult themes. With the *Astro Boy* anime, he also pioneered the art style and production techniques of the television anime industry. On a recommendation from his publisher, he entered the Tokiwa-sou apartment building, and later his publisher sent dozens of manga artists to live there. Although he only lived in the apartment building for one year, he is considered the founder of this commune for manga artists, and he had a great influence on the spirit of community fostered there. There is much more to Osamu Tezuka than can possibly be written in a translation note, but fortunately, much of his library of work has been translated into English, and there are several excellent books about him, including *The Art of Osamu Tezuka: God of Manga* by Helen McCarthy and *The Astro Boy Essays* by Fred Schodt.

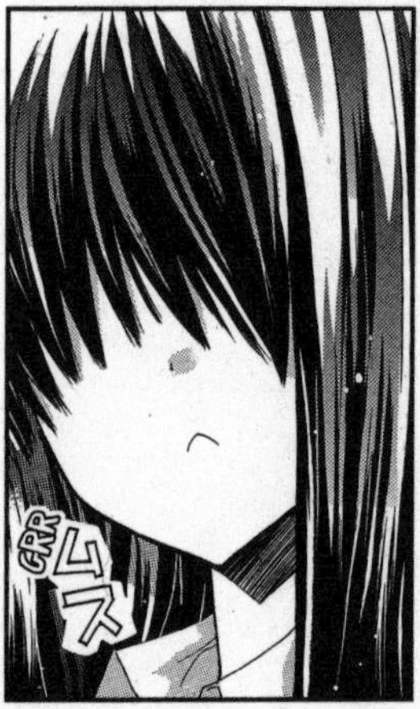
ムス
GRR

Flag (page 14)
Originally a programming term. When all conditions of an event are satisfied, a flag is raised within the program. This term is used in computer games, especially dating simulations. When certain romantic conditions are met, a flag is raised that should lead to the two characters falling in love with each other. It's become shorthand for clichéd events that often occur in fictional romances.

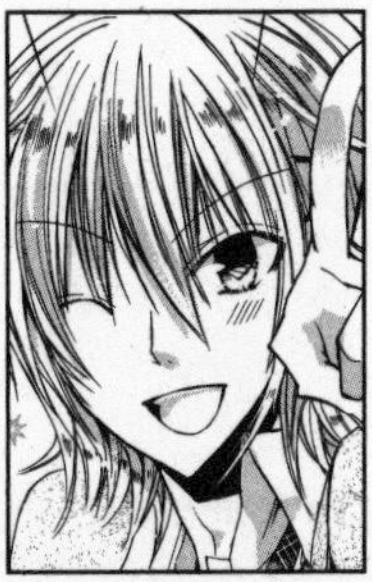

Fumio Akatsuka (page 25)
From Fujio Akatsuka, manga artist of *Tensai Bakabon* and many other top gag manga. He lived in the Tokiwa-sou apartment building along with many other manga artists, first breaking in as a shojo artist, but moving to the shonen magazines when his comedies started selling well. His double-take-like physical gags have even made their way into Godzilla movies, with Godzilla striking his signature pose.

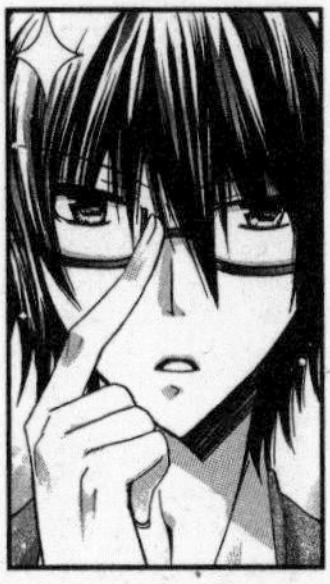

Fujio Fuji (page 25)
From the manga artists known as Fujiko F Fujio, creators of the still massively popular *Doraemon* series. Two other hits of theirs (not quite as ubiquitous as *Doraemon*) were the SF comedy *Perman* and the ghost comedy *Obake no Q-taro*. They were so productive, at one point they had six different manga being serialized at once. In 1963, the pair formed a studio that included both Fujio Akatsuka and Shotaro Ishinomori, among other famous manga artists.

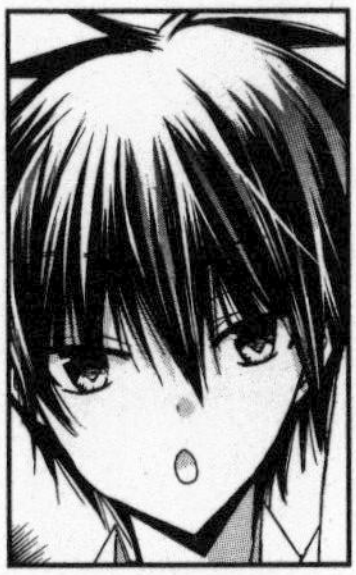

Shota Ishinomori (page 26)
From Shotaro Ishinomori, the famous manga artist and creator of *Cyborg 009* and the *Kamen Rider* series of live-action TV shows. He was also one of the famous residents of the Tokiwa-sou apartment building, assisting other artists and recruiting assistants there. He is credited with coining the Japanese catchphrase *"henshin!"* ("transform!"), used when characters such as Kamen Rider and Kikaider transformed from their human forms to their superhero forms.

Kazuo Umezu (page 29)
Kazuo Umezu is a superstar of Japanese horror manga, author of *The Drifting Classroom*, *Cat-Eyed Boy*, and many others. Now 78, he is still famous for his flamboyant fashion sense and the red-and-white striped house he built in Tokyo's affluent Kichijoji district, causing a minor scandal.

2D (page 33)
Japanese otaku tend to refer to the world of manga and anime as 2D and the real world as 3D.

Lum (page 52)
Perhaps the most popular Shonen Sunday character of the 1980s was Lum-chan (Lum) of Rumiko Takahashi's gonzo romantic comedy *Urusei Yatsura*. She was a mix of a cute girl alien and the traditional Japanese fairy tale villain, the *oni*, with striped horns and tiger-striped clothing. Her violent antics, shooting jealous electric shocks at her constantly philandering "boyfriend," Ataru, made her a fan favorite.

Moe (page 59)
Moe is a Japanese word that comes from the verb *moeru* which means "to bud" as in a flower bud. It refers to young people who display a naïve innocence, but also a certain eagerness for new romantic experiences (too-old or too-mature characters are not considered *moe*). In the middle 2000s, it was estimated that *moe* goods and services accounted for a third of the overall otaku market, but that number is reportedly declining.

Tetsuko Chiba (page 89)
From Tetsuya Chiba, the author of the legendary boxing manga *Ashita no Joe*. Although Tetsuya never lived at Tokiwa-sou, he was known to visit there often and make use of the talents of Fujio Akatsuka and Shotaro Ishinomori to help him meet deadlines.

Stippling (page 90)
This is one way to make gray tones in a manga where the printing process only allows black and white. You draw a tiny dot, then another a fraction of an inch away from the first, then keep repeating the process, eventually creating a region of white with tiny black dots. The sizes of the dots and their spacing are how one varies the color of gray that seems to appear on the page. By the 1980s, this technique had been generally replaced by "screentone," a plastic sheet with adhesive on one side and the dots pre-printed. The same can be done now by computer, thought screentones are still widely used. However, stippling done by hand is nearly extinct.

Shigeru Mizuki (page 91)

This is a reference to an actual manga author who created the famous *GeGeGe no Kitaro* children's horror/comedy manga (available in English as *Kitaro*). Like many of the other authors mentioned here, he is considered "old school" and would include hand stippling in his manga. Several of his fiction and nonfiction works have become available in English in beautifully localized editions in the last few years.

Crosshatching (page 91)

Like stippling, crosshatching is a technique for making gray tones on a black-and-white page. Instead of dots, crosshatching uses short lines that are generally drawn in a checkerboard pattern. Although most crosshatching has been replaced by screentones and computer-generated tones, there is an organic quality to crosshatching that some artists love, so it is still used in manga today. According to some crosshatching advocates, it is also fun work even when an artist is burned out creatively.

Joji Yamauchi (page 150)

From the manga artist Joji Yamauchi (though spelled with different Japanese characters), who was a latecomer to the Tokiwa-sou apartment building. While he was there, he worked as an assistant to Fujio Akatsuka and Shotaro Ishinomori during the last year or two of their respective stays in the building. He later went on to write and draw mainly children's books.

Namu Amida Butsu (page 153)
This is a phrase which means, "In the name of the Amida Buddha," and is a Buddhist religious invocation in Japanese. In this case, it comes out as sort of a Buddhist, "Oh, God!"

Rolling blackouts (page 162)
In 2011, after the 3/11 Tohoku earthquake and subsequent tsunami and nuclear disaster, many of the main generators that fed Tokyo power went offline. For a limited time, portions of Tokyo had to go a few hours a day (or every few days) without power. These blackouts forced many schedule changes among businesses.

Manga Dogs volume 1 is a work of fiction. Names, characters, places, and incidents are the products of the author's imagination or are used fictitiously. Any resemblance to actual events, locales, or persons, living or dead, is entirely coincidental.

A Kodansha Comics Trade Paperback Original.

Published in the United States by Kodansha Comics, an imprint of Kodansha USA Publishing, LLC, New York.

Publication rights for this English edition arranged through Kodansha Ltd., Tokyo.

First published in Japan in 2011 by Kodansha Ltd., Tokyo, as *GDGD-DOGS* volume 1.
ISBN 978-1-61262-903-2

Printed in the United States of America.

www.kodanshacomics.com

9 8 7 6 5 4 3 2 1

Translation: William Flanagan
Lettering: Jennifer Skarupa
Editing: Ben Applegate
Kodansha Comics edition cover design by Phil Balsman

TOMARE!
STOP

You're going the wrong way!

Manga is a completely different type of reading experience.

To start at the beginning,
Go to the end!

That's right! Authentic manga is read the traditional Japanese way—from right to left, exactly the opposite of how American books are read. It's easy to follow: Just go to the other end of the book and read each page—and each panel—from right side to left side, starting at the top right. Now you're experiencing manga as it was meant to be!